Old and New Growth Theories

Old and New Growth Theories

An Assessment

Edited by

Neri Salvadori

Professor of Economics, University of Pisa, Italy

Edward Elgar
Cheltenham, UK • Northampton, MA, USA

Published by
Edward Elgar Publishing Limited
Glensanda House
Montpellier Parade
Cheltenham
Glos GL50 1UA
UK

Edward Elgar Publishing, Inc.
136 West Street
Suite 202
Northampton
Massachusetts 01060
USA

A catalogue record for this book
is available from the British Library

Library of Congress Cataloguing in Publication Data
Old and new growth theories : an assessment / edited by Neri Salvadori.
    p. cm.
  Includes index.
  1. Economic development. I. Salvadori, Neri.

HD75.043 2003
338.9'001—dc21

2002037921

ISBN I 84376 074 6

Printed and bound in Great Britain by MPG Books Ltd, Bodmin, Cornwall

Contents

Figures

Tables

Contributors

Nelson H. Barbosa-Filho (Federal University of Rio de Janeiro, Brasil)

Alberto Bucci (University of Milano, Italy and University of Louvain, Belgium)

Maria Rosaria Carillo (University of Napoli 'Parthenope', Italy)

Ramesh Chandra (University of Strathclyde, Glasgow, UK)

Giacomo Costa (University of Pisa, Italy)

Guido Cozzi (University of Rome 'La Sapienza', Italy)

Amitava Krishna Dutt (University of Notre Dame, USA)

Theo S. Eicher (University of Washington, USA)

Cecilia Garcia-Peñalosa (GREQAM and CNRS, Marseille, France)

Francesco Guala (University of Trento, Italy, and University of Exeter, UK)

Michael A. Landesmann (Vienna Institute for International Economic Studies, WIIW, and Johannes Kepler University, Austria)

Carlo Panico (University of Napoli 'Federico II', Italy)

Andrea Salanti (University of Bergamo, Italy)

Roger J. Sandilands (University of Strathclyde, Glasgow, UK)

Mark Setterfield (Trinity College, CT, USA)

Ian Steedman (Manchester Metropolitan University, UK)

Robert Stehrer (Vienna Institute for International Economic Studies, Austria)

Anthony P. Thirlwall (University of Kent, UK)

Stephen J. Turnovsky (University of Washington, USA)

Alberto Zazzaro (University of Ancona, Italy)

Introduction

Neri Salvadori

The interest in the study of economic growth has experienced remarkable ups and downs in the history of economics. It was central in Classical political economy from Adam Smith to David Ricardo, and then in the critique of it by Karl Marx, but was moved to the periphery during the so-called 'marginal revolution'. John von Neumann's growth model and Roy Harrod's attempt to generalise Keynes's principle of effective demand to the long run re-ignited an interest in growth theory. Following the publication of papers by Robert Solow and Nicholas Kaldor in the mid-1950s, growth theory became one of the central topics of the economics profession until the early 1970s. After a decade of dormancy, since the mid-1980s, economic growth has once again become a central topic in economic theorising. The recent 'new' growth theory (NGT) is also called 'endogenous growth theory', since according to it the growth rate is determined from within the model and is not given as an exogenous variable.

An analysis of recent developments in growth theory, and their status in the history of the field, has been the main goal of a Conference held in Pisa in the autumn of 2001. This book is the main product of the conference. Other papers will soon appear in special issues of three journals: *History of Economic Ideas* (2002), *Metroeconomica* (2003), and *The European Journal of the History of Economic Thought* (2003). The conference was hosted by a research group, and several of the papers elaborated by members of the group were delivered at the conference. The main product of the research group is a companion book on *The Theory of Economic Growth: A 'Classical Perspective* (Salvadori, 2003). There is, of course, no overlapping among all the mentioned publications, which constitute the proceedings of the Conference. In this volume I have inserted the papers with a more direct relation with the title of the Conference, which is also the title of the book. The result is that the book analyses the recent developments in the theory of economic growth and compares them with older theories. I have also inserted a few other papers with the explicit aim to provide on the whole a balanced representation of the views stemming from scholars of different persuasions.

The book opens with a chapter by Stephen J. Turnovsky, who discusses some of the recent theoretical developments in growth theory, tying them to the earlier growth theories. He sets out a general model able to encompass both an endogenous growth model and a non-scale growth model. He shows how the issue of endogeneity of the labour supply is crucial in determining the equilibrium growth rate and its responsiveness to macroeconomic policy. Then we have three short chapters which investigate the new growth theory from a critical point of view. Anthony P. Thirlwall argues that the typical NGT's explanation of non-diminishing returns to capital in terms of externalities of various kinds associated with human capital formation, R&D expenditure etc. is reminiscent of Alfred Marshall's attempt to reconcile increasing returns and competition by means of the concept of external economies. He maintains that Kaldor's technical progress function fully anticipated the NGT's claim that capital accumulation and technical progress are two deeply interrelated processes. Finally, he remarks that the NGT is a supply side theory of growth: no role is left to demand factors such as export growth and balance of payments considerations. The question of demand is also central to the chapter by Carlo Panico. He deals with the role played by aggregate demand in different theories of growth and pays particular attention to those schools of thought, such as the post-Keynesian and Kaleckian ones, which emphasise the influence on growth by the autonomous components of aggregate demand. The triplet is concluded by a chapter by Amitava Krishna Dutt who reviews the NGT from the perspective of post-Keynesian growth theories. He also maintains that the NGT largely ignores issues relating to effective demand and unemployment and shows that its claim to novelty is based on a narrow reading of 'old' growth theory that ignores a number of contributions. A different point of view is expressed in the chapter by Giacomo Costa who recalls from oblivion some results by Trevor W. Swan about the class of production functions which are compatible with steady-state growth in order then to review the recent literature and to provide a generalisation of the 'Swan Proposition'. He also explores the intriguing connection between such a proposition and the 'learning by doing' model by Arrow.

This first part of the book is complemented with two methodological chapters. Francesco Guala and Andrea Salanti first explicate the notion of robustness and articulate it on three different dimensions and then apply it to old and new growth theories. NGT offers a number of possible explanations of mechanisms generating growth processes, but in this case robustness to changes in the implied causal mechanism is more in the nature of a vice than of a virtue, particularly from the perspective of economic policy. Ian Steedman focuses on the analytical treatment of the concept of knowledge within NGT. According to him, no justification is given to the use of this concept as a homogeneous quantity with a cardinal measure.

The second part of the book is concerned with technical change. Theo S. Eicher discusses the microfoundations of technological change in order to integrate the production of new technology into the study of economic growth and compares this approach with previous ideas about technological change since Adam Smith. His main task is a description of plausible mechanics of the research process and the introduction of an evolutionary algorithm as a search procedure for researchers to manage the universe of ideas. The problem of technical change is also central in the chapter by Michael A. Landesmann and Robert Stehrer, who develop a model with classical, Schumpeterian and Keynesian features.

Endogenous growth theory based on R&D purposefully carried out by profit maximising firms in competitive situations has derived much inspiration from Joseph A. Schumpeter's ideas about the innovative process. However, there has been a general theoretical neglect of the role of private money creation in the growth process which Schumpeter considered instead as crucial. Guido Cozzi tries to fill this lacuna. Financial intermediaries lend newly created bank money to R&D firms challenging the current monopolist. This credit creation process fuels obsolescence that limits bank capital and thereby credit. Hence the ultimate variable that equilibrates private money demand and supply is R&D investment. This is the main channel through which Cozzi builds a bridge between modern Schumpeterian theory and Schumpeter's own monetary ideas.

The third part of the book deals with economic policy. Cecilia García-Peñalosa emphasises that NGT extends the scope of economic policy beyond the boundaries imposed by the 'old', Solovian, growth theory. NGT examines how the decisions of agents determine the economy's rate of growth: economic policy, by exerting an impact on these decisions, may significantly affect growth. Moreover, if in a laissez-faire regime the rate of growth is less than socially desirable, as it is usually concluded in most of the literature on NGT, growth-enhancing policies are called forth. Finally, NGT jointly determines factor rewards and growth. Thus, policy may influence the distribution of income across agents. On the other hand, Ramesh Chandra and Roger J. Sandilands investigate empirically the relationship between investment and GDP in India. They find that causality goes from growth to investment and not the other way round as predicted by mainstream development literature. They suggest an approach to Indian development, inspired by Allyn Young's famous theory of increasing returns, that gives greater prominence to demand-side factors.

Finally there are four chapters dealing with various issues in growth economics. Alberto Bucci analyses the steady-state predictions of an endogenous growth model with both purposive R&D activity and human capital accumulation, whereas the majority of models focus on only one of these engines of growth at a time. Starting from a description of the experience of medieval craft guilds, Maria Rosaria Carillo and Alberto Zazzaro present a simple variety-based model of endogenous growth in which they assume that an institution (the craft guild) which represents the interests of the existing industrial élite (the masters) undertakes social and political lobbying to enhance its prestige and prevent the entry of new firms. Nelson H. Barbosa-Filho presents a one-sector model where autonomous expenditure drives growth and determines the level of economic activity and income distribution. The aim is to investigate under which conditions growth can be demand-led and stable. Mark Setterfield introduces variations in the state of long-run expectations into the adjustment dynamics of neo-Kaleckian growth theory and obtains that the outcomes of the model are path dependent and, in particular, that the rate of growth is determined by sequential processes unfolding in historical time. He also re-examines the Kaleckian paradox of costs and shows that changes in the state of long-run expectations may make it harder to generate faster growth by redistributing income towards wages while at the same time reinforcing the negative growth consequences of redistribution towards profits.

Almost all the chapters of this book as well as all the papers included in the mentioned special issues of the three journals have been peer-reviewed (the exceptions are the invited lectures to the conference). I would like to take this opportunity to thank all the referees who contributed to improving the published papers and advised me on the publishability of the papers. The following scholars helped me with this task: Bruno Amable (University of Paris X, France), Kenneth J. Arrow (Stanford University, USA), Roger Backhouse (University of Birmingham, UK), Nelson Barbosa-Filho (Federal University of Rio de Janeiro, Brasil), Enrico Bellino (Università Cattolica del Sacro Cuore, Italy), Daniele Besomi (independent researcher, Gola di Lago, Switzerland), Carlo Bianchi (University of Pisa, Italy), Annetta Binotti (University of Pisa, Italy), Adriano Birolo (University of Padua, Italy), Mark Blaug (University of Amsterdam, Netherlands), Luciano Boggio (Università Cattolica del Sacro Cuore, Italy), Alberto Bucci (University of Milan, Italy), André Burgstaller (Barnard College, USA), Mauro Caminati (University of Siena, Italy), Rabindra N. Chakraborty (University of St. Gallen, Switzerland), Pasquale Commendatore (University of Naples 'Federico II', Italy), Guido Cozzi (University of Rome 'La Sapienza', Italy), Antonio D'Agata (University of Catania, Italy), John Davis (Marquette University, USA), Amitava K. Dutt (University of Notre Dame, USA), Guido Erreygers (University of Antwerpen, Belgium), Rainer Franke (University of Bremen, Germany), Antonio Gay (University of Florence, Italy), Christian Gehrke

(University of Graz, Austria), Gerhard Glomm (Indiana University, USA), Peter D. Groenewegen (University of Sidney, Australia), Harald Hagemann (University of Hohenheim, Germany), Frank H. Hahn (University of Siena, Italy), Geoffrey Harcourt (Cambridge University, UK), Moshe Hazan (Hebrew University, Israel), Eiji Hosoda (Keio University, Japan), Mikio Ito (Keio University, Japan), Peter Kriesler (University of New South Wales, Australia), Heinz D. Kurz (University of Graz, Austria), Christian Lager (University of Graz, Austria), Andrea M. Lavezzi (University of Pisa, Italy), Frederic Lee (University of Missoury, USA), Hongyi Li (Chinese University of Hong Kong, China), Gilberto T. Lima (University of São Paulo, Brazil), Marco Lippi (University of Rome 'La Sapienza', Italy), Alfredo Medio (University of Venice, Italy), Thomas Michl (Colgate University, USA), Juan Carlos Moreno-Brid (CEPAL, Mexico), Marta Nunes Simões (Universidade de Coimbra, Portugal), Antonella Palumbo (University of Rome III, Italy), Carlo Panico (University of Naples 'Federico II', Italy), Howard Petith (Universitat Autonooma de Barcelona, Spain), Fabio Petri (University of Siena, Italy), Francesco Pigliaru (University of Cagliari, Italy), Mario Pomini (University of Verona, Italy), Maurizio Pugno (University of Trento, Italy), Pietro Reichlin (University of Rome 'La Sapienza', Italy), Carlos Ricoy (University of Santiago de Compostela, Spain), J.R. Ruiz-Tamarit (Univesity of Valencia, Spain), Roger Sandilands (University of Strathclyde, UK), Mark Setterfield (Trinity College, USA), Anwar Shaik (New School University, USA), Rodolfo Signorino (University of Naples 'Federico II', Italy), Peter Skott (University of Aarhus, Denmark), Ian Steedman (Manchester Metropolitan University, UK), Antonella Stirati (University of Siena, Italy), Holger Strulik (Hamburg University, Germany), Richard Sturn (University of Graz, Austria), Lance Taylor (New School University, USA), Anthony P. Thirlwall (University of Kent, UK), Stephen J. Turnovsky (University of Washington, USA), Bart Verspagen (Eindhoven University of Technology, The Netherlands), Ferdinando Vianello (University of Rome 'La Sapienza', Italy), Graham White (University of Sydney, Australia), Josef Zweimüller (University of St. Zurich, Switzerland).

Last but not least, I want to thank the members of the Scientific Committee of the Pisa Conference who shared with me the responsibility of selecting the papers to be given at the meeting. They are Giuseppe Bertola (European University Institute and University of Turin, Italy), Theo S. Eicher (University of Washington, USA), Duncan K. Foley (New School for Social Research, USA), and Heinz D. Kurz (University of Graz, Austria). Theo S. Eicher and Heinz D. Kurz provided also advice in choosing referees during the editing of the proceedings.

1. Old and new growth theories: a unifying structure?

Stephen J. Turnovsky

1.1. INTRODUCTION

1.1.1. Some Background

Long-run growth was first introduced by Solow (1956) and Swan (1956) into the traditional neoclassical macroeconomic model by considering a growing population coupled with a more efficient labor force. The direct consequence of this approach is that the long-run growth rate in these models is ultimately tied to demographic factors, such as the growth rate of population, the structure of the labor force and its productivity growth, all of which were typically taken to be exogenously determined. Hence, the only policies that could contribute to long-run growth were those that would increase the growth of population or the efficiency of the labor force. Conventional macroeconomic policy had no influence on long-run growth performance.

Since then, growth theory has evolved into a voluminous literature in two distinct phases. The Solow–Swan model was the inspiration for a first generation of growth models during the 1960s, which, being associated with exogenous sources of long-run growth, are now sometimes referred to as *exogenous growth models*. Research interest in these models tapered off around 1970, as economists turned their attention to other issues, perceived as being of more immediate significance, such as inflation, unemployment, and oil shocks, and the design of macroeconomic policies to deal with them.[1] Beginning with the seminal work of Romer (1986), there has been a resurgence of interest in economic growth theory giving rise to a second generation of growth models. This revival of activity has been motivated by several issues. These include: (1) an attempt to explain aspects of the data not addressed by the neoclassical model; (2) a more satisfactory explanation of international differences in economic growth rates; (3) a more central role for the accumulation of knowledge; and (4) a larger role for the instruments of

1

macroeconomic policy in explaining the long-run growth process (see Romer, 1994). These new models seek to explain the growth rate as an endogenous equilibrium outcome of the behavior of rational optimizing agents, reflecting the structural characteristics of the economy, such as technology and preferences, as well as macroeconomic policy. For this reason they have become known as *endogenous growth models*.

The new growth theory is far-ranging. It has been analysed in both closed economies, as well as in open economies. In fact, one of the characteristics of the new growth theory is that it has more of an international orientation (see e.g. Grossman and Helpman, 1991). This may reflect the increased importance of the international aspects in macroeconomics in general. In comparison with the first generation of growth models, the newer literature places a greater emphasis on empirical issues and the reconciliation of the theory with the empirical evidence. In this respect a widely debated issue concerns the so-called convergence hypothesis. The question here is whether or not countries have a tendency to converge to a common per capita level of income or growth rate.

But new growth theory is also associated with important theoretical advances as well, and one can identify two main strands of theoretical literature, emphasizing different sources of economic growth. One class of models, closest to the neoclassical growth model, stresses the *accumulation of private capital* as the fundamental source of economic growth. This differs in a fundamental way from the neoclassical growth model in that it does not require exogenous elements, such as a growing population, to generate an equilibrium of ongoing growth. Rather, the equilibrium growth rate is an internally generated outcome.

In the simplest such model, in which the only factor of production is capital, the constant returns to scale condition implies that the production function must be linear in physical capital, being of the functional form $Y = AK$. For obvious reasons, this technology has become known as the 'AK model'. As a matter of historical record, explanation of growth as an endogenous process in a one-sector model is not new. In fact it dates back to Harrod (1939) and Domar (1946). The equilibrium growth rate characterizing the AK model is essentially of the Harrod–Domar type, the only difference being that consumption (or savings) behavior is derived as part of an intertemporal optimization, rather than being posited directly. These one-sector models assume (often only implicitly) a broad interpretation for capital, taking it to include both human, as well as non-human, capital (see Rebelo, 1991). A direct extension to this basic model are two-sector investment-based growth models, originally due to Lucas (1988), that disaggregate private capital into human and nonhuman capital (see also Mulligan and Sala-i-Martin, 1993; and Bond et al., 1996).

A second class of models emphasizes the *endogenous development of knowledge*, or research and development, as the engine of growth. The basic contribution here is that of Romer (1990), who constructs a two-sector model in which new knowledge produced in one sector is used as an input in the production of final output. Indeed, the rigorous treatment of the accumulation of knowledge (technology) is viewed by many as being one of the key distinctions between the old and the new growth theory. Early efforts to introduce technology into the original Solow–Swan model assumed that the rate of technological change was exogenous, and the extent to which this was the case, the model could generate exogenous long-run per capita growth. Subsequent authors such as Uzawa (1965) and Shell (1967) endogenized the rate of technological change, though at a purely macroeconomic level without providing any underlying microeconomic foundations. The microeconomic foundations for understanding the evolution of technology were gradually developed later and one of the important contributions of the new growth theory is to incorporate these developments into aggregate growth models in a more rigorous way.

More recently, the knowledge sector has been extended in various directions by a number of authors (see e.g. Aghion and Howitt, 1992, and more recently, Eicher, 1996, among others). A related class of models deals with innovation and the diffusion of knowledge across countries (see Barro and Sala-i-Martin, 1995, Ch. 8).

Despite its attractive features – chiefly the role it gives to macro policy as a determinant of long-run growth – the endogenous growth model is characterized by two aspects, both of which have been the source of empirical and theoretical criticism. First, both classes of models are often characterized by having 'scale effects', meaning that variations in the size or scale of the economy, as measured by say population, affect the size of the long-run growth rate. For example, the Romer (1990) model of research and development implies that a doubling of the population devoted to research will double the growth rate. Whether the AK model is associated with scale effects depends upon whether there are production externalities that are linked to the size of the economy (see Barro and Sala-i-Martin, 1995).

However, empirical evidence does not support the presence of scale effects. For example, OECD data suggest that variations in the level of research employment have exerted no influence on the long-run growth rates of the OECD economies, in contrast to the predictions of the Romer (1990) model (see Jones, 1995b). In addition, the systematic empirical analysis of Backus et al. (1992) finds no conclusive evidence of a relation between US GDP growth and measures of scale. Moreover, Easterly and Rebelo (1993) and Stokey and Rebelo (1995) find at best weak evidence for the effects of tax rates on the long-run rate of growth, although Kneller et al. (1999) argue that these results are biased because of the incomplete specification of the government budget constraint.

The second limitation of recent endogenous growth models is the requirement that to generate an equilibrium of ongoing growth all production functions must in general exhibit constant returns to scale in the factors of production that are being accumulated endogenously. This is a strong condition, one that imposes a strict knife-edge restriction on the production structure, and has been extensively criticized (see Solow, 1994).

These considerations have stimulated the development of non-scale growth models (see Jones, 1995a, 1995b; Segerstrom, 1998; and Young, 1998). The advantage of such models is that they are consistent with balanced growth under quite general production structures. Indeed, if the knife-edge restriction that generates traditional endogenous growth models is not imposed, then any stable balanced growth equilibrium is characterized by the absence of scale effects. From this standpoint, non-scale growth equilibria should be viewed as being the norm, rather than the exception. In this case the long-run equilibrium growth rate is determined by technological parameters, in conjunction with the exogenously given growth rate of labor, and is independent of macro policy instruments.

In light of the empirical evidence, and the theoretical restrictions associated with endogenous growth models, the generality of the production structures compatible with balanced-growth paths in the non-scale growth model enhances the importance of the latter. These models are in many aspects a hybrid of endogenous and neoclassical models.[2] Technology can still be endogenous and the outcome of agents' optimizing behavior, as in Romer's (1990) work, yet the long-run growth rate is determined very much as in the Solow–Swan model, which in fact is an early example of a non-scale model. Thus, one is beginning to see a merger between the old and the new growth theory.

The non-scale model offers advantages on another issue, namely the speed of convergence. This issue is important for the reason that this speed is the crucial determinant of the relevance of the steady state relative to the transitional path. Influential empirical work by Barro and Sala-i-Martin (1992b, 1995), Sala-i-Martin (1994), Mankiw et al. (1992) and others established 2–3 per cent as a benchmark estimate of the convergence rate.[3] But both the one-sector Ramsey growth model and the two-sector Lucas (1988) endogenous growth model generate speeds of convergence that greatly exceed this empirical benchmark, being approximately 7 per cent in the neoclassical model and 10 per cent in the Lucas model. Eicher and Turnovsky (1999b, 2001) show how the two-sector non-scale model can replicate the empirical estimates of the rate of convergence with relative ease.[4]

Interestingly, the speed of convergence offers another connection between the new and the old growth theory. After Solow (1956), Swan (1956), Uzawa (1961) and others established the formal dynamic structure of the neoclassical growth model, other authors including R. Sato (1963), K. Sato (1966), Conlisk (1966), and Atkinson (1969) addressed the question of the speed of adjustment toward the steady state. Already early on, this was recognized as being important, for the reason that this speed is the crucial determinant of the relevance of the steady state relative to the transitional path. The range of estimates of convergence speeds obtained in this early literature was extensive, being sensitive to the specific characteristics of the model, such as the returns to scale, the structure of the technology, the rate of technological progress, and number of sectors.

1.1.2. Scope of this Chapter

It is beyond the scope of this chapter to present an exhaustive discussion of growth theory. For that the reader should refer to Grossman and Helpman (1991), Barro and Sala-i-Martin (1995), and Aghion and Howitt (1998) who provide comprehensive treatments of the subject, albeit from different perspectives. Rather, the purpose of this chapter is to exposit the investment-based growth models, focusing on the common structures between the old and the new growth theories. We shall restrict ourselves to closed economies, although the international aspects of traded and growth are increasingly important.[5]

We begin our discussion in Section 1.2 by expositing a small canonical model of a growing economy, which is sufficiently general to encompass alternative models. Sections 1.3 and 1.4 then consider two alternative versions of the AK growth model as special cases. Such models have been used particularly to analyze the effects of fiscal policy on growth performance.

Section 1.3 begins with the simplest Romer (1986) model with fixed labor supply and then modifies this model to the case where labor is supplied elastically. It emphasizes how going from one assumption to the other dramatically changes the determination of the equilibrium growth rate and the impact of fiscal policy. Section 1.4 discusses the Barro (1990) model where government expenditure is productive and analyzes optimal fiscal policy in that setting.

These initial models have the characteristic that the economy is always on its balanced growth path, and hence abstract from transitional dynamics. This is clearly a limitation and Section 1.5 discusses one straightforward way that transitional dynamics may be introduced. This is through the introduction of government capital, so that in contrast to the Barro model, government expenditure impinges on production as a stock, rather than as a flow. But transitional dynamics can also arise in other ways, and these are discussed in the next two sections.

Section 1.6 discusses the Lucas (1988) model where the production technology is augmented to two sectors, one producing final output and physical capital, the other producing human capital, showing the nature of the dynamics this introduces. Other authors to analyze the two-sector model include Mulligan and Sala-i-Martin (1993), Devereux and Love (1994), and Bond et al. (1996). Section 1.7 considers the non-scale growth model. This is characterized by a higher-order dynamic system than that of the corresponding endogenous growth model, so that even the simplest one-sector model is associated with transitional dynamics.

1.2.   A CANONICAL MODEL OF A GROWING ECONOMY

We begin by describing the generic structure of an economy that consumes and produces a single aggregate commodity. There are N identical individuals, each of whom has an infinite planning horizon and possesses perfect foresight. Each agent is endowed with a unit of time that can be allocated either to leisure, l, or to labour, $(1-l)$. Labor is fully employed so that total labour supply, equal to population, N, grows exponentially at the steady rate $\dot{N} = nN$. Individual domestic output, Y_i, of the traded commodity is determined by the individual's private capital stock, K_i, his labor supply, $(1-l)$, and the aggregate capital stock $K = NK_i$.[6] In order to accommodate growth under more general assumptions with respect to returns to scale, we assume that the output of the individual producer is determined by the Cobb–Douglas production function:[7]

$$Y_i = \alpha(1-l)^{1-\sigma} K_i^{\sigma} K^{\eta} \quad 0 < \sigma < 1, \ \eta \gtrless 0. \tag{1.1a}$$

This formulation is akin to the earliest endogenous growth model of Romer (1986). The spillover received by an individual from the aggregate stock of capital can be motivated in various ways. One is to interpret K as knowledge capital, as Romer suggested. Another is to assume N specific inputs (subscripted by i) with aggregate K representing an intra-industry spillover of knowledge.[8]

Each private factor of production has positive, but diminishing, marginal physical productivity. To assure the existence of a competitive equilibrium the production function exhibits constant returns to scale in the two private factors (Romer, 1986). In contrast to the standard neoclassical growth model, we do not insist that the production function exhibits constant returns to scale, and indeed total returns to scale are $1+\eta$, and are increasing or decreasing, according to whether the spillover from aggregate capital is positive or negative.

As we will show in subsequent sections, the production function is sufficiently general to encompass a variety of models. For example, we will show that the model is consistent with long-run stable growth, provided returns to scale are appropriately constrained. This contrasts with models of endogenous growth and externalities in which exogenous population growth can be shown to lead to explosive growth rates (see Romer, 1990). We should also point out that the standard AK model emerges when $\sigma + \eta = 1$, $n = 0$, and the neoclassical model corresponds to $\eta = 0$.

Aggregate consumption in the economy is denoted by C, so that the per capita consumption of the individual agent at time t is $C/N = C_i$, yielding the agent utility over an infinite time horizon represented by the intertemporal isoelastic utility function:

$$\Omega \equiv \int_0^\infty \frac{1}{\gamma}\left(C_i l^\theta\right)^\gamma e^{-\rho t} dt; \quad -\infty < \gamma < 1; \quad \theta > 0, \ 1 > \gamma(1+\theta), \ 1 > \gamma\theta, \qquad (1.1b)$$

where $1/(1-\gamma)$ equals the intertemporal elasticity of substitution, and θ measures the substitutability between consumption and leisure in utility.[9] The remaining constraints on the coefficients in (1.1b) are required to ensure that the utility function is concave in the quantities C and l. We shall assume that income from current production is taxed at the rate τ_y, while consumption is taxed at the rate τ_c. We shall illustrate the contrasting implications of different models by analyzing the purely distortionary aspects of taxation and assume that revenues from all taxes are rebated to the agent as lump sum transfers T_i. Agents accumulate physical capital, which for simplicity we assume does not depreciate, so that the individual's net rate of capital accumulation is given by his instantaneous budget constraint:

$$\dot{K}_i = (1-\tau_y)Y_i - (1+\tau_c)C_i + T_i - nK_i. \qquad (1.1c)$$

The agent's decisions are to choose his consumption, C_i, leisure, l, and rate of capital accumulation, $\dot{K}_i$, to maximize the intertemporal utility function, (1.1b), subject to the production function, (1.1a), and accumulation equation, (1.1c). The optimality conditions with respect to C_i and l are respectively:

$$C_i^{\gamma-1} l^{\theta\gamma} = \lambda(1+\tau_c) \qquad (1.2a)$$

$$\theta C_i^\gamma l^{\theta\gamma-1} = \frac{\lambda(1-\tau_y)(1-\sigma)Y_i}{(1-l)},$$ (1.2b)

where λ is the shadow value of capital (wealth). Equation (1.2a) equates the marginal utility of consumption to the tax-adjusted shadow value of capital, while (1.2b) equates the marginal utility of leisure to its opportunity cost, the after-tax marginal physical product of labor (real wage), valued at the shadow value of wealth. Optimizing with respect to K_i implies the arbitrage relationship:

$$\rho - \frac{\dot\lambda}{\lambda} = \frac{(1-\tau_y)\sigma Y}{K_i} - n.$$ (1.2c)

Equation (1.2c) is the standard Keynes–Ramsey consumption rule, equating the marginal return on consumption to the growth-adjusted after-tax rate of return on holding capital. Finally, in order to ensure that the agent's intertemporal budget constraint is met, the following transversality condition must be imposed:

$$\lim_{t\to\infty} \lambda K_i e^{-\rho t} = 0.$$ (1.2d)

The government in this canonical economy plays a limited role. It taxes income and consumption, and then rebates the tax revenues. In aggregate, these decisions are subject to the balanced budget condition:

$$\tau_y Y + \tau_c C = T.$$ (1.3)

Aggregating (1.1c) over the N individuals, and imposing (1.3) leads to the aggregate goods market clearing condition, expressed as the growth rate:

$$\frac{\dot K}{K} = \frac{Y}{K} - \frac{C}{K}.$$ (1.4)

The model can thus be summarized by the three optimality conditions (1.2a)–(1.2c), together with the goods market clearing condition (1.4). Many models assume that labor is supplied inelastically, in which case the optimality condition, (1.2b), ceases to be operative.

1.3.   THE ENDOGENOUS GROWTH MODEL

The investment-based endogenous growth model has been the subject of intensive research since 1986, with much of the focus being on the role of fiscal policy on growth and welfare.[10] As we shall demonstrate, the endogeneity (or otherwise) of labor is an important determinant of the equilibrium growth rate, and the effects of policy.

The key feature of the endogenous growth model is that it can generate ongoing growth in the absence of population growth; i.e. if $n = 0$. For this to occur, the production function, (1.1a), must have constant returns to scale in the accumulating factors, individual and aggregate capital, that is:

$$\sigma + \eta = 1. \tag{1.5}$$

Substituting this into (1.1a), this implies individual and aggregate production functions of the form:

$$Y_i = \alpha\big[(1-l)K\big]^\eta K_i^{1-\eta}; \;\; Y = \alpha\big[(1-l)N\big]^\eta K. \tag{1.6}$$

The individual production function is thus constant returns to scale in private capital, K_i, and in labor, measured in terms of 'efficiency units' $(1-l)K$. Summing over agents, the aggregate production function is thus linear in the endogenously accumulating capital stock. Note that as long as $\eta \neq 0$ so that there is an aggregate externality, the average (and marginal) productivity of capital depends upon the size of the population. Increasing the population, holding other technological characteristics constant, increases the productivity of capital and the equilibrium growth rate. The economy is thus said to have a 'scale effect' (see Jones, 1995a). Such scale effects run counter to the empirical evidence and have been a source of criticism of the AK growth models (see Backus et al., 1992). These scale effects can be eliminated from the AK model if either (1) there are no externalities ($\eta = 0$), or (2) if the individual production function (1.1a) is modified to:

$$Y_i = \alpha(1-l)^{1-\sigma}K_i^\sigma\left(\frac{K}{N}\right)^\eta$$

so that the externality depends upon the average, rather than the aggregate capital stock (see Mulligan and Sala-i-Martin, 1993). Henceforth throughout this section, we shall normalize the size of the population at $N = 1$ and thereby eliminate the issue of scale effects.

1.3.1. Inelastic Labor Supply

We begin with the widely discussed case where labor supply is inelastic, i.e.
$l = \bar{l}$. With population normalized, the individual and aggregate production
functions are of the pure AK form:

$$Y_i = AK_i; \quad Y = AK, \tag{1.7}$$

where $A \equiv \alpha\sigma(1-\bar{l})^{1-\sigma}$ is a fixed constant. With the labor supply fixed, both
the marginal and average productivity of capital is constant. The specification
of the technology, consistent with ongoing growth, is a strong knife-edge
condition, one for which the endogenous growth model has been criticized
(see Solow, 1994).[11]

The solution proceeds by trial and error, by postulating a solution of the
form $C = \mu K$, where μ is a constant to be determined. Differentiating (1.2a)
with respect to time, and combining with (1.4) and (1.7) with fixed
employment (and normalized population), leads to the following explicit
solutions for the equilibrium growth rate and consumption/capital ratio:

$$\frac{\dot{C}}{C} = \frac{\dot{K}}{K} \equiv \psi = \frac{A(1-\tau_y)-\rho}{1-\gamma} \tag{1.8a}$$

$$\frac{C}{K} \equiv \mu = \frac{\rho + A(1-\gamma) - A(1-\tau_y)}{1-\lambda}. \tag{1.8b}$$

These two expressions specify the ratio of consumption/capital, and the
rate of growth of capital (and therefore consumption) along the optimal path,
in terms of all exogenous parameters. Noting that $Y = AK$, the right-hand
side of (1.8a) can be written as $(Y/K)(1-C/Y)$. Thus (1.8a) asserts that the
equilibrium rate of growth of capital equals the product of the savings rate,
$(1-C/Y)$, together with the output/capital ratio, precisely as in Harrod
(1939). The difference is – and it is significant – that the savings rate is
endogenously determined through intertemporal optimization, rather than
being assumed exogenously.

In addition, the transversality condition (1.2d) must hold. Using (1.8a),
(1.8b), and the fact that $\dot{\lambda}/\lambda = (\gamma-1)\psi$, this implies the following constraint
on the equilibrium growth rate in the economy:

$$\rho - \gamma\psi > 0 ; \text{ i.e. } \rho > \gamma A(1-\tau_y). \tag{1.8c}$$

Condition (1.8c) is automatically satisfied for $\gamma \le 0$ (thereby including the
logarithmic utility function); otherwise it imposes a constraint on the tax

rate.[12] In any event, the condition (1.8c) for a viable solution is a weak one that any reasonable economy must surely satisfy.

The following general characteristics of this equilibrium can be observed.

1. Consumption, capital, and output are always on their steady-state growth paths, growing at the rate ψ. This is driven by the difference between the after-tax rate of return on capital and the rate of time preference.
2. With all taxes being fully rebated and labour supply fixed, the consumption tax is completely neutral. It has no effect on any aspect of the economic performance and acts like a pure lump-sum tax.
3. An increase in income tax leads to less investment and growth, and more consumption.

A key issue concerns the effects of tax changes, on the level of welfare of the representative agent, when consumption follows its equilibrium growth path. This is given by the expression:

$$\Omega = \int_0^\infty \frac{1}{\gamma} \left[C(0)e^{\psi t} \right]^\gamma e^{-\rho t} dt = \frac{[\mu]^\gamma K_0^\gamma}{\gamma(\rho - \gamma\psi)}. \tag{1.9}$$

Thus, the overall intertemporal welfare effect of any policy change depend upon its effects on (1) the initial consumption level, and (2) the growth rate of consumption. On impact, the higher tax raises current consumption, which is welfare improving in the short run. But at the same time, it reduces the growth rate, and this is welfare deteriorating. Evaluating (1.9) we can show that the overall effect on intertemporal welfare is:

$$\frac{d\Omega}{d\tau_y} \frac{1}{\gamma\Omega} = -\frac{\tau_y A^2}{(1-\gamma)c(\rho - \gamma\psi)} \leq 0.$$

Starting from a zero tax, the imposition of a tax has no effect on welfare; the benefits to current consumption are exactly offset by the discounted adverse effects on the growth rate. But with a positive initial tax. the adverse growth effects dominate and there is a net welfare loss.

1.3.2. Elastic Labor Supply

The endogenous growth model we have been discussing includes two interdependent critical knife-edge restrictions: (1) inelastic labor supply, and (2) fixed productivity of capital. The structure of the equilibrium changes significantly when the labor supply is generalized. This introduces two key changes. The first is that the production function is modified to (1.6), so that the productivity of capital now depends positively upon the fraction of time devoted to labor. Second, the fixed endowment of a unit of time leads to the requirement that the steady-state allocation of time between labor and leisure must be constant.

This latter condition provides a link between the long-run rate of growth of consumption and the rate of growth of output. This can be seen by dividing the optimality condition (1.2a) by (1.2b). On the left-hand side we see that with the allocation of time remaining finite, the marginal rate of substitution between consumption and leisure grows with consumption. On the right-hand side we see that, given the fixed labor supply, the wage rate grows with output. For these condition to remain compatible over time, the equilibrium consumption/output ratio must therefore remain bounded, being given by:

$$\frac{C_i}{Y_i} = \frac{C}{Y} = \left(\frac{1-\tau_y}{1+\tau_c}\right)\left(\frac{l}{1-l}\right)\frac{1-\sigma}{\theta}. \tag{1.10}$$

To obtain the macroeconomic equilibrium we take the time derivatives of: (1) the optimality condition for consumption, (1.2a), (2) the equilibrium consumption/output ratio, (1.10), and, (3) the production function, (1.6). Combining the resulting equations with (1.6) and (1.2c), the macroeconomic equilibrium can be expressed by the differential equation in l:

$$\frac{dl(t)}{dt} = \frac{G(l)}{F(l)}, \tag{1.11}$$

where

$$F(l) \equiv \left[1 - \gamma(1+\theta)\right]\frac{1}{l} + \frac{(1-\gamma)(1-\eta)}{1-l} > 0$$

$$G(l) = \left\{(1-\tau_y)\sigma - (1-\gamma)\left[1 - \left(\frac{1-\tau_y}{1+\tau_c}\right)\left(\frac{l}{1-l}\right)\frac{1-\sigma}{\theta}\right]\right\}\frac{Y}{K} - \rho.$$

1.3.2.1. Balanced-growth equilibrium

Steady-state equilibrium is attained when the fraction of time allocated to leisure (or equivalently to labor supply) ceases to adjust. Setting $\dot{l} = 0$, steady state is characterized by the following balanced-growth conditions:

$$\frac{\dot{C}}{C} = \frac{\dot{Y}}{Y} = \frac{\dot{K}}{K} = -\frac{1}{1-\gamma}\frac{\dot{\lambda}}{\lambda} \equiv \tilde{\psi}.$$

Substituting for (Y/K) from (1.6) into (1.2c) yields:

RR: $$\tilde{\psi} = \frac{1}{1-\gamma}\left[(1-\tau_y)\ (\alpha\sigma(1-\tilde{l})^{1-\sigma} - \rho\right].$$ (1.12a)

Equation (1.12a) describes the tradeoff locus, *RR*, between the equilibrium growth rate, $\tilde{\psi}$, and leisure, $\tilde{l}$, that ensures the equality between the after-tax rate of return on capital and the return on consumption. This curve can be shown to be negatively sloped and concave with respect to the origin (see Figure 1.1). This is because a higher fraction of time devoted to leisure will reduce the productivity of, and return, to capital. For rates of return to remain in equilibrium, the rate of return on consumption must fall correspondingly, and this requires the growth rate of the marginal utility of capital to rise, that is, the balanced-growth rate of the economy must decline.

Similarly, substituting (C/Y) from (1.10) and (Y/K) into (1.4) yields:

PP: $$\tilde{\psi} = \left[1 - \left(\frac{1-\tau_w}{1+\tau_c}\right)\frac{1-\sigma}{\theta}\left(\frac{\tilde{l}}{1-\tilde{l}}\right)\right]\alpha(1-\tilde{l})^{1-\sigma}.$$ (1.12b)

The locus, *PP* describes the trade-off between the equilibrium growth rate and leisure that ensures product market equilibrium is maintained. This, too, is negatively sloped and concave. Intuitively, a higher fraction of time devoted to leisure reduces the productivity of capital. It also increases the consumption/output ratio, thus having a negative effect on the growth rate of capital in the economy. As *l* increases, employment declines, the marginal product of labor increases, and thus the tradeoff along the PP locus becomes steeper.[13]

1.3.2.2. Equilibrium dynamics

We return to the dynamic equation (1.11) and consider its stability in the neighborhood of the balanced-growth equilibrium defined by (1.12a, 1.12b). In steady-state equilibrium, $G(\tilde{l}) = 0$, and the linearized dynamics about that point are represented by:

$$\frac{dl(t)}{dt} = \frac{G'(\tilde{l})}{F(\tilde{l})}\left(l(t) - \tilde{l}\right).$$ (1.13)

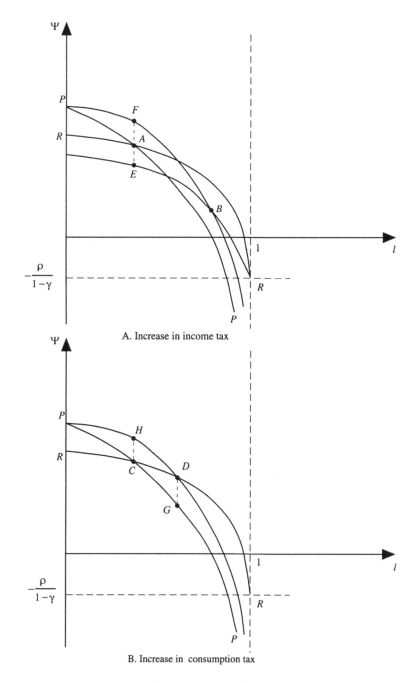

Figure 1.1 Tax changes with endogenous labor

The existence of a balanced-growth equilibrium suffices to ensure that $G'(\tilde{l}) > 0,$ in which case (1.13) is an unstable differential equation. The only solution consistent with a balanced-growth equilibrium is for $l = \tilde{l}$ at all points of time so that the economy is always on the balanced-growth path (1.12a)–(1.12b).[14]

1.3.2.3. Fiscal shocks

The model can be conveniently employed to analyze the effects of various kinds of fiscal disturbances. The qualitative effects of simple changes in the fiscal instruments on the macroeconomic equilibrium are readily obtained by considering shifts in the *RR* and *PP* curves. Others, involving composite changes require more formal analysis.

One important consequence of endogenizing the labor supply is that because of the work–leisure choice, the consumption tax, τ_c is no longer neutral. Indeed it has the same qualitative effect as an increase in the income tax rate, $\tau_y,$ decreasing the fraction of time devoted to work and reducing the equilibrium growth rate. These responses are illustrated in Figure 1.1. Part A illustrates the case of an increase in the income tax, $\tau_y,$ with revenues rebated in lump-sum fashion. To the extent that it is levied on capital income, it leads to a downward rotation in the *RR* locus, which given the fraction of time devoted to leisure, leads to an immediate reduction in the growth rate, as measured by the move from *A* to *E*. This in turn reduces the return on consumption, causing a substitution of leisure for labor, and reducing the rate of return on capital to that of consumption.[15] This decrease in employment reduces output, leading to a further reduction in the growth rate. To the extent that it is levied on wage income, it leads to an upward rotation in the *PP* locus. Given leisure, this leads to an immediate reduction in the consumption/output ratio, and a corresponding rise in the growth rate of output, from *A* to *F*. This raises the return on consumption, causing agents to increase consumption and leisure over work. This causes a reduction in output and the growth rate, leading to a reduction in the return to capital and in consumption. The ultimate shift in equilibrium is thus represented by a move from *A* to *B*, being a combination of the moves EB and FB, with both components of the tax increase reinforcing their common effects on leisure and the growth rate. An increase in the consumption tax leads only to an upward rotation in the *PP* locus, as illustrated in Part B and is therefore equivalent to a wage tax.[16]

1.4.   PRODUCTIVE GOVERNMENT EXPENDITURE

1.4.1.   The Barro Model

Thus far we have focused on the taxation side of the government budget. But most tax revenues are used to finance government expenditures that provide some benefits to the economy. We shall focus on government expenditure that enhances the productive capacity of the economy, identifying such expenditures as being on some form of infrastructure. This model was developed by Barro (1990), and like Barro, we shall make the simplifying assumption that the benefits are derived from the *flow* of productive government expenditures. In Section 1.5 we shall briefly discuss the more plausible case where it is the accumulated *stock* of government expenditure that is relevant.

We abstract from labor (setting $l = 0$) and assume that the production function of the representative firm is now specified by:

$$Y_i = \alpha G_s^\eta K_i^{1-\eta} \equiv \alpha \left(\frac{G_s}{K_i} \right)^\eta K_i, \qquad 0 < \eta < 1, \tag{1.14}$$

where G_s denotes the flow of productive services enjoyed by the individual firm. Thus productive government expenditure has the property of positive, but diminishing, marginal physical product, while enhancing the productivity of private capital. As in Section 1.3, we assume that the population growth $n = 0$.

We shall assume that the services derived from aggregate expenditure, G, are:

$$G_s = G \left(\frac{K_i}{K} \right)^{1-\varepsilon}, \tag{1.15}$$

where K denotes the aggregate capital stock. Most public services are characterized by some degree of congestion and (1.15) provides one convenient formulation that builds on the public goods literature (see Edwards, 1990). The parameter ε can be interpreted as describing the degree of relative congestion associated with the public good and the following special cases merit comment. If $\varepsilon = 1$, the level of services derived by the individual from the government expenditure is fixed at G, independent of both the firm's own usage of capital and aggregate usage. The good G is a non-rival, non-excludable public good that is available equally to each individual; there is no congestion. Since few, if any such public good exist, it is probably best viewed as a benchmark. At the other extreme, if $\varepsilon = 0$, then only if G increases in direct proportion to the aggregate capital stock, K, does the level of the public service available to the individual firm remain fixed. We shall refer to this case as being one of *proportional* (relative) congestion. In that case, the public good is like a private good, in that since $K = NK_i$, the individual receives his proportionate share of services, $G_s = G/N$.

In order to sustain an equilibrium of ongoing growth, the level of government expenditure must be tied to the scale of the economy. This can be achieved most conveniently by assuming that the government sets its level of expenditure as a share of aggregate output, $Y = NY_i$:

$$G = gY. \tag{1.16}$$

In an environment of growth this is a reasonable assumption. Government expenditure thus increases with the size of the economy, with an expansionary government expenditure being denoted by an increase in g.

Summing (1.14) over the N identical agents and substituting (1.15) and (1.16), we obtain:

$$G = \left(\alpha g N^{\eta\varepsilon}\right)^{\frac{1}{1-\eta}} K; \quad Y = \left(\alpha g^{\eta} N^{\eta\varepsilon}\right)^{\frac{1}{1-\eta}} K. \tag{1.17}$$

Aggregate output thus has the fixed AK technology, where the productivity of capital depends (positively) upon the productive government input. Notice that provided $\eta\varepsilon > 0$, the productivity of capital depends upon the size (scale) of the economy, as parameterized by the fixed population, N. This is because the size of the externality generated by government expenditure increases with the size of the economy, playing an analogous role to aggregate capital in the Romer (1986) model. As in that model, this scale effect disappears if $\varepsilon = 0$, so that there is proportional congestion and each agent receives his own individual share of government services, G/N.

We now re-solve the representative individual's optimization problem. In so doing, he is assumed to take aggregate government spending, G, and the aggregate stock of capital, K, as given, insofar as these impact on the productivity of his capital stock. Performing the optimization, the optimality conditions (1.2a) and (1.2b) remain unchanged. The optimality condition with respect to capital is now modified to:

$$\rho - \frac{\dot{\lambda}}{\lambda} = \frac{(1-\tau_y)(1-\eta\varepsilon)Y_i}{K_i}. \tag{1.2c'}$$

The difference is that the private marginal physical product of capital is now proportional to $(1-\eta\varepsilon)$, depending both upon the degree of congestion and the productivity of government expenditure. The less congestion (the larger ε) the smaller the benefits of government expenditure are tied to the usage of private capital, thus lowering the return.

The other modification is to the government budget constraint, (1.4), which becomes:

$$\tau_y Y + \tau_c C = G. \tag{1.3'}$$

1.4.2. Optimal Fiscal Policy

It is clear from Section 1.4.1 that growth and economic performance are heavily influenced by fiscal policy in this model. This naturally leads to the important question of the optimal tax structure. To address this issue it is convenient to consider, as a benchmark, the first-best optimum of the central planner, who controls resources directly, against which the decentralized economy can be assessed. The central planner is assumed to internalize the equilibrium relationship $NK_i = K$, as well as the expenditure rule (1.16). The optimality conditions are now modified to:

$$C_i^{\gamma-1} = \lambda \tag{1.2a'}$$

$$\rho - \frac{\dot{\lambda}}{\lambda} = \frac{(1-g)Y_i}{K_i}. \tag{1.2c''}$$

The key difference is that the social return to capital nets out the fraction of output appropriated by the government.

It is straightforward to show that the decentralized economy will mimic the first-best equilibrium of the centrally planned economy if and only if:

$$(1-g) = (1-\tau_y)(1-\varepsilon\eta). \tag{1.18a}$$

Intuitively, government expenditure, by being tied to the stock of capital in the economy, induces spillovers into the domestic capital market, generating distortions that require a tax on capital income in order to ensure that the net private return on capital equals its social return.

To understand (1.18) better, it is useful to observe that the welfare-maximizing share of government expenditure, is (Barro, 1990):

$$\hat{g} = \eta. \tag{1.19}$$

Substituting (1.19) into (1.18) and simplifying, the optimal income tax can be expressed in the form:

$$\hat{\tau}_y = \frac{g - \eta\varepsilon}{1 - \eta\varepsilon} = \frac{g - \hat{g}}{1 - \eta\varepsilon} + \frac{\hat{g}(1 - \varepsilon)}{(1 - \eta\varepsilon)}. \qquad (1.18a')$$

In order to finance its expenditures, (1.3'), the government must, in conjunction with $\hat{\tau}_y$, set a corresponding consumption tax $\hat{\tau}_c$:

$$\hat{\tau}_c = \frac{\eta\varepsilon(1 - g)}{(1 - \eta\varepsilon)(C/Y)}. \qquad (1.18b)$$

Equation (1.18a') emphasizes how the optimal tax on capital income corrects for two distortions. The first is due to the deviation in government expenditure from the optimum, the second is caused by congestion. Comparing (1.18a') and (1.18b) we see that there is a tradeoff between the income and the consumption tax in achieving these objectives, and that this depends upon the degree of congestion. This tradeoff is seen most directly if g is set optimally in accordance with (1.19). In this case, if there is no congestion, government expenditure should be fully financed by a consumption tax alone; capital income should remain untaxed. As congestion increases (ε declines), the optimal consumption tax should be reduced and the income tax increased until with proportional congestion, government expenditure should be financed entirely by an income tax.

It is useful to compare the present optimal tax on capital with the well-known Chamley (1986) proposition which requires that asymptotically the optimal tax on capital should converge to zero. The Chamley analysis did not consider any externalities from government expenditure. Setting $\eta = 0$, we still find that the optimal tax on capital is equal to the share of output claimed by the government ($\overline{\tau} = g$). The difference is that by specifying government expenditure as a fraction of output, its level is not exogenous, but instead is proportional to the size of the growing capital stock. The decision to accumulate capital stock by the private sector leads to an increase in the supply of public goods in the future. If the private sector treats government spending as independent of its investment decision (when in fact it is not), a tax on capital is necessary to internalize the externality and thereby correct the distortion. Thus, in general, the Chamley rule of not taxing capital in the long run will be non-optimal, although it will emerge in the special case where $g = \eta\varepsilon$, in which case there is no spillover from government expenditure to the capital market.

We conclude by noting two further points. The equilibrium growth rate in the Barro model is:

$$\tilde{\psi} = \frac{(1-g)\left(\alpha g^{\eta}\right)^{\frac{1}{1-\eta}} - \rho}{1-\gamma}.$$

It is straightforward to show that the equilibrium growth rate is maximized at the optimal government expenditure/output ratio. Maximizing the productivity of government expenditure net of resource costs maximizes both the growth rate and utility. The coincidence of the growth-maximizing size of government and its welfare-maximizing size is a strong result, but it is not robust. For example, it ceases to hold if the installation of new capital involves adjustment costs of the type where the productive government investment (plausibly) reduces the costs of adjustment, along with enhancing the productivity of private capital (see Turnovsky, 1996b). It also ceases to apply if the government production good enters the private production function as a stock, rather than as a flow (see Futagami et al., 1993). Third, it ceases to apply to the economy being considered here if that economy is subject to stochastic productivity. This is because growth maximization in general entails too much risk for a risk-averse representative agent (see Turnovsky, 1999a).

The final point is that it is possible to augment this model to include endogenous labor. The qualitative nature of the solution is analogous to that of Section 1.3.2. A detailed analysis of fiscal policy in this case is provided by Turnovsky (2000).

1.5.   PUBLIC AND PRIVATE CAPITAL

The models discussed thus far all have the characteristic that consumption and output (capital) are on their balanced growth paths; there are no transitional dynamics. Instead, the economy adjusts infinitely fast to any exogenous shock, thus contradicting the empirical evidence pertaining to speeds of convergence. As noted, the point of this literature is that the economy adjusts relatively slowly, with the rate of 2 per cent per annum being a benchmark estimate. This implies that the economy is mostly off its balanced growth path, on some transitional path, which only gradually converges to steady state. It is therefore important to modify the model to allow for such transitional dynamics, and this can be achieved in several ways, all of which assign a central role to a second state variable to the dynamics.

In this section, we consider one important modification to the basic model that accomplishes this objective: the introduction of public in addition to private capital. As we will show in Section 1.6 the two-sector endogenous growth model of Lucas (1988), in which the two capital goods are physical capital and human capital, is an alternative way. In both these cases, the stable adjustment path is a one-dimensional locus, implying that all variables converge to their respective long-run equilibrium at the same constant rate. But one further way transitional dynamics can be introduced is through a modification of the technology to allow it to have non-scale growth, along the lines initially proposed by Jones (1995a, 1995b). It is shown that incorporating a more general production technology increases the dimensionality of the transitional path, thus allowing for more flexible dynamic transitional behavior patterns. This model will be discussed further in Section 1.7.

Most models analyzing productive government expenditure treat the current *flow* of government expenditure as the source of contribution to productive capacity. While the flow specification has the virtue of tractability, it is open to the criticism that insofar as productive government expenditures are intended to represent public infrastructure, such as roads and education, it is the accumulated *stock*, rather than the current flow, that is the more appropriate argument in the production function.

Despite this, relatively few authors have adopted the alternative approach of modeling productive government expenditure as a stock. Arrow and Kurz (1970) were the first authors to model government expenditure as a form of investment in the Ramsey model. More recently, Baxter and King (1993) study the macroeconomic implications of increases in the stocks of public goods. They derive the transitional dynamic response of output, investment, consumption, employment, and interest rates to such policies by calibrating a real business cycle model. Fisher and Turnovsky (1998) address similar issues from a more analytical perspective.

The literature introducing both private and public capital into growth models is sparse. Futagami et al. (1993), Glomm and Ravikumar (1994), and Turnovsky (1997a) do so in a closed economy, and an extension to an open economy is developed by Turnovsky (1997b). Private capital in the Glomm–Ravikumar model fully depreciates each period, rather than being subject to at most gradual (or possibly zero) depreciation. This enables the dynamics of the system to be represented by a single-state variable alone, so that the system behaves much more like the Barro model in which government expenditure is introduced as a flow. In particular, under constant returns to scale in the reproducible factors, there are no transitional dynamics and the economy is always on a balanced growth path.

We now outline the main features of such a model, in the simpler case where labor supply is fixed. The key modification to the model is the production function, which is now of the form:

$$Y = \alpha K_g^{\eta} K^{1-\eta} \quad \alpha > 0; \ 0 < \eta < 1, \tag{1.20}$$

where K denotes the representative firm's capital stock of private capital and K_g denotes public (government) capital. The production function is analogous to that introduced in Section 1.4, except that the government input is introduced as a stock, rather than as a flow. Equation (1.20) embodies the assumption that the public capital enhances the productivity of private capital, though at a diminishing rate. Public capital is not subject to congestion and neither form of capital is subject to depreciation.[17] The model abstracts from labor, so that as in the basic AK model of Sections 1.3 and 1.4, private capital should be interpreted broadly to include human, as well as physical, capital.

The other main modification is that government expenditure leads to the accumulation of public capital, and assuming that the government sets its investment as a proportion, g, of output:

$$\dot{K}_g = G = gY \qquad 0 < g < 1. \tag{1.21a}$$

In setting policy, the government is subject to its budget constraint:

$$G = \tau_y Y + \tau_c C + T, \tag{1.21b}$$

where T denotes lump-sum taxes. Summing the private and public budget constraint yields the economy-wide resource constraint:

$$Y = C + \dot{K} + \dot{K}_g. \tag{1.22}$$

To derive the macroeconomic equilibrium, we need to express it in terms of stationary variables. For this purpose it is convenient to express it in terms of quantities relative to the growing stock of private capital, namely, $z \equiv K_g / K$; $c \equiv C / K$. Taking the time derivatives of these quantities and combining with (1.21) and (1.22), together with the optimality conditions for the private agent, the equilibrium dynamics can be represented by:

$$\frac{\dot{z}}{z} = g\alpha z^{\eta-1} - (1-g)\alpha z^{\eta} + c \tag{1.23a}$$

$$\frac{\dot{c}}{c} = \frac{(1-\tau_y)\alpha(1-\eta)z^{\eta} - \rho}{1-\gamma} - (1-g)\alpha z^{\eta} + c. \tag{1.23b}$$

The first of these equations describes the differential growth rate between public and private capital and is obtained from the relationship $\dot{z}/z = \dot{K}_g/K_g - \dot{K}/K$. The second equation determines the differential growth rate between consumption and private capital. It is obtained from the relationship $\dot{c}/c = \dot{C}/C - \dot{K}/K$, where $\dot{C}/C$ is obtained, in turn, from combining the time derivative of (1.2a') with (1.21a) and (1.22).

1.5.1. Steady-state

Steady-state equilibrium is determined by:

$$\tilde{c} = (1 - g)\alpha(\tilde{z})^\eta - g\alpha(\tilde{z})^{\eta-1} \tag{1.24a}$$

$$\frac{(1 - \tau_y)\alpha(1 - \eta)(\tilde{z})^\eta - \rho}{1 - \gamma} - (1 - g)\alpha(\tilde{z})^\eta + \tilde{c} = 0, \tag{1.24b}$$

which jointly determine the equilibrium values of $\tilde{z}$ and $\tilde{c}$. However, equations (1.24a) and (1.24b) define a pair of nonlinear equations in $\tilde{z}$ and $\tilde{c}$, and may or may not be consistent with a well-defined steady state in which $\tilde{c} > 0, \tilde{z} > 0$ (see Turnovsky, 1997a). Having determined these quantities, the corresponding (common) equilibrium growth rate of consumption and the two capital stocks may be expressed in the following equivalent forms:

$$\tilde{\psi} \equiv \frac{\tilde{C}}{C} = \frac{\tilde{K}}{K} = \frac{\tilde{K}_g}{K_g} = g\alpha\tilde{z}^{\eta-1} = (1 - g)\alpha\tilde{z}^\eta + \tilde{c}. \tag{1.25}$$

The long-run effects of fiscal policies on the relative capital stock, $\tilde{z}$, consumption ratio, $\tilde{c}$, and the growth rate, $\tilde{\psi}$, are obtained by considering (1.24a), (1.24b), and (1.25). We shall discuss the effects of changes in (1) the income tax rate and (2) the share of government expenditure, assuming that the government budget constraint is met through an appropriate adjustment in lump-sum taxes. The equilibrium is independent of the consumption tax, τ_c, which therefore operates as a lump-sum tax, and may also serve as the balancing item in the government budget.

Omitting details, the following responses to fiscal policy can be established. An increase in the income tax rate, τ_y, (with tax revenues rebated) reduces the net rate of return to private capital, thereby inducing investors to switch from saving to consumption, thus raising the consumption/capital ratio and decreasing the growth rate of private capital. This negative effect on the return to private capital favors its decumulation and leads to a long-run increase in the ratio of public to private capital. By contrast, an increase in the share of output claimed by the government, financed by a lump-sum tax, raises the equilibrium growth rate of capital unambiguously.[18] The case considered by Futagami et al. (1993), in which government expenditure is determined by tax revenues, corresponds to $g = \tau_y$ and hence $dg = d\tau_y$ and is a hybrid of these two cases. It is straightforward to verify that while the increase in g raises the growth rate, the corresponding increase in τ_y does the opposite, rendering a net effect that depends upon $(\eta - g)$, precisely as in the Barro model, discussed in Section 1.4.1. It then follows that setting $g = \eta$ is growth-maximizing.

1.5.2.   Transitional Dynamics: Tax Cuts

The transitional dynamics for z and c are obtained by linearing (1.23) about (1.24) in the usual manner. And having derived these relationships, one can further derive the linearized dynamics for the growth rates themselves. The formal solutions are provided by Turnovsky (1997a). Figure 1.2 illustrates the transitional dynamics of private and public capital in response to a fiscal expansion taking the form of a permanent cut in the income tax rate, financed by a lump-sum tax.

Suppose that the economy is initially in steady-state equilibrium at the point P, and that a *permanent* tax cut is introduced. The immediate effect of the lower tax is to raise the net return to private capital, inducing agents to reduce their level of consumption and to increase their rate of accumulation of private capital. This increase in the growth of private capital causes the ratio of public to private capital, z, to begin to decline. As z declines, the average productivity of private capital, αz^{η} falls, causing its growth rate to decrease. The transitional adjustment in the growth rate of private capital (ψ_k) is illustrated by the initial jump from P to A, on the new stable arm $X'X'$, followed by the continuous decline AQ, to the new steady state at Q. With the growth of public capital being tied through aggregate output to the capital stocks in accordance with (1.21a), the growth rate of public capital does not respond instantaneously to the lower tax rate, τ_y. The stable arm YY remains fixed. Instead, as z declines, the average productivity of public capital $\alpha z^{\eta-1}$ rises, causing the growth rate of public capital (ψ_g) to rise gradually over time along the path PQ. During the transition, the growth rates of the two capital stocks approach their common long-run equilibrium growth rate from different directions.

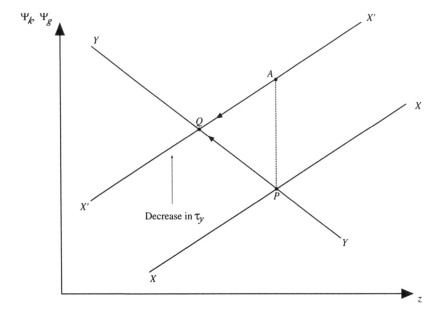

Figure 1.2 Transitional dynamics of capital: tax cut

1.5.3.   Optimal Fiscal Policy

Futagami et al. (1993) analyze the optimal (welfare-maximizing) size of government (optimal income tax) in this economy and show that it is smaller than the growth-maximizing size. This is in contrast to Barro (1990), who, introducing government expenditure as a flow in the production function, finds that the welfare-maximizing and growth-maximizing shares of government expenditure coincide. The difference is accounted for by the fact that when government expenditure influences production as a flow, maximizing the marginal product of government expenditure net of its resource cost maximizes the growth rate of capital. But it also maximizes the social return to public expenditure, thereby maximizing overall intertemporal welfare. By contrast, when government expenditure affects output as a stock, public capital needs to be accumulated to attain the growth-maximizing level. This involves forgoing consumption, leading to welfare losses relative to the social optimum. Intertemporal welfare is raised by reducing the growth rate, thereby enabling the agent to enjoy more consumption.

Turnovsky (1997a) analyzes optimal tax policy in this economy and shows that the first-best tax policy comprises two components, one fixed, the other time-varying. This is because there are two objectives to attain. The fixed component ensures that the steady state of the first-best optimum is replicated, and this has the general characteristics of the optimal tax structure of Section 1.4.2. But because the internal dynamics of the decentralized economy do not in general coincide with those of the first-best optimum, the time-varying component of the optimal tax is necessary to introduce the appropriate correction along the transitional path.

1.6. TWO-SECTOR MODEL OF ENDOGENOUS GROWTH

Two-sector models of economic growth were pioneered by Uzawa (1961), Takayama (1963), and others. In this early literature, the two sectors corresponded to the production of the consumption good and the production of the investment good, respectively. The key results in that early literature focused on the uniqueness and stability of equilibrium, which was shown to depend critically upon the capital intensity of the investment good sector relative to the consumption sector.

In a seminal paper, Lucas (1988) introduced the two-sector endogenous growth model. The model includes two capital goods, physical capital and human capital. The former is produced along with consumption goods in the output sector, using as inputs both human and physical capital. Human capital is produced in the education sector using both physical and human capital. The agent's decisions at any instant of time are: (1) how much to consume, (2) how to allocate his physical and human capital across the two sectors, and (3) at what rates to accumulate total physical and human capital over time. Having two capital goods, this model is characterized by transitional dynamics. However, because two-sector endogenous growth models initially proved to be intractable, much of the analysis was restricted to balanced-growth paths (Lucas 1988; Devereux and Love 1994), or to analyzing transitional dynamics using numerical simulation methods (Mulligan and Sala-i-Martin 1993; Pecorino 1993; Devereux and Love 1994). One important exception to this is Bond et al. (1996) which, by using the methods of the two-sector trade model, provides an effective analysis of the dynamic structure of the two-sector endogenous growth model.[19]

1.6.1. The Two-sector Economy

There is a single, infinitely lived representative agent who accumulates two types of capital for rental at the competitively determined rental rate. The first is physical capital, K, and the second is human capital, H. Neither of these capital goods is subject to depreciation and their accumulation is free of adjustment costs. For expositional simplicity, there is no government.

These two forms of capital are used by the agent to produce a final output good, X, taken to be the numeraire, by means of a linearly homogeneous production function:

$$X = aK_X^\alpha H_X^{1-\alpha} \quad 0 < \alpha < 1, \tag{1.26a}$$

where, K_X and H_X denote the allocations of the two capital goods to the production of final output. Goods may be either consumed, C, or added to the capital stock, which therefore evolves as follows:

$$\dot{K} = aK_X^\alpha H_X^{1-\alpha} - C. \tag{1.26b}$$

The agent also adds to human capital, using an analogous production function:

$$\dot{H} = Y = bK_Y^\delta H_Y^{1-\delta} \quad 0 < \delta < 1. \tag{1.26c}$$

The key feature of the production setup is that the two production functions are linearly homogeneous in the two reproducible factors, K and H. This is critical for an equilibrium with steady growth to exist. This specification is more general than the assumption frequently adopted that physical capital is not an input into the production of human capital (i.e. $\delta = 0$) in (1.26c). Other authors, however, have introduced externalities analogous to those introduced into the one-sector model (see Lucas, 1988), Mulligan and Sala-i-Martin (1993). As Bond et al. note, their approach can be easily extended to include such externalities. Both forms of capital are costlessly and instantaneously mobile across the two sectors, with the sectoral allocations being constrained by:

$$K_X + K_Y = K \tag{1.26d}$$

$$H_X + H_Y = H. \tag{1.26e}$$

The agent chooses the rate of consumption, C, capital allocations K_X, K_Y, H_X and H_Y, and rates of capital accumulation, $\dot{K}$ and $\dot{H}$, to maximize the intertemporal isoelastic utility function subject to the constraints (1.26a)–(1.26e), and the initial stocks of assets, H_0 and K_0. From the optimality conditions we immediately obtain:

$$\frac{\dot{C}}{C} = \frac{r_K(q) - \rho}{1 - \gamma} \equiv \psi(t), \tag{1.27}$$

where q denotes the relative price of human to physical capital. While (1.27) is analogous to previous expressions for the growth rate, for example, (1.8a), in general, q evolves during the transition, thereby rendering the return on capital, r_K, and the growth rate, $\psi(t)$ time-varying.

As Bond et al. (1996) show, the macroeconomic dynamics can be represented by three differential equations in: (1) $k \equiv K/H$, the relative stocks of physical to human capital; (2) $c \equiv C/H$, the ratio of consumption to human capital, and (3) q. As we will see, the steady-state equilibrium will have the characteristic that $\dot{k} = \dot{h} = \dot{c} = 0$, so that consumption and the two types of capital will all grow at an equilibrium rate determined by (1.27), while the relative price of the two types of capital will be constant.

The derivation of the macroeconomic equilibrium proceeds in two stages. The first stage determines the static allocation of existing resources. We express the sectoral capital intensities and marginal physical products of capital in terms of the relative price of nontraded to traded goods, and also express the absolute levels of the allocation of capital in terms of the gradually evolving aggregate stocks, K and H. The second stage then determines the dynamics. As is characteristic of two-factor, two-sector growth models, the dynamics of the system decouple, with the price dynamics evolving independently of the quantity dynamics.

1.6.2. Transitional Dynamics

Working through the model one can show that the linearized transitional dynamics is represented by a matrix equation of the following form:

$$\begin{pmatrix} \dot{q} \\ \dot{c} \\ \dot{k} \end{pmatrix} = \begin{pmatrix} a_{11} & 0 & 0 \\ a_{21} & 0 & a_{23} \\ a_{31} & -1 & a_{33} \end{pmatrix} \begin{pmatrix} q(t) - \tilde{q} \\ c(t) - \tilde{c} \\ k(t) - \tilde{k} \end{pmatrix} \tag{1.28}$$

where the elements of the matrix have the following sign patterns:

$$\operatorname{sgn}(a_{11}) = -\operatorname{sgn}(a_{23}) = -\operatorname{sgn}(a_{33}) = \operatorname{sgn}(\delta - \alpha); \quad a_{31} < 0 \tag{1.29}$$

The characteristic equation to (1.28) can be written as follows:

$$(\mu - \alpha_{11})(\mu^2 - a_{33}\mu + a_{23}) = 0, \tag{1.30}$$

where the factorization of (1.30) reflects the decoupling of the price and the quantity dynamics in (1.28).

As is familiar from two-sector models of international trade, the dynamics depends crucially upon the relative sectoral capital intensity, which in the present context is measured by $\alpha - \delta$. Thus $\alpha > \delta$ corresponds to the output sector being relatively more intensive in physical capital than is the human capital sector, and the common assumption, $\delta = 0$, is an extreme example of this. We now show that irrespective of the relative sectoral intensity condition, $(\alpha - \delta)$, (1.30) always describes a stable saddle path. Two cases must be considered.

First, suppose $\delta > \alpha$. Then (1.29) yields $a_{11} > 0$, $a_{23} < 0$, $a_{33} < 0$. Equation (1.30) then implies that the eigenvalue $\mu = a_{11} > 0$. The remaining two roots are solutions to the quadratic factor in (1.30) and, for the sign pattern noted, one of the roots is positive and the other is negative. The root $\mu = [a_{33} - (a_{33}^2 - 4a_{23})^{1/2}]/2 < 0$ is thus the unique stable root. Second, if $\alpha > \delta$, then $a_{11} < 0$, $a_{23} > 0$, $a_{33} > 0$, so that the eigenvalue $\mu = a_{11} < 0$. Moreover, the two roots to the quadratic factor in (1.30) are now both positive, implying that $\mu = a_{11} < 0$ is the unique stable root. These two alternative cases of capital intensity have important differences for the dynamics that we shall now discuss.

(i) $\delta > \alpha$: *Human Capital Sector Relatively More Intensive in Physical Capital*

In this case the only solution for q consistent with the transversality condition is for q to remain constant at its steady-state value, $\tilde{q}$. The stable solution to (1.28) is thus:

$$q(t) = \tilde{q} \tag{1.31a}$$

$$k(t) - \tilde{k} = (k_0 - \tilde{k})e^{\mu t} \tag{1.31b}$$

$$c(t) - \tilde{c} = \frac{a_{23}}{\mu}(k(t) - \tilde{k}), \tag{1.31c}$$

where $\mu = [a_{33} - (a_{33}^2 - 4a_{23})^{1/2}]/2 < 0$. Note that the consumption/human capital ratio moves directly with the physical to human capital ratio; the stable saddlepath in $c - k$ space is positively sloped. Intuitively, an increase in k results in a decrease in the relative supply of final output when the human capital sector is more intensive in physical capital, so that c must fall to keep the two factors accumulating at the same rate. The constancy in the relative price, q, translates to the constancy in the sectoral physical capital to human capital ratios.

It is convenient to focus on the transitional dynamics of the growth rates. With the relative price q constant, the consumption growth rate is fixed at the common steady-state growth rate:

$$\frac{\dot{C}}{C} \equiv \psi_C(t) = \frac{r_K(\tilde{q}) - \rho}{1 - \gamma} \equiv \tilde{\psi}. \qquad (1.32)$$

By evaluating the expressions for the growth rate of physical capital, $\dot{K}/K \equiv \psi_K$, and human capital, $\dot{H}/H \equiv \psi_H$, and comparing with (1.32) one can establish the following ordering. Assuming that the economy begins from an initial point at which $k_0 < \tilde{k}$, we see from (1.31a)–(1.31c) that the growth rates can be ranked as follows along the transitional paths:

$$\psi_K(t) > \psi_C(t) \equiv \tilde{\psi} > \psi_H(t). \qquad (1.33)$$

The growth rates of physical and human capital approach their common equilibrium growth rate from opposite sides.

(ii) $\alpha > \delta$: *Physical Capital Sector Relatively More Intensive in Physical Capital*

In this case the stable eigenvalue $\mu = a_{11} < 0$, and the stable adjustment path is:

$$k(t) - \tilde{k} = (k_0 - \tilde{k})e^{a_{11}t} \qquad (1.34a)$$

$$q(t) - \tilde{q} = \left[\frac{a_{11}(a_{11} - a_{33}) - a_{23}a_{32}}{a_{11}a_{31} - a_{21}} \right] \left[k(t) - \tilde{k} \right] \qquad (1.34b)$$

$$c(t) - \tilde{c} = \left[\frac{a_{21}(a_{11} - a_{33}) - a_{23}a_{31}}{a_{11}a_{31} - a_{21}} \right] \left[k(t) - \tilde{k} \right]. \qquad (1.34c)$$

The important point is that the relative price, q, is no longer constant, but follows a stable adjustment path. Evaluating the term in brackets in (1.34b), one can establish that the relative price of human to physical capital, q, is an increasing function of the relative stock of physical to human capital, k. The slope of the stable $c - k$ locus includes two conflicting influences: the direct effect as in case (i) and the relative price effect.

One important difference between cases (i) and (ii) is that with the relative price q following a transitional path, the growth rate of consumption now also has the same characteristic:

$$\frac{\dot{C}}{C} \equiv \psi_C = \frac{r_K'(q - \tilde{q})}{1 - \gamma} + \tilde{\psi}. \tag{1.35}$$

For $\alpha > \delta$, we have $r_K' < 0$, so that the growth rate of consumption is a decreasing function of the physical capital to human capital ratio. The adjustment of the relative price has an additional impact on the transitional dynamics of the two types of capital (see Bond et al., 1996).

1.6.3. Fiscal Policy in Two-sector Model

Bond et al. (1996) show that when one introduces distortionary taxes, the dichotomy in the dynamics introduced by the sectoral intensity condition $(\delta - \alpha)$ is somewhat broken. It now becomes possible for the economy to be unstable, but it is also possible for it to have 'too many' stable roots, and for the economy to have a continuum of equilibria, the latter property often being associated with increasing returns and externalities (Benhabib and Perli, 1994). Other authors have also examined fiscal policy in the two-sector Lucas model. Pecorino (1993) has conducted a simulation study of commodities taxes. More recently, Ortigueira (1998) has studied the effects of labor and capital income taxes on the transitional dynamics and determined a measure of inefficiency derived from the taxation of capital income. His analysis is also based primarily on numerical simulations.

1.7. NON-SCALE GROWTH MODEL

As noted, the endogenous growth model has been criticized on both empirical and theoretical grounds. We therefore now turn to an alternative model, the non-scale model, which has been proposed partly in response to these criticisms. The increased flexibility of the production function is associated with higher order dynamics in comparison to the corresponding AK growth model. Thus, in cases where the AK model is always on its balanced growth path, the corresponding non-scale model will follow a first-order adjustment path. The non-scale counterpart to the two-sector Lucas model, which as we have seen follows a one-dimensional stable locus, now follows a two-dimensional path, and so on.

We start our examination of the dynamics by examining the simplest one-sector non-scale model, with inelastic labor supply. The main virtue of this is pedagogic, in that analytical results are easily obtained. The two-sector non-scale model, briefly discussed in Section 1.7.3, is significantly more complex, requiring that we characterize the transition paths numerically.

Our objective is to analyze the dynamics of the aggregate economy about a balanced growth path. Along such an equilibrium path, aggregate output and the aggregate capital stock are assumed to grow at the same constant rate, so that the aggregate output/capital ratio remains unchanged. Summing the individual production functions (1.1a) over the N agents, the aggregate production function with inelastic labor supply is:

$$Y = \alpha(1-\bar{l})^{1-\sigma} K^{\eta+\sigma} N^{1-\sigma} \equiv AK^{\sigma_K} N^{\sigma_N}, \qquad (1.36)$$

where $A \equiv \alpha(1-\bar{l})^{1-\sigma}$, $\sigma_N \equiv 1-\sigma$ = share of labor in aggregate output, $\sigma_K \equiv \eta+\sigma$ = share of capital in aggregate output. Thus $\sigma_K + \sigma_N \equiv 1+\eta$ measures total returns to scale of the social aggregate production function. Taking percentage changes of (1.36) and imposing the long-run condition of a constant Y/K ratio, the long-run equilibrium growth of capital and output, g, is:

$$g \equiv \frac{\sigma_N}{1-\sigma_K} n > 0. \qquad (1.37)$$

Equation (1.37) exhibits the key feature of the non-scale growth model, namely, that the long-run equilibrium rate is proportional to the population growth rate by a factor that reflects the productivity of labor and capital in the aggregate production function. Under constant returns to scale, $g = n$, the rate of population growth, as in the standard neoclassical growth model, to which the present one-sector model reduces. Otherwise g exceeds n or is less than n, that is, there is positive or negative per capita growth, according to whether returns to scale are increasing or decreasing, $n \gtrless 0$. In any event, g is independent of any macro policy instrument, particularly the tax rate. In contrast to the basic AK model of Section 1.3.1 where the growth of output decreases with the tax rate, in the non-scale model, the response to taxes occurs through the gradual adjustment in k. We shall show below that as long as the dynamics of the system are stable, $\sigma_K < 1$, in which case the long-run equilibrium growth is $g > 0$, as indicated.

The implication that long-run growth cannot be sustained in the absence of population growth has itself been criticized. Accordingly, an alternative class of non-scale growth models, that eliminates the effect of country size, but still permits growth in the absence of population growth, has more recently emerged. These models permit at least a limited role for government policy to influence the long-run growth rate, through taxes and subsidies to research and development.[20]

1.7.1. Equilibrium Dynamics

To analyze the transitional dynamics of the economy about its long-run stationary growth path, it is convenient to express the system in terms of the following stationary variables:

$$c \equiv \frac{C}{N^{\frac{\sigma_N}{1-\sigma_K}}} \; ; \; k \equiv \frac{K}{N^{\frac{\sigma_N}{1-\sigma_K}}}.$$

With constant social returns to scale $\left(\sigma_N + \sigma_K = 1\right)$ these reduce to standard per capita quantities; i.e. $c = C/N = C_i$, etc. Otherwise they represent 'scale-adjusted' per capita quantities.

We begin by determining the consumption dynamics. To do so we take the time derivative of (1.2a) and combine with (1.4a) to find that the individual's consumption grows at the constant rate:

$$\frac{\dot{C}_i}{C_i} = \frac{(1-\tau_y)\sigma A K_i^{\sigma-1} K^{\eta} - \rho - n}{1-\gamma} \equiv \psi_i. \tag{1.38}$$

With all individuals being identical, the growth rate of aggregate consumption is $\psi = \psi_i + n$, so that:

$$\frac{\dot{C}}{C} = \frac{(1-\tau_y)\sigma A K^{\sigma_K-1} N^{\sigma_N} - \rho - \gamma n}{1-\gamma} \equiv \psi. \tag{1.39}$$

Differentiating c and using (1.46), the growth rate of the scale-adjusted per capita consumption is:

$$\dot{c} = c\left[\frac{(1-\tau_y)\sigma A k^{\sigma_K-1}}{1-\gamma} - \frac{\rho}{1-\gamma} - \left(\frac{\gamma}{1-\gamma} + \frac{\sigma_N}{1-\sigma_K}\right)n\right]. \tag{1.40a}$$

To derive the dynamics of the scale-adjusted aggregate capital stock we take the time derivative of k and combine with the production market equilibrium condition (1.4) to yield:

$$\dot{k} = k\left[A k^{\sigma_K-1} - \frac{c}{k} - \left(\frac{\sigma_N}{1-\sigma_K}\right)n\right]. \tag{1.40b}$$

The steady-state values of the transformed variables, k and $\tilde{c}$, are given by:

$$\tilde{k} = \left\{ \frac{1}{A\sigma(1-\tau_y)}\left[\rho + \left(\gamma + \frac{(1-\tau_y)\sigma_N}{1-\sigma_K}\right)n\right]\right\}^{\frac{1}{\sigma_K -1}} \qquad (1.41a)$$

$$\tilde{c} = \frac{1}{\sigma(1-\tau_y)}\left\{\rho + \left[\gamma + \left(1-\gamma-(1-\tau_y)\sigma\right)\left(\frac{\sigma_N}{1-\sigma_K}\right)\right]n\right\}\tilde{k} \qquad (1.41b)$$

and we see that the tax rates impinge on the level of activity through k, $\tilde{c}$. Note also that (1.41a) and (1.41b) reduce to the standard expressions for the neoclassical model, in the absence of externalities, when the aggregate production function has constant returns to scale.

Linearizing (1.40a) and (1.40b) around steady state, it is immediately apparent that $\sigma_K < 1$ is a necessary and sufficient condition for saddlepoint stability, in which case (1.37) ensures that the equilibrium growth rate of output, g, is positive. The stability condition asserts $\eta < \sigma_N = 1-\sigma$, so that the share of external spillover generated by private capital accumulation, and hence the overall social increasing returns to scale, cannot exceed the exogenously growing factor's share (labor) in production. Thus stability is consistent with decreasing, constant, or even increasing returns to scale, provided that the latter are not too excessive.

The model we have presented is the direct analogue to the endogenous growth model presented in Section 1.3.1. In contrast to that model, which was always on its balanced growth path, the present model involves transitional dynamics, the linearized approximation to which is described by a first-order path. Thus, whereas in the AK model, a tax increase leads to an instantaneous jump in the price level, in the present model it leads to a gradual decline in the capital stock, with no impact on the long-run growth rate.

1.7.2. Optimal Fiscal Policy

Optimal fiscal policy can be easily characterized in this model. The corresponding first-best equilibrium in the centrally planned economy, in which the central planner internalizes the externalities, is described by:

$$\dot{c} = c\left[\frac{\sigma_K A k^{\sigma_K -1}}{1-\gamma} - \frac{\rho}{1-\gamma} - \left(\frac{\gamma}{1-\gamma} + \frac{\sigma_N}{1-\sigma_K}\right)n\right] \qquad (1.40a')$$

in conjunction with (1.40b). Comparing (1.40a) and (1.40a') we immediately see that the tax rate:

$$\hat{\tau}_y = -\eta / \sigma < 0 \qquad (1.42)$$

will ensure that the decentralized economy replicates the centrally planned economy. The reason that the optimum calls for a subsidy is because aggregate capital generates a positive externality that individual agents fail to take into account. Furthermore, the simple fixed rule (1.42) enables the decentralized economy to mimic the entire optimal dynamic path. Eicher and Turnovsky (2000) have extended this model to include alternative specifications of congestion, including (1.15), and examined optimal policy in this more generalized model.

1.7.3. Two-sector Non-scale Model

The non-scale model was originally introduced by Jones (1995a, 1995b) in the context of Romer's (1990) two-sector model of technological change. As formulated by Romer, his model had an acute scale effect in the sense that it implied that doubling the population and the number of people engaged in research would double the equilibrium growth rate, a proposition that was clearly counterfactual. Jones introduced decreasing returns to knowledge and showed how this leads to an equilibrium in which the long-run growth rates in the two sectors – final output and technology – were independent of the size of the economy. Instead, they were functions of the technological elasticities of production function of the knowledge-producing sector, together with the population growth rate, and as such were a direct generalization of (1.43), the equilibrium one-sector growth rate.

Jones' analysis was based on the specific assumption of constant returns to scale in the final output sector in capital and labour efficiency units. Eicher and Turnovsky (1999a) characterize the equilibrium growth rates under more general conditions with respect to returns to scale in the two sectors. One important conclusion they show is that essentially the only production function consistent with a balanced growth path under arbitrary returns to scale is the Cobb–Douglas. Thus, for example, the CES production function generalized to allow for non-constant returns to scale is inconsistent with a balanced growth path. That is why we have imposed the Cobb–Douglas production function throughout.[21]

Eicher and Turnovsky (1999b, 2001) characterize the transitional dynamics of the two-sector non-scale model in detail, relying extensively on numerical simulation methods. They show how the stable adjustment path, which is a one-dimensional locus in the corresponding endogenous growth model, now becomes a two-dimensional locus in the two-sector non-scale model. This is important for issues pertaining to the speed of convergence. The basic one-sector neoclassical model and the two-sector endogenous growth model both imply speeds of convergence that are generally viewed as implausibly high, around 10 per cent per annum.

The two-sector non-scale models generally imply much slower rates of convergence. In a preliminary examination of this issue, Jones (1995a) obtained excessively slow rates of convergence, mainly because he assumed that the sectoral allocation of each factor remains constant during the transition. Dinopoulos and Thompson (1998) analyze the transition dynamics of the alternative non-scale model numerically to find that the rate of convergence is approximately equal to the rate of population growth, but they do not highlight separate transition paths of output, capital, and technology. Eicher and Turnovsky (1999b) show how the empirical findings regarding the differential rates of convergence of output and technology can be reconciled by introducing a two-sector *non-scale* model of capital accumulation that incorporates endogenous technological change and population growth. Their key contribution is to show how the stable transition path in the two-sector non-scale growth model is characterized by a two-dimensional stable saddlepath, which permits the growth rates and the convergence speeds *to vary both across time and variables*. The presence of a two-dimensional stable manifold introduces important flexibility to the convergence characteristics, by allowing capital, output, and technology to converge at different time-varying rates toward possibly different long-run equilibrium growth rates. These properties are consistent with Bernard and Jones (1996a, 1996b) who show that different sectors exhibit distinctly different convergence time profiles, suggesting that the process of convergence is more complex than indicated by changes in any single aggregate measure. Furthermore, they show that reasonable asymptotic convergence speeds are achieved with a wide variety of parameter values.

1.8.   CONCLUDING COMMENTS

In this chapter we have discussed some of the recent theoretical developments in growth theory, tying them to the earlier growth theories. We have done this by setting out a basic generic model and have shown how it may yield two of the key models that have played a prominent role in the recent literature on economic growth theory, the endogenous growth model and the non-scale growth model. We focused initially on the former, emphasizing how the simplest such model leads to an equilibrium in which the economy is always on its balanced growth path. We have also shown how the endogeneity or otherwise of the labor supply is crucial in determining the equilibrium growth rate and the responsiveness of the equilibrium growth rate to macroeconomic policy.

But transitional dynamics are an important aspect of the growth process and indeed, much of the recent discussion of convergence concerns the speed with which the economy approaches its balanced growth path. We have discussed alternative ways that such transitional dynamics may be introduced. Within the endogenous growth framework this occurs naturally through the introduction of a second capital stock and two such examples have been considered. The first is the introduction of government capital in the one sector model, and the second is the two-sector production model, pioneered by Lucas (1988), in which the two capital goods relate to physical and human capital.

As we have noted, the endogenous growth model has been the source of criticism, leading to the development of the non-scale model. This too is characterized by transitional dynamics, which are more flexible than those of the corresponding endogenous growth model. But the fact that the long-run growth rate is independent of policy in such models does not mean that policy is unimportant. On the contrary, since such models are typically associated with slow convergence speeds (of the order of 2–3 per cent) policy can influence the accumulation of capital for extended periods of time, leading to significant long-run level effects.

We observed at the outset that our discussion is necessarily limited and restricted. We have focused entirely on models where the growth occurs through capital accumulation, emphasizing particularly the role of the technological conditions. We have not addressed issues pertaining to innovation and technology transfer and the related issue of the indigenous development of technology for which the knowledge-based models of Romer (1990), Grossman and Helpman (1991), Eicher (1996), Aghion and Howitt (1998) are particularly relevant. Moreover, our analysis has been restricted to the real aspects, and one can also introduce monetary aspects, including inflation and monetary policy. Some work along these lines has been carried out by Palivos and Yip (1995) and others. Other issues that are important but are not addressed here include the role of fertility and education in the growth process, as well as the relationship between growth, the distribution of income, and income inequality.

As one sorts through the growth literature over the last half century, one sees striking parallels between the old and the new. The structures have many similarities; it is the methods of analysis that have changed, and presumably become more sophisticated. The AK technology of the basic one-sector Barro–Rebelo endogenous growth model is identical to that of the Harrod–Domar model. Furthermore, the equilibrium rate of growth in the AK model can be expressed as the product of the savings rate and the output/capital ratio, and is identical to Harrod's warranted growth rate. Moroever, the rigidities that were associated with the Harrod–Domar technology, and led to the development of the Solow–Swan neoclassical model, have their parallels in the more recent literature. The scale effects identified with the constant returns to scale in innovation in the Romer model led to the more flexible specification of technology in the Jones non-scale model. But this model is just an extension of the Solow–Swan neoclassical model to allow for deviations from returns to scale. Imposing the assumption of constant returns to scale gets us right back to the neoclassical framework. What is new here is the endogeneity of technology and the more serious effort devoted to trying to reconcile the theoretical models with the empirical facts, although that too was important in the early work.

NOTES

1. A comprehensive treatment of the early growth theory through 1970 is provided by Burmeister and Dobell (1970).
2. Jones (1995a) referred to such models as 'semi-endogenous' growth models.
3. Subsequent studies suggest that the convergence rates are more variable and sensitive to time periods and the set of countries than originally suggested and a wider range of estimates have been obtained. For example, Islam (1995) estimates the rate of convergence to be 4.7 per cent for non-oil countries and 9.7 per cent for OECD economies. Temple (1998) estimates the rate of convergence for OECD countries to be between 1.5 per cent and 3.6 per cent and for non-oil countries to be between 0.3 per cent and 6.7 per cent. Evans (1997) obtains estimates of the convergence rate of around 6 per cent per annum. Caselli et al. (1996) obtain an even higher rate of convergence of around 10 per cent.
4. This contrasts with Ortigueira and Santos (1997) who achieve a similar reduction in the rate of convergence in the two-sector endogenous growth model, by introducing appropriate adjustment costs to investment.
5. Turnovsky (2002) provides a parallel discussion to that presented here, describing recent developments of growth theory in an open economy.
6. Since all agents are identical, all aggregate quantities are simply multiples of the individual quantities, $X = NX_i$. Note that since all agents allocate the same share of time to work, there is no need to introduce the agent's subscript to l.
7. When production functions exhibit non-constant returns to scale in all factors, the existence of a balanced growth equilibrium requires the production function to be Cobb–Douglas, as assumed in (1.1a) (see Eicher and Turnovsky, 1999a).
8. A negative exponent can be interpreted as reflecting congestion, along the lines of Barro and Sala-i-Martin (1992a).
9. This form of utility function is consistent with the existence of a balanced growth path (see Ladrón-de-Guevara et al., 1997). The specification in (1.1b) is the case of pure leisure; they also consider the case where utility derived from leisure depends upon its interaction with human capital.
10. See, for example, Barro (1990), Jones and Manuelli (1990), King and Rebelo (1990), Rebelo (1991), Jones et al. (1993), Ireland (1994), Turnovsky (1996a, 2000), Ortigueira (1998).
11. Note that the technology (1.7) is identical to that of the original Harrod–Domar model, to which the AK model is a modern counterpart. It was Harrod, himself, who originally referred to the 'knife-edge' characteristics of his model.

12. The empirical evidence on the intertemporal elasticity of substitution overwhelmingly suggests it is less than unity, i.e. $\gamma < 0$, thus supporting the transversality condition (1.8c).

13. Being nonlinear, (1.12a) and (1.12b) may, or may not, intersect, so that a balanced growth equilibrium may, or may not, exist. A sufficient condition for a unique steady-state balanced-growth path is that $(1 - \tau_y)\,\sigma/(1 - \gamma) - 1 < [\min(1 - \tau_y)\,\sigma/(1 - \tau_c)\,\theta,\ \rho/\alpha]$, and whether this condition is met depends upon tax rates and other parameters.

14. For more general production structures it is possible that (1.13) is stable, giving rise to potential problems of indeterminate equilibria. This may quite plausibly occur for production functions more general than the Cobb–Douglas. In a model with both physical and non-human capital Benhabib and Perli (1994), Ladrón-de-Guevara et al. (1997) show how the steady-state equilibrium may become indeterminate. Other authors have emphasized the existence of externalities as sources of indeterminacies of equilibrium (see Benhabib and Farmer, 1994).

15. The rate of return on consumption equals $\rho - \dot{\lambda}/\lambda$, which varies positively with the growth rate, ψ.

16. The contrast in the effects of tax rates between models having fixed and endogenous labour supply is much more dramatic in an open economy. For example, the effect of an increase in the income tax rate, which reduces growth when labour supply is fixed, is fully borne by labour supply, when labour supply is endogenous, leaving the equilibrium growth rate unaffected (see Turnovsky, 1999b).

17. Turnovsky (1997a) extends the model to allow for congestion, along the lines of the analysis of Section 4.1. Glomm and Ravikumar (1994) make the opposite sign regarding depreciation, namely that capital lasts a single period. This assumption leads to the economy always being on its balanced growth path.

18. This result does not mean that the government can increase the growth rate indefinitely by increasing g indefinitely. There are constraints due to the fact that $g < 1$ and that the transversality conditions must be met.

19. Caballé and Santos (1993) provide an earlier analytical discussion of the transitional dynamics in the two-sector model.

20. Examples of the second form of non-scale model include Young (1998), Aghion and Howitt (1998), Dinopoulos and Thompson (1998), Howitt (1999), and Jones (1999).

21. The existence of a balanced growth equilibrium is consistent with an arbitrary production function if and only if it has constant returns to scale. Eicher and Turnovsky also show that a balanced growth path may arise under a non-constant returns to scale production function provided it is of a specific homogeneously separable form.

REFERENCES

Aghion, P. and P. Howitt (1992), 'A model of growth through creative destruction', *Econometrica*, **60**(2), 323–51.

Aghion, P. and P. Howitt (1998), *Endogenous Growth Theory*, Cambridge, Massachusetts: MIT Press.

Arrow, K.J. and M. Kurz (1970), *Public Investment, the Rate of Return, and Optimal Fiscal Policy*, Baltimore, Maryland: Johns Hopkins University Press.

Atkinson, A.B. (1969), 'The time scale of economic models: how long is the long-run?' *Review of Economic Studies*, **36**, 137–52.

Backus, D., P. Kehoe and T. Kehoe (1992), 'In search of scale effects in trade and growth', *Journal of Economic Theory*, **58**, 377–409.

Barro, R.J. (1990), 'Government spending in a simple model of endogenous growth', *Journal of Political Economy*, **98**, S103–S125.

Barro, R.J. and X. Sala-i-Martin (1992a), 'Public finance in models of economic growth', *Review of Economic Studies*, **59**, 645–61.

Barro, R.J. and X. Sala-i-Martin (1992b), 'Convergence', *Journal of Political Economy*, **100**, 223–51.

Barro, R.J. and X. Sala-i-Martin (1995), *Economic Growth*, New York: McGraw-Hill.

Baxter, M. and R.G. King (1993), 'Fiscal policy in general equilibrium', *American Economic Review*, **83**, 315–34.

Benhabib, J. and R.E.A. Farmer (1994), 'Indeterminacy and increasing returns', *Journal of Economic Theory*, **63**, 19–41.

Benhabib, J. and R. Perli (1994), 'Uniqueness and indeterminacy: on the dynamics of endogenous growth', *Journal of Economic Theory*, **63**, 113–42.

Bernard, A.B. and C.I. Jones (1996a), 'Technology and convergence', *Economic Journal*, **106**, 1037–44.

Bernard, A.B. and C.I. Jones (1996b), 'Comparing apples and oranges: productivity consequences and measurement across industries and countries', *American Economic Review*, **86**, 1216–38.

Bond, E.W., P. Wang and C.K. Yip (1996), 'A general two-sector model of endogenous growth with human and physical capital: balanced growth and transitional dynamics', *Journal of Economic Theory*, **68**, 149–73.

Burmeister, E. and A.R. Dobell (1970), *Mathematical Theories of Economic Growth*, New York: Macmillan.

Caballé, J. and M.S. Santos (1993), 'On endogenous growth models with physical and human capital', *Journal of Political Economy*, **101**, 1042–67.

Caselli, F., G. Esquivel and F. Lefort (1996), 'Reopening the convergence debate: a new look at cross-country empirics', *Journal of Economic Growth*, **1**, 363–90.

Chamley, C. (1986), 'Optimal taxation of capital income in general equilibrium with infinite lives', *Econometrica*, **54**, 607–22.

Conlisk, J. (1966), 'Unemployment in a neoclassical growth model', *Economic Journal*, **76**, 550–66.

Devereux, M.B. and D.R. Love (1994), 'The effects of factor taxation in a two-sector model of endogenous growth', *Canadian Journal of Economics*, **27**, 509–36.

Dinopoulos, E. and P. Thompson (1998), 'Schumpeterian growth without scale effects', *Journal of Economic Growth*, **3**, 313–35.

Domar, E. (1946), 'Capital expansion, rate of growth, and employment', *Econometrica*, **14**, 137–47.

Easterly, W. and S. Rebelo (1993), 'Fiscal policy and growth: an empirical investigation', *Journal of Monetary Economics*, **32**, 417–58.

Edwards, J.H.Y. (1990), 'Congestion function specification and the "publicness" of local public goods', *Journal of Urban Economics*, **27**, 80–96.

Eicher, T.S. (1996), 'Interaction between endogenous human capital and technological change', *Review of Economic Studies*, **63**, 127–44.

Eicher, T.S. and S.J. Turnovsky (1999a), 'Non-scale models of economic growth', *Economic Journal*, **109**, 394–415.

Eicher, T.S. and S.J. Turnovsky (1999b), 'Convergence in a two-sector nonscale growth model', *Journal of Economic Growth*, **4**, 413–28.

Eicher, T.S. and S.J. Turnovsky (2000), 'Scale, congestion, and growth', *Economica*, **67**, 325–46.

Eicher, T.S. and S.J. Turnovsky (2001), 'Transition dynamics in a two-sector nonscale growth model', *Journal of Economic Dynamics and Control*, **25**, 85–113.

Evans, P. (1997), 'How fast do countries converge?', *Review of Economics and Statistics*, **79**, 219–25.

Fisher, W.H. and S.J. Turnovsky (1998), 'Public investment, congestion, and private capital accumulation', *Economic Journal*, **108**, 339–413.

Futagami, K., Y. Morita and A. Shibata (1993), 'Dynamic analysis of an endogenous growth model with public capital', *Scandinavian Journal of Economics*, **95**, 707–25.

Glomm, G. and B. Ravikumar (1994), 'Public investment in infrastructure in a simple growth model', *Journal of Economic Dynamics and Control*, **18**, 1173–88.

Grossman, G.M. and E. Helpman (1991), *Innovation and Growth in the Global Economy*, Cambridge, Massachusetts: MIT Press.

Harrod, R.F. (1939), 'An essay in dynamic theory', *Economic Journal*, **49**, 14–33.

Howitt, P. (1999), 'Steady-state endogenous growth with population and R&D inputs growing', *Journal of Political Economy*, **107**, 715–30.

Ireland, P.N. (1994), 'Supply-side economics and endogenous growth', *Journal of Monetary Economics*, **33**, 559–71.

Islam, N. (1995), 'Growth empirics: a panel data approach', *Quarterly Journal of Economics*, **110**, 1127–70.

Jones, C.I. (1995a), 'R&D based models of economic growth', *Journal of Political Economy*, **103**, 759–84.

Jones, C.I. (1995b), 'Time series tests of endogenous growth models', *Quarterly Journal of Economics*, **110**, 495–527.

Jones, C.I. (1999), 'Growth: with or without scale effects', *American Economic Review, Papers and Proceedings*, **89**, 139–44.

Jones, L.E. and R. Manuelli (1990), 'A convex model of equilibrium growth: theory and policy implications', *Journal of Political Economy*, **98**, 1008–38.

Jones, L.E., R.E. Manuelli and P.E. Rossi (1993), 'Optimal taxation in models of endogenous growth', *Journal of Political Economy*, **101**, 485–517.

King, R.G. and S. Rebelo (1990), 'Public policy and economic growth: developing neoclassical implications', *Journal of Political Economy*, **98**, S126–S150.

Kneller, R., M.F. Bleaney and N. Gemmell (1999), 'Fiscal policy and growth: evidence from OECD countries', *Journal of Public Economics*, **74**, 171–90.

Ladrón-de-Guevara, A., S. Ortigueira and M.S. Santos (1997), 'Equilibrium dynamics in two-sector models of endogenous growth', *Journal of Economic Dynamics and Control*, **21**, 115–43.

Lucas, R.E. (1988), 'On the mechanics of economic development', *Journal of Monetary Economics*, **22**, 3–42.

Mankiw, N.G., D. Romer and D. Weil (1992), 'A contribution to the empirics of economic growth', *Quarterly Journal of Economics*, **107**, 407–37.

Mulligan, C.B. and X. Sala-i-Martin (1993), 'Transitional dynamics in two-sector models of endogenous growth', *Quarterly Journal of Economics*, **108**, 739–75.

Ortigueira, S. (1998), 'Fiscal policy in an endogneous growth model with human capital accumulation', *Journal of Monetary Economics*, **42**, 323–55.

Ortigueira, S. and M.S. Santos (1997), 'On the speed of convergence in endogenous growth models', *American Economic Review*, **87**, 383–99.

Pavilos, T. and C.K. Yip (1995), 'Government expenditure financing in an endogenous growth model: a comparison', *Journal of Money, Credit, and Banking*, **27**, 1159–78.

Pecorino, P. (1993), 'Tax structure and growth in a model with human capital', *Journal of Public Economics*, **52**, 251–71.

Rebelo, S. (1991), 'Long-run policy analysis and long-run growth', *Journal of Political Economy*, **99**, 500–21.

Romer, P.M. (1986), 'Increasing returns and long-run growth', *Journal of Political Economy*, **94**, 1002–37.

Romer, P. (1990), 'Endogenous technological change', *Journal of Political Economy*, **98**, S71–S102.

Romer, P.M. (1994), 'The origins of endogenous growth', *Journal of Economic Perspectives*, **8**, 3–22.

Sala-i-Martin, X. (1994), 'Cross-sectional regressions and the empirics of economic growth', *European Economic Review*, **38**, 739–47.

Sato, K. (1966), 'On the adjustment time in neoclassical growth models', *Review of Economic Studies*, **33**, 263–68.

Sato, R. (1963), 'Fiscal policy in a neoclassical growth model: an analysis of the time required for equilibrating adjustment', *Review of Economic Studies*, **30**, 16–23.

Segerstrom, P. (1998), 'Endogenous growth without scale effects', *American Economic Review*, **88**, 1290–310.

Shell, K. (1967), 'A model of inventive activity and capital accumulation', in K. Shell (ed.), *Essays on the Theory of Economic Growth*, Cambridge, Massachusetts: MIT Press, pp. 67–85.

Solow, R.M. (1956), 'A contribution to the theory of economic growth', *Quarterly Journal of Economics*, **70**, 65–94.

Solow, R.M. (1994), 'Perspectives on growth theory', *Journal of Economic Perspectives*, **8**, 45–54.

Stokey, N.L. and S. Rebelo (1995), 'Growth effects of flat-rate taxes', *Journal of Political Economy*, **103**, 519–50.

Swan, T.W. (1956), 'Economic growth and capital accumulation', *Economic Record*, **32**, 334–61.

Takayama, A. (1963), 'On a two-sector model of economic growth: a comparative statics analysis', *Review of Economic Studies*, **30**, 95–104.

Temple, J.R.W. (1998), 'Robustness test of the augmented Solow model', *Journal of Applied Econometrics*, **13**, 361–75.

Turnovsky, S.J. (1996a), 'Optimal tax, debt, and expenditure policies in a growing economy', *Journal of Public Economics*, **60**, 21–44.

Turnovsky, S.J. (1996b), 'Fiscal policy, adjustment costs, and endogenous growth', *Oxford Economic Papers*, **48**, 361–81.

Turnovsky, S.J. (1997a), 'Public and private capital in an endogenously growing economy', *Macroeconomic Dynamics*, **1**, 615–39.

Turnovsky, S.J. (1997b), 'Public and private capital in an endogenously growing open economy', in B.S. Jensen and K.Y. Wong (eds), *Dynamics, Economic Growth, and International Trade*, Ann Arbor: University of Michigan Press, pp. 171–210.

Turnovsky, S.J. (1999a), 'Productive government expenditure in a stochastically growing economy', *Macroeconomic Dynamics*, **3**, 544–70.

Turnovsky, S.J. (1999b), 'Fiscal policy and growth in a small open economy with elastic labor supply', *Canadian Journal of Economics*, **32**, 1191–214.

Turnovsky, S.J. (2000), 'Fiscal policy, elastic labor supply, and endogenous growth', *Journal of Monetary Economics*, **45**, 185–210.

Turnovsky, S.J. (2002), 'Growth in an open economy: some recent developments', in M. Dombrecht and J. Smets (eds), *How to Promote Economic Growth in the Euro Area?* Cheltenham, UK: Edward Elgar, pp. 9–56.

Uzawa, H. (1961), 'On a two-sector model of economic growth', *Review of Economic Studies*', **29**, 40–47.

Uzawa, H. (1965), 'Optimum technological change in an aggregative model of economic growth', *International Economic Review*, **6**, 18–31.

Young, A. (1998), 'Growth without scale effects', *Journal of Political Economy*, **106**, 41–63.

2. 'Old' thoughts on 'new' growth theory

Anthony P. Thirlwall

The origin of new growth theory (or endogenous growth theory as it is sometimes called) lies in the predictive failure of the neoclassical growth model as originally developed by Solow (1956). Two predictions, in particular, seem to contradict the facts. The first is that how much countries save and invest of their national income does not matter for long-run growth because in the steady state the marginal product of capital falls to zero. The second is that because of diminishing returns to capital, and given the same tastes and technology, poor countries should grow faster than rich countries leading to a convergence of per capita incomes (PCY) in the world economy. In the world as a whole, however, there is no evidence that poor countries are catching up with rich countries, and that the world distribution of income is narrowing. The most comprehensive study to date comes from the Norwegian Institute of International Affairs (2000) which takes 115 countries over the period 1965 to 1997, measuring living standards using purchasing power parity estimates of PCY. The study finds that the gap between the richest and poorest countries has increased and that if China is removed from the sample the Gini ratio as a measure of inequality has stayed the same at 0.59.[1]

The conclusion reached from the above observations, rightly or wrongly, is that the marginal product of capital does not necessarily decline as countries get richer. If this is the case, there will not be convergence of PCYs across the globe, and investment will matter for long-run growth. In this sense, growth is endogenous, and not simply determined exogenously by the (unexplained) growth of the labour force and labour productivity. The explanation given by the new growth theorists for non-diminishing returns to capital is externalities of various kinds associated with human capital formation, research and development (R&D) expenditure, technological spillovers from trade, and so on. In this sense, there is nothing essentially new about the *ideas* of new growth theory. Those of us of an older vintage will remember well the extensive research in the 1950s and 1960s on the contribution of education and R& D to economic growth by scholars such as Schultz (1961), Denison (1967), Griliches (1957), and others. What is new is that the ideas are being modelled in a more rigorous way for a different purpose. And the purpose is not to supplant the neoclassical growth model as a conceptual framework for the analysis of growth, but rather to rehabilitate the neoclassical model to make it compatible with the observation that living standards in the world are not converging. Most new growth theorists are neoclassical economists in disguise e.g. Barro, Mankiw, Lucas and Romer (for a survey of early studies see Thirlwall and Sanna, 1996). The methodology employed of treating human capital formation and R&D as externalities is reminiscent of Alfred Marshall's attempt in the nineteenth century to reconcile the competitive model of the firm with the existence of increasing returns by treating the latter as externalities, thereby preserving the U-shaped cost curve and the notion of a competitive equilibrium. But Marshall's methodology was a fudge, and so, too, is the approach of the new growth theorists who want to preserve the neoclassical growth model (see, for example, Barro, 1991). First, there are many other theories of the growth and development process that can explain why divisions in the world economy continue to persist and even widen, which are much richer in insights and more realistic than new growth theory. Centre–periphery models; models of circular and cumulative causation, and demand-oriented models are much more persuasive (Thirlwall, 2002). Second, the negative sign on the initial level of PCY variable in the new growth theory equations (once differences in levels of education and R&D effort between countries are allowed for) cannot be used as evidence of diminishing returns to capital and a rehabilitation of the neoclassical model because so-called *conditional* convergence is compatible with quite different processes. For example, it could be that conditional convergence is found because of 'catch-up' which involves a shift in the whole production function and has nothing to do with its slope or shape. A negative sign on the initial PCY variable could also be picking up faster structural change in poor countries than in rich countries from low productivity agriculture to higher productivity activities in manufacturing industry and services. To my knowledge, no attempt has been made by new growth theorists to distinguish between these competing possibilities.

Another reason why new growth theory is not particularly new, at least to those familiar with the old growth debates between Cambridge, England and Cambridge, Massachusetts, is that Nicholas Kaldor (1957, 1961) had already pointed out in the 1950s, as one of his (six) stylised facts of capitalist economic growth, that despite continued capital accumulation and increases in capital per head through time, the capital/output ratio has remained broadly the same, implying some form of externalities or constant returns to capital. It is worth quoting Kaldor (1961, p. 178) in full:

> As regards the process of economic change and development in capitalist societies, I suggest the following 'stylised facts' as a starting point for the construction of theoretical models – (4) steady capital/output ratios over long periods; at least there are no clear long-term trends, either rising or falling, if differences in the degree of capital utilisation are allowed for. This implies, or reflects, the near identity in the percentage rate of growth of production and of the capital stock i.e. that for the economy as a whole, and over long periods, income and capital tend to grow at the same rate.

Kaldor's explanation lay in his innovation of the technical progress function (to replace the neoclassical production function with its artificial distinction between movements along the function and shifts in the function), relating the growth of output per man to the rate of growth of capital per man, the slope and position of which determines the long-run equilibrium growth of output. The basic idea is that capital accumulation and technical progress cannot be separated. If investment gets ahead of technical progress, the productivity of capital falls and investment is cut back. If technical progress proceeds faster than investment, the productivity of capital rises which encourages further investment. In other words, capital accumulation adjusts to changes in technical dynamism preserving the rate of profit and the capital/output ratio. New, endogenous growth theory is precisely anticipated (see also Palley, 1996).

What applies to countries through time, applies *pari passu* to different countries at a point in time, with differences in growth rates at the same capital/output ratio being associated with different technical progress functions. To quote Kaldor (1972, pp. 11–12) again:

> A lower capital/labour ratio does not necessarily imply a lower capital/output ratio – indeed, the reverse is often the case. The countries with the most highly mechanised industries, such as the United States, do not require a higher ratio of capital to output. The capital/output ratio in the United States has been falling over the last 50 years whilst the capital/labour ratio has been steadily rising; *and it is lower in the United States today than in the manufacturing industries of many underdeveloped countries.* Technological progress in the present century led to a vast increase in the productivity of labour, but this was not accompanied by any associated reduction in the productivity of capital investment. [emphasis added]

If there are constant returns to capital, and the capital/output ratio is constant, new growth theory boils down to the so-called AK model (where K is capital and A is a constant). The AK model, however, is none other than the Harrod–Domar growth equation. If $Y = AK$, then totally differentiating, and dividing by Y, gives $dY/Y = A(dK/Y) = \sigma(I/Y)$, where Y is output, dY/Y is the growth of output, I/Y is the investment ratio, and σ is the productivity of capital. What this means is that, if this is the model of the economy, all that the empirical counterpart of new growth theory is really doing is attempting to explain differences in the productivity of capital between countries (holding investment constant). In other words, if growth and the investment ratio are not perfectly correlated, there must be differences in the productivity of capital associated with differences in education, R&D, or any other variable that affects the productivity of capital. This highlights the true supply-side nature of these new growth theory equations, and makes them very similar to the old 'growth accounting' equations of Denison (1967) and others which tried to disaggregate the neoclassical residual. From the old neoclassical (Cobb–Douglas) production function can be derived the estimating equation:

$$g = r + a_1 k + a_2 l + a_3 \text{ (education)} + a_4 \text{ (R\&D)} + \text{etc.} \tag{2.1}$$

where g is the growth of output; r is the residual; k is the growth of capital; l is the growth of labour; a_1 and a_2 are the elasticities of output with respect to capital and labour, respectively, and the remaining terms are the contribution of specific factors to growth. From new growth theory, we have the following estimating equation:

$$g = a + b_1 \text{ (initial PCY)} + b_2 (I/Y) + b_3 \text{ (population growth)} \\ + b_4 \text{ (education)} + b_5 \text{ (R\&D)} + \text{etc.} \tag{2.2}$$

The variables are self-explanatory. But notice, there is not much difference between the 'growth accounting' equation (2.1) and the new growth theory equation (2.2). k and I/Y are proxies for each other; so, too, are l and population growth. The only difference is the inclusion of the initial PCY variable in equation (2.2) to test for conditional convergence.

Notice also that there is no role for demand, or demand constraints on growth, in these new growth theory models, except to the extent that the productivity of investment will be affected by demand fluctuations, but this is rarely recognised (an exception in Fischer, 1991). In this sense, new growth theory lies squarely in the orthodox neoclassical camp in which growth is driven from the supply side. Saving leads to investment, a country's balance of payments looks after itself, and countries converge on their own natural rate of growth which is not itself explicitly dependent on the strength of demand within an economy (but see Leon-Ledesma and Thirlwall, 2002). As Kurz and Salvadori (1998, pp. 86–7) have commented: 'It is a major shortcoming both of Solovian and of the NGT (new growth theory) that no serious attempt is made to represent investment and to analyse the interplay between investment and saving. To assume that "Say's Law of Markets" holds is just not good enough'.

The question remains, does investment matter for growth, or do differences in the productivity of investment explain all of the variance between countries? To examine this question, a colleague and I (Hussein and Thirlwall, 2000) recently took a sample of 89 developed and developing countries over the period 1976–95, and applied cross-section and panel data estimating techniques to the whole sample, and to sub-samples of continents. The results are shown in Table 2.1.

Table 2.1   The relation between the investment ratio and the growth of output

---

All countries (89; 1,780 observations)

Cross-section: $\quad\quad\quad\quad\quad\quad\quad\quad\quad g = 0.523 + 0.174\ (I/Y) \quad\quad r^2 = 0.264$
$\quad\quad\quad\quad\quad\quad\quad\quad\quad\quad\quad\quad\ \ (0.7)\quad (5.6)$

Panel: $\quad\quad\quad\quad\quad\quad\quad\quad\quad\quad\quad\quad g = 0.207 + 0.160\ (I/Y) \quad\quad r^2 = 0.068$
$\quad\quad\quad\quad\quad\quad\quad\quad\quad\quad\quad\quad\quad\ \ (0.4)\quad (8.7)$

OECD countries (23; 480 observations)

Cross-section: $\quad\quad\quad\quad\quad\quad\quad\quad\quad g = 1.128 + 0.070\ (I/Y) \quad\quad r^2 = 0.068$
$\quad\quad\quad\quad\quad\quad\quad\quad\quad\quad\quad\quad\ \ (0.5)\quad (1.2)$

Panel: $\quad\quad\quad\quad\quad\quad\quad\quad\quad\quad\quad\quad g = 0.441 + 0.102\ (I/Y) \quad\quad r^2 = 0.028$
$\quad\quad\quad\quad\quad\quad\quad\quad\quad\quad\quad\quad\quad\ \ (0.7)\quad (3.1)$

Asia (16; 320 observations)

Cross-section: $\quad\quad\quad\quad\quad\quad\quad\quad\quad g = -1.347 + 0.268\ (I/Y) \quad r^2 = 0.528$
$\quad\quad\quad\quad\quad\quad\quad\quad\quad\quad\quad\quad\ \ (0.5)\quad (1.2)$

Panel: $\quad\quad\quad\quad\quad\quad\quad\quad\quad\quad\quad\quad g = 1.192 + 0.164\ (I/Y) \quad\quad r^2 = 0.083$
$\quad\quad\quad\quad\quad\quad\quad\quad\quad\quad\quad\quad\quad\ \ (1.0)\quad (3.5)$

Africa (25; 500 observations)

Cross-section: $\quad\quad\quad\quad\quad\quad\quad\quad\quad g = 0.221 + 0.134\ (I/Y) \quad\quad r^2 = 0.302$
$\quad\quad\quad\quad\quad\quad\quad\quad\quad\quad\quad\quad\ \ (0.2)\quad (3.2)$

Panel: $\quad\quad\quad\quad\quad\quad\quad\quad\quad\quad\quad\quad g = 0.212 + 0.134\ (I/Y) \quad\quad r^2 = 0.060$
$\quad\quad\quad\quad\quad\quad\quad\quad\quad\quad\quad\quad\quad\ \ (0.3)\quad (4.7)$

Latin America (17; 340 observations)

Cross-section: $\quad\quad\quad\quad\quad\quad\quad\quad\quad g = 2.284 + 0.024\ (I/Y) \quad\quad r^2 = 0.002$
$\quad\quad\quad\quad\quad\quad\quad\quad\quad\quad\quad\quad\ \ (0.5)\quad (1.2)$

Panel: $\quad\quad\quad\quad\quad\quad\quad\quad\quad\quad\quad\quad g = -1.225 + 0.203\ (I/Y) \quad r^2 = 0.036$
$\quad\quad\quad\quad\quad\quad\quad\quad\quad\quad\quad\quad\quad\ \ (1.0)\quad (3.6)$

As far as long-run growth is concerned, the cross-section results are to be preferred since taking group means irons out the temporary cyclical fluctuations in output growth unrelated to investment, although as Solow (1997) remarks in his Arrow Lectures 'even 30 years (may) not be long enough to distinguish temporary episodes of accelerated growth and increases in the growth rate itself'. Turning to the results in Table 2.1, taking all countries in the sample, we can see that the cross-section estimation indicates that 26 percent of the growth rate variance between countries is related to differences in the investment ratio alone. The regression coefficient is significant at the 99 percent confidence level and indicates a productivity of capital of 17.4 percent. The panel estimation gives a rate of return of the same order of magnitude. It is clear from the table, however, that the significance of investment varies widely between the regional groupings of countries, and regional differences in the productivity of capital are also apparent. In the OECD countries, and in Latin America, there appears to be no long-run relation between investment and the growth of output. This result is surprising, but it might delight old neoclassical growth theorists if 20 years of data are thought to capture the 'steady state'! The implication is that all the variance in growth rates is accounted for by differences in the productivity of capital, but this could have demand-side, as well as supply-side, explanations. By contrast, in Africa and Asia, the proportion of variance in growth rates explained by differences in the investment ratio is much higher – over 50 percent in Asia and 30 percent in Africa. The estimates of the productivity of capital are also well determined. For Asia, the cross-section gives an estimate of 26.8 percent, and the panel an estimate of 16.4 percent. For Africa, both the cross-section and the panel give the same estimate of 13.4 percent. The 16 countries of Asia clearly stand out from all the rest as economies where investment performance seems to have mattered for growth and where the productivity of capital is relatively high.

My final 'old' thought on new growth theory concerns the role of trade and the balance of payments in understanding the growth performance of nations. First, many of the first generation of new growth theory models fail to model trade, as if economies are completed closed, ignoring Marshall's dictum that 'the causes which determine the economic progress of nations belong to the study of international trade'. Later models include a trade variable measured by the share of exports and/or imports in GDP, but invariably it turns out to be insignificant or loses its significance when combined with other variables. On the surface, this is a puzzle because it conflicts with the rich historical literature on the benefits of trade liberalisation and of export-led growth. What appears to be the case in some studies, however, is that the effect of trade works through investment (Levine and Renelt, 1992). Investment is a robust variable in growth equations (but not trade), but trade is a robust variable in explaining investment behaviour between countries. If this is the case, it is an interesting and significant conclusion because it means that many of the studies would support the Keynesian/post-Keynesian position that it is not saving that drives investment, but trade and the growth of output itself.

There is, however, another explanation for the estimated weak impact of trade and that is that the trade variable is measured wrongly. In a growth equation – even in a supply-oriented growth equation – it makes much more sense to include the *growth* of exports rather than the share of exports in GDP, which is a very static measure of the impact of trade. By contrast, the faster export growth is the greater the direct impact of trade on the growth of output, and also the indirect impact by providing the foreign exchange to pay for the import content of other components of demand, particularly investment. In other words, fast export growth can relax a balance of payments constraint on demand which allows other components of demand to grow faster. Also, from the supply side, the faster export growth is the faster import growth can be which will improve the productivity of domestic resources if there are limits to import substitution. If, as argued above, new growth theory equations are picking up reasons why the productivity of capital varies between countries, differences in the growth of exports could be a powerful explanation. The study by Thirlwall and Sanna (1996) includes the growth of exports in a conventional new growth theory estimating equation and gets strong and robust results.

My overall conclusions can be summarised very briefly. New growth theory is hardly new. The true progenitor of new growth theory is Nicholas Kaldor. New growth theory does not rehabilitate the neoclassical growth model as some new growth theorists would like. The AK model of new growth theory is the Harrod–Domar growth equation, so that all that new growth theory equations are really picking up are explanations of differences in the productivity of capital between countries (holding investment constant). If I am right, perhaps future research should focus *directly* on why the productivity of capital varies between countries which would require taking the capital/output ratio as the dependent variable in the equations, not output growth. Estimating indirectly, which is currently the practice, always runs the risk of omitted variable bias, as in Barro's (1991) original study which attempts to rehabilitate the neoclassical growth model by including only differences in education between countries in the equation (omitting investment). The sign on the initial PCY variable turns negative (which Barro wants) and the significance of education looks high. Only at the end of a very long paper is investment included in the equation and education loses much of its significance. What is still missing are demand-side explanations of differences in growth performance, and export growth is one missing variable. In my recent book *The Nature of Economic Growth: An Alternative Framework for Understanding the Performance of Nations*, I provide a critique of new growth theory in these terms.

NOTE

1. With China in the sample, the Gini ratio is 0.52 in 1997. On the other hand, the inclusion of China in the sample increases the degree of global inequality, which takes account of the distribution of income within countries, because there has been a widening income gap between rural and urban China (see Milanovic, 2002).

REFERENCES

Barro, R. (1991), 'Economic growth in a cross section of countries', *Quarterly Journal of Economics*, May, 407–443.

Denison, E. (1967), *Why Growth Rates Differ: Post-war Experience in Nine Western Countries*, Washington, DC: Brookings Institution.

Fischer, S. (1991), 'Growth, macroeconomics and development', *NBER Macroeconomics Annual*, New York: NBER, 329–379.

Griliches, Z. (1957), 'Hybrid corn: an exploration in the economics of technological change', *Econometrica*, October, 501–522.

Hussein, K. and A.P. Thirlwall (2000), 'The AK model of "new" growth theory is the Harrod–Domar growth equation: investment and growth revisited', *Journal of Post Keynesian Economics*, Spring, 427–435.

Kaldor, N. (1957), 'A model of economic growth', *Economic Journal*, December, 591–624.

Kaldor, N. (1961), 'Capital accumulation and economic growth', in F.A. Lutz and D.C. Hague (eds), *The Theory of Capital*, London: Macmillan, pp. 177–222.

Kaldor, N. (1972), 'Advanced technology in a strategy of development: some lessons from Britain's experience', in *Automation and Developing Countries*, Geneva: ILO, pp. 3–16.

Kurz, H.D. and N. Salvadori (1998), 'The "new" growth theory: old wine in new goatskins', in F. Coricelli, M. di Matteo and F.H. Hahn (eds), *New Theories in Growth and Development*, London: Macillan, pp. 63–94.

Leon-Ledesma, M. and A.P. Thirlwall (2002), 'The endogeneity of the natural rate of growth', *Cambridge Journal of Economics*, July, 441–459.

Levine, R. and D. Renelt (1992), 'A sensitivity analysis of cross-country growth regressions', *American Economic Review*, September, 942–963.

Milanovic, B. (2002), 'True world income distribution 1988 and 1993: first calculations based on household surveys alone', *Economic Journal*, January, 51–92.

Norwegian Institute of International Affairs (2000), *Globalisation and Inequality: World Income Distribution and Living Standards 1960–1998*, Report to the Norwegian Ministry of Foreign Affairs: Report 66: 2000.

Palley, T (1996), 'Growth theory in a Keynesian mode: some keynesian foundations for new endogenous growth theory', *Journal of Post Keynesian Economics*, Fall, 113–135.

Schultz, T. (1961), 'Investment in human capital', *American Economic Review*, March, 1–17.

Solow, R. (1956), 'A contribution to the theory of economic growth', *Quarterly Journal of Economics*, February, 65–94.

Solow, R. (1997), *Learning from 'Learning by Doing': Lessons for Economic Growth*, Stanford, California: Stanford University Press.

Thirlwall, A.P. (2002), *The Nature of Economic Growth: An Alternative Framework for Understanding the Performance of Nations*, Cheltenham, UK and Northampton, Massachusetts: Edward Elgar.

Thirlwall, A.P. and G. Sanna (1996), 'The macrodeterminants of growth and 'new' growth theory: an evaluation and further evidence', in P. Arestis (ed.), *Employment, Economic Growth and the Tyranny of the Market: Essays in Honour of Paul Davidson*, Vol. 2, Cheltenham, UK and Brookfield, Massachusetts: Edward Elgar, pp. 131–156.

3. Old and new growth theories: what role for aggregate demand?

Carlo Panico

3.1. INTRODUCTION

This chapter deals with the role played by aggregate demand in the theories of growth that have historically emerged. Its aim is to attract the attention of the readers to those parts of the economic literature, which emphasize that the autonomous components of aggregate demand have an influence on growth. There is a tendency in modern literature to disregard this influence and to accept Say's Law, which has constantly enjoyed a large consensus in the history of economic thought. Yet, as will be argued in the following pages, the validity of Say's Law has always been disputed and, for some decades after the Great Depression, it was denied by most of the profession. Since the 1970s, the Law has been regaining consensus and nowadays represents by far the prevailing view. Thus, in the New Growth Theories, which are the most established theories of growth in modern literature, Say's Law holds and autonomous demand has no influence on the rate of growth, because of the assumption that investment decisions are directly generated by saving decisions.

3.2. GROWTH IN CLASSICAL THEORY

The determinants of growth were a major concern of the classical political economists. They related growth to income distribution. The latter affected the savings decisions of the different classes and, according to some, their investment decisions too. Others, like Malthus, Sismondi and Marx, however, denied the validity of Say's Law and explored a possible influence of demand. The presence of their analyses within classical political economy makes it possible to say that this tradition was 'open' to the influence on growth of the autonomous components of aggregate demand.

In their writings on the growth process Smith and Marx also highlighted the role of technical progress, presenting on this subject a broad analysis, which can be considered an antecedent of the modern cumulative causation and evolutionary approaches. Efficiency, they claimed, is enhanced by division of labour, which, according to them, depends on the expansion of the markets (see Ricoy, 1998). Changes in demand, whether autonomous or induced by changes in production, can thus affect growth by favouring division of labour and technical progress. This kind of influence of demand does not require the rejection of Say's Law, as confirmed by its presence in New Growth Theories, where variations in demand are induced by variations in production.

3.3.   THE RISE OF THE NEOCLASSICAL SCHOOL

The rise of the neoclassical school in the second half of the nineteenth century brought about a change of perspective in economic theory. Allocation of resources became the major concern and the problem of distribution but one aspect of the general pricing and allocation process. Neoclassical economists argued that competitive forces, operating through variations in relative prices and factor substitution, generate a tendency to full employment and to the exploitation of the growth potentials of the economy. In the writings of these authors, Say's Law took a new form, which made it coincide with the tendency to full employment. Moreover, the possibility of referring to the influence of the autonomous components of demand on long-term growth, which was present in the classical tradition, disappeared.

The problems related to the operation of these market forces were examined by neoclassical economists in what Keynes called the 'real department of economics'. The 'monetary department' dealt instead with business fluctuations, arguing that the working of the credit system cause them. Following this approach, Hayek, Keynes, Robertson and others in the 1920s tried to identify a 'neutral monetary policy', i.e. a policy that can prevent monetary and credit disturbances from amplifying the fluctuations of the economy.

3.4.   KEYNES AND HARROD ON EFFECTIVE DEMAND AND GROWTH

The severity of the 1929 Great Depression changed the course of these events. As Harrod pointed out in an unpublished 1933 essay reported by Young (1989, pp. 30–8), the previous recessions had not led the economy too far from full employment, nor had they cast doubts on the belief that the economy is able to return to it. The Great Depression, instead, put in danger political stability and raised the problem of a new political approach and of a new economic theory able to clarify whether market forces can lead the economy towards full employment or whether Government intervention is required to restore it.

Moving along these lines, Keynes introduced in 1932 the concept of 'monetary theory of production' in order to part with the neoclassical separation between the real and the monetary departments of economics and with the idea of a tendency to full employment. The notion of 'effective demand' and its influence on economic activity became the central theme of *The General Theory*.

Harrod, on the other hand, began in 1933 to develop economic dynamics. His contributions to this subject have been misinterpreted for a long time. First of all, it was thought that they had been stimulated by his work on imperfect competition and his dissatisfaction with the Austrian trade cycle theory put forward by Hayek (see Kregel, 1980 p. 98; 1985, pp. 66–7). The analysis of Harrod's papers, recently become available at the Chiba University of Commerce in Ichikawa (Japan), has instead pointed out that his efforts in this direction were stimulated by his contacts with Keynes and by his desire to extend the ideas of the Cambridge economist to the long-period dynamic context (see Young, 1989, pp. 15–50). His seminal 'An essay in dynamic theory' conceived of modern growth theory as a Keynesian theory. It developed the views that the economic system does not tend necessarily to full employment and that the rate of growth may be affected by three sources of autonomous demand, coming from the government sector, the private sector, in the form of autonomous investment, and the foreign sector.

The analysis of Harrod's papers also confirms the limits of the widespread interpretation that he developed his analysis of growth by assuming an absence of monetary influences, constant technical coefficients and a constant saving propensity, in order to bring out the famous 'knife-edge problem'.[1] Harrod worked out his views without denying that the rate of interest has some influence on saving and investment decisions. In 1939 he made some reference to the influence of the interest rate on the propensity to save (see Harrod, 1939, p. 276) and, in his following writings, he recalled the possibility of using Ramsey's inter-temporal approach as the foundation of this part of his analysis.[2] Moreover, dealing with investment, he recognized the possibility of substitution between factors of production and the existence of decreasing marginal returns,[3] although he was sceptical as to the possibility that the operation of these forces would lead the economy towards the full employment (or 'natural') steady growth path. He considered, following the results reached by the Oxford Research Group in which he actively participated, that this kind of substitution was low and that the rate of interest does not tend to undergo large variations since it depends on the conduct of monetary policy, which, according to the Oxford economist, operates by stabilizing this rate at some specified level.[4]

3.5.   GROWTH IN NEOCLASSICAL THEORY

To oppose Harrod's views, Solow (1956) and Swan (1956) presented a dynamic version of neoclassical theory. They argued that variations in relative prices and factor substitution lead the economy to a full employment steady growth path. The debates on capital theory, started by J. Robinson (1953) and enhanced by the publication in 1960 of Sraffa's *Production of Commodities by Means of Commodities*, scrutinized Solow's conclusions. Some outstanding neoclassical economists acknowledged the validity of some criticisms raised against their theory. Samuelson recognized, in the summing up of the 1966 Symposium in the *Quarterly Journal of Economics*, that in the long-period analysis of an economy where more than one commodity is produced, the occurrence of the 'reverse capital deepening' is the general case. This conclusion undercut the neoclassical 'parables' that extend to a multi-commodity economy the conclusions of the analysis of a one-commodity world and challenged the view that price variations and factor substitutions lead the economy to full employment.

3.6.   GROWTH IN POST-KEYNESIAN THEORY

During the same years, Kaldor (1955–56) and Pasinetti (1962) developed the post-Keynesian theory of growth and distribution by assuming that market forces operate along lines, which are different from those envisaged by neoclassical authors and similar to those described by the classical political economists. Like the latter, Kaldor and Pasinetti assumed that the propensities to save of different income earners (or classes, or sectors of the economy) are not equal, and argued that variations in income distribution bring about variations in total saving and aggregate demand, leading the economy to steady growth. The post-Keynesian theory of growth and distribution introduced the 'Cambridge equation' and the 'Pasinetti theorem', which state that in steady growth the rate of profits is equal to the ratio between the rate of growth and the capitalists' propensity to save, and does not depend on technology and on the workers' propensity to save. Samuelson and Modigliani (1966) challenged this conclusion and proposed an 'anti-Pasinetti' or 'dual' theorem. They argued that in steady growth, if the capital owned by the capitalists' class is zero, the capital/output ratio is equal to the ratio between the workers' propensity to save and the rate of growth, while the rate of profits depends on the technological relation connecting this variable to the capital/output ratio. The occurrence of the 'Pasinetti' or of the 'dual' theorem depends on this technological relationship too.

By focusing on the role of income distribution in the growth process and underlining the links with classical political economists and the differences with neoclassical authors, the theory proposed by Kaldor and Pasinetti failed to emphasize the idea that the tendency to full employment does not necessarily operate. However, developments of this theory, which examine the role of the demand coming from the government sector, make good for this failure.

Kaldor's 1958 Memorandum to the Radcliffe Commission shows many similarities with the views on the role of Government policy proposed by Harrod and other Keynesian authors. Kaldor considered Government policies *necessary* to pursue stability and growth. For him, monetary policy is the appropriate tool against the fluctuations of the economy, while fiscal policy is the appropriate tool to use in the pursuit of the long-range objective of sustained growth.

He argued that monetary policy has to stabilize the short-term interest rates in order to avoid some 'undesirable consequences'. The instability of the interest rates enhances financial speculation and reduces the ability of the markets to convey financial resources towards productive enterprises. Moreover, it raises the risk premium to be paid on loans of longer maturity and leads to higher long-term interest rates. Higher long-term interest rates, in turn, cause difficulty to the management of Government debt and increase the probability that firms may not be able to pay back their loans, making lending institutions and financial markets more fragile. Finally, they tend to cause economic stagnation.

To justify the tendency to stagnation Kaldor made explicit reference to his theory of growth and distribution and to the Cambridge equation.

In a steadily growing economy the average rate of profit on investment can, in the first approximation, be taken as being equal to the rate of growth in the money value of the gross national product divided by the proportion of profit saved ... To keep the process of investment going, the rate of profit must exceed the (long-term) interest rates by some considerable margin. (Kaldor [1958] 1964, pp. 137–8)

A monetary policy causing unstable interest rates can raise the long-term rates to a level considered by investors too high to keep accumulation going. Under these circumstances, stagnation prevails, unless the rate of profits is raised too. According to Kaldor, this can be done through fiscal policy.

> If the rate of interest were higher than (the level that keeps investment going), the process of accumulation would be interrupted, and the economy would relapse into a slump. To get it out of the slump it would be necessary to stimulate the propensity to consume – by tax cuts, for example – which would raise the rate of profit and thus restore the incentive to invest. (Kaldor [1958] 1964, p. 138)

Kaldor thus proposed to use the equilibrium condition of the commodities' market and the Cambridge equation to determine the intensity of fiscal policy compatible with a desired rate of growth and the rate of interest fixed by the monetary authority. In making this proposal he showed awareness of the complexity of the growth process, since he made some anticipations of the view, developed some years later, that an expansive fiscal policy may cause problems for the international competitiveness of the economy and for the maintenance of sustained growth in the future. This solution, Kaldor ([1958] 1964, pp. 136–7) said, has the drawback that in time of inadequate demand the Government gradually transforms the economy into one of high consumption and low investment, with some undesirable consequences for long-run growth.

Kaldor did not present his positions on the role of Government policy in a formalized way. His reference to the Cambridge equation must then be considered, as he himself stated, a first approximation rather than the result of a thorough treatment of this problem.

Steedman (1972) provided the first formal presentation of the post-Keynesian theory of growth and distribution, which explicitly introduces the Government sector. He assumed a balanced Government budget to show that the Cambridge equation – in a revised form that takes into account the existence of taxation – holds in a larger number of cases than the dual theorem of Samuelson and Modigliani. Some years later, Fleck and Domenghino (1987) and Pasinetti (1989) started a debate on the validity of the Cambridge equation when the Government budget is *not* balanced. The debate examined a large number of cases, showing when the Cambridge equation holds and confirming the conclusions previously reached by Steedman (for a review of this debate, see Panico, 1997). Its results describe how the views presented by Kaldor to the Radcliffe Commission can be formally developed, by clarifying the different ways in which the demand coming from the Government sector can influence growth and distribution. In the Memorandum the lack of a formal analysis of how Government intervention can affect growth and distribution led Kaldor to refer to a version of the Cambridge equation, which does not include the tax rate. As a consequence, he conceived of the influence of tax variations on growth in terms of their effect on the propensities to save. The debate on the role of the Government sector in the post-Keynesian theory of growth and distribution has, instead, clarified that Government intervention can affect demand and growth independently of changes in the propensities to save and in the capital/output ratio. This kind of influence of demand is not to be found in other literature on growth. The New Growth Theories, for instance, tend to focus on the effect of taxation and Government expenditure on the propensity to save and on the capital/output ratio, disregarding the direct influence of Government intervention on the rate of growth and the rate of profits.[5]

Finally, the debate on the role of the Government sector in the post-Keynesian theory of growth and distribution has pointed out the existence of some other common elements between the classical and the Keynesian traditions, allowing the reconciliation of the two approaches to distribution, which had previously been considered as alternative. These are the approaches proposed by Kaldor and Pasinetti in their theory of growth and distribution and that implied by Sraffa's hint in *Production of Commodities* (1960) to take the rate of profits, rather than the wage rate, as the independent variable (determined, in turn, by the money interest rates) in the classical theory of prices and distribution.

3.7. THE INFLUENCE OF THE DEMAND FOR INVESTMENT ON GROWTH

Within the post-Keynesian literature on growth it is possible to find two other lines of development attributing a primary role to autonomous demand. They contribute to the improvement of the analysis of the growth process, by describing its different aspects and the diverse kinds of influence that the autonomous components of aggregate demand can have on the rate of growth.

A first line of development focuses on the demand coming from the private sector in the form of autonomous investment, i.e. of investment not generated directly from previous saving decisions. This literature presents several investment-driven growth theories based on different specifications of the investment function and different solutions to the problem of income distribution.

The neo-Keynesian theory, proposed by Joan Robinson (1956, 1962) and Kaldor (1957, 1961), assumes a direct functional relationship between investment and the rate of profit. The theory, which determines growth and distribution simultaneously, extends to long-period analysis the 'paradox of thrift', according to which an increase in the propensity to save causes a reduction in the rate of profits and in the rate of growth. Moreover, it underlines the existence of an inverse relationship between the real wage rate and the rate of growth.

The Kaleckian theory, inspired by Kalecki and Steindl, which attracts the attention of a large number of Keynesian researchers (see, among others, Rowthorn, 1981; Dutt, 1984, 1987, 1990; Bhaduri and Marglin, 1990; Lavoie, 1992, 1995), assumes that (1) productive capacity is not utilized at its 'normal' level, (2) the profit margin is an exogenous variable depending on the degree of monopoly enjoyed by oligopolistic firms, (3) prices are determined through a mark-up procedure, and (4) investment is positively related to the rate of profits, which stands in for the state of expected profitability and the availability of internal finance, and to the degree of capacity utilization, which reflects the state of aggregate demand. This theory confirms the neo-Keynesian conclusion on the paradox of thrift but argues, in opposition to the neo-Keynesian theory, for the existence of a positive relationship between the real wage rate and the rate of growth in the presence of long-run under-utilization of production plants. This result, known as the 'paradox of costs', is due to the fact that the rise in the real wage rate brings about an increase in demand and capacity utilization, which has a positive effect on the rate of profits and on investment.

The Kaleckian theory has been recently amended by the works inspired by Bhaduri and Marglin (1990), which take into account the different effects produced on investment by the rate of profits, the profit margin and capacity utilization. By introducing an investment function positively related to the profit margin and to capacity utilization, these works identify a wage-led and a profit-led growth regime. In both cases, a rise in the real wage rate reduces the profit margin and increases capacity utilization. In the wage-led regime the overall effect of an increase in the real wage rate on growth is positive, as in the Kaleckian paradox of costs, because the positive effect on growth generated by the increase in capacity utilization is greater than the negative effect on growth generated by the decrease in the profit margin. In the profit-led regime, the opposite result holds because the positive effect on growth generated by the increase in capacity utilization is lower than the negative effect generated by the decrease in the profit margin.

Finally, an attempt has been made in recent literature to develop a neo-Ricardian theory of growth, which incorporates a classical theory of prices and distribution (see, among others, Vianello, 1985, 1989, 1996; Ciccone

1986, 1987). This theory, in opposition to the neo-Keynesian and Kaleckian theories, assumes that the investment function depends on the discrepancies between actual and normal capacity utilization and underlines the need to develop the analysis of growth through the comparison of long-period positions. Moreover, it makes the rate of profits depend on the money rates of interest, as suggested by Sraffa in *Production of Commodities*.

3.8. THE INFLUENCE OF GROWTH OF THE DEMAND COMING FROM THE FOREIGN SECTOR

A second line of development of Keynesian literature focuses on the influence on growth of the demand coming from the foreign sector, a problem already considered by Harrod in the 1930s. This literature, which has provided some renowned contributions to the empirical analysis of open economies, plays down the role of distributive variables and is intertwined with the analysis of growth as a 'cumulative process'.

In a series of essays, written between 1966 and 1972, Kaldor used the notion of 'cumulative causation' to describe the actual performance of the economies. He attributed to the demand coming from the foreign sector the primary role in setting in motion the growth process. The domestic sources of demand mainly influence, instead, the competitiveness of the economy and the intensity with which the external stimulus is transmitted to the rate of growth. According to Kaldor (1971), the composition of output and demand has an important influence on the rate of change of productivity, owing to the presence of variable returns in the different sectors of the economy and to the fact that increasing returns mainly occur in the manufacturing sector generally and especially in the capital goods sector. For Kaldor, high quotas of investment to aggregate demand and of the capital goods sector in the productive structure enhance productivity changes, which, in turn, improve the international performance of the economy setting up and intensifying the cumulative processes. He distinguished between the concepts of 'consumption-led' and 'export-led' growth. The latter, he argued, is more desirable than the former, which tends to have negative long-run effects on productivity and international competitiveness, since it increases the weight of non-increasing return sectors in the productive structure of the economy. This distinction was at the basis of Kaldor's claim, recalled above, that the maintenance of sustained growth in the future may be endangered by the use of fiscal policy, which, according to him, tends to increase the proportion of consumption in aggregate demand.

In 1975 Dixon and Thirlwall presented an 'export-led growth model', which formalized some aspects of Kaldor's views. Thirlwall (1979) and

Thirlwall and Hussein (1982) made important contributions to this subject by working out a dynamic analysis, which shows how growth may be constrained by the equilibrium of the balance of payments, playing down the operation of cumulative causation processes. In spite of this simplification, the empirical applications of the new analysis, which are able to account for the difference in the rates of growth among countries and the cumulative divergence in their GDP levels, have produced more satisfactory results than those of the 1975 export-led model. Recently Moreno Brid (1998–99) and McCombie and Thirlwall (1999) have extended Thirlwall's new analysis to take into account the impact of the persistent accumulation of external debt on the economy's long-term rate of expansion. These extensions have opened new areas of research into the financial restrictions imposed by international credit institutions on the long-term economic growth of countries with persistent trade balance deficits.

3.9.   CONCLUSIONS

In spite of the consensus enjoyed nowadays by Say's Law and by the theories adopting it, there is a large amount of literature that focuses on the role of the autonomous components of demand on the rate of growth of the economy. This literature, by dealing with aspects of the growth process that are overlooked by other traditions, can provide a set of articulated ideas and analyses, which contribute to a wider view of the growth process. The aim of this chapter has been to attract the attention of readers to these parts of economic theorizing.

NOTES

1. The major reference for the 'knife-edge' interpretation is Solow (1956; 1970). For an opposite interpretation, see Eisner (1958), Asimakopulos and Weldon (1965), Kregel (1980), Asimakopulos (1985).
2. See Harrod (1948, p. 40; 1964, pp. 903 and 905–6). The similarity between Harrod's and Ramsey's analysis of saving is underlined by Asimakopulos and Weldon (1965, p. 66). Harrod (1973, p. 20) also clarifies that 'what each person chooses in regard to saving is governed by various institutional arrangements, which differ from country to country and from time to time. There is the question of what the State will provide for future contingencies – old age, ill health, unemployment, etc. – by current transfer payments as and when they arise. The more ground that the State covers, the less will the individual feel it incumbent to provide for himself by saving. Personal saving will also be affected by the degree the education of one's children is subvented by the public authorities'.
3. See Harrod (1939, pp. 258, 259 and 276). On page 276, in particular, Harrod explicitly referred to an inverse relationship between v and r. In the 1930s the neoclassical assumption

of decreasing marginal returns was generally accepted. Sraffa's critique of the neoclassical theory of capital had not yet been presented. Within Sraffa's papers, the first written evidence of this critique is dated 1942. (See Panico, 1998, p. 177, fn. 55; and Panico, 2001, pp. 300 and 308–9 fn. 59, 60 and 61.) As is well known, it was published in 1960 and discussed at length in the following decades.

4. Harrod (1948, p. 83) points out that his analysis of the warranted rate assumes the rate of interest to be constant. He referred to the realism of Keynes's view on the behaviour of the interest rate (pp. 64–5), agreeing that this rate may be rigid (pp. 56–7) and unable to decrease in such a way as to lead to full employment (pp. 70–1; 83–4; 97; 99).

5. Barro (1990) follows such a line in his analysis of Government spending in an endogenous growth model.

REFERENCES

Asimakopulos, A. (1985), 'Harrod on Harrod: the evolution of "a line of steady growth" ', *History of Political Economy*, **17**(4), 619–35.

Asimakopulos, A. and J.C. Weldon (1965), 'A synoptic view of some simple models of growth', *Canadian Journal of Economics and Political Science*, **31**, February, 59–79.

Barro, R.J. (1990), 'Government spending in a simple model of endogenous growth', *Journal of Political Economy,* **98**(5), S103–25.

Bhaduri, A. and S. Marglin (1990), 'Unemployment and the real wage: the economic basis for contesting political ideologies', *Cambridge Journal of Economics*, **14**(4), 375–93.

Ciccone, R. (1986), 'Accumulation and capital utilization: some critical considerations on Joan Robinson's theory of distribution', *Political Economy*, **2**(1), 17–36.

Ciccone, R. (1987), 'Accumulation, capacity utilization and distribution: a reply', *Political Economy*, **3**(1), 97–111.

Dixon, R. and A.P. Thirlwall (1975), 'A model of regional growth-rate differences on Kaldorian lines', *Oxford Economic Papers*, **27**, 201–14.

Dutt, A.K. (1984), 'Stagnation, income distribution and monopoly power', *Cambridge Journal of Economics*, **8**(1), 25–40.

Dutt, A.K. (1987), 'Alternative closures again: a comment on "Growth, Distribution and Inflation" ', *Cambridge Journal of Economics*, **11**(1), 75–82.

Dutt, A.K. (1990), *Growth, Distribution and Uneven Development*, Cambridge: Cambridge University Press.

Eisner, R. (1958), 'On growth models and the neoclassical resurgence', *Economic Journal*, **68**, December, 707–21.

Fleck, F.H. and C.M. Domenghino (1987), 'Cambridge (UK) versus Cambridge (Mass.): a Keynesian solution to the "Pasinetti paradox" ', *Journal of Post Keynesian Economics*, **10**(1), Fall, 22–36.

Harrod, R.F. (1939), 'An essay in dynamic theory', *Economic Journal*, **49**, March, 14–33. Reprinted in R.F. Harrod, *Economic Essays*, second edition, London: Macmillan, 1972, pp. 254–77.

Harrod, R.F. (1948), *Towards a Dynamic Theory*, London: Macmillan.

Harrod, R.F. (1964), 'Are monetary and fiscal policies enough?', *Economic Journal*, December, 903–15.

Harrod, R.F. (1969), *Money*, London: Macmillan.

Harrod, R.F. (1973), *Economic Dynamics*, London: Macmillan.

Kaldor, N. (1955–56), 'Alternative theories of distribution', *Review of Economic Studies*, **23**(2), 83–100.

Kaldor, N. (1957), 'A model of economic growth', *Economic Journal*, **67**, 591–624.

Kaldor, N. (1961), 'Capital accumulation and economic growth', in F.A. Lutz and D.C. Hague (eds), *The Theory of Capital*, London: Macmillan, pp. 177–222.

Kaldor, N. (1964), 'Monetary policy, economic stability and growth', in *Essays on Economic Policy*, vol. I, Duckworth, London, pp. 128–153, originally presented as 'A Memorandum submitted to the Radcliffe Committee on the Working of the Monetary System', 1958, June 23, first published in Principal Memoranda of Evidence, Cmnd 827, HMSO, London, 1960.

Kaldor, N. (1971), 'Conflicts in national economic objectives', *Economic Journal*, **81**, 1–16, reprinted in N. Kaldor (1978), *Further Essays on Economic Theory*, London: Duckworth.

Keynes, J.M. (1936), *The General Theory of Employment, Interest and Money*, in D. Moggridge (ed.), *The Collected Writings of J.M Keynes: The General Theory and After. Part I: Preparation,* vol. XIII, London: Macmillan Press, 1973.

Kregel, J.A. (1980), 'Economic dynamics and the theory of steady growth: an historical essay on Harrod's "Knife-edge" ', *History of Political Economy*, **12**(1), 97–123.

Kregel, J.A. (1985), 'Harrod and Keynes: increasing returns, the theory of employment, and dynamic economics', in G.C. Harcourt (ed.), *Keynes and his Contemporaries*, Macmillan: London, pp. 66–88.

Lavoie, M. (1992), *Foundations of Post-Keynesian Economic Analysis*, Aldershot: Edward Elgar.

Lavoie, M. (1995), 'The Kaleckian model of growth and distribution and its Neo-Ricardian and Neo-Marxian critiques', *Cambridge Journal of Economics*, **19**, 789–818.

McCombie, J. and A.P. Thirlwall (1999), 'Growth in an international context: a post Keynesian analysis, in J. Deprez and T.J. Harvey (eds), *Foundations of International Economics: Post Keynesian Perspectives*, London: Routledge.

Moreno Brid, J.C. (1998–99), 'On capital flows and the balance-of-payments constrained growth model', *Journal of Post Keynesian Economics*, 21, 283–98.

Panico, C. (1997), 'Government deficits in the post Keynesian theories of growth and distribution', *Contributions to Political Economy*, **16**, 61–86.

Panico, C. (1998), 'Le questioni monetarie negli scritti di Sraffa', *Il Pensiero Economico Italiano,* **VI** (1), 123–55.

Panico, C. (1999), 'The government sector in the post Keynesian theory of growth and personal distribution', in G. Mongiovi and F. Petri (eds), *Value, Distribution and Capital, Essays in Honour of P. Garegnani,* London: Routledge, pp. 339–53.

Panico, C. (2001), 'Monetary analysis in Sraffa's writings', in T. Cozzi and R. Marchionatti (eds), *Piero Sraffa's Political Economy: A Centenary Estimate,* London: Routeledge, pp. 285–310.

Pasinetti, L.L. (1962), 'Rate of profit and income distribution in relation to the rate of economic growth', *Review of Economic Studies,* **29**, 267–79.

Pasinetti, L.L. (1989), 'Government deficit spending is not incompatible with the cambridge theorem of the rate of profit: a reply to Fleck and Domenghino', *Journal of Post Keynesian Economics,* **11**(4), Summer, 640–7.

Ricoy, C. (1998), 'Cumulative causation', in H.D. Kurz and N. Salvadori (eds), *The Elgar Companion to Classical Economics,* vol. I, Cheltenham: Edward Elgar, pp. 202–8.

Robinson, J.V. (1953), 'The production function and the theory of capital', *Review of Economic Studies,* **21**(2), 81–106.

Robinson, J. (1956), *The Accumulation of Capital,* London: Macmillan.

Robinson, J. (1962), *Essays in the Theory of Economic Growth,* London: Macmillan.

Rowthorn, R.E. (1981), 'Demand, real wages and economic growth', *Thames Papers in Political Economy,* Autumn, 1–39.

Samuelson P.A. (1966), 'A summing up', *Quarterly Journal of Economics,* **80**(4), November, 568–83.

Samuelson, P.A. and F. Modigliani (1966), 'The Pasinetti paradox in neoclassical and more general models', *Review of Economic Studies,* **33**(4), October, 269–302.

Solow, R. (1956), 'A contribution to the theory of economic growth', *Quarterly Journal of Economics,* 70, February, 65–94.

Solow, R. (1970), *Growth Theory: An Exposition,* Oxford: Oxford University Press.

Sraffa, P. (1960), *Production of Commodities by Means of Commodities,* Cambridge: Cambridge University Press.

Steedman, I. (1972), 'The state and the outcome of the Pasinetti process', *Economic Journal,* **82**(328), December, 1387–95.

Swan, T.W. (1956), 'Economic growth and capital accumulation', *Economic Record,* 32, November, 334–61.

Thirlwall, A.P. (1979), 'The balance of payments constraint as an explanation of international growth rate differences', *Banca Nazionale del Lavoro Quarterly Review,* 128. Reprinted in A.P. Thirlwall, *Macroeconomic Issues from a Keynesian Perspective,* Cheltenham: Edward Elgar, 1997, pp. 45–53.

Thirlwall, A.P. and M.N. Hussain (1982), 'The balance of payments constraint, capital flows and growth rate differences between developing countries', *Oxford Economic Papers,* **34**, 498–509.

Vianello, F. (1985), 'The pace of accumulation', *Political Economy*, **1**(1), 69–87.

Vianello, F. (1989), 'Effective demand and the rate of profit: some thoughts on Marx, Kalecki and Sraffa', in M. Sebastiani (ed.), *Kalecki's Relevance Today*, New York: St. Martin's Press, pp. 164–190.

Vianello, F. (1996), 'Joan Robinson on normal prices (and the normal rate of profits)', in M.C. Marcuzzo, L.L. Pasinetti and A. Roncaglia (eds), *The Economics of Joan Robinson*, London and New York: Routledge, pp. 112–120.

Young W. (1989) (eds), *Harrod and his Trade Cycle Group*, London: Macmillan.

4. New growth theory, effective demand, and post-Keynesian dynamics

Amitava Krishna Dutt*

4.1. INTRODUCTION

What is called new growth theory or endogenous growth theory appears to have changed the face of modern macroeconomics and the study of economic growth since the late 1980s.

After enormous enthusiasm and excitement from the late 1930s to the mid-1960s, the subfield of growth economics became a dormant one. Solow (1982), one of the major contributors to growth theory in these early glory days, wrote in the late 1970s that:

> I think there are definite signs that (growth theory) ... is just about played out, at least in its familiar form. Anyone working inside economic theory these days knows in his or her bones that growth theory is now an unpromising pond for an enterprising theorist to fish in. (Solow, 1982, cited in Solow, 1991, p. 393)

Undergraduate intermediate macroeconomic texts, usually quite quick to incorporate major recent developments in the subject, normally only devoted a brief chapter to growth economics tucked away towards the end of the book. This chapter contained a brief description of Solow's (1956) neoclassical growth model and some growth accounting related to it, and perhaps made some mention of Harrod and Domar's pioneering contributions. To be sure, there were some economists who were working on growth-theoretic issues in heterodox traditions (see, for instance, Harris, 1978; Marglin, 1984; and Taylor, 1983), but they were well outside the mainstream of the subject.

The publication of the papers by Romer (1986) and Lucas (1988) has changed all this. There has been an enormous outpouring of research on new growth theory. The number of papers published on growth economics in the leading economics journals has ballooned, and a new journal devoted solely to the study of economic growth has emerged, entitled *Journal of Economic Growth*. Several new textbooks on growth theory have appeared, and a popular graduate macroeconomics text by David Romer (1996) begins with the study of economic growth. Undergraduate texts have also adopted this procedure, moving their discussion of growth to a prominent spot towards the beginning of the book before getting down to the analysis of the determination of output and prices in the short run. Growth has been put on center stage.[1]

Although this 'new' growth theory has certainly made a positive contribution by placing growth back on the agenda of mainstream economics, questions can and have been raised about how new it really is, and regarding the extent to which it makes a useful contribution to understanding the phenomenon of growth. This chapter will follow some recent critics of new growth theory and argue that although there are some contributions to the new theory that can be said to be major new contributions, its newness has been greatly exaggerated by its proponents. Moreover, new growth has not adequately captured some of the issues regarding the growth process and left out some others completely, and therefore made rather limited contributions to our understanding of the phenomenon of economic growth. The central argument of this chapter is that a large part of the problem of new growth theory lies in its failure or unwillingness to examine issues relating to effective demand and unemployment. Since these are issues stressed in post-Keynesian dynamic models, these models are well placed to overcome some of the problems faced by new growth theory. However, these models can also profitably draw from new growth theory as well.

The rest of this chapter proceeds as follows. Section 4.2 provides a quick summary of what new growth theorists call old growth theory and contrasts it to an earlier view of growth theory. Section 4.3 reviews the contributions of new growth theory, and discusses its criticisms, including its neglect of unemployment and aggregate demand. Section 4.4 provides a brief discussion of post-Keynesian growth theories. Section 4.5 points out some new issues in post-Keynesian growth theory concerning technological change because it raises questions related to those raised in new growth theory.

4.2.   'OLD' GROWTH THEORY

An analytical history of what is now often referred to as 'old' growth theory, that is, the theory of growth prior to the advent of 'new' growth theory, goes something like this (see, for instance, Sen, 1970; Solow, 1994, pp. 45–7).[2]

Harrod (1939), who laid the foundation of modern growth theory, focused on two major problems of growth.[3] The first was the knife-edge instability problem of the destabilizing consequences of the divergence between planned investment (represented by the accelerator) and saving (represented by a Keynesian saving function) which would make the economy move further away from its warranted growth path (at which there is saving/investment equilibrium). The second was the long-run problem of equality of the warranted rate of growth that determined the rate of growth of labor demand (with a fixed labor/output ratio) with the natural rate of growth that determined the rate of growth of effective labor supply. The warranted rate of growth is determined by s/v, where s and v are the constant saving/income and capital/output ratios, and the natural rate of growth by $n + \lambda$, where n and λ are the given rates of growth the given rate of growth of labor supply and labor productivity. Since there is no reason for s/v and $n + \lambda$ to be equal, the economy would either experience persistent increases in unemployment or excess demand for labor.

Most subsequent contributions to growth theory can be seen as reactions to Harrod's problems, especially to his long-run problem. The Solow–Swan neoclassical growth theory with full employment growth can be seen as 'solving' the long-run problem by allowing for capital/labor substitution by cost-minimizing, perfectly competitive, firms, which brought about adjustments in v; Solow (1956) in fact motivates his model in this manner. Kaldor (1955–56) and others developed models allowing the saving rate to change in response to changes in the distribution of income, given differential propensities to save for different income groups. This Cambridge model, like the neoclassical model, assumes full employment growth, although Kaldor tried to provide reasons based on the buoyancy of investment rather than neoclassical wage/price flexibility to do the job. He also pointed out that if income distribution could not be changed due to wage or profit constraints, the adjustment mechanism need not work and unemployment could result. A third set of models – such as those of Kahn (1959) and Robinson (1962) – accepts the Harrodian conclusion and examines actual growth paths which may not make the economy grow at its natural rate. Other models which determine capital accumulation by saving, but assume that distribution is exogenously determined and that unemployed labor exists in the economy – that is, models in the Marx–von Neumann tradition – also imply that the economy grows at its rate of capital accumulation, which is different from the rate of growth of labor supply. These, of course, do not exhaust all possibilities. For instance, changes in s caused by factors other than distributional shifts, in v due to technological change, and in n due to changes in labor supply (as in the classical models of

Malthus and Ricardo), can also solve Harrod's problem and make the economy eventually grow at its natural rate.

But what of Harrod's knife-edge instability problem? Neoclassical growth theory simply assumes the problem away by making investment identically equal to saving and by assuming that factor/price flexibility and smooth substitution in a frictionless model always ensures full employment, not just in the long run. As discussed earlier, the Kaldor model also assumes full employment in the long run, though not in terms of the neoclassical adjustment story but by arguing that investment demand will be buoyant enough to produce full employment during the growth process. Kaldor therefore allows for investment and saving to be different from each other, but argues that investment will be sufficient to generate full employment in the long run, and that distribution will adjust to bring saving into equality with investment. Thus the Harrodian knife-edge is averted by assuming the economy to be at full employment and examining changes in the price level and distribution in response to goods market disequilibria: investment is fixed while saving adjusts to it. Robinson (1962) and others who have analyzed actual growth paths, which do not imply full employment, have assumed that desired investment and saving depend on the rate of profit (as in Robinson's banana diagram), ensuring stability by making saving respond more strongly to changes in the profit rate than investment. In the neoclassical Keynesian version the real interest rate or the asset price of capital (or Tobin's q) is introduced into the investment function to bring saving and investment to equality at full employment, at least on a long-run growth path. Thus, different contributions have bypassed (in the case of the neoclassical model) or overcome (in the case of the Cambridge, Robinsonian, and neoclassical Keynesian models) Harrod's knife-edge instability problem in different ways.

Following the emergence of the Solow–Swan growth model, there developed a large neoclassical literature extending that model, all of it assuming continuous full employment. A few of these contributions relevant for our subsequent discussion may be briefly discussed. Solow (1956) had extended his model to allow for technological change in his original paper. Using a Cobb–Douglas formulation with the production function given by:[4]

$$Y = A K^{\alpha}(EL)^{1-\alpha} \tag{4.1}$$

where K (sweeping problems of heterogeneity and measurement under the rug, but see Kurz and Salvadori, 1995 for a recent discussion) denotes capital stock, L the employment of labor, and E the labor-augmenting productivity parameter, that model can be expressed in terms of its dynamic equation involving $k = K/EL$, as:

$$\hat{k} = s\,Ak^{\alpha-1} - n - \hat{E},\qquad(4.2)$$

where n is the exogenously fixed rate of growth of labor supply and employment (under conditions of full employment), and overhats denote rates of growth. Solow assumed that $\hat{E}$ is exogenously given at the rate λ, so that this equation becomes:

$$\hat{k} = s\,Ak^{\alpha-1} - n - \lambda.\qquad(4.3)$$

The model implies that in steady state, with $\hat{k} = 0$, $Y/EL = Ak^{\alpha}$ becomes a constant, so that per capita income, $y = Y/L$, grows at the rate λ, the exogenous rate of technological change. Several contributions have modified the assumption of exogenous technological change.

Arrow (1962) examined the case of learning by doing, in which labor productivity depends on cumulative experience, measured by cumulative gross investment. Altering his assumption of the fixed coefficients production function with vintage capital to that of a Cobb–Douglas production function with homogeneous capital, and writing the learning function as:

$$E = \zeta K^{\eta}\qquad(4.4)$$

where ζ and η are positive parameters of the learning function and K denotes cumulative gross investment (assuming away depreciation), equation (4.2) becomes:

$$\hat{k} = s(1-\eta)Ak^{\alpha-1} - n.\qquad(4.5)$$

Under Arrow's assumption that $\eta < 1$, which reflects diminishing returns to learning, equation (4.5) determines the steady state level of k, given by:

$$k^{*} = \left[\frac{n}{(1-\eta)sA}\right]^{-\frac{1}{(1-\alpha)}},$$

at which $Y/EL = Ak^{\alpha}$ becomes a constant, implying that per capita income, $y = Y/L$, grows at the rate $\hat{E}$, which from equation (4.3) is seen to be given by $\eta n/(1-\eta)$. Uzawa (1965) examined the case in which the growth of E is related to education. In particular, he assumed that $\hat{E}$ depends positively on the proportion of labor devoted to education, which we express in iso-elastic form as:

$$\hat{E} = \tau\left(\frac{L_E}{L}\right)^{\epsilon}.\qquad(4.6)$$

Assuming that labor engaged in education does not produce final output, that output is given by:

$$Y = AK^{\alpha} (EL_p)^{1-\alpha},$$

where L_p denotes labor engaged in production, with $L_p + L_E = L$, and continuing to assume that a fixed fraction s of output is saved and invested, and that L_E/L is fixed at the level u (in contrast to Uzawa's interest in finding the optimal time path of production by choosing s and u at every point in time), equation (4.2) can be written as

$$\hat{k} = sAk^{\alpha-1}(1-u)^{1-\alpha} - n - \tau u^{\varepsilon}. \tag{4.7}$$

Solving for the steady state level of k as before we find that the rate of growth of per capita output at this steady state is given by τu^{ε}. It may be noted that we can think of the 'education' sector alternatively as the 'research' sector, implying that greater research effort implies faster technological change.

Other contributions modified the assumption of a given saving rate with that of optimizing consumer-households. This was done in two ways. One class of models assumes that infinitely lived dynasties have instantaneous utility given by a function of the form:

$$u(c) = \frac{c^{1-\upsilon}}{1-\upsilon} \qquad \text{for } \upsilon \neq 1$$

$$= \ln c \qquad \text{for } \upsilon = 1$$

and maximize:

$$U = \int_0^{\infty} u\,(c(t))\, e^{nt}\, e^{-\rho t}\, dt$$

with the fixed rate of time preference ρ, taking into account family size growing at the rate n. Another class uses the overlapping generations (OLG) structure, with individuals maximizing their present utility over two periods, working and saving in the first and retired and dissaving in the second. These models, assuming that labor-augmenting technological change occurs at the exogenous rate λ, also imply that at steady state per capita income grows at this exogenous rate, so that in this sense they are no different from the standard Solow model with a fixed saving rate with exogenous technological change.[5] However, they come closer to the neoclassical methodological ideal of explaining all behavior in terms of the optimizing agent.

4.3.   'NEW' GROWTH THEORY

The essence of new growth theory is captured by the simple AK model, in which output, Y, is assumed to be related to 'generalized' capital, K, by a fixed coefficient, A, in terms of the production function:

$$Y = AK. \tag{4.8}$$

It should be noted that this function states that output can be increased indefinitely, without experiencing diminishing returns, with the accumulation of generalized capital and that, moreover, output cannot be expanded by increasing labor employed. In its intensive form, it can be written as:

$$y = Ak \tag{4.9}$$

where k now denotes K/L, and the efficiency factor for labor, E is fixed and set equal to 1.[6] If we assume that a constant fraction, s, of output and income is saved and automatically invested, and assume away depreciation, the equation of motion of k is given by:

$$\hat{k} = sA - n. \tag{4.10}$$

Assuming that $sA > n$, we see that k does not reach a steady state value but grows continuously at the rate $sA - n > 0$. Equation (4.9) then implies that per capita income grows forever at this same rate, $\hat{y} = sA - n$. Equation (4.10) differs from equation (4.3) of the Solow model by ignoring exogenous technological change, setting $\lambda = 0$, and more importantly, by setting $\alpha = 1$, which implies doing away with diminishing returns to capital while maintaining constant returns to scale. It is this latter assumption that is crucial for generating a constant rate of growth of k rather than reaching a constant value of it in steady state. In general, new growth models require that the returns to endogenously accumulable factors is non-diminishing. In this simple model, labor is not endogenously accumulable – in the sense that the growth rate of labor supply is fixed exogenously – and capital is, so that the condition for endogenous growth is that we do not have diminishing returns to capital, an assumption which is satisfied because we have constant returns to capital. If we have diminishing returns to capital and the marginal product of capital approaches zero, as in the Solow model, in steady state, the exogenously fixed rate of growth of labor supply (in effective units) determines the rate of output growth.

Two comments should be made about this model. First, it does not require the assumption of full employment of labor: since labor is not productive, the level of employment of labor does not matter; indeed some versions of the model can omit labor altogether. Second, the AK form is not necessary to generate 'endogenous' growth. A production function of the form:

$$Y = AK + BK^\alpha L^{1-\alpha}$$

yields the equation of motion:

$$\hat{k} = s(A + Bk^{\alpha-1}) - n.$$

As long as $sA > n$, this equation will not yield a steady state value of k, and the growth rate of k and hence y will asymptotically tend to the value $sA - n$. This implies that endogenous growth is consistent with diminishing returns to the accumulable factor, provided that there is some lower bound to diminishing returns. Moreover, the model can even allow for increasing returns to capital, in which case the growth rate of k and y will increase over time. The usual problem arises of making increasing returns consistent with the perfect competition assumption. But this problem is not insurmountable, as the subsequent discussion will clarify.

The AK formulation, of course, is new growth theory in a skeletal form. Many of the major contributions to the new growth theory can be seen as putting muscle on these bare bones, although they appeared before the AK. One formulation interprets K as generalized capital including some sort of technology stock with positive externalities across producers. This is the interpretation of Romer (1986), who essentially uses a production function of the form given by equation (4.1) with K interpreted as the stock of knowledge (ignoring measurement problems) and assumes that:

$$E = K^A. \tag{4.11}$$

Here K^A denotes the economy's aggregate stock of capital, reflecting how technology improves when the aggregate stock of knowledge (which is a public good) increases, whereas K in the individual firm's production function given by (4.1) denotes private knowledge. The firm invests in research and development expenditures to increase their private knowledge stock, on which they earn the rental rate equal to its marginal product; note that we have diminishing returns to private capital. However, as the knowledge stock of all firms grows, the aggregate stock of capital contributes to increasing productivity from non-excludable knowledge. Since the sum of all private capital (which we also denote by K, assuming for simplicity that there is only one representative firm) is equal to aggregate capital, equation (4.11) implies:

$$E = K, \tag{4.12}$$

so that $\hat{A} = \hat{K}$. This equation is seen simply to be a special case of Arrow's learning equation (4.4) with $\eta = 1$, that is, with no diminishing returns to learning. Substituting equation (4.12) into equation (4.1) we obtain:

$$Y = AKL^{1-\alpha},$$

which yields the AK model as long as labor supply is constant (which is what Romer assumes in his basic model) and we assume that full employment of labor prevails.[7] It should be noted that since we have diminishing returns to private capital, the model is consistent with perfect competition. We find that Arrow's model, with a slight change in assumptions ($\eta = 1$ rather than $0 < \eta < 1$), implies the Romer (1986) model (and therefore also the AK model), although Romer uses the infinite horizon optimizing framework, and assumes K increases due to research and development expenditures rather than learning by doing. Another formulation, that of Lucas (1988), includes two types of capital – physical and human capital. The structure of Lucas's model is in fact identical to that of Uzawa's, with two differences: he assumes $\varepsilon = 1$ in his technical change function given by equation (4.6), and he introduces externalities due to human capital accumulation, captured by introducing an aggregate human capital formation term in the production function. The presence of externalities, as in the Romer model, makes this model consistent with perfect competition despite the presence of increasing returns. This formulation yields 'endogenous' growth but, as we saw earlier, so did Uzawa's model. But it does not yield the AK model. That model, however, can be generated with models with two types of capital – human and physical capital – where both are accumulated and both have similar production conditions, and where raw labor is therefore not a constraint on production. Physical and human capital together exhibit non-diminishing returns, and both are endogenously accumulable.

Yet other formulations allow for new products, either as new consumer goods (which in some versions expand the number of goods which consumers consume, and in others replace older goods with higher quality goods), or as new intermediate goods used in production (see, for instance, Aghion and Howitt, 1998). The development of new products or better technology in these models is modeled as being the result of research and development activities of inventor/innovators who involve themselves in research activity rather than in production. Although these models do not necessarily introduce stocks of capital, they produce results that are similar to the AK model because they have production or utility functions of the Dixit–Stiglitz type where variety adds to production or to utility. These models are also different from the Solow model because they introduce imperfect competition, thereby allowing them to have neoclassical optimization microfoundations with increasing returns even without externalities, and also derive (at least temporary) returns from innovations that subsequently become public goods. It should be noted that all of these versions of new growth theory assume explicitly that labor is fully employed: for instance, in models with research and development activity, the total labor force at any moment in time is engaged either in production or in research and development.

Most endogenous growth theory models do not assume given saving rates as in the *AK* model discussed above, but allow infinitely lived consumers (one representative consumer or dynasty is considered) to maximize their present discounted utility level over their lifetime under the assumption of perfect foresight. Solow has repeatedly criticized this practice. In Solow (1997, p. 12) he writes: 'I find that I resist this practice instinctively. It seems to me foolish to interpret as a descriptive theory what my generation learned from Frank Ramsey to treat as a normative theory, a story about what an omniscient, omnipotent, and nevertheless virtuous planner would do'. One can argue that at best what these models do is to allow a comparison of the actual outcome for economies with some social optimum. But even here its value is limited by its assumption that preferences are given, whereas during the growth process one can expect preferences to change, arguably in unknowable ways. In any case, this approach is not unique to endogenous growth theory, even before its appearance, optimizing growth models were already in vogue. Solow (1994, p. 49) also argues that the intertemporally optimizing agent also has the effect of 'encumbering it [the growth model] with unnecessary implausibilities and complexities'. Finally, this assumption makes no real difference in terms of results. As Solow (1997, p. 12) notes, comparing the optimizing model with models with behavioral saving functions, '[i]t is not a matter of great importance for growth theory. The two approaches come to the same thing in the long run, although they can differ in the short run'. These comments apply not just to new growth theory models, but also earlier neoclassical models with infinite horizon optimizing agents, but can be said to apply more strongly to the former because of the more pervasive presence of this kind of agent. We will return to this theme later.

Its proponents claim that new growth theory, unlike old growth theory, determines growth endogenously even in the long run (hence its alternative name, endogenous growth theory) and, in particular, makes long-run growth depend on the saving and investment rates (which is consistent with empirical work based on cross-country regressions). These claims have some truth to them, but are exaggerated. The element of truth is that most old neoclassical growth theories imply that long-run growth depends only on exogenously given rates of technological change (as for instance in the basic

Solow model) or parameters of technological change functions (as in the Arrow model), and is independent of the saving and investment rates. However, it is untrue for a number of reasons. First, at least for Uzawa's optimization model, growth depends on the allocation of labor between production and education sectors, which is affected by the rate of time preference for consumers-workers which determines saving behavior. Second, as Srinivasan (1995) reminds us, there are old neoclassical models in which no steady state may exist, so that rate of growth is endogenous even in the long run, and is affected by saving and investment rates. For instance, in the Solow model (as he himself notes) if the Inada condition (which requires the marginal product of capital tend to zero as the capital/labor ratio tends to infinity) is not satisfied, the existence of a steady state is not guaranteed, even if the marginal product of capital is strictly diminishing. Third, this view involves a drastic reinterpretation of old growth theory.

Old growth theory was not just neoclassical growth theory in which growth in the long run was (apart from the exceptions just noted) exogenous and in particular independent of saving and investment rates. It also included other growth theories that allowed the rate of growth to be different from its natural rate in the long run (see Srinivasan, 1995). In Robinson's model, for instance, if the investment rate increased due to an upward shift in the desired accumulation function, the rate of growth would increase in the long run. Models in the Marx–von Neumann tradition also implied that a rise in the saving rate out of the surplus would increase the saving rate, capital accumulation, and the rate of growth (von Neumann, 1945; Mahalanobis, 1955; Marglin, 1984). These models produced endogenous growth because they assumed that the only possibly endogenously non-accumulable factor – labor – was not a binding constraint on production even in the long-run not because it was not productive in the sense of the *AK* model, but because there existed unemployed labor. It is by reinterpreting 'old' growth theory in a way that obliterates these theories that new growth theory can claim to be the first to endogenize long-run growth rates. Romer (1995), however, defends new growth theory from these charges by arguing that although endogenous theories of growth did exist in earlier times, they did not draw attention to the important forces driving technological change.

Is it possible that new growth theory is new in some other senses, for instance for highlighting the major forces driving technological change? Here also the degree of novelty may have been exaggerated.

First, the main insights of new growth theory such as: technical change is largely endogenous to the economic system; technology is at least partly proprietary; market structures supporting technical advance are imperfectly competitive; growth fueled by technical advance involves externalities and increasing returns; the investment rate affects growth in the long run – have been well known to students of economic growth and technical change (see Nelson, 1997), including Adam Smith, Karl Marx, Young (1928), Kaldor (1966, 1970) to name just a few, so that there is little which is really new in 'new' growth theory in this sense. It can be argued, of course, that it is one thing to know about concepts, but quite another to actually formalize them into models of growth. However, there were a number of old growth theories that treated endogenous technological change, externalities, and increasing returns in a formal manner, both in the neoclassical (see, in addition to Arrow and Uzawa, Ahmad, 1966 and Kennedy, 1964) and non-neoclassical (see Kaldor, 1957, 1961) traditions.

Second, many of the ways these ideas have been formalized into growth models are hardly different from ways that they were in earlier growth models (see also Bardhan, 1995). For instance, our earlier discussion has shown that Romer's (1986) early growth model was little different from Arrow's (1962) learning by doing model in what may be considered its essence, except for the removal of one restriction in the technological progress parameter, while Lucas's (1988) model is very similar to Uzawa's (1965) model with an education sector, except for removing a parameteric restriction similar to the way in which Romer's analysis changed Arrow's, and for modeling the behavior of agents rather than the social planner (who can in any case be interpreted as a representative agent). However, there are some important developments as well: models with new products which allow for imperfect competition in production, and allow for profit-seeking research and development expenditures are genuinely new. But it should be pointed out that some features of these developments were modeled earlier, for instance, imperfect competition; the newness lies in large part in making these ideas consistent with models of maximizing behavior with explicitly defined market forms, and in modeling new product development.

Third, it can be argued that some basic analytical properties of endogenous growth models were well known earlier, although in some cases not emphasized because they were considered to be unrealistic. Kurz and Salvadori (1998, 1999) point out that versions of the linear AK model can be found in the writings of Ricardo, Knight, and in a more complicated form in von Neumann. For instance, in Ricardo's model, since labor is an endogenously accumulable factor due to endogenous Malthusian dynamics, if land is free or omitted from the model, we have endogenous growth. Kurz and Salvadori argue that the classical notion of endogenously accumulable labor has the analogue in the new growth theory models with human capital that effective labor supply becomes an endogenously accumulable factor due to human capital accumulation. Smith's analytical framework, in which the productivity of labor grew indefinitely due to the division of labor (when output increased), also allowed for endogenous growth in the sense that growth was unbounded and the rate of growth increased with the saving rate. This insight seems to have been used in the model with increasing numbers of intermediate goods.

Beyond the charge of lack of novelty, critics have drawn attention to some other weaknesses of new growth theory. First, as Skott and Auerbach (1995) and Nelson (1997) argue, the way in which the insights regarding technological change are incorporated into the models are often incorrect and seriously incomplete. The models do not take into account some of the main features of technology (including the fact that a great deal of hands-on learning is often required to gain mastery over technology), of firms and their organization and management, and of institutions (including universities, government agencies and banks and banking institutions) and of cultural factors determining technological dynamism. Moreover, in analyzing technological change they abstract from true uncertainty, assuming either perfect foresight or that uncertainty can be treated in terms of probabilistic risk. Much of this is the result, Nelson argues, of constraining the models to remain as close as possible to the canons of general equilibrium theory. Second, the ability of new growth models to explain empirical growth patterns has been questioned. As Pack (1994) argues, new growth theory provides relatively few insights for the understanding of actual trends in productivity growth in OECD countries or in the Asian NICs, or of international productivity differences. Srinivasan (1995) provides a review of the results of empirical growth equations which cast doubts on the factors stressed in new growth theory as the important determinants of growth, especially for the Asian NICs.

We eschew the task of evaluating more fully these charges against new growth theory – most of which have been made before – except to note that taken together, they cast serious doubts about its newness and relevance. Instead, we turn to a third criticism which is related to several of the criticisms just discussed, that is, new growth theory abstracts away from issues relating to Keynesian effective demand and unemployment.[8] By following the neoclassical tradition of assuming that the labor market clears due to wage flexibility and that all saving is automatically invested, new growth theory models assume that the economy is always at full employment. This sets them apart from those segments of old growth theory that allowed long-run growth to be determined by effective demand considerations and assumed that full employment does not always prevail. Intermediate macro texts, which often discuss new growth theory right at the start, have to introduce effective demand issues for short-run models. In this approach, the reason for unemployment and the determination of output by aggregate demand is short-run money wage rigidity. In the long run, when the money wage is flexible, the economy tends to full employment.

Therefore, in the long-run analysis of growth, so the story goes, we are entitled to ignore these considerations. Even if money wage flexibility is not enough to quickly take us to full employment, government policies can be relied upon to achieve that.

Many non-orthodox economists, of course, have been wary of this kind of distinction between the short run and the long run. Kalecki (1971), for instance, has argued that the long run is nothing but a succession of short runs. Much of this wariness comes from the lack of confidence among these economists in the ability of either markets or the state to push the economy to full employment. Keynes (1936) had argued that wage reductions would not necessarily guide the economy to full employment if one takes into account its demand side – as well as its cost side – effects. Expectational factors, and redistribution from debtors to creditors, would depress aggregate demand, preventing the interest rate mechanism (paradoxically known as the Keynes effect) from increasing demand. Wage flexibility, in fact, is likely to increase uncertainty, and thereby reduce aggregate demand and increase the demand for money. Post-Keynesian economics have also stressed the fact that income redistribution away from wages also reduces demand, while the endogeneity of money prevents adjustments in interest rates due to excess liquidity in the economy. Moreover, the role of deflation in reducing investment has been stressed by writers of very different stripes – from Fisher to Minsky. Turning to the government, their ability to manipulate aggregate demand to restore full employment should not be overestimated, as should be clear from the ineffectiveness of recent efforts of the US Federal Reserve, and from those of the Japanese government. Kalecki (1943) has also drawn attention to the political obstacles to full employment policies, due to the opposition of 'industrial leaders' to government interference as such, to government spending, and of the consequences of maintaining full employment because of its effect on worker discipline. One may add to these obstacles those emphasized in political business cycle theory, and to the fears (whether justified or not) of what inflation may do to financial markets if aggregate demand is allowed to expand.

It is not only non-orthodox economists who have raised the issue of the neglect of unemployment in growth models. Even in his paper that laid the foundations of neoclassical growth theory with full employment, Solow (1956, p. 91) noted that his model:

> is the neoclassical side of the coin. Most especially it is full employment economics – in the dual aspect of equilibrium condition and frictionless, competitive, causal system. All the difficulties and rigidities which go into modern Keynesian income analysis have been shunted aside. It is not my contention that these problems don't exist, nor that they are of no significance in the long run. My

purpose was to examine what might be called the tight-rope view of economic growth and to see where more flexible assumptions about production would lead in a simple model. Underemployment and excess capacity or their opposite can still be attributed to any of the old causes of deficient or excess aggregate demand, but less readily to any deviation from a narrow 'balance'.

Solow (1982), after his comments on the stagnation of growth theory noted in the introduction, stated that he did not confidently expect that state to last. He states that 'A good new idea can transform any subject; in fact, I have some thoughts about the kind of new idea that is needed in this case'. Writing after the advent of new growth theory, Solow (1991, p. 394) says that its basic idea of the endogenous determination of the long-run rate of growth through increasing returns to scale at the macroeconomic level due to externalities in research and development and human capital accumulation was 'not the sort of "new idea" I had been hoping for in 1982. I had in mind the integration of equilibrium growth theory with medium-run disequilibrium theory so that trends and fluctuations in employment and output can be handled in a unified way. That particular idea has not yet made its appearance'. Indeed, he has consistently opined that growth theory should pay more attention to demand issues and unemployment. In his Nobel lecture (Solow, 1988, p. 309) he admits of his own models that 'I think I paid too little attention to the problems of effective demand', and criticized 'a standing temptation to sound like Dr. Pangloss, a very clever Dr. Pangloss. I think that tendency has won out in recent years'.

Is it fair to say that unemployment and effective demand are completely neglected in new growth theory? A perusal of textbooks and journals on the subject suggest that this is not entirely accurate, but more or less true. Barro and Sala-i-Martin (1995) have no discussion of unemployment or aggregate demand: according to them even the Harrod and Domar models are treated basically as a neoclassical growth model with a fixed coefficient production function, with all saving automatically invested. Aghion and Howitt (1998) devote an entire chapter to unemployment and growth in which they allow workers to become unemployed due to the scrapping of the capital, but unemployment is due to frictions in the matching of workers to plants. In this chapter Aghion and Howitt discuss the role of the creation of new jobs through the stimulation of demand, but it is only due to intersectoral complementarities in demand among intermediate goods, rather than to Keynesian aggregate demand issues. A chapter on growth and cycles discusses the long-run effects of temporary shocks by introducing aggregate demand into the analysis and shows how aggregate demand shocks can affect long-run growth by changing the level of output and the learning that results from it. But output fluctuations are possible due to surprise supply functions, rather than due to standard Keynesian output adjustments (though some of the effects that are considered in the chapter would work with such adjustments as well). A perusal of the papers in the *Journal of Economic Growth* reveal little that has to do with unemployment and aggregate demand. I examined its contents over the five years of its existence and found only two papers that seemed to have some promise of dealing with these issues on account of the fact that they referred to business cycles or demand constraints, namely Fatas (2000) and Mani (2001). The former introduces aggregate demand considerations and allows for long-run effects of short-run fluctuations, but has no unemployment, while the latter focuses on the composition of demand, and does not incorporate aggregate demand and unemployment.

As far as I know, there are only two major contributions to recent growth theory that may be called neoclassical in the sense that they explicitly consider optimizing agents, which explicitly deal with what can be called Keynesian unemployment. Ono (1994) uses the infinite horizon optimization model but departs from the Ramsey framework by assuming that the household's instantaneous utility depends on real money balances in addition to consumption, and that the marginal utility of real balances remains positive even when they become infinitely large. Introducing money in the utility function implies that the household's optimization conditions gives the interest rate an intra-temporal dimension (which equates it to the liquidity premium on money) in addition to the traditional intertemporal dimension. Assuming that inflation is determined by the level of excess demand in the economy, Ono shows that it is possible to have a steady state with market disequilibrium in the sense that consumption is less than the exogenously given level of output. He also extends the analysis to allow for production, employment, the wage and investment.

Since the marginal utility of money tends to a positive constant as real money holding tends to infinity, households keep accumulating real balances without increasing consumption, implying that excess supply persists indefinitely, in contrast to his version of the neoclassical models in which deflation increases consumption since the marginal utility of money tends to zero. Ono therefore shows how short-circuiting the real balance effect with his restriction on the utility of money can prevent an otherwise neoclassical economy from reaching full employment despite the flexibility of the wage and the price level. Indeed, Ono (1994, p. 64) shows that greater price (and wage in a more general model) flexibility can hurt, rather than help, in attaining full employment.

Hahn and Solow (1995) use the OLG model and introduce real money balances using a variant of the Clower constraint rather than directly in the utility function like Ono to produce results similar to Ono's – for instance, that wage and price sluggishness can be stabilizing – but in a much more complicated model which is analysed with simulation techniques.

Although these two models confirm some of the issues relating to the ability of economies to attain full employment, they become rather unwieldy, primarily due to their optimizing assumptions, and introduce money into the models in arguably artificial ways. Furthermore, they have nothing at all to do with new growth theory models. Although Ono cites the work of Romer and Lucas, his models do not introduce technological change, and Hahn and Solow's list of references do not cite any new growth theory contribution at all, probably seeing itself as a contribution to medium-run macroeconomics rather than growth theory proper (although dealing with all aspects of growth theory other than technological change).

4.4. POST-KEYNESIAN GROWTH THEORY

In contrast to old neoclassical and new growth theory models, post-Keynesian models of growth bring effective demand issues to center stage. They build on the contributions of Robinson and others who modeled the actual path of dynamic economies that did not grow at their natural rate even in the long run and draw on the contributions of the Cambridge growth theorists, Kalecki, and other writers. These models are built using macroeconomic accounting relations, behavioral equations, and mechanisms governing how markets adjust. Since they start with macroeconomic relations and market adjustment mechanisms they can be called 'systemic' – as opposed to individual-based – models. Since they start with behavioral equations not explicitly based on optimizing behavior on the part of economic agents, they depart from the standard neoclassical optimizing agent approach. This does not imply that these models do not have proper microfoundations. They are microfounded by modeling firms, consumers-savers and other agents based on empirically observable behavior patterns and stylized facts, rather than from a deductive optimizing approach. Some, especially those brought up in the mainstream neoclassical tradition, may find this approach incomplete, and specific post-Keynesian models can no doubt be improved by making their microfoundations more explicit, a point to which we will return at the end of the following section.

Although several versions of post-Keynesian growth models are available in the literature, we present a simple model drawing on the work of Kalecki (1971) and Steindl (1952).[9] Assume that output is produced with capital and labor with a fixed labor/output ratio, b, and a fixed capital/potential output ratio, a.[10] Following Kalecki (1971) it is assumed that the price of the representative firm is set as a mark-up on variable costs, assumed for simplicity to be only labor costs, so that:

$$P = (1 + z) bW,$$

where P is the price level, and W the money wage. The mark-up rate, z, is assumed to be a constant, representing Kalecki's (1971) degree of monopoly: it is determined by factors related to industrial organization, such as the degree of industrial concentration, and the labor market, such as the relative bargaining power of workers and firms.[11] Firms are assumed to adjust output in response to effective demand, and to maintain excess capacity, so that actual output is not at its potential level, given by K/a, but less than it. Employment, which is determined by labor demanded, given by bY, is less than labor supply and the money wage is assumed fixed for simplicity. The supply of labor is assumed to be fixed at a point and time and growing at a given rate over time. Assuming that there are only two factors of production – labor and capital – and that all non-wage income goes to profits, this equation implies that the profit share is given by:

$$\sigma = \frac{z}{1+z}.$$

Workers are assumed to spend all their income while profit recipients are assumed to save a constant fraction, s, of profits, so that we have consumption given by:

$$C = (1 - \sigma)Y + (1 - s)\,\sigma Y, \qquad (4.13)$$

where the first term is the labor share in output and income and the second term capitalist consumption. Assuming a closed economy and no government fiscal activity, the only other source of aggregate demand is investment demand. We assume that investment demand is exogenously fixed at a point in time. We denote the investment/capital ratio which, in the absence of depreciation, is the rate of growth of capital stock, by:

$$\frac{I}{K} = g, \qquad (4.14)$$

where I and K are real investment and the physical stock of capital. In the longer run we assume that firms adjust their investment rate to their desired rate of investment, which we formalize with the equation:

$$\frac{dg}{dt} = \Lambda(g_d - g), \qquad (4.15)$$

where Λ is a positive constant and where g_d is the desired rate of investment. Following Robinson (1962), Kalecki (1971), and especially Steindl (1952), we assume that desired investment depends positively on the rate of profit and on the rate of capacity utilization, which we measure as $u = Y/K$.[12] Since the profit share, σ, is constant as long as the mark-up, z, is constant, the profit rate is proportional to the rate of capacity utilization and given by σu. For simplicity we therefore write the desired investment function as:

$$g_d = \gamma_0 + \gamma_1 u, \qquad (4.16)$$

where γ_i (for $i = 0, 1$) are positive investment parameters.

In the short run we assume that g and the stock of capital, K, are fixed and that the level of output adjusts to meet effective demand, given by the sum of consumption and investment demand, so that in short-run equilibrium:

$$Y = C + I.$$

Substituting from equations (4.13) and (4.14), dividing by Y and solving for u, we get the short-run equilibrium value of capacity utilization, given by:

$$u = \frac{g}{s\sigma}. \qquad (4.17)$$

We constrain g to be always positive, so that equilibrium u will be positive, and if output adjusts to excess demand, the short-run equilibrium will be stable. We also assume that there is enough capital (as well as labor) available not to be a constraint on production.

In the longer run we assume that K and g can change. Assuming away depreciation, we have the rate of growth of capital given by g. The dynamics of g are given by equation (4.15) with equations (4.16) and (4.17) holding at every instant. Substituting these equations into equation (4.15) we get:

$$\frac{dg}{dt} = \Lambda\left(\gamma_0 + \gamma_1 \frac{g}{s\sigma} - g\right), \qquad (4.18)$$

which can be used to find the long-run equilibrium value of g, given by:

$$g = \frac{s\sigma\gamma_0}{s\sigma - \gamma_1}. \qquad (4.19)$$

The existence and stability of this long-run equilibrium requires that $s\sigma > \gamma_1$, which is the familiar macroeconomic stability condition of Keynesian models, that is, the responsiveness of saving to changes in the adjusting variable (in this case the capacity utilization rate) is greater than the corresponding responsiveness of investment. It may be noted that the long-run equilibrium rate of growth depends inversely on the capitalist saving rate and the profit share, and positively on the investment parameters. The result that growth depends negatively on the profit share – which follows from the fact that an increase in the profits share reduces consumption demand, capacity utilization and hence investment demand (see Dutt, 1984; Rowthorn, 1982) – can be altered if one amends equation (4.16) to make desired investment also depend positively on the profit share (as is done by Bhaduri and Marglin, 1990).

Alternative models in heterodox traditions can be thought of as special limiting cases of this model.[13] If aggregate demand is high enough so that in the short run the economy reaches full capacity utilization, output can no longer adjust in response to excess demands. If the price level adjusts to clear the market, then in effect the mark-up rate, z, and hence income distribution, σ, vary to clear the market. With output always at full capacity, the model becomes the Robinsonian model, or what Marglin (1984) calls the neo-Keynesian growth model. This model assumes that the real wage can attain whatever level is necessary to clear the goods market. If, however, the real wage reaches a floor before the goods market clears, and reductions in the real wage lead to increases in the money wage due to wage resistance, the goods market cannot clear to bring aggregate demand and output to equality. One way to ration demand is to assume that actual investment is determined by savings, and that the gap between desired and actual investment (or saving) only results in inflationary pressures which do not affect the actual rate of accumulation. This model, in which the real wage (and hence distribution) is fixed due to wage resistance and accumulation is savings driven, can be thought of as the classical-Marxian model, which Marglin (1984) calls the neo-Marxian model. In all of these models we have unemployed workers, and in that sense they all deviate from neoclassical models.[14]

It may be argued that it is inappropriate to have models like these, in which capital, output and employment grow at a rate different from the rate of growth of labor supply, since that implies that the unemployment rate will continuously rise or fall during the growth process. This implication may be considered to be theoretically implausible and empirically unrealistic. Against this it may be said that the rate of unemployment in capitalist economies has been known to fluctuate, increasing and staying at high levels for relative long periods of time, and remaining low at other periods. It can also be argued that the unemployment rate is actually kept within bounds for a number of reasons, such as government policies (which do not necessarily maintain full employment), the nature of technological change (which affects the growth of labor demand), and factors affecting the supply of labor. The latter include: changes in social norms (women joining the workforce); labor legislation (restricting hours worked, or child labor); individual responses to changes in real wages; migration (including illegal immigration facilitated by changes in the degree of laxity in the enforcement of immigration laws); and discouraged worker and deskilling effects. This is a 'problem' that is faced by many heterodox models, including neo-Marxian ones, and not just the post-Keynesian model discussed here, and 'solutions' to it can be sought in the rich analysis provided by these approaches (see Marglin, 1984, for instance).

More specific to the post-Keynesian model discussed here, it may be objected that it is inappropriate to have the rate of capacity utilization endogenously determined in long-run equilibrium, rather than be at some exogenously given desired or normal rate. This issue has attracted a fair amount of attention in the discussion regarding this post-Keynesian model. Some authors argue that even if in the short run, deviations from some exogenously given 'normal' capacity are permissible, in the long run the economy must adjust so that actual and 'normal' capacity utilization are equalized. Others argue in favor of the endogenous determination of capacity utilization even in long-run equilibrium, on the grounds that firms may not have a unique level of normal capacity utilization but be content if it remains within a band, or that 'normal' or 'desired' capacity utilization itself may be endogenous (see, for instance, Dutt, 1990 and Lavoie, 1995).

This skeletal post-Keynesian model, or those very much like it, have been modified in numerous ways to examine a host of issues relevant for both advanced and developing economies. This has been done by introducing inflation, asset markets, the rentier class, government expenditures, non-industrial or primary producing sectors, sectoral interaction involving different types of sectors, technological change, open economy considerations, and trade between developed and developing countries.[15] For present purposes it suffices to discuss only one such modification, involving the incorporation of technological change, to which we now turn.

4.5. TECHNOLOGICAL CHANGE, POST-KEYNESIAN GROWTH THEORY AND NEW GROWTH THEORY

As just stated, the incorporation of technological change in post-Keynesian growth models is not new. As in the neoclassical approach, such changes can be incorporated into the post-Keynesian model of the previous section in terms of changes in the efficiency of labor. Labor productivity can be measured in the previous model by $A = 1/b$, where it will be recalled that b is the unit labor requirement used in the mark-up equation. Technological change, then, can be seen as a rise in A or a fall in b. Equations (4.17) and (4.19) show that such an exogenous parametric shift will have no effect on the rate of capacity utilization in the short run (the growth of capital stock is given in the short run), and on the rates of capacity utilization and capital growth in the long run. If we assume that technological change results in an exogenously given rate of growth of labor productivity at the rate $\hat{A} = -\hat{b}$, and that it affects no other parameters of the model (including the parameter a), g and u will be unaffected by technological change both in the short or long runs. This result may be taken to imply that technological change has no effect in the post-Keynesian growth model. Since the rate of growth of output is unaffected by the rate of technological change, the effect of a higher rate of technological change is merely to reduce the rate of growth of labor demand, resulting in a faster increase in the unemployment rate over time.

This result, however, depends on the assumption that none of the other parameters in the model change when the rate of technological progress changes. Post-Keynesians have long argued that changes in the rate of technological progress will alter some of the other parameters in the model directly and indirectly.

First, and perhaps most importantly, a higher rate of technological change will have a positive effect on investment as firms need to invest in order to make use of new technology embodied in new machines, to use new processes, and to produce new products. This was an important theme in the work of Kalecki (1971), and this effect has been incorporated into numerous post-Keynesian models (see Rowthorn, 1982; Dutt, 1990). Thus, higher rates of technological change push the desired investment upwards, implying higher rates of investment and capacity utilization in the long run.

Second, a higher rate of technological change can also reduce the saving rate of capitalists, if it increases the variety of goods available to capitalist consumers, thereby increasing capacity utilization in the short run, and both growth and capacity utilization in the long run.

Third, a higher rate of technological change can change the mark-up rate charged by firms, z, and hence, σ.[16] Suppose that faster technological change implies that firms increase their degree of monopoly by allowing technological leaders to weed out competitors, which increases the mark-up. A higher mark-up in the model presented above, however, has the somewhat counterintuitive effect of reducing the degree of capacity utilization in the short run and reducing both capacity utilization and the rate of growth in the long run, because of the redistribution of income from workers to profit recipients which reduces aggregate demand. But modifications of the desired investment function represented by equation (4.16) can lead to different conclusions. For example, with the Bhaduri and Marglin (1990) desired investment function mentioned above, an increase in σ (due to the faster rate of technological change and consequent increase in the mark-up) will reduce the rate of capacity utilization in the short run due to the fall in consumption demand, but will have an ambiguous effect on the rate of desired accumulation, having a positive effect due to the increase in σ and a negative effect because of the short-run fall in u. The eventual long-run impact on growth and capacity utilization could be positive if the positive impact of the profit share on desired investment is strong enough.

In the discussion so far I have assumed that the rate of technological change is given exogenously. Post-Keynesian growth theory has also endogenized the rate of technological change by assuming that $\hat{A}$ depends on economic variables. They have followed the lead of Kaldor (1957, 1961), who argues that capital accumulation and technological change are necessarily interdependent. He formalizes the dependence of the latter on the former with a technical progress function that makes labor productivity growth a positive function of the rate of growth of the capital/labor ratio. Using a linear functional form, we assume:

$$\hat{A} = \tau_0 + \tau_1 \hat{k}.$$

Noting that $\hat{k} = \hat{K} - \hat{L} = \hat{K} - \hat{Y} - \hat{A}$, we can rewrite this equation as:

$$\hat{A} = \left(\frac{\tau_0}{1-\tau_1}\right) + \left(\frac{\tau_0}{1-\tau_1}\right)\left(\hat{K} - \hat{Y}\right).$$

In long-run equilibrium u attains its equilibrium level, so that $\hat{K} = \hat{Y}$, implying that:

$$\hat{A} = \frac{\tau_0}{1-\tau_1},$$

or in other words, that the rate of labor productivity growth is determined only by the parameters of the technical progress function. In the model, therefore, in the long run, the rates of growth of capital and output per capita are endogenous, but the rate of growth of output per worker remains exogenous in the sense that it depends only on the parameters of the technological change function. However, this property is not present in all post-Keynesian models. For instance, for a model which incorporates Arrow's learning by doing function given by equation (4.4), so that we have $A = \zeta K^\eta$, we get:

$$\hat{A} = \eta g,$$

which can be analyzed as follows.

This learning by doing function is shown as the positively sloped line $g = (1/\eta)\hat{A}$ in Figure 4.1: it shows the rate of labor productivity change due to learning by doing for any given rate of growth of capital, g, the causality running from capital growth to productivity growth. This relationship can be combined with the rest of the post-Keynesian model by using the curve $g = g_d$, which shows the long-run relation between $\hat{A}$ and g from the model of the previous section. From equation (4.15), (4.16) and (4.17), with equation (4.16) replaced by:

$$g_d = \gamma_0 + \gamma_1 u + \gamma_2 \hat{A}$$

to take into account the positive effect of technological change on desired investment, as discussed earlier in this section, we obtain the equation for the curve:

$$g = s\sigma \frac{\gamma_0 + \gamma_1 \hat{A}}{s\sigma - \gamma_1}$$

which replaces equation (4.19), and shows that a higher rate of technological change increases investment, increases aggregate demand, and thereby directly and indirectly, through its effect on u, increases g. The direction of causation here runs from technological change to the growth rate of capital stock. The intersection of the two curves in Figure 4.1 shows how $\hat{A}$ and g are jointly determined in the long run.[17] In this model, not only changes in the parameters of the technological progress (or learning) function, but also the saving and investment parameters, affect the long-run values of the growth rate of capital and output, as well as labor productivity growth.[18]

Drawing on this brief discussion of the treatment of technological change in post-Keynesian models it is possible make several observations on the relationship of the post-Keynesian approach to new growth theory.

First, the dramatic change that has occurred within neoclassical growth theory due to the changes in the assumptions regarding technological change made by new growth theory do not result in any corresponding change in the post-Keynesian approach. For neoclassical theory we found that almost all formulations of technological change (Uzawa excepted) long-run growth is determined by forces exogenous to the economy, and in particular, saving and investment parameters had no effect on long-run growth. In the Arrow model, for instance, with $\eta < 1$, the long-run growth rate was independent of the saving rate. New growth theory in essence removed the restriction that $\eta < 1$ and the result was that the long-run rate of growth of the economy

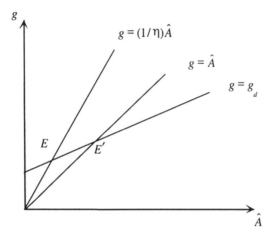

Figure 4.1   Post-Keynesian model with endogenous technological change

became endogenous as in the *AK* model (for the case of $\eta = 1$). For post-Keynesian theory, the change in the value of η from less than one to one creates no qualitative change. In both cases the rate of growth and the rate of productivity growth are endogenous and not independent of saving and investment parameters. The assumption that $\eta = 1$ merely shifts the technological change curve to the one denoted by $g = \hat{A}$ in Figure 4.1, merely increasing the rates of growth of capital and productivity.[19]

Second, post-Keynesian growth models with technological change, by allowing aggregate demand to play a major role and incorporating unemployment, have important implications for economic policy regarding saving and investment. New growth theory does not distinguish between saving and investment, and argues that faster growth and technological change requires policies to increase saving and investment. Post-Keynesian models, however, distinguish between the effects of saving and investment parameters: while policies to increase investment can increase growth and technological change, those to increase the saving rate of capitalists can depress aggregate demand and reduce the rate of growth.[20]

Third, post-Keynesian models, unlike most new growth theory models, imply that not all kinds of technological change will increase the rate of growth of the economy. Post-Keynesian models imply that certain kinds of technological changes, which do not significantly affect investment or consumer demand or industrial structure (which affects the mark-up), are likely to have the primary impact of displacing labor without speeding up growth. By increasing unemployment and depressing aggregate demand, they may in fact have the consequence of slowing down growth. Other kinds of technological changes, which set in motion major changes in investment demand or consumer demand (involving new products and new processes requiring new machines) or shake up industrial structure, thereby having profitability and demand effects, can lead to increases in the rate of growth. This distinction can be said to formalize Baran and Sweezy's (1966) distinction between 'normal' and 'epoch making' innovations, a distinction that is not to be found in a qualitative sense in new growth theory models.

Fourth, post-Keynesian models can bring into consideration a number of mechanisms of technological change not addressed in new growth theory. For instance, You (1994) makes labor-saving technological change depend on labor shortages as captured by the rate of change in the wage, while Lima (1997) examines the interaction between market concentration, industrial innovation and growth in an attempt to synthesize post-Keynesian macrodynamics with evolutionary and neo-Schumpeterian ideas. Freed from the straightjacket of optimization with specific market structures based on market demand based on explicit utility functions that individuals maximize over infinite horizons,[21] post-Keynesian models have been able to incorporate arguably more realistic features from stylized facts about actual economies.

Although the discussion so far argues that post-Keynesian models have some advantages over new growth theory models, it would be incorrect to infer that the former can learn nothing at all from the latter. The careful treatment of microfoundations in new growth theory can certainly provide insights from which post-Keynesian growth theories can draw. Rejection of the requirement that all growth models use the dynamic optimization method should not imply that all new growth theory contributions concerning the modeling of firm and innovator behavior should be jettisoned as well. Three issues in particular deserve mention.

First, new growth theory models often give careful attention to externalities between firms, taking care to distinguish between firm level variables and economy wide variables (as in the Romer model which distinguishes between private and aggregate capital, although this attention is also to be found in the old neoclassical growth model of Arrow). Post-Keynesian models can do the same, distinguishing more carefully between (say) their own profit rates and aggregate rate of capacity utilization (as an index of the state of the macroeconomy), when they specify behavioral functions which include these variables as arguments.

Second, new growth theories derive the values of certain key variables from explicit optimizing decisions, while post-Keynesian models usually take these variables to be exogenously given. Although it is quite legitimate to do this, and perhaps preferable to endogenize these parameters using empirical regularities rather than arbitrary deductive models, it is advisable to check relations based on these regularities against the deductive models. One example is the treatment of the mark-up rate which is often taken to be given and sometimes taken to be a function of other variables such as the rate of technological change in post-Keynesian models, but can be derived from explicit profit-maximizing decisions of firms operating in markets with clearly specified structures. Another example is the treatment of consumer demand parameters from explicit utility functions, which may be particularly useful for the case of the introduction of new products.

Third, given the focus of new growth theory on technological change, a great deal of research has been done modeling mechanisms of technological innovation and diffusion, including research and development activities aiming to make profits and education (although the extent to which these contributions are truly new is debatable). Post-Keynesian growth theory can usefully draw on some of these contributions, although not confining attention to only those mechanisms.

4.6.   CONCLUSION

This chapter has examined the contributions of new growth theory from the perspective of post-Keynesian growth theory. Its main conclusions regarding the two theories are as follows.

The advent of new growth theory has resulted in a tremendous resurgence of mainstream growth theory because of its alleged advance over old growth theory by endogenizing the rate of growth of the economy in the long run, making it depend on economic behavior. However, the claims of newness of new growth theory for this reason is based on an extremely narrow reading of 'old' growth theory that ignores not only some neoclassical contributions but also many non-neoclassical contributions to growth theory. The latter, by allowing for the existence of unemployed labor in the long run, did make long-run growth depend on economic behavior such as investment and saving. Moreover, a careful reading of new growth theory and a comparison with earlier writing on growth and technological change suggests that it has made relatively little progress in terms of addressing new ideas, of developing new ways of modeling macroeconomic dynamics and the mechanisms of technological change, and of understanding the actual growth experiences of capitalist economies regarding productivity changes. Moreover, by assuming away unemployment problems due to the lack of effective demand, it has failed to come to grips with an important feature of the growth process: the integration of medium-run macroeconomic phenomenon with long-run issues, which are arguably not as separate as is often assumed in mainstream macroeconomic theory.

The chapter then presents an alternative to new growth theory in the form of post-Keynesian growth theory, which gives a central place to effective demand and unemployment, and which draws on some of the non-neoclassical contributions to 'old' growth theory. It uses this approach to analyse the interaction between technological change and capital accumulation, showing that new growth theory appears far less revolutionary than it claims when seen in terms of this approach, and that while the post-Keynesian approach can learn some things from new growth theory, it can arguably analyze technological change in a more satisfactory way.

We end with two concluding remarks. First, it should be observed that by overemphasizing issues relating to technological change and neglecting effective demand and unemployment, new growth theory diverts attention from other important issues such as financial issues and firm and consumer debt, and their relation to the growth process. Post-Keynesian models have been, and can further be, used to rectify this problem. We have not dealt with this issue here because it is far removed from the concerns of new growth theory (but see Taylor, 1991, for instance). Second, seen from a new growth theory perspective post-Keynesian growth theory may be able to analyze the implications of technological change and financial factors, but only in an ad hoc manner, since it departs from the model of the dynamically optimizing agent. However, this departure may well be an important strength of post-Keynesian growth models which, by breaking free of the straightjacket of implausible dynamic optimizing myths, offers the flexibility to develop simple models incorporating important issues which are relevant for understanding the growth process of actual economies.

NOTES

*   I am grateful to an anonymous referee and to participants at a session at the Conference for very useful comments and suggestions.

1.   The entire credit for this change does not necessarily lie with new growth theory. A general interest in the problem of economic growth in the West as a result of slow economic growth along with high growth in East Asia certainly had a part to play, as did the appearance of the purchasing power parity adjusted internally comparable data in the form of the Penn Tables. Nevertheless, the nature and direction of the revival of growth economics can largely be explained by the advent of new growth theory.

2.   The following analytic history, which concentrates on Harrod's growth problems and their resolution, is by no means the only one that can be told. An alternative history, suggested by an anonymous referee, underlines the shift from models focusing on production over time, which were related to development planning – when professional communication between classical and neoclassical paradigms was intense, to models of intertemporal consumption efficiency, when there occurred a decisive break between paradigms. While this distinction – and the dogma that the most important requirement of growth models is that individuals optimize utility intertemporally – has constituted the major *methodological* divide between (old and new) neoclassical growth theorists and heterodox ones, and will be reflected in the following discussion, the history concentrates on Harrod's problems because they point

naturally to the major *substantive* differences between alternative growth theories and their views of the growth process (for instance, whether growth occurs with full employment or with unemployment), which are the focus of this chapter.

3. Domar's influential paper, which is bracketed with Harrod's in the so-called Harrod–Domar model, does not figure prominently in this story, and had an arguably greater influence on early development economics and planning (leading to the emphasis on policies for increasing the saving rate and reducing the capital/output ratio) than on the evolution of growth theory.

4. In presentations of the neoclassical and new growth theory models we will, for simplicity, assume the Cobb–Douglas formulation throughout this chapter, except where noted to the contrary. More general constant returns to scale formulations do not change most of the main results, provided E is interpreted as the Harrod–neutral technical progress parameter. One result that it does preclude, however, is the possibility that no steady state may exist in the old neoclassical model due to the violation of the Inada condition, an issue to which we will turn later.

5. The OLG models, however, may not have a stable steady state equilibrium, and may even imply chaotic dynamics.

6. Assuming that the efficiency of labor grows at an exogenously fixed rate will not change the nature of our conclusions.

7. If we wish to allow for population growth, it is easy to check that if equation (4.12) is replaced by $A = K/L$, then we will obtain the production function AK for this model, yielding exactly the AK model. In this modified formulation what is relevant for productivity increases is not the stock of knowledge but the stock per unit of labor.

8. This point has been noted earlier by several authors, including Palley (1996) and Kurz and Salvadori (1998), but in my opinion not adequately explored.

9. See Rowthorn (1982) and Dutt (1984) for the original models, and Taylor (1983, 1991), Dutt (1990) and Lavoie (1992) for further analysis.

10. These coefficients are partly determined by technology and partly by social factors such as work practices and organization. A harmless simplification – for our purposes – is to assume that they represent fixed coefficients, constant returns (Leontief) technology. Since firms are assumed to hire and fire labor according to their demand for workers, we assume that there will never be any excess labor hired by firms beyond what is necessary for production; hence the potential and actual labor/output ratio are the same. Since capital, once installed, must be held by firms, they may have excess capacity.

11. A narrow interpretation, based on profit-maximizing models of imperfect competition, can make the mark-up depend solely on the perceived elasticity of demand (assumed constant) of monopolistic competitors, but Kalecki (1971) had a broader interpretation in mind.

12. The rate of capacity utilization can alternatively be measured as the ratio of actual output to potential output, which is $Y/(K/a)$, which is proportional to u, since we assume throughout that the capital/potential output ratio is constant.

13. See Dutt (1990) for a discussion and comparison of these alternative models.

14. Some of alternative models, such as the neo-Marxian one, do not take account of effective demand considerations explicitly. The foregoing discussion explores how, starting with an analysis which explicitly incorporates the role of effective demand, one can obtain models in which effective demand does not necessarily influence long-run growth in special situations.

15. For a discussion of a number of such models see Dutt (1990) and Taylor (1991) and for a recent survey, see Dutt (2001).

16. It is not possible to assert whether a faster rate of technological change will affect the mark-up positively, negatively or not at all: the direction of change will depend on how technological change affects the various determinants of the mark-up, such as the degree of

industrial concentration. Note that any change in the mark-up is a consequence of a change in the rate of technological change, and such a change is unrelated to the motivations individual firms have of introducing new technology. Technological change, other things constant, increases the profits of the firm which experiences it (and this is sufficient to explain the motivation behind technological change), but these other things may not ultimately be constant due to various systemic consequences (such as changes in industrial concentration).

17. Willy Cortez's unpublished dissertation written at the University of Notre Dame earlier used this diagram for a related post-Keynesian model.

18. The model discussed here has the property that the saving and investment rates (as a proportion of output) are not positively associated with the rate of growth or the rate of growth of productivity, contrary to the usual empirical evidence which finds that higher saving and investment rates are positively related to growth. This can be seen as follows. The equilibrium saving and investment rates in this model are given by $I/Y = S/Y = g/u$. Equation (4.17) implies that $g/u = s\sigma$, which implies that the only parameters that increase the saving and investment rate, that is, s and σ, also reduce the rate of growth, g. An upward shift in the investment parameters, such as γ_0, has no effect on the saving and investment rate, although it increases g, because it increases u equiproportionately. This anomaly, however, depends on certain simplifying assumptions of the models. For instance, if the capitalist saving function is given by:

$$S = s\sigma Y - \beta K,$$

with $\beta > 0$ to capture the positive effect of wealth in the form of capital on capitalist consumption, we get $g = s\sigma u - \beta$. This implies that $g/u = s\sigma - \beta u$. An upward shift in the investment function will now increase u and g, but increase g/u and hence the saving and investment rates. Note now, however, that the precise relation between the saving and investment rates and the growth rate depends on what causes changes in both. For instance, contrary to the case of the increase in the investment parameters, an increase in s can increase the saving and investment rates and reduce the rate of growth of the economy.

19. See Palley (1996) for an earlier attempt to develop a synthesis of Keynesian and new growth approaches. This earlier contribution, however, suffers from at least two problems in characterizing both new growth and Keynesian approaches. First, Palley assumes that in old neoclassical growth theory labor productivity growth is exogenous, while in new growth theory it depends, among other things, on the capital/labor ratio. This way of distinguishing old from new growth theory is incorrect, given that old growth theory did endogenize technological change, but generally found it to be exogenous in long-run equilibrium. Second, and more importantly for our discussion, the model does not allow effective demand to determine output, which is still determined by a production function in which labor grows at the rate of growth of the exogenously-given supply of labor although capital grows according to investment demand (with the role of saving ignored). Effective demand is introduced into the model by specifying that changes in effective demand growth are caused by deviations of output growth from effective demand growth, and by assuming that the investment rate depends on the growth of effective demand. In the Keynesian framework adopted in the model here, output is determined by effective demand, and both saving and investment functions play a role in determining output and its growth.

20. It should be noted that merely distinguishing between saving and investment functions is not sufficient for allowing effective demand to affect long-run growth or for generating unemployment. This should be obvious from the neoclassical Keynesian macroeconomic models of textbooks which produce full employment in the long run with wage flexibility through Keynes (or interest rate) and real balance effects despite their having investment

functions, and the neoclassical Keynesian growth model with Tobin's q. For examples of growth models with separate investment and saving functions which produce supply-determined full employment growth, see Dixit (1990) and Palley (1996).

21. A similar comment can be made about overlapping generations models, which in addition to optimization insert a rigid dynamic framework in which individuals live for two periods.

REFERENCES

Aghion, P. and P. Howitt (1998), *Endogenous Growth Theory*, Cambridge, Massachusetts: MIT Press.

Ahmad, S. (1966), 'On the theory of induced innovation', *Economic Journal*, **76**, 344–57.

Arrow, K.K. (1962), 'The economic implications of learning by doing', *Review of Economic Studies*, **29**, 155–73.

Baran, P. and P. Sweezy (1966), *Monopoly Capitalism*, New York: Monthly Review Press.

Bardhan, P. (1995), 'The contributions of endogenous growth theory to the analysis of development problems: an assessment', in J. Behrman and T.N. Srinivasan (eds), *Handbook of Development Economics*, Vol. 3B, Amsterdam: North Holland, pp. 2983–98.

Barro, R. J. and Sala-i-Martin, X. (1995), *Economic Growth*, New York: McGraw-Hill.

Bhaduri, A. and S.A. Marglin (1990), 'Unemployment and the real wage: the economic basis of contesting political ideologies', *Cambridge Journal of Economics*, **14**(4), 375–93.

Dixit, A. (1990), 'Growth theory after thirty years', in P. Diamond (ed.), *Growth, Productivity and Unemployment*, Cambridge, Massachusetts: MIT Press, pp. 3–22.

Dutt, A.K. (1984), 'Stagnation, income distribution and monopoly power', *Cambridge Journal of Economics*, **8**(1), 25–40.

Dutt, A.K. (1990), *Growth, Distribution and Uneven Development*, Cambridge: Cambridge University Press.

Dutt, A.K. (2001), 'Kalecki and the Kaleckians: The relevance of Kalecki today', published in Portuguese, in L. Pomeranz, J. Miglioli and G. Lima (eds), *Dinamica economica do capitalismo contemporaneo: Homenagen a M. Kalecki*, São Paulo: EDUSP, FAPESP, pp. 21–68.

Fatas, A. (2000), 'Do business cycles cast long shadows? Short-run persistence and economic growth', *Journal of Economic Growth*, **5**, June, 147–62.

Hahn, F. and R.M. Solow (1995), *A Critical Essay on Modern Macroeconomic Theory*, Cambridge, Massachusetts: MIT Press.

Harris, D.J. (1978), *Capital Accumulation and Income Distribution*, Stanford, California: Stanford University Press.

Harrod, R.F. (1939), 'An essay in dynamic theory', *Economic Journal*, **49**, 14–33.

Kahn, R.F. (1959), 'Exercises in the analysis of growth', *Oxford Economic Papers*, **11**, 143–56.

Kaldor, N. (1955–56), 'Alternative theories of distribution', *Review of Economic Studies*, **23**(2), 61, 83–100.

Kaldor, N. (1957), 'A model of economic growth', *Economic Journal*, **67**, 591–624.

Kaldor, N. (1961), 'Capital accumulation and economic growth', in F.A. Lutz and D.C. Hague (eds), *The Theory of Capital*, London: Macmillan, pp. 177–222.

Kaldor, N. (1966), *Causes of the Slow Rate of Economic Growth in UK*, Cambridge: Cambridge University Press.

Kaldor, N. (1970), 'The case for regional policies', *Scottish Journal of Political Economy*, **18**(3), 337–48.

Kalecki, M. (1943), 'Political aspects to full employment', *Political Quarterly*, reprinted in *Selected Essays on the Dynamics of the Capitalist Economy*, Cambridge: Cambridge University Press, 1971.

Kalecki, M. (1971), *Selected Essays on the Dynamics of the Capitalist Economy*, Cambridge: Cambridge University Press.

Kennedy, C. (1964), 'Induced bias in innovation and the theory of distribution', *Economic Journal*, **74**, 541–7.

Keynes, J.M. (1936), *The General Theory of Employment, Interest and Money*, London: Macmillan.

Kurz, H.D. and N. Salvadori (1995). *Theory of Production: A Long-period Analysis*, Cambridge: Cambridge University Press.

Kurz, H.D. and N. Salvadori (1998), 'The "new" growth theory: old wine in new goatskins', in M. Coricelli, M. di Matteo and F. Hahn (eds), *New Theories of Growth and Development*, London: Macmillan, pp. 63–94.

Kurz, H.D. and N. Salvadori (1999), 'Theories of "endogenous" growth in historical perspective', in R.S. Murat (ed.), *Contemporary Economic Issues, Vol. 4, Economic Behaviour and Design*, London: Macmillan in association with International Economic Association, pp. 225–61.

Lavoie, M. (1992), *Foundations of Post-Keynesian Economic Analysis*, Aldershot: Edward Elgar.

Lavoie, M. (1995), 'The Kaleckian model of growth and distribution and its neo-Ricardian and neo-Marxian critiques', *Cambridge Journal of Economics*, **19**(6), 789–818.

Lima, G. (1997), 'Market concentration and endogenous technological innovation in a model of growth and distributional dynamics', unpublished paper, University of Notre Dame, published in Portuguese, in L. Pomeranz, J. Miglioli and G. Lima (eds), *Dinamica economica do capitalismo contemporaneo: Homenagen a M. Kalecki*, São Paulo: EDUSP, FAPESP, 2001, pp. 129–55.

Lucas, R.E. (1988), 'On the mechanics of economic development', *Journal of Monetary Economics*, **22**, 3–42.

Mahalanobis, P.C. (1955). 'The approach of operational research to planning in India', *Sankhya: Indian Journal of Statistics*, **16**, 3–62.

Mani, A. (2001), 'Income distribution and the demand constraint', *Journal of Economic Growth*, **6**, June, 107–33.

Marglin, S.A. (1984). *Growth, Distribution and Prices*, Cambridge, Massachusetts: Harvard University Press.

Nelson, R. (1997), 'What is new in new growth theory?' *Challenge*, **40**(5), September–October, 29–58.

Ono, Y. (1994), *Money, Interest, and Stagnation: Dynamic Theory and Keynes's Economics*, Oxford: Clarendon Press.

Pack, H. (1994), 'Endogenous growth theory: intellectual appeal and empirical shortcomings', *Journal of Economic Perspectives*, **8**(1), Winter, 55–72.

Palley, T.I. (1996), 'Growth theory in a Keynesian mode: some Keynesian foundations for new endogenous growth theory', *Journal of Post Keynesian Economics*, Fall, **19**(1), 113–35.

Robinson, J. (1962), *Essays in the Theory of Economic Growth*, London: Macmillan.

Romer, D. (1996), *Advanced Macroeconomics*, New York: McGraw-Hill.

Romer, P.M. (1986), 'Increasing returns and long-run growth', *Journal of Political Economy*, **94**, 1002–37.

Romer, P.M. (1995), 'Comment', in T. Ito and A.O. Krueger (eds), *Growth Theories in Light of the East Asian Experience*, Chicago: University of Chicago Press, pp. 71–5.

Rowthorn, R. (1982), 'Demand, real wages and growth', *Studi Economici*, **18**, 3–54.

Sen, A. (1970), 'Introduction', in A. Sen (ed.), *Growth Economics*, Harmondsworth: Penguin, pp. 9–40.

Skott, P. and P. Auerbach (1995), 'Cumulative causation and the "new" theories of economic growth', *Journal of Post Keynesian Economics*, Spring, **17**(3), 381–402.

Solow, R.M. (1956), 'A contribution to the theory of economic growth', *Quarterly Journal of Economics*, **70**, 65–94.

Solow, R.M. (1982), 'Some lessons from growth theory', in W.F. Sharpe and C.M. Cootner (eds), *Financial Economics: Essays in Honor of Paul Cootner*, Englewood Cliffs, New Jersey: Prentice-Hall, pp. 246–59.

Solow, R.M. (1988), 'Growth theory and after', *American Economic Review*, **78**, 307–17.

Solow, R.M. (1991), 'Growth theory', in D. Greenaway, M. Bleaney and I.M.R. Stewart (eds), *Companion to Contemporary Economic Thought*, London and New York: Routledge, pp. 393–415.

Solow, R.M. (1994). 'Perspectives on growth theory', *Journal of Economic Perspectives*, **8**(1), Winter, 45–54.

Solow, R.M. (1997). *Learning from 'Learning by Doing': Lessons for Economic Growth*, Stanford, California: Stanford University Press.

Srinivasan, T.N. (1995), 'Long-run growth theories and empirics: anything new?', in T. Ito and A.O. Krueger (eds), *Growth Theories in Light of the East Asian Experience*, Chicago: University of Chicago Press, pp. 37–70.

Steindl, J. (1952), *Maturity and Stagnation in American Capitalism*, Oxford: Blackwell.

Taylor, L. (1983), *Structuralist Macroeconomics: Applicable Models for the Third World*, New York: Basic Books.

Taylor, L. (1991), *Income Distribution, Inflation and Growth*, Cambridge, Massachusetts: MIT Press.

Uzawa, H. (1965), 'Optimum technical change in an aggregative model of economic growth', *International Economic Review*, **6**(1), January, 18–31.

von Neumann, J. (1945), 'A model of general equilibrium', *Review of Economic Studies*, **13**, 1–9.

You, J.-I. (1994), 'Endogenous technical change, accumulation and distribution', in A.K. Dutt (ed.), *New Directions in Analytical Political Economy*, Aldershot: Edward Elgar, pp. 121–47.

Young, A. (1928), 'Increasing returns and economic progress', *Economic Journal*, **38**, 527–42.

5. Exogenous and endogenous growth in the Solow and Arrow models, and the Swan proposition

Giacomo Costa

5.1. INTRODUCTION

In this chapter, some of the earlier papers on neoclassical growth theory will be reconsidered in the light of the more recent ideas on endogenous growth. This subject has already been discussed by several authors, including Aghion and Howitt (1998) and Solow (1992), and I will take note of their observations, with special but not exclusive emphasis on Solow's. In Section 5.2, I review the basic neoclassical growth model and recall the proposition by Swan (1963) about the general class of production functions which is compatible with steady-state growth (where output and the reproducible factor grow at an equal proportional rate). In Section 5.3, a suggestion by Solow about the logic of endogenous growth is discussed. I explore first, under the assumption of constant returns to scale, the connection between the strict positivity of the lower bound of the marginal product of capital, the tendency of the competitive capital share to approach 1 when the growth rate of output and capital is higher than the natural rate of growth, the possible non-existence of a balanced growth equilibrium (where factors and product grow at a common proportional rate), and endogenous growth, i.e. a type of growth where the dynamics of output is driven by and ultimately converges to the dynamics of capital. It is shown that under constant returns to scale, endogenous growth is only possible if labour is an inessential factor of production. In Section 5.4, I consider the endogenization of technical progress *à la* Arrow. The most general type of production functions is sought, allowing learning of the Arrow type, which is compatible with steady-state growth. In Section 5.5, I show that the resulting class of production functions, although not at first sight of the Swan type, can be represented in that way and offer an alternative representation of it. In Section 5.6, the Arrow–Solow learning parameter is allowed to assume the value for which there is no steady state, and find an endogenous asymptotic rate of growth. Section 5.7 is devoted to a scrutiny of Arrow's own production functions. The question of the admissible values of Arrow's learning parameter is discussed in the light of the Swan Proposition. In Section 5.8, I discuss the problem of finding a Swan-like proposition for endogenous growth, and suggest an asymptotic vindication for the 'AK' model. The various observations made in the chapter are brought together in Section 5.9.

5.2.   INCREASING RETURNS AND THE SWAN PROPOSITION

The basic growth model is made up of the two equations:

$$Y = F(K,N,t), \tag{5.1}$$

$$\dot{K} = sY, \quad 0 < s < 1, \tag{5.2}$$

where Y is output, F is the production function, K is capital, N is the labour force, and t is the time index. All variables are functions of time; in particular, N depends on t only and is exponential with exponent $n > 0$. Parameter s is the average savings propensity. The system is completed by specifying initial conditions for the factors of production, K and N.

There is some discussion in the literature as to the significance of a change from constant to increasing returns to scale in generating endogenous growth. For example, starting with a production function:

$$Y = F(K,(AN)^h), \tag{5.3}$$

first degree homogeneous in its two arguments, and $h > 1$, so that F is increasing returns to scale in K and N, and A is an exponential function of time with exponent a, Solow finds the steady-state rate of growth:

$$g = (a+n)h > (a+n), \tag{5.4}$$

where $(a+n)$ is the 'natural' rate of growth. He observes (1992, p. 8) that 'if there are increasing returns to scale in the only form that allows for exponential steady state, then you get a rate of growth that is exogenous'.

Let's explain: the rate of growth given by (5.4) is exogenous because it is independent of s. That *the class of functions (5.3), with F constant returns to scale in its two arguments, and h positive, exhausts the functions compatible with steady-state growth*, is the content of a mathematical proposition that was, to my knowledge, first advanced by T.W. Swan in (1963), and that I suggest calling 'Swan's Proposition'.[1] This proposition will play an important role in the discussion that follows.

5.3. SOME EQUIVALENT CONDITIONS FOR ENDOGENOUS GROWTH IN SOLOW'S OWN MODEL

Setting $h = 1$ in (5.3), we obtain:

$$Y = F(K, AN), \qquad (5.5)$$

the standard production function of the old neoclassical growth theory.[2] By differentiating with respect to time the production function (5.5), and using (5.2), we can obtain:

$$\frac{\dot{Y}}{Y} - (a+n) \equiv g - (a+n) = sF_K - \beta(a+n), \qquad (5.6)$$

where we set:

$$\beta = 1 - \alpha = \frac{KF_K}{Y}, \quad \alpha = \frac{ANF_{AN}}{Y}. \qquad (5.7)$$

Equation (5.6) neatly expresses, according to Solow (1992, p. 40), the challenge that any theory of endogenous growth must meet:[3]

> If output only grows at a rate equal to $(a + n)$, then this a model of exogenous growth. There is endogenous growth only when the left hand side, and therefore the r.h.s., is positive. Generally what makes the r.h.s. not to be positive is that F_K falls as capital accumulates. Thus we can say that the job of any model of endogenous growth is simply to keep the marginal product of capital from falling too fast as capital accumulates.

A somewhat more complete account of the problem may be given as follows. Equation (5.5) implicitly defines, by constant returns to scale, the function $Y/K = \varphi(AN/K)$, $\varphi' > 0$. Then we can rewrite (5.6) as:

$$g - (a+n) = \beta \left[s\varphi\left(\frac{AN}{K}\right) - (a+n) \right]. \qquad (5.8)$$

Suppose there is no positive balanced growth ratio AN/K, i.e.

$$\varphi\left(\frac{AN}{K}\right) > \frac{a+n}{s} \quad \text{for all } \frac{AN}{K} > 0, \tag{5.9}$$

so that $\lim_{(AN/K)\to 0} \varphi(AN/K) \geq (a+n)/s$. Then we will have an *asymptotic* rate of growth:

$$\lim_{t\to\infty} g(t) = s\varphi(0) \quad \text{if and only if} \quad \lim_{AN/K\to 0} \beta = 1, \tag{5.10}$$

and, since in steady state, the K/Y ratio will be constant, by (5.7) the function F_K will be bounded from below at a positive level. Let us now recall the concept of essentiality of a factor of production.[4] Labour is *essential* in (5.1) if $F(K, 0, t) = 0$ for all K and t.

It turns out that conditions (5.9) and (5.10) are both related to this property, according to the following:[5]

Lemma 1: *If for some (positive) values of the parameters a, n, s, there is no positive AN/K balanced growth ratio, then labour is an inessential factor of production.*

Lemma 2: *If labour is an inessential factor of production, the competitive capital share tends to 1 as the ratio AN/K tends to zero.*

Combining the two lemmas, we obtain the following proposition, which gives a sufficient condition for endogenous growth:

Proposition 1: *If there is no balanced growth equilibrium (i.e., if $\varphi(0) \geq (a+n)/s$), there is an asymptotic steady state where the competitive capital share absorbs the whole output and capital and output grow at a rate higher than the natural rate of growth if $\varphi(0) > (a+n)/s$), equal to it if $\varphi(0) = (a+n)/s$).*

Notice that an asymptotic steady state is not exactly the same as a steady state. Of course in a sense all steady states are asymptotic, for if the system is not in one of them, it will (if stable) come back to it only in an infinite time. But while in a model with a steady state there are initial conditions that allow the economy to be in it all the time, this possible constancy over time is missing in an asymptotic steady state.

Conversely, suppose labour is an essential factor of production. Then we can assert:

Lemma 3: *Essentiality of labour implies the existence of a positive balanced growth AN/K ratio.*

What does essentiality of labour imply for the behaviour of β? A partial answer is:

Lemma 4: *When labour is essential, and* $\lim_{(AN/K)\to 0} F_{AN}(1, AN/K)$ *is finite, then* $\lim_{(AN/K)\to 0} \alpha = 1$ *(and therefore* $\lim_{(AN/K)\to 0} \beta = 0$*).*

However, as the example provided by the Cobb–Douglas production function illustrates, if $\lim_{(AN/K)\to 0} F_{AN}(1, AN/K)$ is infinite, $\lim_{(AN/K)\to 0} \alpha$ may assume a value in the open interval $(0, 1)$.[6] What is more, examples can be provided of constant returns to scale production functions with essential labour, marginal product of labour tending to infinity, and for which the competitive effective labour share tends to zero as $(AN/K)\to 0$.[7] It is definitely not true that $\lim_{(AN/K)\to 0} \beta = 1$ *only* if labour is inessential. We can assert, however, the following:

Lemma 5: *Under essentiality of labour, an asymptotic steady-state rate of growth higher than or equal to the natural rate is impossible.*

Thus if labour is essential, by Lemma 3 there is certainly a balanced growth equilibrium AN/K ratio, and, by Lemma 5, there can be no asymptotic steady state, i.e., there cannot be endogenous growth. We can then conclude with a proposition and a corollary:

Proposition 2: *In the context of the Solow model, there is an asymptotic steady state, where the competitive capital share absorbs the whole output and capital and output grow at a rate, higher than or equal to the natural rate of growth, if and only if there is no positive balanced growth AN/K ratio.*

Corollary: *In the context of the Solow model there can be endogenous growth only if labour is inessential.*[8]

One implication of Proposition 1 is that by choosing a sufficiently high rate of savings, an economy can free itself from the shackles of the natural rate of growth and grow at a 'warranted rate' of its choice. Moreover, as is made clear from (5.8), it can do so even if the natural rate of growth is zero, or indeed negative, a circumstance that is the hallmark of endogenous growth![9] In a sense, this is not surprising. By our Corollary, a necessary condition for endogenous growth is that labour be an inessential factor of production. This is why the reproducible factor, K, is able to grow faster than $(a + n)$, and to draw the growth of output.[10]

5.4.   ENDOGENIZING TECHNICAL PROGRESS À *LA* ARROW

'Another more interesting way to proceed, is genuinely to endogenize technological progress', Solow observes. 'What one could do is to suppose that the level of technology A depends on the amount of capital that has been accumulated'.[11] Let us then consider the Arrow–Solow production function:

$$Y = F(K, A^*(t, K)N), \qquad (5.11)$$

that allows both an exogenous and an endogenous component in the labour productivity function A^*. We can prove the following:

Proposition 3: *A production function of type (5.11) is compatible with steady-state growth only if the function A^* takes the form*

$$A^*(t, K) = K^b A, \qquad b > 0,$$

where A is the usual exponential function.

The growth equation becomes:

$$g = \left[\beta + (1-\beta)b\right]\frac{\dot{K}}{K} + (1-\beta)(a+n), \qquad (5.12)$$

and we see from (5.12) that there will be a steady-state rate of growth (where $g = \dot{K}/K$) only if $b < 1$. The solution is:

$$g = \frac{a+n}{1-b}. \qquad (5.13)$$

For $b = 1$, the rate of growth of output is infinite; for $b > 1$, only if effective labour grew at a negative rate, i.e. $(a + n) < 0$, could there be a steady-state solution. Formula (5.13) is completely analogous to Swan's (5.4) of Section 5.2. There is no dependence of g on β, a parameter that summarizes the properties of the production function F; no dependence on the savings propensity, s, either. Hence, by Solow's own suggested definitions, even if $g > (a + n)$, *we are still in the realm of exogenous growth.* Notice that if $(a + n) = 0$, $g = 0$. Only if the natural rate of growth is positive can there be a positive (if greater) steady-state rate of growth. This too can be considered as a property of exogenous growth. Endogenous growth, therefore, should allow $(a + n) = 0$ and $g > 0$.

5.5.   EQUIVALENT REPRESENTATIONS OF THE PRODUCTION FUNCTION IN THE SWAN PROPOSITION

The Arrow–Solow production function discussed in the preceding section

$$Y = F(K, K^b AN), \quad 0 < b < 1 \tag{5.14}$$

exhibits increasing returns to scale in the variables K and AN. It does not at first sight appear to be of the class (5.3). Is this then a class of functions that has somehow managed to slip through the mesh of the Swan Proposition? Of course not. One can easily prove the following 'equivalent representation proposition':

Proposition 4: *A production function can be expressed in the form (5.14) if and only if there exists a constant returns to scale function G and a value of the parameter* q, q = 1/(1 – b) > 1, *such that:*

$$F(K, K^b AN) = G(K, (AN)^q).$$

We are now in the position to assess the second part of Solow's 'general point'. If F is first degree homogeneous in its two arguments, F_K is zero degree homogeneous, i.e., depends on the ratio K/AN only. F_K can only be constant over time, therefore, if K grows at the same proportional rate as AN, and therefore, if Y grows at the natural rate $(a + n)$. Increasing returns of the form (5.14) do not, as we have seen, disturb the constant returns to scale property of the F function with respect to its two arguments, K and $K^b AN$. It follows that F_K will be constant over time if the ratio $K/K^b AN$ can be kept constant, i.e., if g satisfies equality (5.13). This is the arithmetical way in which Solow's suggested route 'to keep the marginal product of capital from falling too fast as capital accumulates' works in the model with endogenous technical progress. 'The job of any model of endogenous growth' has been carried out by a model of endogenous productivity growth. By merely constraining it to yield a steady-state solution, it has been turned into a model of exogenous growth, with increasing returns to scale of the 'right' (i.e. Swan) type.

5.6.   ENDOGENOUS GROWTH IN THE ARROW–SOLOW MODEL

But of course we are free to dismiss that self-imposed constraint: what happens if we do so, i.e. if we agree to consider $b = 1$? That a steady state is impossible does not mean that the economy cannot operate ... and grow. Equation (5.14) becomes:

$$Y = F(K, KAN),\tag{5.15}$$

and by constant returns to scale, (5.15) takes the fateful, almost 'AK' form:

$$Y = KF(1, AN)\tag{5.16}$$

whose associated growth equation is:

$$g = \frac{\dot{K}}{K} + \alpha(a+n) = sF(1, AN) + \alpha(a+n),\tag{5.17}$$

so that, if:

$$\lim_{(AN/K) \to 0} \alpha = 0, \quad \lim_{AN \to \infty} F(1, AN) = c < \infty,\tag{5.18}$$

there will be an asymptotic steady state $g = sc$, i.e., the rate of growth is endogenous. Let us state it as our:

Proposition 5: *Those production functions (5.15) which satisfy (5.18) generate an endogenous asymptotic rate of growth.*

Thus, endogenization of technical progress *à la* Arrow does give an endogenous growth model: it does so in the same way as any other model of endogenous growth – for just one real value of some crucial parameter.[12]

Suppose that in (17) $(a + n) = 0$. Then AN is constant over time, and, by (17), $g = g(t) = sF(1, AN)$, the *current rate of growth* is constant over time (but depends on AN, the 'scale effect'[13]). Current and long-run rates of growth coincide. Conditions (5.18) need not be assumed or invoked. This is the concept of solution to a growth model which is presently most popular among applied new growth theorists.[14] It is a new knife-edge, a knife-edge on a knife-edge.

5.7.   THE ARROW PRODUCTION FUNCTIONS AND THE SWAN PROPOSITION

Let's consider Arrow's own rather formidable looking production function:[15]

$$Y = aK\left[1-\left(1-\frac{N}{cK^{1-m}}\right)^{\frac{1}{1-m}}\right] \equiv F(K,N).\qquad(5.19)$$

As Arrow points out (1962, p. 159), $F(K, N)$ has increasing returns to scale for all positive real values of m. It can also be observed that since $F(K, 0) = 0$ for all K, labour is certainly essential in the Arrow production function (5.19). We notice that its two variants:

$$Y = aK\left[1-\left(1-\frac{N^{1-m}}{cK^{1-m}}\right)^{\frac{1}{1-m}}\right] \equiv F^1(K,N)$$

and:

$$Y = aK\left[1-\left(1-\frac{N}{cK}\right)^{\frac{1}{1-m}}\right] \equiv F^2(K,N)$$

are both constant returns to scale functions. Also:

$$F^1(K, N^q) = F(K, N), \quad \text{with } q = \frac{1}{1-m},$$

and:

$$F^2(K, K^b N) = F(K, N), \quad \text{with } b = m.$$

By the last two equalities, we have managed to express the Arrow production function (5.19) in either of the forms indicated in our 'alternative representation' proposition. From equation (5.4), or from (5.13), we can compute immediately the steady-state rate of growth of the Arrow model:

$$g = \frac{a+n}{1-m}.$$

For $0 < m < 1$ then, and only for m in this interval, the Arrow model falls within the Swan Proposition. We are now ready to make the following:

Proposition 6: *Only if* m < 1 *does the production function (5.19) allow for a proportional rate of growth of the same sign as the natural rate of growth.*

Arrow (1962, p. 159) thought that his model would have a steady-state solution *for all* positive real values of m. The above analysis shows quite well what happens: as m goes through 1, the rate of growth goes through infinity, and comes back to ... reality, so to speak (to the real numbers), but with the opposite sign to that of the natural rate of growth.[16] Thus there is a non-Swan steady state for $m > 1$. Its interpretation, of course, is not that sufficiently fast learning, with its associated sufficiently strong increasing returns to scale, turns the rate of growth of output from positive to negative, but that only with a decreasing working population can there be a steady state with a positive rate of growth of output when learning is faster than the watershed value, $m = 1$. Indeed, it can be easily checked that the variant of (5.19) that can be obtained by letting $m \to 1$ has the form (5.16) and satisfies both conditions (5.18).[17]

5.8.   TOWARDS A SWAN-LIKE PROPOSITION FOR ENDOGENOUS GROWTH

A Swan-like proposition for endogenous growth would answer the following question: what is the most general type of production function allowing for essential labour and endogenous growth? Our only example so far has been the class of production functions mentioned in Proposition 5. As is clear from (5.16), all production functions of this class, because of their very special separable structure, have $\beta = 1$. It might seem that endogenous growth is either robust, but implies inessential labour, as in Section 5.3, or allows essential labour, but then is a knife-edge, as in Section 5.6. Can't we have increasing returns and $\beta \to 1$? Consider the following production function:

$$Y = F(K, AN) = cK \left[1 - \exp\left(-\frac{(AN)^p}{K} \right) \right],$$ (5.20)

where c is a positive constant and $p \geq 1$ is a parameter. If $p = 1$, (5.20) is constant returns to scale. Let's assume $p > 1$. Then (5.20) is increasing returns to scale: for a proportional increase in K and AN, the term $((AN)^p/K)$ increases, the term $\exp(-(AN)^p/K)$ decreases, the whole expression within square brackets therefore increases. Thus, the increase in Y is more than proportional to the increase in K and AN that produces it. Some easy computations allow us to verify:

Proposition 7: *The class production functions (5.20), parameterized by p, allows for endogenous growth at the asymptotic rate* $\lim_{t \to \infty} g(t) = sc$ *under condition* $(a + n) < sc < p(a + n)$.

This example is interesting not only because it consists of a one parameter family of production functions rather than just a single, isolated function on the brink of non-existence like (5.16), but also because the emancipation of the warranted from the natural rate of growth is incomplete here: for Proposition 7 requires $(a + n) > 0$. No such requirement is needed for endogenous growth when the production function is:

$$Y = F(K, AN) = cK\left[1 - \exp(-ANK)\right],\qquad (5.21)$$

an example that is worth mentioning because the α and β associated to it depend on ANK rather than K/AN, and reach their limiting values 0 and 1 for $(ANK) \to \infty$, a condition that is implied by $(AN/K) \to \infty$ since the natural rate of growth $(a + n)$, is finite. Moreover, the β associated to (5.21) approaches 1 from the right,[18] a possibility that under constant returns to scale cannot arise.

The class of production functions with essential labour which are compatible with endogenous growth has some features that by now should be clear: as $AN/K \to 0$, β should tend to 1, α to 0. As a consequence, $(\alpha + \beta)$ tends to 1: the increasing returns production function should gradually but inexorably turn into a constant returns to scale function of the simple form $Y = cK$. It has not been established above that a functional form of the separable type $Y = F(K, AN) \equiv KG(K, AN)$, with $G(K, 0) = 0$, like (5.19), is necessarily implied by these conditions. To this extent, the 'Swan problem for endogenous growth' remains open.

5.9.   CONCLUSIONS

In the context of the old neoclassical theory, endogenous growth can be obtained with $\beta = 1$, but, if we insist on maintaining one of its main ingredients, constant returns to scale, we must resign ourselves to very simplistic production functions; or we can settle for $\beta \to 1$, which opens up a broader parametric range for endogenous growth. But this is all confined to *inessential labour*. We can endogenize technical progress *à la* Arrow, but 'the job to keep the marginal product of capital from falling too fast as capital accumulates' turns out to be 'the job of any theory where capital grows faster than the natural rate', and this includes the old growth theory if we abandon the assumption of constant returns to scale, as in fact we must when we endogenize technical progress. It is true that increasing returns to scale is an assumption which proves to be neither necessary (Sections 5.3) nor sufficient (Sections 5.2, 5.4 and 5.7) for endogenous growth. However, if we insist on essentiality of labour then increasing returns to scale becomes a necessary condition for endogenous growth.

Another aspect of the comparison between exogenous and endogenous growth theory that our discussion has shed some light on is strictly grammatical. The new growth theorists, in defending the special assumptions they need, usually point out that they are no more arbitrary than the other assumptions needed for steady-state growth.[19] The steady states of the old and new growth theory are not, however, the same. The importance of the Swan Proposition is that it is an 'if and only if' proposition. If we want a steady state, our production function will have to be of type (5.3).[20] That the Arrow production function does fall within it shows that the endogenization of productivity increases does not in itself have anything to do with the algebraic format of the growth model.[21] But it is new formats that are needed if the equilibrium rate of growth is to be freed from its multiplicative dependence on population growth. Thus new types of solution concepts have been introduced, such as asymptotic steady states, and, more often, constant current growth rates. The contribution of the endogenous growth theorists has been to play a game with slightly altered, and perhaps a little more liberal, grammatical rules. The knife-edge nature of many 'new growth' models seems to contradict this impression of greater freedom, but as we have seen in our attempt to extend the Swan Proposition in Section 5.8, it is not perhaps a necessary feature of the new theory.

Finally, our discussion allows us to comment on the relationship between those two admirable, momentous papers, Swan's and Arrow's. Both were published in the early 1960s, and neither author knew of the other's work. Arrow (1962, p. 168) found that 'as in many growth models, the rates of growth of the variables in the system do not depend on savings behaviour; however, their levels do', and did not explain why; Swan on the other hand did give the explanation, i.e., the Swan Proposition; but did not provide a concrete production model which had a steady-state growth at a rate higher than $(a + n)$. Thus, they nicely complement each other in clearing the ground for endogenous, as well as exogenous, growth theory.

NOTES

1. See also Chilosi and Gomulka (1974) for this attribution.
2. It is typically assumed that $F(K, AN)$ is increasing in both its arguments, is differentiable, and has not only first but also second partial derivatives. Both $F_{K,K}$ and $F_{AN,AN}$ are assumed to be negative. (The marginal product of either factor is positive but decreasing in the amount of the own factor.)
3. This is Solow's 'general point on endogenous growth models' that should establish a bridge between 'old' and the 'new' growth theories.

4. See Burmeister and Dobell (1970, p. 30) for a definition and discussion of this concept.

5. See Costa (2001) for proofs of the Lemmas, Propositions, and other statements made in this chapter.

6. Let's take $F(K,AN) = K^b(AN)^{1-b}$, $0 < b < 1$. Then $F_K = b(AN/K)^{1-b}$, $F_{AN} = (1-b)(K/AN)^b$, so that $\lim_{(AN/K) \to 0} F_{AN} = \infty$, and, as is well known, $\alpha = 1-b$.

7. Let us write the production function in the intensive form $y = f(x)$, where $Y = Y/K$, $x = AN/K$. Then our assumptions on the production function can be expressed by the assumptions (1) $f(x)$ exists and is continuous for $x \geq 0$; (2) $f(0) = 0$; (3) $f'(x) > 0$ for $x > 0$; (4) $f''(x) < 0$ for $x > 0$; (5) $\lim_{x \to 0} f'(x) = \infty$. Consider the function $f(x) = [-1/\log x]$ for x in the semi-closed interval $[0, A)$, $A = \exp(-2)$; $f(x) = 0$ for $x = 0$. It can be checked that $f(x)$ satisfies all the properties (1)–(5). At $x = A$, $f''(x) = 0$, but the function can be extended to the right of $[0, A)$ without impairing conditions (1), (3), and (4). It can be easily checked that $f(x)$ is a solution to the differential equation $xf'(x) = f^2(x)$. Therefore, $\lim_{x \to 0} xf'(x)/f(x) = \lim_{x \to 0} f(x) = 0$, q.e.d. I owe this example to Mr Carlo Viola of the Dept of Mathematics of the University of Pisa.

8. The paper by Chilosi and Gomulka (1974) might be taken as an exception to this statement. They argue that one can have a steady state $g = (n + a)$ with $a = a(K/Y)$, $a' > 0$. But since $s = (K/Y)g$, a higher s results in a higher (K/Y) and a higher g. Thus they, and their teacher M. Kalecki, are among the precursors of endogenous growth theory. But their production function is not quite of type (5.5).

9. Notice however that in the growth equation $g(t) = \beta s \varphi(AN/K) + (1-\beta)(a+n)$, a simple rearrangement of (5.8), the *current* rate of growth of output, $g(t)$, is not independent of time. Of course the *asymptotic* rate of growth, $\lim_{t \to \infty} g(t) = s\varphi(0)$, is independent of time.

10. See Costa (2001) for a detailed analysis of a special case of endogenous growth, given by the production function $Y = BK + K^b(AN)^{1-b}$, $B > 0$, $0 < b < 1$. This example is also discussed by Solow (2000, pp. 138–40, 144–47).

11. Solow (1992, p. 41) writes: 'It is perfectly possible for the quantity $A(K)$ to grow fast enough as capital accumulates to keep F_K from going to zero'. And he adds (2000, p. 147): 'The details can be left as an exercise; the economically interesting thing is the story told about $A(K)$'. Our answer is Proposition 3.

12. Consider the following remark by Aghion and Howitt (1998, p. 23): 'The Arrow model ... was fully worked out only in the case of a fixed capital–labor ratio and fixed (but vintage specific) labor requirements. This implied that in the long run the growth of output was limited by the growth in labor, and hence was independent of savings behavior, as in the Solow–Swan model'. As the analysis of the Arrow–Solow production function makes clear, whether the Arrow model generates exogenous or endogenous growth depends on the value of b, and on no other aspect of the production conditions.

13. See Solow (2000, p. 167) or Turnovsky (2003, p. 3).

14. See Bertola (1993) or Turnovsky (2001). An example is provided by the function $Y = KN^\alpha$, $0 < \alpha < 1$, currently highly popular among new growth theorists. It satisfies neither of the conditions (5.18).

15. We are indicating Arrow's learning parameter as 'm' rather than 'n', as in the original, in order to maintain consistency with our previous notation.

16. It can be checked that the β associated to (1A) is less than 1 only for $m < 1$. But the advantage of the Swan Proposition is that by applying it one does not have to undertake the computations of β!

17. See Costa (2001) for the detailed calculations. See also Solow (1997, pp. 11–12).

18. It can be easily checked that $\beta = 1 + ANK \exp(-ANK)/[1 - \exp(-ANK)]$.

19. See for example Aghion and Howitt (1998, p. 15).

20. A recent example is the prototype of 'non-scale growth model' discussed by Turnovsky (2001).
21. Perhaps we should ask of any serious growth model that it should be compatible, like Arrow's, with both exogenous and endogenous growth.

REFERENCES

Aghion, P. and P. Howitt (1998), *Endogenous Growth Theory*, Cambridge, Massachusetts: MIT Press.

Arrow, K.J. (1962), 'The economic implications of learning by doing', *Review of Economic Studies*, **29**, 155–73.

Bertola, G. (1993), 'Factor shares and savings in endogenous growth', *American Economic Review*, **83**(5), 1184–98.

Burmeister, E. and A.R. Dobell (1970), *Mathematical Theories of Economic Growth*, New York: Macmillan.

Chilosi, A. and S. Gomulka (1974), 'Technological conditions for balanced growth: a criticism and restatement', *Journal of Economic Theory*, **9**(2), 171–84.

Costa G. (2001), 'Solow on exogenous and endogenous growth, and the Swan Proposition', Working paper no. 83 of *Studi e ricerche del Dipartimento di Scienze Economiche dell'Università di Pisa*.

Solow, R.M. (1992), 'Siena lectures on endogenous growth theory', *Collana del Dipartimento di Economia Politica*, no. 6, Siena.

Solow, R.M. (1997), *Learning from 'Learning by Doing': Lessons for Economic Growth*, Stanford, California: Stanford University Press.

Solow, R.M. (2000), *Growth Theory: An Exposition*, second edition, London: Oxford University Press.

Swan, T.W. (1963), 'Golden ages and production functions', in K.E. Berrill (ed.), *Economic Development with Special Reference to East Asia*, London: Macmillan and St. Martin's Press, and in A. Sen (ed.), *Growth Economics*, Harmondsworth: Penguin, 1970, pp. 203–18.

Turnovsky, S.J. (2003), 'Old and new growth theories: a unifying structure?', this volume, pp. 1–44.

6. Model robustness in 'old' and 'new' growth theory*

Francesco Guala and Andrea Salanti

6.1. INTRODUCTION

Scientific progress is often supposed to consist of the discovery of 'better and better' theories within a particular field of research. How to characterise a 'better' theory is nonetheless far from obvious. Plausible candidates may be an increased power in the prediction, explanation, and control of real-world phenomena. In economics, where *models*, rather than theories, are the fundamental unit of appraisal, practitioners seem to hold in high esteem the criterion of *'robustness'* (as it can be detected in the literature or during seminars and workshops). A 'model economy', or 'model' for short, is a simple object that stands for (in some way to be specified) a real-world economic system. Models can be abstract or (rarely) concrete objects, which can be studied and manipulated on paper, by means of thought experiments, or concretely, with the ultimate goal of discovering interesting facts about the real-world system they are representative of.[1] A 'better' model, then, is a 'more robust' one – but robust *to what*? In this chapter we would like to do two things: first, we shall try to explicate the notion of robustness, and articulate it on three different dimensions. Second, we shall apply these notions of robustness to a historical case, in order to show their relevance to concrete economic practice. 'Old' and 'new' growth theory (OGT and NGT respectively, from now on) stimulate interesting methodological reflections, as we shall see. Special attention will be paid to the robustness of the implied causal mechanisms, due to its substantial role concerning the possibility of deriving sound policy prescriptions from models.

6.2.   THREE DIFFERENT NOTIONS OF ROBUSTNESS

Robustness is a comprehensive term under which various different concepts are subsumed. However, since different kinds of progress are associated with different kinds of robustness, it is important to distinguish between them properly. In Guala and Salanti (2001), we identify three main different meanings of the term: (1) robustness to changes in the model's 'idealisations'; (2) robustness to changes in the 'background' conditions (usually, but somewhat improperly, referred to as *ceteris paribus* clauses); (3) robustness to changes in the implied causal mechanism(s).[2]

The first two notions emerge from considering that models provide simplified representations of real entities and systems in roughly two ways, by distortion and, often at the same time, by omission of some aspects of reality. The terms '*idealisation*' and '*abstraction*' are meant to refer to these two distinct facets of model-building activity respectively.[3]

Every model incorporates (possibly highly) idealised descriptions of some real-world feature (entity, system, or property). These descriptions capture just one of the several possible forms that each single feature can take in the real world. A typical idealisation is involved for example when a result[4] (e.g. a steady-state equilibrium with its associated properties) is proved to hold for a one-sector, or a two-sector (or even a two-class) model-economy, although we in fact know that the number of 'sectors' or 'classes' in the real world almost certainly differs from what is assumed in that model. Many other examples of idealisations within ('old' or 'new') growth theory could be easily provided. Think of, for instance: Harrod's (or Hicks's, for that matter) definition of neutral technical progress within OGT; the assumption of constant returns to scale in capital and labour; the notion of optimal consumption for an infinitely lived (representative) household; two-period overlapping generations models; and so on.

Increasing robustness to changes in idealisations is taken as an indication of progressiveness on the basis of the presumption that a given result has been rigorously demonstrated with respect to a very specific model-economy only for reasons of simplicity, clarity, or mathematical tractability, but the validity of the result itself should not depend on any of the specific idealisations used in the proof. This independence may be self-evident to the specialist or hinted at by the author. In any case, what characterizes idealisations is that they are explicitly (and rigorously) enunciated and very often they are also highlighted as such.[5]

At the same time, models usually depart from reality also by deliberately omitting some features (abstractions). The crucial point to be noted is that the abstracted features do not appear in the model-economy, although sometimes they may be mentioned in the informal interpretation that goes with it. The omitted aspects are kept 'in the background' as conditions, factors, etc. which are supposedly irrelevant for the purpose at hand.[6] Sometimes successive approximations (or 'concretisations') permit the omitted feature to be added back in and thus test the robustness of the result to changes in the degree of abstraction. If carried on, however, eventually the process of concretisation will lead from the theoretical to the empirical realm. This is why to establish the robustness (in the previous senses) of a model is often supposed to be a preliminary step towards (but sometimes even a partial substitute for) identifying a structural relation in the real world.

A third kind of model-robustness we may encounter in economics is robustness to changes in the implied causal mechanism, where progress is identified with the proliferation of models featuring *different* causal mechanisms.[7] Perhaps economists rely on an argument of the same sort as the one used for 'robustness to changes in idealisations': if conclusions do not change very much under different assumptions, this means that that particular detail is not so important after all. In some cases, this may be true. If the only aim is to predict, assuming that not much will change in the institutional set-up, an instrumentalist attitude may be justified. In this case, in other words, robustness may refer to the conclusions but by no means to the explicative power of the various models that have been employed to justify them.[8] But in many other circumstances, particularly when the possibility of deriving policy prescriptions is concerned, reliance on such a kind of 'robustness' seems to be seriously misplaced. When this is the case, the proliferation of models is just evidence of our inability to detect the best unique representation of the situation we want to investigate and/or the true mechanism at work. For each real-world situation, indeed, at most only one of these models can tell the true causal story; the fact that we have many alternatives converging on the same result does not, *per se*, imply that we are getting closer to the truth at all.[9]

6.3.   'OLD' VS. 'NEW' GROWTH THEORY

Growth theory has traditionally been based on highly idealised, caricatured models (in the sense of Gibbard and Varian, 1978). Because of this feature – which is generally recognised by its proponents as well as by its critics – it constitutes an appropriate case study for our purposes. We would like first to separately appraise OGT and NGT according to the different criteria of robustness we have previously summarised, and then try to figure out in which respects exactly we can speak of a progressive shift from the old to the new 'programme'.[10]

OGT represented from its very outset an explicit attempt to extend the domain of macroeconomics to the analysis of long-period mechanisms of growth. Its first important results were pessimistic conclusions about the stability of growth paths, grounded on the 'knife-edge' properties of equilibrium path as emerging from the Harrod–Domar model. This result, however, was quite soon shown to be fragile: small changes in the idealisations and abstractions (concerning either the form of technology as in the neoclassical approach, or the form of the saving function as in the neo-Keynesian formulation) suffice to produce much more favourable conclusions about the stability (convergence to steady states) of equilibrium paths.

Both these approaches (the neoclassical and the neo-Keynesian), separately considered, seem to be fairly robust according to our first two definitions of robustness. Within each of them we may find indeed a great variety of models (based on different idealisations and abstractions[11]), leading to similar conclusions. But our third robustness criterion (namely, robustness to changes in the implied causal mechanism) provides some food for thought. If the ultimate goal in growth theory is the discovery of some effective set of policy recommendations suited to promote economic growth, then robustness to changes in idealisations or abstractions is only part of the story. It also matters, eventually, how much reliance we can place on the actual functioning of the mechanisms represented in our models. The problem is that, even if it is not always acknowledged, different idealisations and abstractions often involve different causal mechanisms as well. This is what happens, in neoclassical models, when the assumption of an exogenously fixed propensity to save in the Solow–Swan model is replaced either by a representative household maximising utility over an infinite horizon, or by an overlapping generations mechanism (and, incidentally, it is not clear at all how such particular mechanisms might be exploited in order to enhance the rate of growth in actual economies). Moreover, neoclassical and neo-Keynesian approaches envisaged deeply different causal mechanisms behind the growth process. In fact, the fierce debates during the 1960s and the 1970s between the advocates of the two approaches involved a fundamental disagreement about one of the most important causal mechanisms embodied in those models, i.e. the causal link between accumulation and distribution. However, even neo-Keynesian models of growth, by leaving virtually unexplained the determinants of distribution, were unable to offer secure prescriptions on policy matters.

The highly idealised character of (all) models within OGT, together with a significant amount of uncertainty about the 'true' causal mechanisms, prompted many scholars to regard those models as no more than a first step towards a satisfactory explanation of economic growth. During the 1960s and

1970s, caveats about the limitations of growth theory were indeed very common. It was usually maintained that its content was neither a satisfactory description of actual growth processes or development experiences, nor a useful starting point for policy recommendation, but simply a first step towards a better understanding of some fundamental mechanisms (primarily the accumulation of capital) affecting economic growth. As Frank Hahn (1971, p. vii) puts it:

> The theory of growth is not a theory of economic history. It is of no help in answering Max Weber's famous question and only of marginal use in understanding, say, the Industrial Revolution. Where the theory is to be taken descriptively, it takes the institutional setting for granted and highly idealises it. The parts of the theory which are to be understood as prescriptive have hardly anything to say on either the actual problems of 'control' or on the society to be controlled.

In this respect, new growth theorists display a different and much more ambitious attitude. Consider, for instance, the following quotation from Aghion and Howitt (1998, pp. 6–7), a recent and widely acclaimed advanced textbook on NGT:

> Because of its explicit emphasis on structural aspects of the innovation process, endogenous growth theory makes it possible to bridge the gap between theory and various strands of empirical and historical literature. ... Thus one of our primary motivations in developing the model ... with capital accumulation and population growth is to show that when these other important aspects of growth are taken into account, our approach becomes broadly consistent with the empirical observations that have been adduced to refute it.

Behind this sharp change in perspective[12] lies a firm belief in the possibility of deriving some reliable prescriptions of policy designed to raise the growth rate of actual economies.[13] Accordingly, one of the most apparent differences between OGT and NGT is that the latter places much more emphasis than its precursor upon its descriptive adequacy and, consequently, the reliability of policy recommendations coming from it.

Moreover, while OGT had to resort to some form of what we may now recognise as piecemeal theorising, the most recent approaches are more akin to the neoclassical view on theory-making, according to which all economic models must be built on the common basis of a few basic premises (individual maximising rationality and subjectivistic equilibrium being the best known). We find here, incidentally, paradigmatic examples of the two principal ways in which the term '*ad hocness*' is used in economics. Both are fairly different from the standard philosophical definition of 'being able to account for the empirical data only after the latter have been observed'.[14] OGT was '*ad hoc*' in the sense that it relied on a number of non-robust assumptions (primarily the view of technical progress as exogenous), a change in which was sufficient to make the whole theoretical structure crumble. It also appeared inadequate because the explanation of some assumptions about exogenous variables was implicitly or explicitly deferred to other pieces of theory.

NGT, in contrast, supports a different choice of what is to be regarded as exogenous, probably more coherent with its own methodological premises. The price to be paid, however, is twofold: (1) the old distinction between 'development' and 'growth' virtually vanishes, but the underlying problem reappears in the form of the heterogeneity of structural parameters when cross-section analyses are performed; (2) the usual economists' list of 'fundamentals' does not seem sufficient for an adequate explanation of growth and a rapidly growing number of other exogenous variables is necessary. Because some of these do not fall within the traditional boundaries of the discipline, in addition to the problem of their selection, we have to face the even bigger question of the demarcation of 'economic' from other generically 'social' phenomena. More than that, the proliferation of possible determinants of growth brings with it a proliferation of possible causal mechanisms that is beginning to cause some embarrassment among practitioners.

A possible 'ecumenical' solution would be this: to acknowledge that different causal mechanisms actually *are* at work in real-world economies and that observed rates of growth are a (possibly very complicated) combination of all their effects. A proliferation of models could be considered progressive in so far as it approximates real-world diversity and pluralism. The problem here is that to recognise the contemporary presence of different causal mechanisms at work is more typical of historical than economic interpretations. As we may find in a recent review of two books on NGT (Agliardi, 2001, p. F773):

> Endogenous growth theory has tried to understand the interplay between knowledge and structural characteristics of the economy, and how such interplay results in economic growth. A somewhat disturbing feature of the recent work has been a proliferation of special models, each with its own assumptions. This proliferation is, for the most part, a healthy thing, an indication that old assumptions are being challenged and that innovation is taking place. However, it becomes necessary a synthesis that defines the common elements in the variety of new models and, at the same time, re-establishes some continuity with older traditions.

Given the ubiquitous claim that NGT provides for better interpretations of the relevant facts about growth and development, what the reviewer points out as the most urgent need within this field of research simply misses the point. What is needed, indeed, is not so much a theoretical 'synthesis of the common elements' as a selection, among all the available ones, of the effectively operating mechanisms.

When it comes to choosing between mutually exclusive mechanisms, it is empirical evidence, obviously, that becomes decisive. This opens the problem of appraising the body of empirical research related to NGT. The shift from OGT to NGT can be regarded, at most, as theoretically progressive in the light of the first two of the robustness criteria identified above, but it came with a price. In particular, it made the business of empirical testing much more complicated than it used to be. First, it must be noticed that with the advent of NGT the facts (whether stylised or not) to be explained have changed, particular emphasis being placed on the growth of some per capita magnitudes as a result of possibly different sources of increasing returns.

Second, while empirical applications associated with OGT were scarce and almost limited to estimating Solow's residual and/or total factor productivity (and cross-country data were regarded as highly suspicious if not totally useless), with the advent of NGT the amount of applied research (together with the number of supposedly relevant variables) has enormously increased. As a consequence, NGT markedly departs from the classical tradition, to which the OGT was still somehow linked, of trying to focus on the fundamental mechanisms capable of fostering growth or, in other words, on the fundamental laws of motion of industrial economies.[15]

The problem here is that the empirical evidence,[16] which according to its advocates should support NGT, at a closer scrutiny appears to be far from decisive. Steven Durlauf (2000a) has recently pointed out the inconclusiveness of much recent empirical work intended to exploit a number of insights provided by NGT. He goes beyond some criticisms previously set forth in Durlauf and Quah (1998),[17] with an admittedly 'provocative purpose – namely to argue that the econometric component of the new growth literature has done little to adjudicate leading growth questions' (p. 249). In his opinion, because almost all variables employed to explain growth in real per capita income are probably endogenous (and possible instrumental variables, due to the open-endedness of growth theories, are likely to be correlated with the error term), we cannot easily jump from finding statistical correlations to claiming stable causal links. Moreover, discriminating between competing explanations of growth would require reliable criteria for sorting out the relevant variables, but statistical robustness does not seem to be attainable through the actually available procedures of variable selection.[18]

6.4. FINAL REMARKS

Despite the (sometimes bold) claims in favour of NGT, this approach has failed so far to detect the fundamental determinants of growth and to provide firm empirical evidence of the relevant links among variables. Consequently it has also failed to provide precise and reliable prescriptions about policies intended to foster economic growth (an issue whose practical importance can hardly be underestimated).

NGT offers a number of possible explanations of mechanisms generating (more or less directly) cumulative processes, but in this case (assuming the possibility of deriving sound policy prescriptions as the pre-eminent target) robustness to changes in the implied causal mechanism(s) is more a problem than a virtue. A problem, unfortunately, which still has to be solved. Of course, growth theory remains a field of research worthy of serious attention. After all, in the long run it is not so much the optimal allocation of given resources or the effectiveness of counter-cyclical policies, as the rate of growth of per-capita magnitudes, that, given a reasonable degree of inequality in the distribution of individual incomes, determines people's standard of life.

Our main point is that the three notions of robustness highlight some of the methodological problems within growth theory (and other sub-fields in economics, although we cannot show it here) that traditional philosophical accounts leave somewhat unaccounted for. Take, for instance, the classic Popperian notion of '*ad hocness*' as *post-hoc* accommodation of previously observed evidence. If taken seriously, such a criterion would condemn almost all of what economic theorists usually consider progressive in economic history.[19] At a closer scrutiny, economists' attempts to refine growth theory display a more articulated situation: the development of growth theory was progressive on the first two robustness dimensions (robustness to different idealisations and abstractions), but problematic on the third dimension (due to the proliferation of alternative causal mechanisms). Such a trade-off between different methodological criteria (robustness criteria, in this case) is the price to be paid for abandoning 'monistic' methodological frameworks such as the Popperian one. But it pays off by reducing the gap between economists' practice and abstract philosophical theorising.

NOTES

*   We would like to thank, with the usual caveat about responsibility, Giacomo Costa and Stephen Turnovsky for the useful comments made at the Conference. The final version has benefited from comments and suggestions by Roger Backhouse and two anonymous referees. Grants from, respectively, the Cognitive Science Laboratory of the University of Trento and the Department of Economics of the University of Bergamo are gratefully acknowledged.

1. See Morgan and Morrison (1998) for a general account of modelling along these lines.

2. This categorisation owes substantially to the work of Cartwright (1989) and, more recently, Woodward (2000) on causation. Their approach, in turn, borrows from the notion of 'structural' relation introduced by early econometricians like Haavelmo and Frisch.

3. This terminology is by no means standard in philosophy of science or methodology of economics. The lack of a shared convention can be appreciated for example by looking at the essays in Hamminga and de Marchi (1994). Here we adopt Cartwright's convention (1989, Ch. 5).

4. The term 'result' is here employed according to common scientific jargon, i.e. somehow loosely. It may indeed refer to theorems, predictions, existence or non-existence proofs, but also to the demonstration of the existence of a (causal) relation between modelled entities.

5. This does not mean, however, that all the idealised features have the same status. With different terminology, several authors have pointed out the distinction between 'core relations' and 'boundary' conditions (indeed, the distinction goes back to at least Machlup, 1955). As Roger Backhouse pointed out to us, ideally we would like a result to be completely independent from boundary assumptions, but to a certain extent dependent on the core assumption of the model. If a result holds independently of a core assumption, then that assumption seems pretty useless. (When the assumptions are variables which can take different numerical values, the issue becomes more complicated. We shall bracket such subtleties here, but see Guala and Salanti, 2001.)

6. Economists often express this idea by saying that a theoretical result is valid *ceteris paribus* (other things being equal). It would be perhaps more appropriate to say that such a result holds *ceteris absentibus* (other things being absent) or *ceteris neglectibus* (other things being neglected). With reference to economic theory, Musgrave (1981) was the first to point out the difference between these kinds of assumption (although the terminology he used was different). On such distinctions see also Mäki and Piimies (1998) and Boumans and Morgan (2001).

7. It is far from easy to define precisely what is a 'mechanism'. For the present purposes, we shall define it as a path through a sequence of causal links, connecting one or more parent variables to one or more descendants. For an application to a specific economic issue (based on a slightly different definition of the concept), see also Salmon (1998) and the following discussion.

8. See Rosenberg (1978, p. 683 and 1992, pp. 84–5).

9. See Cartwright (1991) for a very similar argument. In the terminology of Backhouse (1997, pp. 100–1), we may say that robustness to the causal mechanism increases the *generality* of a result, but diminishes its *scope*. (Where the 'scope' is the class of *identifiable* situations of applicability.)

10. The problem of what exactly is scientific progress has been widely debated in the philosophy of science literature. For interesting discussions focused on economics cf., for instance, Boland (1989) and Backhouse (1997). By focusing on 'robustness', we try in this chapter to propose yet another set of criteria for progress, which we feel is more in line with economists' practice and intuitions. As we shall see, to establish robustness in a model is regarded as a preliminary step to (but sometimes even a substitute for) establishing a structural relation in the real world. Robustness, in other words, may be regarded as a property of either theoretical models or empirical generalisations.

11. The neoclassical version of OGT supports, for instance, models with one or two sectors, with vintage or non-vintage capital goods, and so on: see Burmeister and Dobell (1970) or

Wan (1971). On models in the neo-Keynesian tradition, see Harris (1978) or Marglin (1984).

12. For an intermediate position on the applicability of (old) growth theory, see Solow (1970).
13. The same attitude may be found, for instance, in Shaw (1992) and Crafts (1996).
14. See for instance Popper (1963, Ch. 10) and Laudan (1977, p. 115). For a survey of the notion of ad hocness in the Popperian tradition, see Hands (1988).
15. When we see studies on the relation between, say, personal distributions of income, levels of democracy, or different tax systems, and growth, can we still legitimately speak of 'fundamental' laws?
16. For a recent survey of such a 'new growth evidence', see Temple (1999).
17. See also Durlauf (2000b and 2001).
18. More technical objections concern, on one hand, models with multiple steady states, for which the usual specification of empirical models based upon linearisation may lead to misleading conclusions about convergence issues. On the other hand, assuming an invariant statistical model when performing cross-section analyses of growth amounts to completely disregarding the important question of parameter cross-country heterogeneity (while both econometrics and historical analyses lead to regarding heterogeneity as a key feature of country-specific patterns of growth).
19. This is indeed the conclusion forcefully stated in Blaug (2000), where NGT is portrayed as nothing but a further – albeit brilliant – exercise in neoclassical theory, lacking any convincing explanation of empirical evidence and bringing no real improvement on OGT.

REFERENCES

Aghion, P. and P. Howitt (1998), *Endogenous Growth Theory*, Cambridge, Massachusetts: MIT Press.

Agliardi, E. (2001), 'Book Review: *Endogenous Growth Theory*. By Aghion (Philippe) and Howitt (Peter), MIT Press, 1998 and *New Growth Theory: An Applied Perspective*. By Sengupta (Jati K.), E. Elgar, 1998', *Economic Journal*, **111** (Nov.), F773–75.

Backhouse, R.E. (1997), *Truth and Progress in Economic Knowledge*, Cheltenham, UK and Lyme, USA: Edward Elgar.

Blaug, M. (2000), 'Endogenous growth theory', *Research Memoranda in History and Methodology of Economics*, 00–7, Universiteit van Amsterdam.

Boland, L.A. (1989), *The Methodology of Economic Model Building*, London and New York: Routledge.

Boumans, M. and M. Morgan (2001), '*Ceteris paribus* conditions: materiality and the application of economic theories', *Journal of Economic Methodology*, **8**(1), 11–26.

Burmeister, E. and A.R. Dobell (1970), *Mathematical Theories of Economic Growth*, London: Macmillan.

Cartwright, N. (1989), *Nature's Capacities and their Measurement*, Oxford: Oxford University Press.

Cartwright, N. (1991), 'Replicability, reproducibility, and robustness: comments on Harry Collins', *History of Political Economy*, **23**, 143–55.

Crafts, N. (1996), 'Post-neoclassical endogenous growth theory: what are its implications?', *Oxford Review of Economic Policy*, **12**, 30–47.

Durlauf, S.D. (2000a), 'Econometric analysis and the study of economic growth: a sceptical perspective', in R. Backhouse and A. Salanti (eds), *Macroeconomics and the Real World. Vol. I: Econometric Techniques and Macroeconomics*, pp. 249–61.

Durlauf, S.D. (2000b), 'Review of Ph. Aghion and J.G. Williamson, "Growth, inequality and globalization: theory, history and policy"', *Journal of Economic Literature*, **38**(3), 637–8.

Durlauf, S.D. (2001), 'Manifesto for a growth econometrics', *Journal of Econometrics*, **100**(1), 65–9.

Durlauf, S.D. and D. Quah (1998), 'The new empirics of economic growth', *NBER Working Paper n. 6422*.

Gibbard, A. and H. Varian (1978), 'Economic models', *Journal of Philosophy*, **75**(11), 664–77 (Reprinted in B. Caldwell (ed.), *The Philosophy and Methodology of Economics*, Cheltenham: Edward Elgar, 1993. Vol. III, pp. 401–14).

Guala, F. and A. Salanti (2001), 'On the robustness of economic models', mimeo.

Hahn, F. (1971), *Readings in the Theory of Growth*, London: Macmillan.

Hamminga, B. and N. de Marchi (eds) (1994), *Idealization VI: Idealization in Economics* (Poznan Studies in the Philosphy of Sciences and Humanities, 28), Amsterdam and Atlanta: Rodopi.

Hands, D.W. (1988), 'Ad Hocness in economics and the Popperian tradition', in N. de Marchi (ed.), *The Popperian Legacy in Economics*, Cambridge: Cambridge University Press, pp. 121–39.

Harris, D.J. (1978), *Capital Accumulation and Income Distribution*, London: Routledge & Kegan Paul.

Laudan, L. (1977), *Progress and Its Problems*, Berkeley: University of California Press.

Machlup, F, (1955), 'The problem of verification in economics', *Southern Economic Journal*, **22**(1), 1–21.

Mäki, U. and J.-P. Piimies (1998), 'Ceteris paribus', in J. Davis, D.W. Hands and U. Mäki (eds), *The Handbook of Economic Methodology*, Cheltenham, UK and Northampton, Massachusetts: Edward Elgar, pp. 55–9.

Marglin, S.A. (1984), *Growth, Distribution and Prices*, Cambridge, Massachusetts: Harvard University Press.

Morgan, M.S. and M. Morrison (eds) (1998), *Models as Mediators*, Cambridge: Cambridge University Press.

Musgrave, A. (1981), 'Unreal assumptions' in economic theory: the F-twist untwisted', *Kyklos*, **34**(3), 377–87.

Popper, K.R. (1963), *Conjectures and Refutations: The Growth of Scientific Knowledge*, London: Routledge & Kegan Paul.

Rosenberg, A. (1978), 'The puzzle of economic modeling', *Journal of Philosophy*, **75**(11), 679–83.

Rosenberg, A. (1992), *Economics – Mathematical Politics or Science of Diminishing Returns?*, Chicago: University of Chicago Press.

Salmon, P. (1998), 'Free riding as mechanism', in R.E. Backhouse, D.M. Hausman, U. Mäki and A. Salanti (eds), *Economic and Methodology. Crossing Boundaries.* London: Macmillan, IEA Series, pp. 62–87.

Shaw, G.K. (1992), 'Policy implications of endogenous growth theories', *Economic Journal*, **102**, 611–21.

Solow, R.M. (1970, *Growth Theory: An Exposition*, Oxford: Oxford University Press.

Temple, J. (1999), 'The new growth evidence', *Journal of Economic Literature*, **37**, 112–56.

Wan, H.Y. Jr. (1971), *Economic Growth*, New York: Harcourt Brace Jovanovich.

Woodward, J. (2000), 'Explanation and invariance in the special sciences', *British Journal for the Philosophy of Science*, **51**, 197–254.

7. On 'measuring' knowledge in new (endogenous) growth theory

Ian Steedman

7.1. INTRODUCTION

In many contributions to New (Endogenous) Growth Theory – though not in all – central reference is made to 'a stock of knowledge', a 'stock of ideas', etc., this variable featuring centre-stage in the analysis. Yet it is immediately apparent that this is far from being a crystal-clear concept. Is knowledge a homogeneous quantity of which there is simply more or less? Clearly not. How then, in constructing a measure of the total stock, is one to select:

> the weights (prices) with which an idea in carbon chemistry, say, is to be combined with an idea in the production of insurance services. It is not obvious what the weights are, and they certainly are not to be found in market prices. (Metcalfe, 2001, p. 580)

One may also wonder to what extent knowledge is truly non-rivalrous, as opposed to being specific to sets of individuals (Metcalfe, 2001, p. 569) and, to the extent that knowledge *is* held in common, whether one ought not to think of the 'total' stock as being the union rather than the sum of 'individual stocks' (Olsson, 2001, pp. 10–11).

Even if 'knowledge' either is or can be rendered homogeneous – and that is a very big 'if' – the question arises whether there exists any *cardinal* measure of the single stock of knowledge. Yet it is common in the New Growth Theory (NGT) literature to treat the 'stock of knowledge' *as if* it were a single magnitude with a cardinal measure, without any justification being given for this highly dubious assumption.

7.2. CARDINALITY

Few if any authors indeed state explicitly that they suppose the stock of knowledge to be cardinally measurable. Yet they often assert this by implication. Let A represent the stock of knowledge. We read many times that a function with A as one of its arguments does (or does not) exhibit constant returns to scale. But either assertion is entirely meaningless if A is measurable only ordinally. Again, we frequently read that, in such a function, A has a decreasing (or increasing) marginal product – i.e., that *equal* successive increments in A yield decreasing (or increasing) increments in output. By the very meaning of ordinality, however, *no meaning* can be attached to the claim that successive increments in (ordinal) A are (or are not) equal.

Yet again, the relevant literature frequently presents equations in which $(\mathrm{d}A/\mathrm{d}t)$ is set equal to some *power* of A multiplied by other variables. These equations too are meaningless unless A is cardinally measurable. And yet they are never supported by any indication of how such a cardinal measure may be found or constructed.

This is certainly not 'measurement without theory'; it is theory without the minimal conceptual clarity required to make that theory coherent. No amount of 'sophisticated' mathematical analysis can derive valid and meaningful conclusions from conceptual confusions. As pointed out by Aghion and Howitt (1998, p. 435, quoted below), neither theory nor measurement can be adequate in the absence of conceptual clarity.

Lest any reader of an instrumentalist inclination should take our reference to 'valid and meaningful conclusions' to mean merely 'testable predictions', we may make two brief remarks. The first is that incoherent assumptions yield no valid conclusions at all – and it would be a diehard instrumentalist indeed who responded, 'who cares about logical validity?' The second remark is that, as noted at the beginning of this section, the NGT writings in question definitely *do* make a testable prediction – namely, that the 'stock of knowledge' has a cardinal measure. And this prediction may well be false. (As Samuelson famously pointed out in his critique of the 'F-twist', one cannot sensibly worry about the potential (dis-)confirmation of *some* of a theory's predictions and yet shrug off as irrelevant the disconfirmation of others.)

7.3.   SELECTED QUOTATIONS FROM THE LITERATURE

We should now perhaps establish that our critical remarks are not directed to a pure figment of our imagination – and recognize that worries about the measurement of knowledge can indeed be found within the NGT literature. The following examples are far from being exhaustive, of course, and it is not implied that every NGT model involves the kind of difficulty we are considering. Our examples are presented in historical order – which will make it clear that there has not been clear-cut progress in conceptual clarity about measuring knowledge!

In his famous 'learning-by-doing' paper (1962), Arrow painted a 'picture of technical change as a vast and prolonged process of learning about the environment in which we operate' (p. 155). He went straight on, however, to refer to a variable 'so difficult to measure as the quantity of knowledge' (ibidem). Sensibly, therefore, Arrow did *not* make any 'amount of knowledge' a central variable in his analysis but used, rather, cumulative gross investment – a measurable variable taken to be positively related to the acquisition of knowledge. Not everyone, alas, has followed Arrow's excellent (and very early) lead.

Romer (1986) begins his formal analysis with a two-period model in which 'production of consumption goods in period 2 is a function of the state of knowledge, denoted by k, and a set of additional factors ... denoted by a vector x' (p. 1014). This knowledge is produced 'from forgone consumption in period 1' (p. 1015). We then read that output in firm i is given by $F(k_i, \Sigma k_j, x_i)$, where $F(\ )$ is assumed to be *concave in k_i*, and that, 'Without this assumption, a competitive equilibrium will not exist in general' (p. 1015). But this crucial assumption involves a purely meaningless assertion (*re* concavity) unless the 'state of knowledge', k_i, is a cardinally measurable variable. And as to what might be the cardinal measure of the 'state of knowledge', Romer gives us no indication. Nothing daunted, he assures us that the production function exhibits 'global increasing marginal productivity of knowledge from a social point of view' (p. 1015). Talk of increasing (or decreasing, or constant) marginal productivity is, of course, empty talk *unless* the 'knowledge' variable has a cardinal measure.

Exactly comparable issues arise as Romer goes on to develop a continuous time, infinite horizon analysis (p. 1019 ff.) but we may conclude here by noting his later reference to a 'model in which knowledge and capital are used in fixed proportions' (pp. 1034–5); what could that reference possibly *mean* unless both knowledge and capital have cardinal measures?

In his 1988 contribution Lucas reasons in terms of 'human capital' rather than 'knowledge' and, as is well known, these two variables can be significantly different with respect to both rivalry and excludability. It may nevertheless be useful here to note some of his remarks relating to cardinality and measurability. Thus Lucas writes (p. 17): 'By an individual's 'human capital' I will mean ... simply his general skill level, so that a worker with human capital $h(t)$ is the productive equivalent of two workers with $\frac{1}{2}h(t)$ each, or a half-time worker with $2h(t)$'. What, one may wonder, is the cardinal measure of 'general skill level' that renders possible Lucas's statements about productive equivalence? His formal analysis certainly depends on the existence of such a measure, since his equation (13) (on p. 19):

$$\dot{h}(t) = \delta h(t)\big[1 - u(t)\big]$$

would be meaningless without it.

We do not suggest that Lucas is unaware of the measurement problem, however. To the contrary, he observes that 'we can no more directly measure the amount of human capital a society has, or the rate at which it is growing, than we can measure the degree to which a society is imbued with the Protestant ethic' (p. 35). After referring to human capital as a 'force, admittedly unobservable' (ibidem), he goes on to suggest that, 'Physical capital, too, is best viewed as a force, not directly observable, that we postulate in order to account in a unified way for certain things we *can* observe' (p. 36). *Even if* we admit these mysterious 'forces' a place in formal economic analysis, we may still be unconvinced that they can be represented in that analysis by cardinal measures exhibiting constant-returns-to-scale, diminishing/increasing marginal products, etc. Analogously, it is one thing to say that (exogenously or endogenously) increasing knowledge is important to economic growth; it is quite another to include it in references to returns-to-scale, variable marginal products, etc.

Romer's (1990) paper makes little advance over (1986) with respect to the issues at hand. At first we find a rather abstract discussion (p. S76) of the relations:

$$F(\lambda A, \lambda X) > \lambda F(A, X)$$

and:

$$F(A, X) < A\,\frac{\partial F}{\partial A} + X\frac{\partial F}{\partial X}$$

where A represents non-rival inputs and X rival inputs. But by (p. S77) we are reading of non-rival knowledge and of A as 'the benefits of research and development'. Are 'knowledge' and 'the benefits of R&D' synonymous expressions? Either way, are there cardinal measures of these magnitudes?

In his Section III, Romer explains that, 'The four basic inputs in this model are capital, labour, human capital, and an index of the level of technology' (pp. S78–79). It is noteworthy that Romer makes fairly clear remarks on how to measure the first two 'inputs', some vaguer remarks on measuring the third 'input' – and says nothing whatever on how to measure the fourth!

Romer presses on. The 'existing stock of knowledge' is an input in the research sector (p. S79) and the product of the research sector is *designs* for new producer durables (p. S79) or, by the next page, 'new designs or knowledge' (p. S80). At this stage in Romer's analysis A becomes *an integer*; but he is not really claiming to have produced a cardinal measure of the level of technology/knowledge/designs, of course. The integer nature of A is a mere artefact. Subsequently, in equation (3) of (p. S83):

$$\dot{A} = \delta H_A A,$$

where H_A is human capital in research and A is 'the total stock of designs and knowledge'. This equation is meaningless unless there are cardinal measures for both H_A and A.

In their discussion of 'Models with Learning-by-Doing and Knowledge Spillovers', Barro and Sala-i-Martin (1995) consider a production function for firm i:

$$Y_i = F(K_i, A_i L_i)$$

'where L_i and K_i are the conventional inputs, and A_i is the index of knowledge available to the firm' (p. 146; by p. 147, A_i has become the firm's 'stock of knowledge'). We are told that 'a steady state exists when A_i grows at a constant rate' (p. 146). And what can that *mean* when A_i is an 'index' or a 'stock of knowledge'? Nothing; unless A_i has a cardinal measure and, once again, we are told nothing of how such a measure may be found or constructed.

A ray of hope in the general gloom of conceptual vagueness has been provided recently by Aghion and Howitt, who offer a 14-page appendix 'On Some Problems in Measuring Knowledge-Based Growth' (1998, pp. 435–448; 14 pages, that is, in a volume of 694 pages). They note immediately that 'we do not have any generally accepted empirical measures of such key theoretical concepts as the stock of technological knowledge, human capital … the rate of obsolescence of old knowledge, and so forth' (p. 435). And they make it perfectly clear that the problem is not a purely empirical or data problem:

It would be more accurate to say that formal theory is ahead of conceptual clarity. As the English side of the Cambridge capital controversy used to insist, the real question is one of meaning, not measurement. Only when theory produces clear conceptual categories will it be possible to measure them accurately. (Aghion and Howitt, 1998, p. 435)

Aghion and Howitt do not pretend to have resolved all the relevant issues – far from it – but they do identify the problem at hand and begin to think it through. (It is to be hoped that their attempt attracts more attention than did Arrow's clear (1962) warning!) They conclude:

If the critical component of our discussion in this appendix has been larger than the constructive component, this is mainly attributable to the fact that what is at issue is not something likely to be fixed by minor tinkering with national income accounting practices ... a better conceptual foundation is needed before we know just what magnitudes to look at and how. (p. 447)

These warnings seem to have come too late for Jones (1999), however. Surveying 'The Romer/Grossman–Helpman/Aghion–Howitt Models' he writes (p. 140):

$$Y = A^\sigma L_Y$$

and:

$$\dot{A} / A = \delta L_A,$$

where A is 'the stock of ideas'. (These equations are also said (p. 141) to reappear in 'The Young/Peretto/Aghion–Howitt/Dinopoulos–Thompson Models' with a variable number of products.) And with respect to 'The Jones/Kortum/Segerstom Model' he states (p. 140) that the second equation is replaced by:

$$\dot{A} = \delta L_A A^\varphi,$$

where $\varphi < 1$ may be positive or negative. Nowhere is it even mentioned that these equations have no meaning if there is not a cardinal measure of 'the stock of ideas'.

7.4.   CONCLUDING REMARKS

A surprisingly high proportion of the NGT literature involves the elaborate analysis of models based on completely unclear assumptions, offering for example (non-) constant returns and variable marginal products with respect to variables one of which – the stock of knowledge – has not been shown to be, and may well not be, cardinally measurable. This is greatly to be regretted, since the analysis of equations having no meaning cannot yield convincing conclusions. One must hope that the clear warnings sounded 40 years ago by Arrow and, more recently, by Aghion and Howitt, will at last begin to be taken seriously.

REFERENCES

Aghion, P. and P. Howitt (1998), *Endogenous Growth Theory*, Cambridge, Massachusetts: MIT Press.

Arrow, K.J. (1962), 'The economic implications of learning-by-doing', *Review of Economic Studies*, **29**(1), 155–73.

Barro, R.J. and X. Sala-i-Martin (1995), *Economic Growth*, New York: McGraw-Hill.

Jones, C.I. (1999), 'Growth: with or without scale effects?', *American Economic Review (Papers & Proceedings)*, May, 139–44.

Lucas, R.E. (1988), 'On the mechanics of economic development', *Journal of Monetary Economics*, **22**, 3–42.

Metcalfe, J.S. (2001), 'Institutions and progress', *Industrial and Corporate Change*, **10**(3), 561–85.

Olsson, O. (2001), 'The appearance of knowledge in growth theory', *Economic Issues*, **6**(1), 1–20.

Romer, P.M. (1986), 'Increasing returns and long-run growth', *Journal of Political Economy*, **94**, 1002–37.

Romer, P.M. (1990), 'Endogenous technical change', *Journal of Political Economy*, **98**, S71–S102.

8. On the mechanics of technical change: new and old ideas in economic growth[*]

Theo S. Eicher

8.1. INTRODUCTION

This chapter discusses microfoundations of technological change in order to systematically integrate the production of new technology into the study of economic growth. The issue is not whether technology is generated endogenously or exogenously, but rather the task is to describe plausible mechanics of the research process.

Technical change has been an integral part of the economic growth literature from the very beginning. The most prominent examples might be Smith's pin factory, Ricardo's discussion of labour augmenting technical change and its effects on growth and distribution. However, the salient feature of technology in the discussion of economic growth has been the researchers' willingness to treat the mechanics of technical change itself as exogenous.

Even the earliest reference of the impact of technical change on growth lack specifics, for example, Adam Smith thought that technological innovations simply arise from workmen who become specialists without any clear notion of the actual process of innovation, i.e., whether it is due to learning by doing, to apprenticeship programmes, or formal education. This tradition continued to the Solow model which takes an even more agnostic stand – casually labelling the 'residual' (the 87.5 percent of growth not explained by the model, Solow 1957) 'technical change'. The *mechanics* of technical change were not nearly as important to the classical and neoclassical growth theorists as the study of the comparative statics *effects* of technical change.

It is easy to argue that the study of the effects of technical change is a natural starting point – but that does not explain satisfactorily why the mechanics of new technology development were never tackled in a formal manner. How detrimental the absence of endogenous technical change can be to the validity of the implications of the model has been proven many times over, most notably by Thomas Malthus.

In this sense the new growth theory – commencing with Paul Romer's (1983) PhD Thesis at the University of Chicago – deserves its name; it is not an immediate extension of any previous branch of the growth literature as it incorporates a fundamental break with the past with its emphasis on the exact properties and characteristics of endogenous technological change. Key to understanding the innovations contained in R&D-based growth models is an appreciation of the differences between technology and human capital on the one hand, and labour and physical capital on the other.

The earlier discussions of growth models from Smith and Ricardo to the formal models of Harrod (1960), Domar (1946), and Solow (1956), share their focus on capital accumulation and as the engine of per capita growth. Unfortunately, the notion of 'capital' was often a loosely defined concept that usually referred to physical capital, but which could also include knowledge, human capital or technology at times. Solow (1957) tested the historical approach, which postulated that growth was driven by physical capital deepening. In a stunning find he discovered that only 12.5 percent of US growth in output between 1909 and 1949 could be attributed to physical capital accumulation and population growth.

Leaving such a large share of growth unexplained implicitly assigned a large role to technological progress to account for US growth. Today it seems obvious that the prime candidate to fill the void would be technological change. Grossman and Helpman (1991a) point out that economists did not necessarily consider the evolution of technology as part of economic analysis. State of the art were pure growth accounting exercises that sought to simply measure the unexplained residual, which would then be labelled technological change. Kaldor (1957) countered the residual approach to technology by introducing a Technical Progress Function where productivity growth is related to gross investment, much like Arrow (1962). While Kaldor and Arrow emphasize the importance of integrating technology as part of a fully specified economic model, their mechanics of technical change do not recognize that technology might be a fundamentally different factor, as its accumulation is specified to be largely a by-product of physical capital investment. Shell (1966) introduced a formal technology sector, however, the decision to innovate is taken by a planner, without formal structure to decentralize the innovation decision.

On a simple technical level there were seemingly insurmountable modelling obstacles to introducing intentional R&D into a model with perfect competition and constant returns to scale. Solow spent years collaborating with the GM research and development team to study the mechanics of technical change, but finally concluded that he could not meaningfully discuss the subject.

Eventually growth theory became increasingly technical, some suggest it lost touch with the empirical applications (Barro and Sala-i-Martin, 1995 p. 12). The oil shocks of the 1970s certainly altered the focus from long-run growth to short-run fluctuations, and from infinite, balanced growth to the study of exhaustible resources and business cycles. To address the shortcomings of the purely capital/investment based approach to economic growth, an alternative was sought that was to be based explicitly on a well-specified process of technical change, determined within the model, by profit maximizing agents. Romer (1987, 1990), Grossman and Helpman (1990, 1991b), Segerstrom et al. (1990) and Aghion and Howitt (1989, 1992) developed similar approaches to endogenize technology in a growth model. The break with the past was drastic. Leaving constant returns and perfect competition behind, the new models rely on monopolies, oligopolistic competition, or monopolistic competition to allow firms to recapture research outlays. Instead of relying on population growth or exogenous technology parameters, the growth rate of the models is now determined by research effort and the determinants of success in R&D.

Fundamental to the development of the new class of R&D-based growth models was the insight that the characteristics of technology and physical capital differ profoundly. First, technology has a distinct, non-rival nature, which implies that its use in one activity does not necessarily preclude its utilization in another. Second, technology may also be to some degree non-excludable, since the owners of patents usually face great difficulties preventing competitors from also using the technology (i.e. to discover even better technologies). Third, there is ample reason to justify the existence of positive long-run growth rates based on innovation. Knowledge is neither an exhaustible resource, nor does it face the same obvious limits to accumulation as physical capital.

Within the literature of R&D-based growth models, two approaches resulted. First, Judd (1985), Romer (1986) and Grossman and Helpman (1991b) developed models based on increasing product varieties, then followed the quality ladder models of Aghion and Howitt (1989, 1992) and Segerstrom et al. (1990). Models based on product variety assume agents' love of variety, so that continuous innovations of new product varieties sustain growth in the long run. A powerful interpretation of the product variety approach is that it formalizes the idea that continued specialization of labour across different varieties of activities generates economic benefits. Aghion and Howitt (1989) instead focus exclusively on quality ladder models, which they label 'The Schumpeterian Approach'. In quality ladder models, ever-new technology improvements generate positive growth rates of income and consumption. The strands of the literature have been unified recently and the current state of the art is an amalgam of the product variety and quality ladder approach, where products experience not only increases in varieties, but also changes in production costs, or qualities; see Young (1998), Howitt (1999) and Eicher and Kim (2003).

The fundamental drawback of this new growth literature is that – while technology is endogenous – only residual interest focuses on the actual process of technology creation and evolution. Consequently technology is customarily modelled much like any other factor of production. Research functions in R&D-based growth models are thus at best reduced forms that focus on blueprint accumulation by simply mapping input quantities into blueprints, instead of representing a process of technology creation that takes into account how new technologies come about. Weitzman (1998) criticizes this approach as 'technological progress in a black box', lamenting that ' "new ideas" are simply taken to be some exogenously function of "research effort" in the spirit of a humdrum conventional relationship between inputs and outputs'.

Unconstrained by modelling limitations, the descriptive literature on the nature of the invention process extends far beyond a list of determinants of blueprint accumulation. Real world observations emphasize the stochastic, trial-and-error nature of generating and managing new ideas. In this chapter I seek to suggest a structure of the actual research process. To endogenize research productivity, I describe an evolutionary search algorithm that has found widespread applications in the (social) sciences. Based on the principle of the survival of the fittest, Holland (1970) developed this algorithm to emulate biological search and selection processes. It can be interpreted as a variant of adaptive learning, or as an augmented combinatorial optimization process. Due to its origins in evolutionary biology, it was originally entitled genetic algorithm.

The novel implications that result from the application of the evolutionary search algorithm are pertaining to the determinants of economic growth. Aside from the parameters that determine the growth rate in previous R&D-based growth models, I show that the mechanics and efficiency of the search process now influence the growth rate. The new research specification is shown to generate distinct research productivities among parametrically identical countries – productivities that signify the trials and errors involved in learning and managing new ideas. This model allows also for convergence and leapfrogging due to an international exchange of ideas between high and low growth countries. Finally, evolutionary search breaks the direct relationship between scale and growth, since the share of the factor allocated to R&D is now a function of endogenous research productivity.

8.2.   THE EVOLUTIONARY APPROACH

The evolutionary approach to search in research can be seen as a formalization and extension of Romer's (1993) toy model, a first attempt to highlight the complexity of the search problem researchers face. Below technology is created by two types of inputs: (1) the usual factor of production (labour), and (2) ideas. Instead of the constant and exogenous research productivity in previous growth models, I assume researchers manipulate the universe of ideas according to the evolutionary search algorithm to alter the research productivity.

Ideas and researchers interact. As time and research progress, and as researchers select relatively more successful ideas more often (selection), proven ideas become more prevalent over time as they are imitated with increasing frequency (reproduction).[1] Researchers also experiment by combining elements of different ideas to generate completely new ideas (crossover or recombination) in a manner that has been shown to mimic human behaviour. Experimentation provides structure to the process by which an individual idea might initially not be the most productive, but in combination with another idea it may generate extremely high research productivity. Over time, the universe of ideas changes as the experimentation, selection and reproduction criteria generate an increased uniformity of ideas, until all researchers adopt the same way of thinking. At this point the algorithm (and research productivity) achieves a steady state.

The evolution of a universe of ideas takes place within a multimodal search space (or, landscape, see Krugman, 1994). This contrasts sharply with the well-behaved, single-peaked research functions in the common R&D-based growth model. The fundamental advantage of the evolutionary search algorithm is its ability to allow for a vast diversity of ideas at initial stages of development, as well as its capability to manage an increased dominance of highly productive ideas via experimentation and learning on the part of the researchers.

Versions of the evolutionary algorithm have been used extensively in the social sciences in general and in economics specifically. A survey of seminal papers is provided by Riechmann (1999) and Clemens and Riechmann (1996). However, previous applications have been limited to utilizing the algorithm's excellent search properties in selecting optimal numerical solutions among alternative rational expectation equilibria, as for example in cases of indeterminacy (e.g. Marimon et al., 1990), or to optimize functions in econometrics. I do not employ the algorithm in order to aid an optimization process, but to provide a structure to the process by which ideas are produced and selected in research. Much like Vriend (1995), who uses such an evolutionary algorithm to explain self-organizations of markets, I employ the algorithm to provide microfoundations to search in research.[2] Birchenhall (1995) used evolutionary algorithms to examine the economic implications of 'modular technology' where the production function depends on a number of ideas or technologies that are distributed across an economic population; evolutionary learning is then a process of population learning.

Previous models of endogenous technical change that allow for stochastic innovation are for the most part based on a Poisson process to permit analytical tractability rather than to reflect realism (see Aghion and Howitt, 1992).[3] In equilibrium, deterministic and Poisson innovation processes generate largely identical implications for the determinants of growth rates. Hence experimentation, guessing, creative exploring, and imitating has not been an explicit part of the research modelling.[4]

Most similar to my approach to search in research is the combinatorial approach of Weitzman (1998) and the adaptive learning featured in Jovanovic and Nyarko (1996). Jovanovic and Nyarko rely on Baysian learning to provide structure to learning by doing, where agents do not know the true productivity of an existing technology, but where continued usage reveals further information. Analogously, the evolutionary search algorithm I employ below provides structure to the research process that generates technical change, since I allow for completely new ideas to be introduced as part of the research process. Weitzman (1998) also provides microfoundations to the knowledge producing function in the R&D-based growth model, to investigate the resulting properties of growth rates. His Recombinant Growth model relies on reconfigured old ideas; the selection and reproduction properties of the evolutionary algorithm employed below are absent. Hence the management of diversity becomes the limiting factor in his model of recombinant growth. Our result confirms Weitzman's (1992) earlier insight that there may exist optimal levels of diversity. The mechanics of the evolutionary algorithm introduced below have been shown to efficiently manage the trade-off between recombination and diversity.

Reaching equilibrium on a local maximum is a distinct possibility in evolution as well as in the economy described below, as the algorithm trades diversity for quality over time. Each time a low quality idea is discarded and lost, as a higher quality idea is imitated, the lost diversity limits the future scope of experimentation. Hence the ideas needed to propel the research effort to global maxima may have either never been discovered, or their individual quality or prevalence at the time of discovery was initially comparatively small. Thus ideas may be washed out by the strong prevalence of initially more successful ideas. The Brazilian rainforests motivate a good example, where the current destruction of biodiversity to satisfy present-day manufacturing may limit future welfare, as important but undiscovered chemical compounds may be destroyed forever.

As a consequence of the trade-off between quality and variety, parametrically identical countries may not converge to identical growth rates. The intuition relies on the well-known result that, when as technical change is no longer assumed to be deterministic, it is also no longer guaranteed that the research process converges quickly to a maximum (see Aghion and Howitt, 1998). Most interesting are the implications for cross-country convergence. If a high and low growth country (*A* and *B* respectively) have not attained the most effective idea in research, they may well benefit from globalization, the worldwide exchange of ideas. Even if Country *B* uses ideas that exhibit lower productivity in research than Country *A*, the high growth country may still gain from the exchange of ideas because of increased diversity. This is because less productive ideas from Country *A* at time *t* might generate improved research productivity in the high growth country via experimentation, as parts of ideas from both countries are combined. Such search dynamics may lead to convergence or overtaking, if the laggard actually gains more from the leader's idea than vice versa.[5] The alternative may, however, also be true, in that ideas promulgated by globalization might also lower the growth rate. Immiserizing globalization occurs when foreign ideas do not combine well with the domestic ideas. In this case unusually prevalent foreign ideas may slowly extinguish the domestic best practice.

Divergence due to globalization is quite common in the trade and growth literature, where it is usually due to trade-induced reduction of one country's production of the high learning (growth) content good. Convergence can be achieved through international spillovers (see, for example, Howitt 2000), but overtaking is much rarer. In Jovanovic and Nyarko (1996) the possibility of overtaking also exists, and Xie (1994) also features overtaking in the Lucas model, but has to rely on complex dynamics. Brezis et al. (1993) actually allow for leapfrogging, a more dramatic form of overtaking. Their model shows that Ricardian technology, together with differential technology adoption costs, can even lead to cycles in technological leadership. In the model below the origin of overtaking (and divergence) is simply the exchange of ideas and the differential gain in productivity achieved by differential degrees of complementary of ideas, and because of the inherent randomness of the search process.

8.3. THE MODEL

Without exception, R&D-based growth models represent technical change with increased product quality or variety (or both). At the same time, however, this class of models is largely agnostic about the determinants of research productivity, or of the invention process. Hence research productivity is assumed to be exogenous and constant. To highlight the impact of this assumed exogeneity I present the bare bones of a standard growth model first, together with the determinants of equilibrium growth. Then I introduce the evolutionary search algorithm to provide microfoundations to the research process in a model and in simulations. The novel implications regarding the resulting growth rate and the effects of openness to foreign ideas can then be discussed.

I introduce evolutionary search into a Schumpeterian model of economic growth. The starting point is a simple quality ladder model of technical change. The economy produces one final good that uses technology and an intermediate good. New technology is developed by the fraction of the population devoted to research, and a successful innovation together with one unit of labour generates a higher quality intermediate good. Economic growth is thus the result of a sequence of quality improving innovations. Details and extensions of the basic quality ladder model can be obtained from the original Aghion and Howitt (1992) paper; and real world realism can (and has been) added to extend the base model in multiple dimensions (for a summary, see Aghion and Howitt, 1998). None of these extensions alter the impact of evolutionary search on economic growth; all the qualitative results reported below are robust.

8.3.1. Bare Bones

We abstract from capital formation, and assume a constant labour force, L. At time τ, infinitely lived households maximize utility:

$$U(y_\tau) = \int_0^\infty e^{-r\tau} y_\tau d\tau, \tag{8.1}$$

Output of a consumption good, y, is produced in a competitive sector with technology, A, and an intermediate input, x:

$$y_\tau = A_\tau x_\tau^a, \quad \alpha < 1. \tag{8.2}$$

The production of a unit of x requires one unit of labour. Whenever a better quality intermediate good becomes available, it replaces the old and raises the technological efficiency, A, by a constant amount g.[6] If n units of labour are devoted to research, $a \cdot n$ innovations result, where $a > 0$ is the productivity parameter of labour in research.[7] It is this productivity parameter, which will be endogenized below with the aid of an evolutionary search algorithm.

When a firm invents a new technology, it obtains an infinitely lived patent to become the monopoly supplier of the intermediate good. Given the labour constraint:

$$L = x_\tau + n_\tau,$$ (8.3)

the amount of labour devoted to research is determined by the incentive condition that, at the margin, the discounted expected value of a future innovation, V_{t+1}, must equal today's unit cost of research, w_t:

$$w_t = aV_{t+1},$$ (8.4)

To simplify matters, we add notation; while τ above represents real time, t now represents the duration between innovations. We unify the representation in terms of real time when we discuss the growth rate below.

The expected value of an innovation depends on the discounted monopoly profits derived from manufacturing the intermediate good minus the discounted expected capital loss. The latter is given by the probability that more sophisticated inputs fully destruct the current monopolist supplier's profits:

$$V_{t+1} = \frac{\left(\pi_{t+1} - an_{t+1}V_{t+1}\right)}{r}.$$ (8.5)

Profit maximization for the monopolist is entirely standard. Given the demand curve derived from the final goods, the optimal quantity of the intermediate input can be written in terms of the productivity adjusted wage, $\omega \equiv w/A$:

$$x_t = \left(\frac{\alpha^2}{\omega_t}\right)^{\frac{1}{(1-\alpha)}},$$ (8.6)

which implies a level of profits:

$$\pi_t = w_t x_t \left(\alpha^{-1} - 1\right),$$ (8.7)

Equations (8.6 and 8.7) express the common result that the volume of intermediate good production and profits are a decreasing function of the productivity-adjusted wage. Higher demand for future labour, generated by a more productive blueprint, decreases the profit flow of future innovators.

8.3.2. Stationary Equilibrium

I focus on the stationary state where $\omega_t = \omega_{t+1} = \omega^*, n_t = n_{t+1} = n^*$ (see Aghion and Howitt, 1992, for the dynamics). Equations (8.5) and (8.7) can be substituted into the incentive and labour constraints to yield the steady-state wage and the share of labour in research. Placing these values into the production function renders the average growth rate, β, determined by:

$$\beta = an^* \ln g \tag{8.8}$$

The determinants of the growth rate imply that the performance of countries varies according to (1) their exogenous productivity in research, (2) their exogenous incremental increase in technology when new innovations arrive, and (3) the share of labour in R&D. The latter quantity is endogenously determined by the interest rate, the elasticity of demand, the size of the population, and by the productivity in research.

The point of this chapter is not to outline the exact parameters that determine growth rates; these are in part dependent on the exact microfoundations of the model, as Aghion and Howitt (1998) and Jones and Williams (1998) amply lay out. The purpose is to attract attention to the implications that are directly contingent on the reduced form of the research function and on the exogeneity of the research productivity, a. Once exogenous differences in preferences and in the underlying parameters (in the simple case above, g, r, L) are accounted for, R&D-based growth models predict that all countries grow at the same steady-state rate. In this case, the absence of some basic understanding of the determinants of research productivity voids any chance of explaining cross-country variations in terms of research or total factor productivity growth.

More dramatic are the implications for international flow of knowledge. The evidence strongly suggests significant spillovers between countries, although the impact of such spillovers varies across countries (Eaton and Kortum, 1997). When a country opens to the outside world of ideas, the mechanism by which ideas are incorporated, developed and propagated becomes a crucial factor. While models of endogenous technical change allow for endogenous growth, they provide no insight into how exactly the exchange of ideas across countries may or may not be beneficial.

Specifically, the model predicts that when two identical countries, (A, B), open up to the ideas of the outside world, the growth rate simply doubles in both countries (assuming away duplication etc.):

$$\beta_{A,B} = a\left(n_A^* + n_B^*\right)\ln g = a2n^* \ln g. \tag{8.8'}$$

From (8.8') it is easily to see the common conclusion of the endogenous growth literature that even parametrically distinct countries with very different growth rates will both gain from opening to the world of ideas, if both continue to conduct research (for exceptions to these general results see Rivera-Batiz and Romer, 1994, and Feenstra, 1996). While the change in the growth rates does not necessarily have to be identical (depending on how countries differ in the underlying parameters), overtaking is, in general, impossible in this setup (exceptions are discussed in the introduction).

These properties of the growth rate highlight that the reduced form of the R&D function leaves much room for interpretation, which does not increase but limit the generality of the models. For example, the returns to scale in the research sector are dictated by the assumption of whether or not the factors in R&D are modelled endogenously or not (see Jones 1995). The absence of substance in the R&D sector that would explain how international ideas are integrated into domestic thinking is not due to sloppy modelling, however. The descriptive literature is vast and empirical guidance to judge the relative importance of the different approaches for different levels of aggregation is scant.

The key problem in the empirical work has been how to measure R&D outputs and inputs. Hence without comprehensive guidance from the empirical literature, constant productivity may simply be an acceptable first approximation.[8] It is important to keep in mind, however, that the assumption of constant productivity in research drives important conclusions of the model, the convergence implication in particular.

The alternative to employing an agnostic approach to modelling research is to apply search algorithms that have been proven to be efficient, relevant and applicable in a wide range of areas in the social sciences. Indeed the evolutionary algorithm below was developed to replicate the genetic selection process and soon found widespread application as a search process in the social sciences, too.

8.4.   ENDOGENOUS PRODUCTIVITY IN RESEARCH

In this section I introduce the mechanics of the evolutionary search algorithm. To preserve maximum simplicity while integrating endogenous search into the above model of endogenous technical change, I adopt the same model as above with the modification that research productivity, now $a(t)$, is endogenously determined by the search algorithm. Without loss of generality, the algorithm outlined below is stripped of all unnecessary layers of complexities that have been added to in the literature.

The evolutionary algorithm describes the means by which one universe (or set) of ideas is transformed into another as time progresses. To achieve this transformation the algorithm dictates researchers a set of rules based on learning/imitation and experimentation.

8.4.1. Formal Definitions of the Evolutionary Algorithm

An idea, i, is represented by a bit string of length q, which contains an array of information, for example, a list of rules (the formalization of the algorithm here follows Riechmann, 1999). I adopt a binary representation, which Holland (1975) argues to be the most general. Let the value of a binary number, $\gamma(i,t)$, determine the quality of idea i in terms of productivity in research at time t.[9] Given the choice of a binary representation, the set of all possible different ideas of length q is then given by $S \in \{0,1\}^q$, which implies that there are at most $|S| \equiv N = 2^q$ different ideas.

I assume that the universe of ideas available to any particular research sector is of size Z, which may or may not exceed N, since Z may contain several identical ideas in contrast to N. I also assume $Z < \infty$, which implicitly imposes a resource constraint. A simple way to motivate a limited number of ideas in the universe at each time, t, is to assume that each researcher can only manage ξ ideas in each period so that $Z = \xi n$. Such an assumption would, however, only complicate the simulations, not the quality of the results.

The absolute frequency of ideas of type i at time t is denoted by $m(i,t)$, which allows us to represent the universe of ideas as a vector, $\bar{m}(t) = (m(1,t), ..., m(N,t))$. I assume that the research productivity is a function of the average quality of the ideas circulating in research:

$$a_t = \frac{1}{Z}\sum_i^Z \gamma_t^i, \tag{8.9}$$

where a_t now reflects the mechanics of search, the efficiency of search, and the size and properties of the search space. Since the output of the research activity is new blueprints, researchers are paid according to their productivity in terms of blueprints generated. The marginal product of researchers is thus a_t, which rewards researchers for their sorting and experimentation efforts that result in $a_t n_t$ innovations.

8.4.2. Learning by Imitation

To provide a mechanism for 'natural selection' among ideas, the evolutionary algorithm offers several methods of learning. We start with the simplest method in which unproductive ideas are de-emphasized and eventually discarded, while successful ideas are increasingly imitated. Learning by imitation determines whether a specific idea is used again in the future (reproduction), and how widespread its usage should be (selection).[10]

Through imitation the old universe of ideas is transformed into a new one from period t to $t+1$. Essentially imitation is the process by which researchers select relatively more productive ideas more frequently over time. Formally, imitation is characterized by 'drawing' ideas (with replacement) from the old universe of ideas for use in the next period. The chance of any one idea in $\bar{m}(t-1)$ to be imitated, $P_1\left(i \mid \bar{m}(t-1)\right)$, to be part of the universe of ideas at time t is:

$$P_1\left(i \mid \bar{m}(t-1)\right) = \frac{m(i,t-1)\gamma(i,t-1)}{\sum_{j \in S^N} m(j,t-1)\gamma(j,t-1)} \qquad (8.10)$$

Hence the likelihood that any given idea being imitated is a function of the idea's relative quality and frequency. In terms of research, this process can be interpreted as researchers discarding ideas that produce relatively low research productivity, and imitating ideas that are relatively more successful. Note that this specification does permit propagation of a bad idea, especially if by some strange fluke the use of that type of idea was frequent or widespread in the past.

The evolution of the universe of ideas from $t-1$ to t can be represented by the transition probability of a transition matrix describing the algorithm as a Markov process:

$$P_1\left(\bar{m}(t) \mid \bar{m}(t-1)\right) = \frac{Z\,!}{\prod_{i \in S}\{m(i,t-1)\}!} \prod_{i \in S} P_1\left(i \mid \bar{m}(i,t-1)\right)^{m(i,t-1)} \qquad (8.11)$$

Essentially (8.11) gives the probability of each possible outcome of a multinomial distribution. The equation specifies how a new universe of ideas is formed from the ideas that are imitated. Drawing from the pool of imitated ideas with replacement, $P_1\left(\bar{m}(t) \mid \bar{m}(t-1)\right)$ gives the probability that any vector $\bar{m}(t)$ will result.

The research process reaches its steady state as relatively unproductive and infrequently used ideas are continuously discarded, while relatively better and prevalent ideas become more frequently used. In the steady state, one idea, i^*, establishes itself as the best practice. Every universe that consists of only one type of an idea is a steady state, and since there is a total of 2^q possible different ideas, there are at most that many possible steady states. Since every steady state can be reached from at least one of the remaining transient states, the Markov process will inevitably end up in one steady state. The evolutionary algorithm thus always leads to a uniform universe of ideas, $m(i^*) = Z$, with constant R&D productivity, $a^* = \gamma(i^*)$.

The fact that not only quality but also frequency counts implies that researchers may not find the most productive idea. In effect this simplest version of the evolutionary search algorithm may be stuck in a local maximum, since the best idea may not have been prevalent enough in the early stages of development. An additional drawback is that the search is constrained by the set of initially available ideas, Z, which may not contain the entire possible best of ideas, N. Hence in this version of the algorithm no truly new discoveries are made, and researchers are only provided with a mechanism for achieving a best practice. The natural extension of this simple evolutionary search algorithm for the research sector is thus to allow for experimentation.

8.4.3 Learning by Imitation and Experimentation

Experimentation allows for a meaningful exchange of ideas among researchers within a lab or a country (and even between countries, as discussed below). Weitzman (1998) previously introduced experimentation via recombination, where two old ideas form a new hybrid. The evolutionary algorithm is more general, since it allows researchers to take any part of one idea and combine it with some part of another idea to create an entirely new idea. The share of each old idea that forms any new idea is, for simplicity, assumed to be random.[11] In addition, after experimentation the algorithm provides a procedure to examine the quality of the new idea and thus its ability to be imitated in the future.

Formally, experimentation in the evolutionary search algorithm can be expressed as a function, $I(i, j, k, p)$, which returns the value 0 or 1. The ideas chosen as inputs for the experimentation process are i and j, respectively, and k identifies the resulting new idea. How much of each old idea becomes part of the new idea k is determined by $p \in \{1, 2, ..., q-1\}$. In the bit string formulation of evolutionary algorithms, p, is the crossover point that indicates the length of the first (second) part of i and the second (first) part of j if $I(.)$ returns 1(0). The Appendix provides an example. It is important that experimentation combines two parts of two ideas, but the productivity of the new idea may be related to neither parent. Experimentation thus allows that new ideas are more than the combined total of the previous ideas. A new idea may actually break entirely new ground and be many times more successful (or worse) than either one of its predecessors.

The probability of any one idea being chosen for experimentation is χ, and the probability of obtaining an idea k from a palette of ideas via imitation and experimentation is:

$$P_2\big(k \mid \bar{m}(t-1)\big) = (1-\chi)P_1\big(k \mid \bar{m}(t-1)\big) +$$

$$+\chi\sum_{i\in S}\sum_{i\in S}P_1\big(i \mid \bar{m}(t-1)\big)P_1\big(j \mid \bar{m}(t-1)\big)\frac{\displaystyle\sum_{p=1}^{q-1}I(i,j,k,p)}{q-1}, \qquad (8.12)$$

which is the probability that an idea is not chosen for experimentation but still selected for imitation, plus the probability that an idea that is the product of experimentation is chosen for imitation. Similarly to the case of pure imitation, the probability of any universe of ideas $\bar{m}(t+1)$ becoming the successor of the universe $\bar{m}(t)$ by reproduction and selection is given the transition probability:

$$P_2\big(\bar{m}(t) \mid \bar{m}(t-1)\big) = \frac{Z!}{\displaystyle\prod_{i\in S} m(i,t-1)!}\prod_{i\in S}P_2\big(i \mid \bar{m}(i,t-1)\big)^{m(i,t-1)} \qquad (8.13)$$

Managing the multimodal search space with this evolutionary algorithm is often compared to a hill-climbing exercise, as the topographic representation of the search space resembles a rugged mountain terrain. The highest peak is the global maximum of the research productivity. Given the evolutionary search process outlined above, even with experimentation it is still possible that the search stops prematurely, at a local maximum. Local maxima may now occur for two reasons. First, as in the case of pure imitation, the best idea may not be frequent enough at the crucial stage of development. Second, and more importantly, as old and unproductive ideas are de-emphasized and eventually discarded, the pool of ideas loses precious diversity. Only sufficient diversity allows for the possibility that future experimentation leads down to form a local maximum and towards more efficient ideas. For example, an idea may not have been the most productive at the time it is discovered, but it may have held information that could, in combination with another idea, generate the most productive idea of all. Hence, the drive towards a best practice idea comes at the cost of forgone diversity and potential future productivity, as in the case of the Brazilian rainforest mentioned above.[12]

In terms of the equilibrium properties, experimentation does not change the qualitative implication of the algorithm; the system still attains one unique stationary state that is characterized by a homogeneous set of ideas. Experimentation does allow, however, for inventions of new ideas that potentially expand the initial pool of ideas significantly, hence it extends the search time and space relative to the pure imitation-based search algorithm. Hence experimentation generates a higher expected productivity of the equilibrium best practice. With endogenous research productivity, the new growth rate of a country is now:

$$\beta = \gamma(i^*)n^* \ln g$$

where $\gamma(i^*)$ is the quality of the best practice idea and the efficiency in research as determined by the evolutionary algorithm.

8.5. IMPLICATIONS

The search algorithm augments the previous results of the literature. The growth rate is constant along the balanced growth path, and determined by the underlying economic parameters outlined above. What is new is that the endogeneity of the research productivity affects the growth rate not only directly, but also through n^*, which now depends positively on a^* (given (8.3)–(8.7) and (8.9)). Also new is that even parametrically identical countries may exhibit different growth rates, if their productivities in research differ due to different outcomes in their evolutionary optimization. This result follows in part from the rugged search space, and also from the character of the search activity, which trades diversity for quality. Not reaching the global maximum is, however, never the result of bounded rationality, or sub-optimal search. Instead local maxima reflect the trade-off between diversity (maintaining a large set of different ideas for experimentation) and uniformity (selecting higher quality ideas more frequently) to develop the most efficient common practice in research.

These results highlight that fast convergence to the eventual steady state is not necessarily an advantageous characteristic of an economy, because it implies that the country quickly trades diversity for quality of ideas. If the quality level chosen is a local minimum, the country is no better off than a country that searches for a long time and maintains diversity and climbs slowly to the global maximum.

Finally, it is noteworthy to point out that globalization raises n^* in the basic Aghion and Howitt model, simply because the size of the market increases. Here, the share of factors allocated to the R&D sector is a positive function of the average productivity of research, hence an increase in n^* is no longer guaranteed. Certainly the size of the market will again have a positive influence on n^*, but we now must also consider the direct effect of the research productivity, which may be negative as pointed out above. Hence the direct relation between size and growth rate is severed and it is now dominated by the relative quality and by the interaction between domestic and foreign ideas.

8.6.   CONCLUSION

The chapter seeks to illuminate part of the black box that is commonly associated with the formal modelling of technical change. Instead of specifying a simple input–output relationship between researchers and new technologies, I introduce an evolutionary algorithm as a search procedure for researchers to manage the universe of ideas. In that sense the model provides additional structure or microfoundations to the innovation process.

The introduction of the search algorithm to research has two distinct advantages. First, it introduces a truly stochastic nature to the search process, a process in which diversity of ideas matters as much as continued selection and imitation of higher quality ideas. Second, it allows for gains from informational exchange between countries, as the exchange of ideas may be beneficial to both leader and laggard countries. Most interesting is the interaction of the ideas and the role that the information exchange plays. In essence opening to another economy's world of ideas increases the diversity of ideas and allows for more fruitful experimentation and possible the development of higher quality ideas.

The application of the algorithm to search is not limited to explaining worker productivity. Once can easily imagine that alternatively the size of the innovation, or the productivity of a blueprint in output could be explained by the algorithm. Only the interpretation, but none of the results, would change. This highlights that the range of applications of the algorithm is quite wide, and that I have chosen in this chapter to provide only one example, one in which research productivity is endogenized. I judge this example to be the most natural one, but by no means the only application of the algorithm to economic growth.

APPENDIX

The Evolutionary Research Algorithm Instructions

1.   Create a new universe of ideas (draw ideas from the past universe, given (8.11) or (8.13))
2.   Evaluate universe of ideas (establish the quality of each idea)
3.   Experiment with ideas (choose any pair of ideas with probability χ)
4.   Imitate ideas (replicate ideas that have proven successful given (8.10) or (8.12))
5.   Evaluate the universe of ideas
6.   Find the average quality, a_i
7.   Produce a blueprint

NOTES

*   I thank Klaas Van't Veld, Christiane Clemens, Eric Zivot, Cecilia García Peñalosa and Uwe Walz for early discussions on the topic and for helpful comments on this version; any errors are my own.

1. The terms in brackets show the algorithms' roots in evolution and natural genetics.
2. Further introductions of life sciences algorithms into economics can be found in the resource–growth literature, where natural resource regeneration is modelled according to biological regeneration functions (Copeland and Taylor, 1995), and in the financial markets literature, which uses epidemiologists' contagion models (Shiller and Pound, 1989).
3. There is no evidence that innovations evolve according to Poisson distributions.
4. More sophisticated research processes have been introduced by models of General Purpose Technology (see Helpman, 1998) and by Aghion and Howitt's (1998) model of basic and applied research. These models are primarily interested in how the different natures of technologies (basic, applied, process, product) affect growth rather than how innovations come about, which is the topic in this chapter.
5. An analogy would be the manufacturing developments in the 1980s where West (assembly plant production) met East (teamwork) and both sides flourished by adopting some principal ideas from the other. Even the Ford Motor Company, the quintessential inventor of the assembly line that propelled Western manufacturing into a new era, did import Japanese managers to improve efficiency with teamwork concepts.
6. The constancy of *g* implies that the research does not actually alter the incremental increase in technology; rather that research changes the time interval at which new blueprints arrive. It is possible to endogenize the incremental increase in technology, *g*, as shown by Aghion and Howitt (1992). None of the results below would change.
7. Aghion and Howitt (1992) assume a Poisson arrival rate to proxy uncertainty in the innovation process. As mentioned in the introduction, the qualitative results are identical to assuming exogenous, constant innovation.
8. The empirical literature is marred by data problems related to measuring technical change and determining the factors that influence technical change. The best approximation seems to be Caballero and Jaffe (1993).
9. Complications that reflect more complex mappings from the value of the binary number into research productivity would not alter the results.
10. A step-by-step scheme of search in research is given the Appendix.
11. Directed learning would only improve the efficiency of the algorithm but not the qualitative nature of the results.
12. I excluded the possibility of completely random accidents (*mutation*). If random accidents dominate the algorithm to affect the results, the structure of research as presented above loses its substantive interpretation, since random effects then drive productivity. Mutations do not necessarily lead to the global maximum and lead to a constant probability distribution, a 'corridor of social behavioral patterns' (Riechmann, 1999) instead of one best practice.

REFERENCES

Aghion, P. and P. Howitt (1989), 'A model of growth through creative destruction', Working papers of the Massachusetts Institute of Technology (MIT).

Aghion, P. and P. Howitt (1992), 'A model of growth through creative destruction', *Econometrica*, **60**(2), 323–51.

Aghion, P. and P. Howitt (1998), *Endogenous Growth Theory*, Cambridge, Massachusetts: MIT Press.

Arrow, K. (1962), 'The economic implications of learning by doing', *Review of Economic Studies*, **29**, 155–73.

Barro, R. and X. Sala-i-Martin (1993), *Economic Growth*, Cambridge, Massachusetts: MIT Press.

Bengtsson, M.G. (1999), 'Genetic algorithms', *Swedish National Defence Research Establishment Working Paper*.

Birchenhall, C. (1995), 'Modular technical change and genetic algorithms', *Computational Economics*, 8, 233–53.

Brezis, E.S., P. Krugman and D. Tsiddon (1993), 'A theory of cycles in national technological leadership', *American Economic Review*, **83**(5), 1211–19.

Caballero, R.J. and A.B. Jaffe (1993), 'How high are the giants' shoulders: an empirical assessment of knowledge spillovers and creative destruction in a model of economic growth', in O.J. Blanchard and S. Fischer (eds), *NBER Macroeconomics Annual 1993*, Cambridge, Massachusetts and London: MIT Press, pp. 15–74.

Clemens, C. and T. Riechmann (1996), 'Evolutionary optimization methods and their application to economics', *Discussion paper 195*, University of Hannover.

Copeland, B.R. and M.S. Taylor (1995), 'Trade and the environment: a partial synthesis', *American Journal of Agricultural Economics*, **77**(3), 765–71.

Domar, E. (1946), 'Capital expansion, rate of growth, and employment', *Econometrica*, **14**, April, 137–47.

Eaton, J. and S. Kortum (1997), 'Engines of growth: domestic and foreign sources of innovation', *Japan and the World Economy*, **9**(2), 235–59.

Eicher, T.S. and S.C. Kim (2003), 'Market structure and innovation revisited: endogenous productivity, training and market shares', in M. Boldrin, B-L. Chen and P. Wang (eds), *Human Capital, Trade and Financial Development in Rapidly Growing Economies: From Theory to Practice*, Northampton, MA, USA: Edward Elgar, forthcoming.

Feenstra, R.C. (1996), 'Trade and uneven growth', *Journal of Development Economics*, **49**(1), 229–56.

Grossman, G.M and E. Helpman (1990), 'Trade, innovation, and growth', *American Economic Review*, **80**(2), 86–91.

Grossman G.M. and E. Helpman (1991a), *Innovation and Growth in the Global Economy*, Cambridge, Massachusetts: MIT Press.

Grossman, G.M and E. Helpman, (1991b), 'Quality ladders and product cycles', *Quarterly Journal of Economics*, **106**(2), 557–86.

Harrod R.F. (1960), 'A second essay in dynamic theory', *Economic Journal*, **70**, pp. 277–93.

Helpman, E. (1998), *General Purpose Technologies and Economic Growth*, Cambridge, Massachusetts and London: MIT Press.

Holland, J.H. (1970), 'Robust algorithms for adaptation set in a general formal framework', in *Proceedings of the IEEE Symposium on Adaptive Processes: Decision and Control*, New York: Inst. Electrical and Electronic Engineering.

Holland, J.H. (1975), *Adaptation in Natural and Artificial Systems*, Ann Arbor: University of Michigan Press.

Howitt, P. (1999), 'Steady endogenous growth with population and R&D inputs growing', *Journal of Political Economy*, **107**, 715–30.

Howitt, P. (2000), 'Endogenous growth and cross-country income differences', *American Economic Review*, **90**, 829–46.

Jones, C.I. (1995), 'R&D-based models of economic growth', *Journal of Political Economy*, **103**(4), 759–84.

Jones, C.I., and J. Williams (1998), 'Measuring the social return to R&D', *Quarterly Journal of Economics*, 113, 1119–35.

Jovanovic, B. and Y. Nyarko (1996), 'Learning by doing and the choice of technology', *Econometrica*, **64**(6), 1299–310.

Judd, K. (1985), 'On the performance of patents', *Econometrica*, **53**, 298–319.

Kaldor, N. (1957), 'A model of economic growth', *Economic Journal*, **67**, 591–624.

Krugman, P. (1994), 'Complex landscapes in economic geography', *American Economic Review*, **84**(2), 412–16.

Marimon, R., E. McGrattan and T. Sargent (1990), 'Money as a medium of exchange in an economy with artificially intelligent agents', *Journal of Economic Dynamics and Control*, **14**(2), 329–73.

Riechmann, T. (1999), 'Learning and behavioral stability: an economic interpretation of genetic algorithms', *Journal of Evolutionary Economics*, **9**(2), 225–42.

Rivera-Batiz, L. and P.M. Romer (1994), 'Economic integration and endogenous growth', *Quarterly Journal of Economics*, **109**(1), 307–8.

Romer, P.M. (1986), 'Increasing returns and long-run growth', *Journal of Political Economy*, **94**, 1002–37.

Romer, P.M. (1987), 'Growth based on increasing returns due to specialization', *American Economic Review*, **77**(2), 56–62.

Romer, P.M. (1990), 'Endogenous technological change', *Journal of Political Economy*, **98**(5), S71–102.

Romer, P.M. (1993), 'Two strategies for economic development: using ideas vs. producing ideas', in L.H. Summers and S. Shah (eds), *Proceedings of the World Bank Annual Conference on Development Economics 1992: Supplement to The World Bank Economic Review and The World Bank Research Observer*, Washington, DC: World Bank, pp. 63–91.

Segerstrom, P.S., T.C.A. Anant and E. Dinopoulos (1990), 'A Schumpeterian model of the product life cycle', *American Economic Review*, December 1990, 1077–91.

Shell, K. (1966), 'Towards a theory of inventive activity and capital accumulation', *American Economic Review*, **56**, 62–8.

Shiller, R.J. and J. Pound (1989), 'Survey evidence on diffusion of interest and information among investors', *Journal of Economic Behavior and Organization*, **12**(1), 47–66.

Solow, R.M. (1956), 'A contribution to the theory of economic growth', *Quarterly Journal of Economics*, **70**, 65–94.

Solow, R.M. (1957), 'Technical change and the aggregate production function', *Review of Economics and Statistics*, **39**, 312–20.

Vriend, N. (1995), 'Self-organization of markets: an example of a computational approach', *Computational Economics*, **8**(3), 205–31.

Weitzman, M.L. (1992), 'On diversity', *Quarterly Journal of Economics*, **107**(2), 363–405.

Weitzman, M.L. (1998), 'Recombinant growth', *Quarterly Journal of Economics*, **113**(2), 331–60.

Xie, D. (1994), 'Divergence in economic performance: transitional dynamics with multiple equilibria', *Journal of Economic Theory*, **63**(1), 97–112.

Young, A. (1998), 'Growth without scale effects', *Journal of Political Economy*, February, 41–63.

9. Technical change, effective demand and economic growth

Michael A. Landesmann and Robert Stehrer

9.1. INTRODUCTION

The model developed in this chapter has distinctly classical, but also Schumpeterian and Keynesian features. The analysis is explored in an aggregate (one good) setting, but many of the results carry over to a multisectoral setting (for the latter see Landesmann and Stehrer, 2000; Stehrer 2002). Sections 9.2 and 9.3 present the main components of the model in its equilibrium setting. Here we show the classical wage–profits and consumption vs. investment/growth trade-offs. We also show the conditions which have to be satisfied for full employment growth. Important are distributive requirements – particularly the determination of the real wage – which allow the economy to achieve full employment in the face of (positive) productivity shocks and changes in the available labour force. This issue is further explored in Section 9.4 in the context of changing (exogenous) growth rates of productivity and labour force growth. Real wage adjustments are also required if the economy is to remain on a full employment path and profit-receivers change their behaviour with respect to investment vs. consumption spending. Section 9.5 moves to discuss off-steady-state analysis and introduces further components into the model. In 'disequilibrium' there is no immediate price-to-cost adjustment; thus Schumpeterian rents emerge and we allow for some bargaining between workers and capitalists over these rents. The impact of the unemployment rate also features in the wage equation. Hence, as the economy absorbs a (positive) productivity shock, there is a shift of income shares towards 'rents', and different distributive scenarios of such rents can emerge. The next important ingredient to understand the growth implications is to look at the 'spending' pattern out of these rents: these can go into consumption spending, investment spending or they 'leak out' of the real system (e.g. into liquid or financial assets). We show that the classical results obtained earlier with regard to wage–profit consumption–growth trade-offs can be seriously modified when such 'off-equilibrium' dynamics are explored. Here, both Schumpeterian and Keynesian features emerge. Section 9.6 attempts to model the interaction between the financial and the real sector of the economy more fully. We discuss not only the 'leakage' effects but also the role which pre-financing of investments by financial institutions plays in absorbing productivity shocks and affecting economic growth. Finally, we introduce endogenous (productivity) growth features into the model. Section 9.7 illustrates further some of the features of the model through simulations. One of the motivations behind the study is to arrive at an understanding of the so-called 'Solow Paradox', i.e. that there might be evidence of a strong positive technology boost which, however, does not translate – at least for some time – into higher economic growth.

There exists, of course, an immense literature dealing with the questions which are discussed within the modelling framework of this chapter. These questions have been at the heart of economic theory since the beginning. There are a number of recent publications applying a classical framework and using different closures of the model (for some of the principal contributions, see e.g. Marglin, 1984; Dutt, 1990; Taylor, 1981). While most of these previous contributions work in the context of comparative static analysis, our analysis adopts a fully fledged dynamic formulation. The essence of our analysis lies in the focus on disequilibrium (or transitory) dynamics, while the earlier contributions mostly refer to 'equilibria' (e.g. of the classical, Keynesian, and Marxian type). In our approach, it is in the transitory dynamics, where we demonstrate Schumpeterian and Keynesian features of our model. On the other hand, the model is robustly anchored in dynamic steady-state properties but the emphasis lies in the reactive processes which emerge when there are 'shocks' (particularly productivity shocks) to which the steady-state structures are exposed. Previous contributions by the authors (Landesmann and Stehrer, 2000; Stehrer, 2002) have shown the usefulness of this type of approach to studying the ways that structural change can impinge on the growth features of the system. Thus the model has proved useful when studying the interaction between macroeconomic dynamics and structural change within the context of a multisectoral model (for earlier contributions see Goodwin, 1986; Pasinetti, 1981; Goodwin and Punzo, 1987).

In this chapter, in contrast, we follow up a number of features of the macroeconomic dynamics in more detail in the context of an aggregate model. The chapter extensively discusses the properties of the model in the steady-state (stationary or growing) with the aim of setting up a dynamic framework which is also applied for disequilibrium states and transitory (i.e. between steady-states) dynamics. As will be seen, we first analyse the model as far as possible in the case of steady-state growth. Although some analytical results can be derived for transition paths we also use simulations to show the dynamics of the model in disequilibrium states. The study of the steady-state properties of the model (i.e. the existence of solutions and the stability properties) is important for a proper understanding of the transitory and out-of-equilibrium dynamics of the model. We are able to show that both the long-run outcome of output and employment paths as well as the transitory dynamics depend heavily on behavioural adjustments in the transitory phases, particularly in phases of rapid technological progress. This is where we think the contribution of this chapter lies in relation to the other literature in this field.

As mentioned above, in Sections 9.6 and 9.7 we discuss the integration of a financial sector on the performance of the real sector. Although we do not set up a complete model of the financial sector the effects on real growth and distribution are emphasized. This part thus contributes to the literature on interactions between the real and the financial sector. For important recent statements of the financial–real interaction in a Keynesian framework see e.g. Flaschel et al. (1997) and Foley (1986).

9.2.   THE MODEL

In this chapter we explore a one-good model. Most results can be extended to the multisectoral case (see Landsmann and Stehrer, 2000; Stehrer 2002). In this section we present the main accountancy relationships of the model.

9.2.1.   Technology

Technology is denoted by a pair of input coefficients a and b where a denotes the input coefficient of intermediate goods and b the input coefficient for labour. The standard relationships are:

1. $aq(t)$ is the intermediate demand for production of output $q(t)$
2. $(1-a)q(t)$ is the amount of output q not used as intermediate input
3. $(1-a)^{-1}f(t)$ gives the necessary gross production for a final demand $f(t)$

The labour input coefficient b is assumed to be strictly positive (thus we assume that some labour is always used in production). Labour productivity is then b^{-1}. As indicated by the time indexing, we shall take account of changes in labour productivity $b^{-1}(t)$, but assume that the input coefficient a remains fixed.

9.2.2.   Wages, Unit Labour Costs, Costs and Prices

The (nominal) wage rate is denoted by $w(t)$ and unit labour costs are defined as $b(t)w(t)$.

Total unit costs are then $c(t)=p(t)a + w(t)b(t)$ and prices are given by $p(t) = (1+\pi)c(t)$, where π refers to a long-run mark-up ratio. This formulation implies that wages are paid at the beginning of the period, i.e. *ante factum*.

The equilibrium of the price system can easily be determined in the case where the coefficient a, and w, b and thus the unit labour costs wb and the mark-up ratio π are exogenously given and constant. The equilibrium price is:

$$p = \frac{(1+\pi)b}{1-(1+\pi)a}w.$$

In the special case where $w/p = 0$ we obtain the maximum mark-up rate $\pi^{max} = (1/a) - 1$.

9.2.3.   Profits and Rents

The per unit (equilibrium) profit is defined as a mark-up on costs:

$$r(t)=\pi\ c(t)=\pi[p(t)a+w(t)b(t)].$$

In the case that the price is not at the equilibrium level there arise per-unit rents which are defined as:

$$s(t)=p(t)-(1+\pi)c(t) = p(t)[1-(1+\pi)a]-(1+\pi)w(t)b(t).$$

In equilibrium these rents are zero. In the following we define a scalar $m(t)$ which adds up profits $r(t)$ and rents $s(t)$, which we refer to as 'total profits':

$$m(t)=r(t)+s(t)=p(t)-c(t)=p(t)(1-a)-w(t)b(t).$$

In equilibrium total profits per unit in real terms are:

$$\frac{m}{p}=\frac{r}{p}=(1-a)-\frac{w}{p}b=(1-a)-\frac{1-(1+\pi)a}{1+\pi}=\frac{\pi}{1+\pi}.$$

9.2.4.   Demand Components and Total Demand

Next we turn to the quantity system. Total supply/production is denoted by $q(t)$. Demand consists of three different components: demand for (1) intermediate goods, (2) consumption goods, and (3) investment goods. We shall discuss them in detail below.

Demand for intermediate goods used in production is $aq(t)$. Intermediate goods can be interpreted as capital stock, which in this model consists only of circulating capital.

Workers earn a nominal wage rate $w(t)$ and thus total nominal wage income is $w(t)b(t)q(t)$ as $l(t) = b(t)q(t)$ is labour demand. In real terms this is:

$$f_w(t) = \frac{w(t)}{p(t)} b(t)q(t) = \frac{w(t)}{p(t)} l(t).$$

With constant b, w, π, a, p, demand out of wage income depends only on the equilibrium real wage and the quantity of labour demanded:

$$f_w(t) = \frac{w}{p} bq(t) = \frac{w}{p} l(t).$$

We shall henceforth assume in classical fashion that all labour income is spent on consumption. By this assumption, $f_w(t)$ also denotes the amount of goods demanded by workers.

The nominal total profit income is $m(t)q(t)$. Expressed in real terms this is:

$$f_m(t) = \frac{m(t)}{p(t)} q(t) = \frac{p(t)(1-a) - w(t)b(t)}{p(t)} q(t) = \left[(1-a) - \frac{w(t)}{p(t)} b(t) \right] q(t).$$

In fact, this is the residual real income, i.e. total output $q(t)$ minus demand for intermediate inputs and real wage income. How income from profits is turned into spending on investment goods and thus affects the growth of output is specified below (Section 9.3.2). Until Section 9.3.5 we shall (again in classical fashion) assume that all profits are spent on investment. In the case that $m(t) = 0$ one gets $1 - a = [w(t)/p(t)]b(t)$ which means that the workers in the economy attain the maximum amount of consumption.

If all incomes are spent then total demand $d(t)$ is the sum of the three components:

$$d(t) = aq(t) + f_m(t) + f_w(t).$$

In equilibrium total demand equals total supply:

$$q(t) = aq(t) + f_m(t) + f_w(t) = aq(t) + \left[(1-a) - \frac{w(t)}{p(t)}b(t)\right]q(t) + \frac{w(t)}{p(t)}b(t)q(t).$$

The types of demand and shares of income (intermediate, demand from profit receivers and demand from workers) in real terms are given by:

$$1 = a + \left[(1-a) - \frac{w(t)}{p(t)}b(t)\right] + \frac{w(t)}{p(t)}b(t).$$

Before presenting the solutions to this model we specify labour demand and supply and hence unemployment.

9.2.5. Labour Demand and Supply

As already mentioned above, labour demand is given by $l(t) = b(t)q(t)$. We denote labour supply by $k(t)$. We define the unemployment rate as $u(t) = (k(t) - l(t))/k(t)$.

9.3. EQUILIBRIUM SOLUTIONS

9.3.1. Existence

In equilibrium total supply must equal total demand, $q(t) = d(t)$. The condition stated above may be rewritten as:

$$q(t) = d(t) = \left[a + \frac{m(t)}{p(t)} + \frac{w(t)b(t)}{p(t)}\right]q(t).$$

Rearranging this condition yields:

$$\left[(a-1) + \frac{m(t)}{p(t)} + \frac{w(t)}{p(t)}b(t)\right]q(t) = 0.$$

In the case that all income is spent this condition holds at each point in time t (i.e. even in the case that the price system is not in equilibrium) as:

$$0 = (a-1) + \frac{w(t)}{p(t)}b(t) + \frac{p(t)(1-a) - w(t)b(t)}{p(t)} =$$

$$= (a-1) + \frac{w(t)}{p(t)}b(t) + (1-a) - \frac{w(t)}{p(t)}b(t).$$

It is clear that the level of output cannot be determined by this condition alone.

9.3.2.   Steady-state (Classical) Growth

In order to examine the steady-state we take the input coefficients a and b as constant. Wage rates and prices are at their equilibrium values, respectively. Further, rents s are equal to zero and real per-unit profit is $\pi/(1 + \pi)$ as shown above, hence $m = \pi c$. Further we assume that all incomes are spent and that there is no shortage of labour. The demand for labour which equals supply is given by:

$$k(t) = l(t) = bq(t).$$

Returning to demand out of profits and assuming that $(m/p)q(t)$ is fully reinvested, the demand and supply for inputs will be growing at a rate:

$$\frac{f_m(t)}{aq(t)} = \frac{1}{a}\frac{m}{p} = \frac{1}{a}\frac{\pi}{1+\pi} \equiv \gamma_{aq} = \gamma_q.$$

In this model with circulating capital this represents the (gross and net) accumulation rate (a positive depreciation rate can be easily inserted). The growth path of the economy can then be written as:[1]

$$\dot{q}(t) = \frac{(1+\gamma_q)[f_m(t)+f_w(t)]}{1-a} - q(t) = \frac{(1+\gamma_q)f_w(t)}{1-(1-\gamma_q)a} - q(t).$$

By using $[f_m(t)+f_w(t)] = (1-a)$ this yields:

$$\frac{\dot{q}(t)}{q(t)} = \gamma_q = \frac{1}{a}\frac{\pi}{1+\pi}.$$

This dynamic equation shows that profit receivers finance accumulation out of the current income. If $\pi = 0$ the economy remains stationary (all surplus $(1-a)q(t)$ being consumed). Note that for $\pi = \pi^{max} = (1/a) - 1$, i.e the maximum mark-up rate, this reduces to:

$$\gamma_q^{max} = \pi^{max}.$$

In this case the economy grows at the maximum rate which is equal to the profit rate.[2]

9.3.3. Full-employment Solution

In the steady-state full employment is guaranteed when labour supply equals demand at the initial point of time $k(0) = l(0) = bq(0)$ and there are neither labour supply restrictions nor insufficient labour demand in the course of growth, i.e.:

$$\frac{\dot{k}(t)}{k(t)} = \frac{\dot{l}(t)}{l(t)} = \frac{\dot{q}(t)}{q(t)}.$$

9.3.4. Exogenous Technical Progress

We first introduce a growth of labour productivity at a constant exogenously given rate γ_b which implies that the input coefficient is decreasing:

$$\dot{b} = -\gamma_b b.$$

Under the assumptions that $\pi = 0$ and that the labour supply is constant $\dot{k} = 0$, using the full-employment assumption[3] implies that:

$$\frac{\dot{l}}{l} = \frac{\dot{b}}{b} + \frac{\dot{q}}{q} = 0$$

and thus:

$$-\frac{\dot{b}}{b} = \frac{\dot{q}}{q} \quad \text{or} \quad \gamma_b = \overline{\gamma}_q.$$

This means, that for keeping employment at the initial full-employment level, output has to grow at the same rate as labour productivity ($\overline{\gamma}_q$ refers to 'full employment output growth'). To guarantee that output grows at this rate two conditions must be met: first, enough demand has to be created and, second, enough resources have to be reinvested. As shown above, the condition:

$$\overline{\gamma}_q = \frac{1}{a} \frac{m(t)}{p(t)}$$

has to be satisfied, but now with $\overline{\gamma}_q$ given (rather than π given). Rearranging gives:

$$\overline{\gamma}_q = \frac{1}{a} \frac{m(t)}{p(t)} = \frac{1}{a} \frac{p(t) - p(t)a - w(t)b(t)}{p(t)} = \frac{1}{a}\left[(1-a) - \frac{w(t)b(t)}{p(t)}\right].$$

As γ_q and $(1-a)$ are constant, $w(t)b(t)/p(t)$ also has to be constant, thus:

$$0 = \frac{\dot{w}}{w} + \frac{\dot{b}}{b} - \frac{\dot{p}}{p}$$

$$\gamma_w - \gamma_p = \gamma_b.$$

This means that the real wage has to grow at the rate of productivity γ_b. This condition assures that consumption demand rises in line with productivity growth. If it rose beyond productivity growth there would not be enough profits to allow the required net accumulation to take place to assure full employment. If it grew below that rate a mismatch between net accumulation (i.e. increase in productive capacity) and final consumption demand would take place.

We can also see that the ratio of unit labour costs to price has to be lower than it would be if the economy would not undergo positive productivity growth. We get:

$$\overline{\gamma}_q = \frac{1}{a}\left[(1-a) - \frac{w(t)}{p(t)}b(t)\right].$$

Rearranging this expression yields:

$$\frac{w(t)}{p(t)}b(t) = (1-a) - a\overline{\gamma}_q = (1-a) - a\gamma_b.$$

This condition assures that enough resources are available for keeping the economy growing at the full employment path.

9.3.5. Exogenous Population Growth

Next, we turn to a situation where the labour force is growing at an exogenously given and constant rate, γ_k. For keeping the economy at the full employment level, this means that labour demand must rise with the (exogenously given) rate of the labour supply:

$$\gamma_k = \gamma_l$$

and thus the growth rate of output must be:

$$\overline{\gamma}_q = \gamma_k + \gamma_b.$$

Again, as γ_b and $(1-a)$ are assumed to be constant, the term $w(t)b(t)/p(t)$ has to be constant which analogously to above yields:

$$\gamma_w - \gamma_p = \gamma_b$$

i.e. the real wage has to grow at the rate of productivity. But, different from above, the ratio of unit labour costs to price will have to be even lower, as:

$$\gamma_k + \gamma_b = \frac{1}{a}\left[(1-a) + \frac{w(t)}{p(t)}b(t)\right]$$

or equivalently:

$$\frac{w(t)}{p(t)}b(t) = (1-a) - a(\gamma_k + \gamma_b).$$

This implies that the consumption level must be lower to 'save' relatively more output for reinvestment and hence for an expansion of capacity. Output must be growing not only to keep employment at a constant level (thus only capturing the labour-saving effects of technical progress) but also to create employment for the growing labour force (population). The balance between necessary total demand and the growth of productive capacity is created by adjustments in the real wage and the demand from new workers.

9.3.6.   Endogenous Technical Progress

In the simulations below we also introduce endogenous technical progress along the Kaldor–Verdoorn mechanism. Labour input coefficients are assumed to be falling as a function of the growth rate of output (or of intermediate inputs, i.e. investments; within the specification of the model, the two cases have the same dynamic implications):

$$\dot{b} = -\kappa_b a \frac{\dot{q}}{q}b = -\kappa_b a \, \gamma_q b,$$

where $\kappa_b \geq 0$ denotes the 'Kaldor–Verdoorn parameter'.

To simplify we also assume that profit margins are constant. In equilibrium, with m/p constant, the growth rate of the economy is given by $\gamma_q = (1/a)(m/p)$ and productivity growth is given by $\dot{b}/b = -\kappa_b(m/p)$. For profit per unit $m/p = (1-a) - (wb/p)$ to be constant, the labour share has to be constant too, i.e.:

$$\frac{\dot{w}}{w}+\frac{\dot{b}}{b}-\frac{\dot{p}}{p}=0 \quad \text{or} \quad \frac{\dot{w}}{w}-\frac{\dot{p}}{p}=\kappa_b a\gamma_q$$

i.e. the real wage rate grows in line with productivity. In equilibrium, labour demand grows at a rate determined by the difference of the growth of output and the growth of productivity. Assuming full employment und using the (dynamic) full-employment condition yields:

$$\frac{\dot{l}}{l}=\frac{\dot{b}}{b}+\frac{\dot{q}}{q}=-\kappa_b a\gamma_q+\gamma_q=(1-a\kappa_b)\gamma_q=\frac{\dot{k}}{k}.$$

Thus for $\kappa_b=0$ labour demand (supply) must rise at the same rate as output, as shown in Section 9.3.3. With $\kappa_b>0$ this condition is relaxed as part of the additional labour necessary for keeping the economy growing at a rate γ_q comes from labour-saving (endogenous) technical progress. For $\kappa_b=1/a$ the growth rate of employment is zero and the result is similar to the case of exogenous productivity growth in Section 9.3.4 (the labour cost share becomes $(wb/p)=(1-a)-(m/p)$).

The demand condition is satisfied as there are additional workers and as real wages are rising, the relative weights of these factors being determined by the value of κ_b. Note that in this case, output, employment and the real wage grow at different rates.

9.3.7. Consumption out of Profits

So far we have assumed that workers income is spent on consumption and income out of profits is spent on investment. We now relax this assumption and consider the case in which profit earners spend part of their income on consumption and the other part on investment. The part of income spent on consumption is denoted by κ_m with $0\leq\kappa_m\leq1$.

In steady-state growth the demand and supply for inputs will in this case be growing at the rate:

$$(1-\kappa_m)\frac{f_m(t)}{aq(t)}=(1-\kappa_m)\frac{1}{a}\frac{m}{p}=(1-\kappa_m)\frac{1}{a}\frac{\pi}{1+\pi}\equiv(1-\kappa_m)\gamma_q,$$

where $\gamma_q=(1/a)[\pi/(1+\pi)]$. Thus the growth rate of the economy is reduced relative to the case in which all profits were reinvested. The growth path of the economy is then:

$$\dot{q}(t) = \frac{1+(1-\kappa_m)\gamma_q}{1-a}\left[\underbrace{(1-\kappa_m)f_m(t)}_{\text{Investment demand}} + \underbrace{\kappa_m f_m(t) + f_w(t)}_{\text{Consumption demand}}\right] - q(t).$$

Also in the case of exogenous technological progress and population growth one has to take into account that part of total profit income is spent on consumption. The condition for full-employment remains:

$$\overline{\gamma}_q = \gamma_k + \gamma_b.$$

For the economy to provide enough resources to grow at the rate $\overline{\gamma}_q$ the condition becomes:

$$\overline{\gamma}_q = (1-\kappa_m)\frac{1}{a}\frac{m(t)}{p(t)} = (1-\kappa_m)\frac{1}{a}\left[(1-a)-\frac{w(t)}{p(t)}b(t)\right],$$

which yields a per unit real wage:

$$\frac{wb}{p} = (1-a) - a\frac{\gamma_k + \gamma_b}{1-\kappa_m},$$

where:

$$(1-a) \geq a\frac{\gamma_k + \gamma_b}{1-\kappa_m}$$

has to be satisfied. This condition says that given that there is consumption out of profits; some of the required extension of capacities has to be financed by lower real wage income. (In the case that $\kappa_m = 1$ there would be no possibility for the economy to grow whatsoever.)

9.4.   UNDEREMPLOYMENT EQUILIBRIA

9.4.1.   Stationary Economy

In this section we return to an economy in which all profits are invested. In such an economy, with no technical progress, no exogenous population growth and $\pi = 0$, the equilibrium of the economy is given by $\gamma_q = 0$ and $(1-a) = (w/p)b$. The output is allocated to (intermediate) investment and consumption demand so that the economy exactly reproduces itself over time. If $(1-a) < (w/p)b$ the economy would contract and if $(1-a) > (w/p)b$ the economy would be able to grow.

What happens if the economy starts in an unemployment situation $u(t) > 0$? The answer is quite simple: nothing, as long as the fact of unemployment has no impact on the other variables. One way out of the unemployment situation will be (this is shown below in the disequilibrium dynamic model), that the wage rate falls, rents emerge and these rents enable the economy to grow until it reaches the full-employment equilibrium. The same situation is reached if prices are growing which again leads to emerging rents via falling real wages. These two processes both have in common that the real wage has to be lower (at least temporarily) to reach the full-employment situation. An analogous analysis can be derived for an influx of new labour (migration).

Another possibility to reach full-employment seems to be to switch to more labour-intensive production techniques, which implies a rising b. But this alone does not do the job! With sticky real wages this measure would only raise the ratio $(w/p)b$ which would lead to a contraction of the economy in the long run. Only if the real wage rate is adjusted for lower productivity so that $(w/p)b$ remains constant might unemployment diminish. Note that this solution implies that the real wage is lower for all time.

9.4.2.   Constant Growth Economy

Above we have seen that – given initial conditions – the model exhibits a full-employment growth path at a growth rate:

$$\gamma_q = \gamma_b + \gamma_k.$$

Further the condition:

$$\frac{wb}{p} = (1-a) - a(\gamma_b + \gamma_k)$$

has to be satisfied. Analogously to the constant economy case we can state that the economy is growing at a lower rate if:

$$(1-a) - a(\gamma_b + \gamma_q) < \frac{w}{p}b$$

and the economy has the potential to grow faster if:

$$(1-a) - a(\gamma_b + \gamma_q) > \frac{w}{p}b.$$

In the case that the economy is starting at the full-employment level this means, in the first case, that the actual growth rate is lower than the necessary growth rate to keep the economy at the full-employment level (the economy is constrained by the available intermediate inputs). In the second case the potential growth rate of the economy is higher than the necessary growth rate to keep the economy at the full-employment level. In this situation the economy is in a sense constrained by a labour (and consumption) shortage. Profit-receivers can react to this by investing less than is available as retained earnings (rents) and the difference between profits and required investments may be consumed, exported, or saved in some form which does not lead directly to additional productive investment.

9.4.3.   Technology Shocks and Emerging Unemployment Equilibria

We first discuss the case with $\gamma_k = \gamma_b = 0$ and with the economy at the full-employment level. What happens if there is a sudden and once and for all rise in the productivity level to $b_1 < b_0$? First of all $(w/p)b$ would fall and thus $(1 - a) > (w/p)b_1$. Thus there would be a potential for growth as inputs are saved. If these are actually reinvested the economy may expand and come back to full employment. Now assume that the nominal wage rate is adjusted to this increase in labour productivity such that $(w_1/p)b_1 = (w_0/p)b_0$. In this case the economy would produce exactly the same amount as before the technological shock but there are less workers employed. If these unemployed workers have no influence on wage setting they will remain unemployed forever.

In a growing economy the implications are similar. A sudden rise of the productivity level would imply that the economy may expand faster because of the emergence of rents. If real wages adjust immediately to the increase in labour productivity (and hence no rents emerge) then the economy would continue to grow at the same (long-term) rate of growth as before but at a lower (but not constant) level of employment.[4]

9.4.4.   Conclusions

What can be learned from this? To achieve full-employment in an economy which has to change its growth path (due to increased productivity or population growth) two conditions have to be satisfied:

1. Rents have to emerge (in our model by falling real per-unit wages) to enable the economy to grow at a higher rate.
2. These rents have to be reinvested despite (temporarily) falling real wages and thus (in the short run) lower consumption demand. Higher effective

demand then comes from investment which widens the productive capacities and thus creates the condition for employment absorption.

9.5.   OUT-OF-EQUILIBRIUM DYNAMICS

In this section we shall first restate the dynamic full employment conditions when productivity and labour force growth change over time and then introduce some further behavioural ingredients into the model which characterize out-of-equilibrium behaviour.

9.5.1.   Full-employment Path

Above we have seen that keeping the economy at the full employment level the (dynamic) condition $\overline{\gamma}_q = \gamma_b + \gamma_k$ has to be satisfied. In this section we discuss the implications for the wage movements in the case that technical progress and labour force growth is not constant but that the growth rates change over time. As we are focusing on transitory dynamics in the following we simplify the analysis by setting the long-run mark-up to zero, i.e. $\pi = 0$. In a situation where all investment spending occurs from (transitory) rents $s(t)$, the dynamic full employment condition requires that:

$$\overline{\gamma}_q(t) = \frac{1}{a}\frac{m(t)}{p(t)} = \frac{1}{a}\frac{(1-a)p(t)-w(t)b(t)}{p(t)} = \frac{1}{a}\left[(1-a)-\frac{w(t)}{p(t)}b(t)\right]$$

has to be satisfied. In the rest of this section we assume that prices are fixed, i.e. $\dot{p} = 0$, to study the implications for wage setting. For fixed prices this can also be seen as real wage policy. Thus the condition above reduces to:

$$\overline{\gamma}_q(t) = \frac{1}{a}\left[(1-a)-\frac{w(t)}{p}b(t)\right]$$

and thus:

$$w(t) = \frac{1}{b(t)}p\left[(1-a)-a\overline{\gamma}_q(t)\right]$$

i.e. the wage rate at time t is determined by the productivity level and the growth rates gamma $\overline{\gamma}_q(t) = \gamma_b(t) + \gamma_k(t)$.

Differentiating with respect to time gives:

$$\dot{w}(t) = -p\frac{a(\dot{\gamma}_b + \dot{\gamma}_k)b(t) - a\dot{b}(t)(\gamma_b + \gamma_k) + \dot{b}(t)(1-a)}{b(t)^2} =$$

$$= -p\frac{a(\dot{\gamma}_b + \dot{\gamma}_k) - a\gamma_b^2 - a\gamma_b\gamma_k + \gamma_b(1-a)}{b(t)}.$$

Rearranging and using the condition $(w(t)/p)b(t) = (1-a) - a(\gamma_b + \gamma_k)$ yields:[5]

$$\frac{\dot{w}}{w} = -\gamma_b - \frac{a(\dot{\gamma}_b + \dot{\gamma}_k)}{(1-a) - a(\gamma_b + \gamma_k)}.$$

Note, that for $\dot{\gamma}_b = \dot{\gamma}_k = 0$ these conditions are the same as stated in Sections 9.3.4 and 9.3.5, respectively.

9.5.2.   Dynamic Formulation of Prices and the Emergence of Rents

Price adjustment can be modelled as a price to cost (plus normal mark-up) adjustment:

$$\dot{p}(t) = \delta_p\left\{(1+\pi)\left[p(t)a + w(t)b(t)\right] - p(t)\right\}$$

with $0 < \delta_p \le 1$ being the adjustment parameter. With $\delta_p < 1$ and a positive technology shock (a or $b(t)$ falling) rents emerge in addition to profits.[6]

We now model the distribution of rents. As rents emerge, a certain proportion of such rents gets distributed to workers; this proportion depends on the bargaining strength of workers. In that case the portion of rents at the disposal of capital owners is:

$$(1 - \kappa_s)s(t) = (1 - \kappa_s)[p(t) - (1 + \pi)\,c(t)],$$

where $0 \le \kappa_s \le 1$ denotes the share of unit rents which goes to workers (see also the wage equation below). Total profits then have a normal mark-up and a rent component:

$$m(t) = r(t) + (1 - \kappa_s)s(t)$$

to which we refer as 'retained profits'. Out of these, $\kappa_m m(t)q(t)$ is spent for consumption and $(1-\kappa_m)m(t)q(t)$ for investment.

9.5.3.   Labour Market Dynamics

The (out-of-equilibrium) dynamics of the wage rate is now modelled as follows:

$$\dot{w} = \kappa_s \frac{s(t)}{b(t)} + \kappa_u u(t)w(t),$$

where $u(t)$ denotes the unemployment rate $u(t)=[k(t)-l(t)]/k(t)$. We assume that $0 \le \kappa_s \le 1$ and $\kappa_u \le 0$. The first term means that part of transitory rents are distributed to workers (e.g. for compensating them for the increases in productivity) and the second term imposes a negative effect of unemployment on the growth of the nominal wage rate.

For reasons which will become clear below we assume that population $n(t)$ grows at a constant rate γ_n, i.e. $\dot{n}(t)/n(t) = \gamma_n$. Then labour supply is modelled as:

$$\dot{k}(t) = \delta_k \left[l(t)-k(t)\right] + \delta_n \left[k(t)-\zeta n(t)\right],$$

where ζ is the long-run participation rate.[7]
We assume that:

$$\delta_k = \begin{cases} \delta_{k,IN} > 0 & \text{if } l(t)-k(t) > 0 \\ \delta_{k,OUT} \ge 0 & \text{if } l(t)-k(t) < 0. \end{cases}$$

This formulation allows for an asymmetric adjustment of the actual participation rate to positive or negative excess demand for labour (in general, one would expect a faster adjustment to positive excess demand and a relatively slow adjustment to negative excess demand). The actual participation rate may differ in the short to medium run from the long-term rate ζ and is defined as:

$$\frac{k(t)}{n(t)} = \frac{l(t)+u(t)}{n(t)}.$$

Of course, the absolute constraint of labour supply is $k(t) \le n(t)$.

9.5.4.   Quantity Dynamics

We now come to the dynamics of the quantity system outside the steady-state.

With the assumption that all incomes are spent the growth path is determined as before, i.e.:

$$\dot{q}(t) = \frac{(1+\gamma_q)\left[(1-\kappa_m)f_m(t) + \kappa_m f_m(t) + f_w(t)\right]}{1-a}q(t) - q(t),$$

where the modification lies in the determination of spending on accumulation and the part of rents distributed to wages:

$$\gamma_q = (1-\kappa_m)\frac{1}{a}\frac{f_m(t)}{q(t)} = (1-\kappa_m)\frac{1}{a}\frac{m(t)}{p(t)} = (1-\kappa_m)\frac{1}{a}\frac{r(t)+(1-\kappa_s)s(t)}{p(t)}.$$

This expression can be further rearranged to:

$$\gamma_q = (1-\kappa_m)\frac{1}{a}\left\{(1-a) - \frac{w(t)b(t)}{p(t)} - \kappa_m(1+\pi)\left[\frac{1-(1+\pi)a}{1+\pi} - \frac{w(t)b(t)}{p(t)}\right]\right\}.$$

In equilibrium, i.e. $wb/p = \left[1-(1+\pi)a\right]/(1+\pi)$, the economy is growing at the rate $\bar{\gamma}_q = (1-\kappa_m)(1/a)\left[\pi/(1+\pi)\right]$. This can be verified by inserting the equilibrium real per-unit wage in the equation above. In general, the emergence of rents $s(t)$ allows the economy to grow faster as more intermediate goods are available for investment allowing a faster growth rate. On the other hand the real wage will be lower than the equilibrium real wage. Note that the (supply equal) demand condition is satisfied in any case as it does not matter whether it is demand for consumption or for investment.

In disequilibrium with $s(t)>0$ and thus with actual real wages below the equilibrium level, i.e. $w(t)b(t)/p(t) < \left[1-(1+\pi)a\right]/(1+\pi)$, the economy is able to grow faster. However, if part of the rents are (immediately) redistributed to workers as $\kappa_s > 0$, this lowers the growth rate as can be seen in the equation above. For $\kappa_s = 0$ the equation reduces to the cases discussed above. For $\kappa_s = 1$, which means that all rents are distributed to the workers, the equation reduces to:

$$\gamma_q = (1-\kappa_m)\pi\frac{1}{a}\frac{p(t)a + w(t)b(t)}{p(t)} = (1-\kappa_m)\pi\left(1+\frac{1}{a}\frac{wb}{p}\right).$$

In equilibrium this reduces to the growth rate:

$$\gamma_q = (1-\kappa_m)\frac{1}{a}\frac{\pi}{1+\pi}.$$

9.6. FINANCIAL ASSETS, DISTRIBUTIONAL DYNAMICS AND EFFECTIVE DEMAND

In this section we continue with transitional dynamics where we again focus on the impact of technical change. We shall show that the impact of technical change on the growth path of an economy depends on the parameters which determine the distribution of rents through price adjustments and adjustments in the labour market. We shall then show that the distribution of rent income between workers and capitalists has further repercussions on the growth path if the assumption is dropped that all income is being spent. We introduce a 'leakage-factor' which reflects the relative attractiveness of investing into the real or financial assets and/or the hesitancy of capitalists to proceed with ('real') investment spending when the growth of demand is not assured. Dropping the assumption that all incomes are being spent on goods leads us to introduce the possibility of saving in the form of the acquisition of financial assets.

9.6.1. Saving in Financial Assets Out of Retained Earnings

We now allow for the possibility that capitalists are not spending all their income on goods purchases. So far, we have discussed that earnings from total profits are either reinvested or consumed. Both have exerted a demand effect (either for investment goods or consumption goods). The effect was that consumption out of profits reduces the growth rate of the economy as less is reinvested. We now introduce the possibility that part of the earnings are invested in financial assets and thus do not have a direct demand effect. This represents a 'leakage' from the real part of the economy. It also expresses the potential instability of investment demand, i.e. the hesitancy of ploughing back income into productive investment when there is no assurance of rising demand. This further contributes to the possibility that actual growth falls short of potential growth.

The retained earnings are distributed across different uses in the following way:

1. Spending for consumption: $\kappa_m [r(t) + (1 - \kappa_s)s(t)]q(t)$.
2. Spending for investment: $(1 - \kappa_m)[r(t) + (1 - \kappa_s)s(t)]q(t)$.
   Investment is either in productive capacities or in financial assets ($\eta^+ \geq 0$ denotes the share of investments in financial assets):
   (a) productive capacities: $(1 - \eta^+)(1 - \kappa_m)[r(t) + (1 - \kappa_s)s(t)]q(t)$;
   (b) financial assets: $\eta^+(1 - \kappa_m)[r(t) + (1 - \kappa_s)s(t)]q(t)$.

To concentrate on the effects of the factor η^+ we assume that $\kappa_m = 0$ and $\kappa_s = 0$. Demand for investment goods in the real sector reduces to $(1-\eta^+)[m(t)/p(t)]q(t)$ and the investment ratio which determines the growth rate is $(1-\eta^+)(1/a)[m(t)/p(t)]$.

We now examine the impact of 'leakage' (i.e. investments in liquid assets) on the growth path of the economy. The growth path of the economy (with b constant) becomes:

$$\dot{q}(t) = \left[1+(1-\eta^+)\frac{1}{a}\frac{m}{p}\right]\frac{1}{1-a}\left[(1-\eta^+)\frac{m}{p}+\frac{w}{p}b\right]q-q.$$

With $m/p > 0$ and constant real unit labour costs one can use:

$$\frac{w}{p}b = (1-a)-\frac{m}{p}.$$

Inserting into the growth equation and rearranging yields:

$$\frac{\dot{q}}{q} = \left[1+(1-\eta^+)\frac{1}{a}\frac{m}{p}\right]\frac{1}{1-a}\left[(1-a)-\eta^+\frac{m}{p}\right]-1=$$

$$= \frac{1-a-\eta^+}{a(1-a)}\frac{m}{p}-\frac{\eta^+(1-\eta^+)}{a(1-a)}\left(\frac{m}{p}\right)^2.$$

This implies an inverse U-shaped relationship between η^+ and retained (profit) earnings m/p (see Figure 9.1). Setting $\dot{q}/q = 0$ gives the critical value of real retained earnings: larger retained earnings would mean a negative growth rate. This critical value is given by:

$$\left(\frac{m}{p}\right)^{cr} = \frac{(1-a)-\eta^+}{\eta^+(1-\eta^+)}$$

(for $\eta^+ > 0$). Positive growth of output requires that $\eta^+ < 1-a$. Differentiating the growth rate with respect to m/p and setting to zero yields the growth maximising (the second derivative is negative) real retained earnings:

$$\left(\frac{m}{p}\right)^{max} = \frac{(1-a)-\eta^+}{2\eta^+(1-\eta^+)}.$$

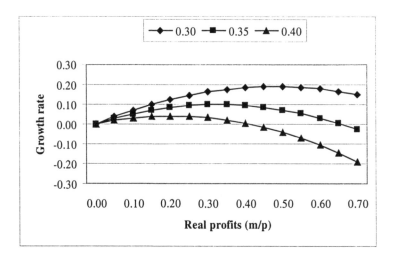

Figure 9.1   Relationship between (per-unit) profit share and growth rate at different values of η^+

The reason for an inverse U-shaped relationship between m/p and $\dot{q}/q$ is the following: on the one hand we know that, given the classical assumption that all investment spending is made out of profits, there can be no positive growth without profit income. Consequently, initially, a redistribution from wages to profits must generate growth if all profits are reinvested. A positive value of η^+ reduces the growth rate, because less is invested which implies that less capacities are being built up and less workers are employed which means that the growth of the volume of wage income is reduced. At positive values of η^+ the 'leakage' out of profits reduces the level of 'effective demand'. On the other hand, wage income which in the above formulation is specified as the residual income always has a real demand effect albeit being spent only on consumption. The consequence is that with a given 'leakage' factor η^+ there will be a positive net accumulation and hence growth only when profits are a positive, but – on the other hand – a too high distributive share of profits depresses 'effective demand' (because of the leakage) and hence becomes counter-productive for growth.

With leakage there is excess supply of goods given by $\eta^+(m/p)q$. We assume that these goods vanish immediately. Furthermore, we have not so far discussed that ownership claims on actual output are emerging from the investments into financial assets, which may also bear interest rate payments. We shall consider this issue below.

9.6.2. Schumpeterian (ex-ante) Financing of Innovative Investment

In this section we look at the opposite of 'leakage', i.e. investors raising loans from banks.

Investments of these loans raise the rate of investment (and hence adds to the existing stock of intermediate goods aq) and enables the economy to grow faster. Income will also be rising as more workers are employed and the volume of retained earnings mq is rising; consequently, demand is increasing as well.

There is however a physical constraint: in equilibrium we have $q = aq + (m/p)q + (wb/p)q$ which implies a growth rate of $(1/a)(m/p)$. The necessary additional resources for investment to enable the economy to grow faster can therefore only come from:

- workers incomes (forced saving)
- exogenous resources (e.g. foreign countries or unused inventories)
- a higher productivity of the system (i.e. a lower coefficient a)

The last point would mean that from the stock of inputs available for production at time t a higher output can be produced. This could be justified by the assumption that 'normal' productivity is lower than the (technically) feasible productivity of the system, i.e. $a^{max} < a$.

In either case there would be additional physical resources available which can be used by entrepreneurs. Financing the mobilization of these resources has to occur via credits. The additional investment goods enable the economy to grow at a faster rate which (in the continuous time model) immediately raises the volume of profits mq; by the assumption that labour supply is infinitely elastic with respect to labour demand, the demand for consumption $wbq = wl$ will also be growing. This ensures that the demand condition is satisfied.

With a pre-financing of productive investment through credits from the banking sector the total nominal sum available for buying investment goods including credit financing now becomes:

$$mq + \eta^- pq,$$

where the additional finance for investment is modelled as a share η^- of the nominal value of production pq. In this case the growth path of the economy becomes:[8]

$$\dot{q} = \left[1 + \frac{1}{a}\left(\frac{m}{p} + \eta^- \right) \right] \underbrace{\frac{1}{1-a}\left(\frac{m}{p} + \frac{w}{p}b \right)}_{1-a} q - q,$$

which yields a growth rate of the economy:

$$\frac{\dot{q}}{q} = \frac{1}{a}\left(\frac{m}{p} + \eta^-\right).$$

We can see that pre-financing of productive investment can boost economic growth (an important role emphasized by Schumpeter). This is quite important in the case that the economy operates below its full capacity level or credits are financing productivity enhancing investments.

If the economy, however, operates at the full capacity level there are constraints on mobilizing the additional investment goods. First, there could be a constraint from the financial sector which may not be willing to extend finance much in such circumstances.[9] Second, there are constraints from the physical side of the economy. This physical constraint requires an explicit consideration concerning the specific source of the additional physical goods. If these are coming via forced savings of workers the natural constraint is given by $(wb/p)q$. In the case that there are exogenous resources (imports, inventories) the amount of these imposes a natural constraint. In the third case, finally, the physical constraint is the maximum productivity of the system given by $1/a^{max}$.

9.6.3.   Accumulation of Assets and Debts

So far we have neglected that assets and debts accumulate. The growth of financial assets amounts to:

$$\dot{h}^+ = \eta^+ mq + (\rho^+ - \vartheta^+)h^+$$

ρ^+ denotes the interest rate on assets and $\vartheta^+ h^+$ are the flows from the financial sector back to the real sector which will be discussed below in more detail. In real terms this amounts to a long-term claim of $h^+ p_{h^+}$ where p_{h^+} refers to the relative price of financial (h^+) versus productive asset holdings (paq) as it developed from the time of its purchase. Over time we assume that the financial asset holders will be realizing their claims (i.e. demand in the real sector) which implies a transversality condition $\lim_{t \to \infty} p_{h^+} h^+ = 0$. Thus if h^+ remains positive for whatever reason, the price of the asset must approach zero. We shall, however, assume subsequently that the stock of financial assets will tend towards zero in the long run.

We now turn symmetrically to the accumulation and repayment of loans: so far we have assumed that the investor can borrow without paying interest and without having to pay back the loans. Taking these into consideration, the outstanding claim of the financier (the debt of the investor) accumulates over time with:

$$\dot{h}^- = \eta^- pq + (\rho^- - \vartheta^-)h^-,$$

where ρ^- is the interest on loans and $\vartheta^- h^-$ are repayments of the principal. The claim in real terms of the financiers (e.g. banks) are given by $h^- p_{h^-}$ where p_{h^-} refers to the relative value of (one unit of) credit claims. To avoid unlimited indebtedness we again introduce a transversality condition as:

$$\lim_{t \to \infty} p_{h^-} h^- = 0.$$

As before, we assume that the transversality condition is satisfied.[10]

9.6.4.   Growth Effects of Asset Decumulation and Loan Repayments

Let us now focus on financial asset decumulation, i.e. $\dot{h}^+ < 0$. For simplicity we also assume that no further financial asset accumulation takes place, i.e. $\eta^+ = 0$. These assumptions together with the transversality condition imply that $\rho^+ - \vartheta^+ < 0$. We have to consider various possibilities.

As pointed out above, the realization of ownership claims from financial assets depends on the valuation of financial assets as defined by the relative price p_{h^+}. The realization of the ownership claims at any point of time, given by $p_{h^+}h^+$, may be introduced through an adjustment of either wage income or profit income or both. We assume that the economy operates at the full capacity level. Other mechanisms discussed above in the case of credit financing would be possible as well (e.g. exogenous resources, unused capacities, higher productivity of the system). These would have partly different implications for growth and consumption. The impact on economic growth will depend on whether the liquidation of financial assets adds to consumption or investment:

1. (a) Let us start with the case that forced saving is imposed on the workers and that the claims are used for consumption. The growth path of the economy then becomes:

$$\dot{q} = \left(1 + \frac{1}{a}\frac{m}{p}\right)\frac{1}{1-a}\left[\frac{m}{p} + \frac{\tilde{w}b}{p} + \frac{\vartheta^+(p_{h^+}h^+)}{pq}\right]q - q,$$

where $\tilde{w} = w - \left[(\vartheta^+ p_{h^+}h^+)/bq\right] = w - (\vartheta^+ p_{h^+}h^+/l)$. Note that in this case the growth rate of the system is not reduced. Workers, however, get a lower actual real income. We can see here that per-worker actual real income falls by $\vartheta^+ p_{h^+}h^+/l$, i.e. the amount required to satisfy the real claims of financial asset holders who wish to realize at a point of time $\vartheta^+ h^+$ portion of their financial asset.

(b) The second case is that the claims are financed by forced savings of workers but are used for investment.

$$\dot{q} = \left(1 + \frac{1}{a}\frac{m}{p} + \frac{\vartheta^+ h^+}{paq}\right)\frac{1}{1-a}\left[\frac{m}{p} + \frac{\tilde{w}b}{p} + \frac{\vartheta^+(p_{h^+}h^+)}{pq}\right]q - q,$$

where again $\tilde{w} = w - \left(\vartheta^+ p_{h^+} h^+ / l\right)$. In this case there is a higher growth rate financed by the workers.

2. In the second case the claims of the financial asset holders are financed from the entrepreneurs' incomes. Here again there are two subcases depending on whether the financial asset holders spend the realization from these claims on consumption or investment.

   If they spend it on consumption the growth effects are equivalent to the earlier case where profit-receivers spend a proportion of their income on consumption rather than on investment (i.e. $\kappa_m > 0$) while in the second case no change in growth takes place.

Of course, various combinations of the above possibilities can also be considered.

The issue of loan repayments and their impact on growth can be dealt with in the same or symmetric manner as in the cases discussed above (financial asset accumulation or decumulation) depending on the expenditure/savings behaviour of the creditors (which are being repaid). We do not treat this any further.

9.7. SIMULATION STUDIES

In this section we explore the quantity, price, wage and employment dynamics through simulations of the model. The purpose of these simulations is to show the sensitivity of transition paths with respect to particular behavioural parameters in the model especially with respect to the investment behaviour in liquid or financial assets and the financing of investment via credits. In these simulations we abstract from exogenous growth of population and do not restrict the dynamics to a given labour supply. Further we assume that $\delta_{k,OUT} = 0$, which means that there are no effects of unemployment on the labour supply. This assumes that participation increases in line with labour demand, i.e. $\delta_{k,IN} = 1$, and does not converge to an exogenous level. We set the long-run mark-up rate $\pi = 0$. This implies that in equilibrium the economy is stationary. (The simulations below could then also be interpreted as deviations from a long-term growth path.) The parameters and starting values of the scenarios are reported in Tables 9.1 and 9.2, respectively. The starting values are equilibrium values for the given parameters. We model the technological shock as a logistic pattern which implies a time path of the labour input coefficient as shown in Figure 9.2.

Table 9.1   Parameter values used in simulations

Parameter	Scenario 1	Scenario 2	Scenario 3	Scenario 4	Scenario 5
a	0.500	0.500	0.500	0.500	0.500
π	0.000	0.000	0.000	0.000	0.000
δ_p	0.250	0.250	0.250	0.250	0.250
κ_s	0.000	0.000	0.000	0.000	0.000
κ_m	0.000	0.000	0.000	0.000	0.000
δ_{LIN}	1.000	1.000	1000	1000	1000
δ_{LOUT}	0.000	0.000	0.000	0.000	0.000
κ_u	–0.010	–0.010	–0.010	–0.010	–0.010
η^+	0.000	0.485	0.485	0.000	0.485
η^-	0.000	0.000	0.300	0.000	0.300
κ_b	0.000	0.000	0.000	0.050	0.050

Table 9.2   Starting values used in simulations

Variable	Values	Variable	Values
b	1.000	q^c	0.500
w	1.000	q	1.000
v	1.000	l	1.000
p	2.000	k	1.000
c	2.000	u	0.000
r	0.000	γ_q	0.000
s	0.000	n	2.000
q^l	0.000		

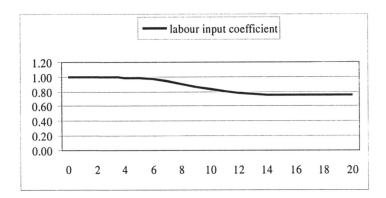

Figure 9.2 Labour input coefficient

9.7.1. Technical Progress and Effective Demand

In the first scenario we assume that all emerging rents are reinvested, whereas in the second scenario a large part of the emerging rents is invested in financial assets, $\eta^+ = 0.485$. In the third scenario, however, there is additionally to the investment into the financial sector, an active banking sector which supports investments via credit finance, i.e. $\eta^- = 0.300$.

Figure 9.3 shows the trajectories of several variables. In the first and the third scenario there is no unemployment (or even slightly excess demand for labour) and the nominal wage rate is almost stable. In the second scenario, however, the wage rate is falling due to high unemployment. The reason for the behaviour of the unemployment rate can be found in the output dynamics (as the effect of technological progress on output per worker is the same in all three scenarios). In the first scenario (with no investment into liquid assets), output growth is highest as all emerging rents are reinvested which also boosts demand for labour with no unemployment arising. In the second scenario, unemployment is rising as output is not growing (output growth is even slightly negative at the beginning) but output per worker is rising due to the exogenous technical progress. Finally, in the third scenario, the inflow of financial capital used for additional investment helps to keep unemployment at a very low level. In all three scenarios there are positive rents emerging. These are highest in the second scenario due to a depressing effect of unemployment on the wage rate and almost identical in the first and the third scenarios.

There is a small albeit important difference in real wages in the three scenarios. Although the parameter of the Phillips-curve effect is small in the

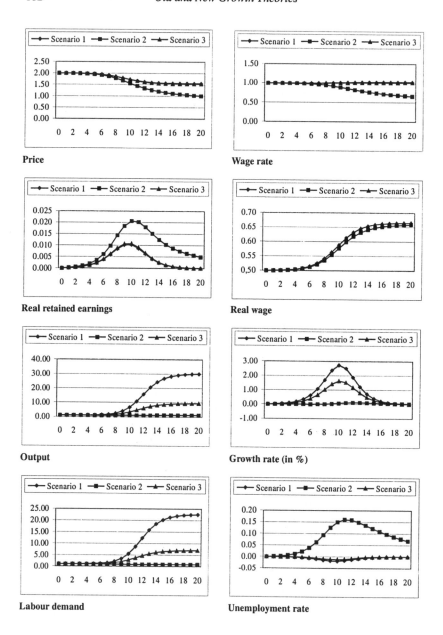

*Figure 9.3 Simulations with leakages and injections to/from the financial
          sector*

simulations, $\kappa_u = -0.01$, together with the bargaining parameter set to zero, $\kappa_s = 0$, the high unemployment rate in the second scenario leads to lower real wages which feeds back into higher real rents.

These simulations, which are in accordance with the analytical results, but derived from a richer model with wage, rent, and output dynamics may give a first understanding of the 'Solow-paradoxon': even if there are high rents due to technical progress these need not lead immediately to a higher growth rate of the economy. A pre-financing of investments may, however, help to contribute to higher output growth.

9.7.2. Endogenous Productivity Growth and the Solow Paradoxon

So far we have argued that growth paths of an economy exposed to an exogenous technology shock are a function of distributional and expenditure dynamics induced by such a shock. However, in all the scenarios described in the previous section, productivity growth remained unaffected, as it was exogenously determined. We now introduce the simple specification of endogenous productivity growth following a Kaldor–Verdoorn formulation in which productivity growth is a function of output growth (see also Section 9.3.6 above). The dynamics of the labour input coefficient then become $\dot{b}/b = -\kappa_b a(\dot{q}/q)$ where $\kappa_b > 0$ can be referred to as the Kaldor–Verdoorn parameter, translating the effect of output growth (or, more precisely, the growth rate of working capital or investment) into (labour) productivity growth. Differences in scenarios regarding output growth will therefore further affect productivity growth and through this again distributional rent dynamics and expenditure growth.

It is in this context that we can show that technology shocks affect not only output dynamics – depending on the effective demand issues discussed in the previous section – but also productivity dynamics. The latter were the focus of Solow's remarks about developments in the 1980s.

Figure 9.4 shows the results of two simulations with endogenous productivity growth in which scenario 4 shows a simulation without any leakage (i.e. all income is spent on goods) and scenario 5 shows a simulation with leakage (i.e. some investment into a non-interest bearing liquid asset). We can see – as before – that leakage has an impact on output growth, but in this case with endogenous productivity growth also a (negative) impact on productivity development. Notice that such a detrimental effect on productivity growth takes place in spite of the simulation runs 'with leakage' showing up higher per-unit profits than the simulation without leakage. The reason for this is of course the wage-depressing effect of higher unemployment levels.

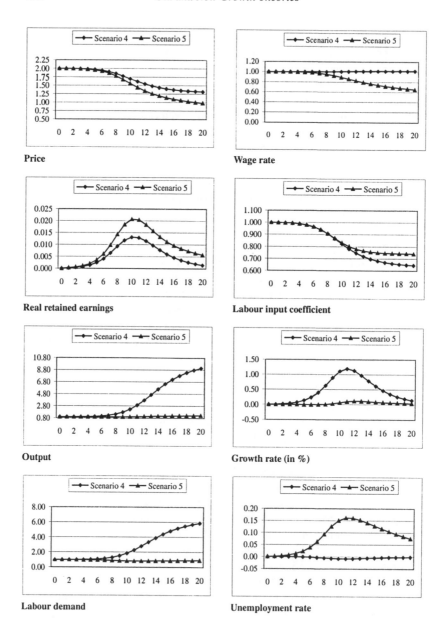

Figure 9.4 Simulations with endogenous productivity growth

Hence this version of the model tracks well the 'stylized facts' of the 1980s: a positive shift in GDP towards profits, but a relatively low[11] output and productivity performance in a period in which the economy is exposed to a (positive) technology shock. We can also easily show that the presence of venture capital (such as in the USA) which amounts to a scenario with injections from the banking sector stimulating real investments can turn the situation towards a better exploitation of the productivity potential; this is the story of the USA in the 1990s.

9.8.   CONCLUSIONS

We have shown the following in this chapter. We started with a classical model in which the well-known classical results concerning a wage–profit consumption–investment/growth trade-off emerged. We showed that the full employment condition required an increase in the profit share when there was a higher rate of (labour-saving) technical progress or an increase in the (actual) labour force. Also an increase in the share of profits spent on consumption had to be accommodated by a fall in the wage share if full employment was to be obtained. We then introduced some Keynesian elements into the analysis to show that these 'classical' results get modified when a 'whimp' factor gets introduced in terms of a hesitancy to spend on productive investment on the part of profit receivers. In this case we could show that an increase in the profit share above a certain level depresses economic growth. Next we modelled more extensively the relationships between the financial and the real sector of the economy. We showed the impact on economic growth both of 'leakage' effects from shifting investment spending towards financial assets as well as the role which financial institutions can play in pre-financing productive investments in the real sector (a role which J. Schumpeter emphasized). In a number of simulations we show the qualitative behaviour of the model as it absorbs 'technology shocks'. We show that the features of the model are quite able to explain how a positive 'technology shock' could lead to effective demand problems which keep the actual growth rate substantially below the potential growth rate. The model thus serves as a way to understand the underlying factors which could explain the so-called 'Solow paradoxon' much discussed in the 1970s and 1980s.

APPENDIX

A. Stability analysis

The model can be summarized with the following system of differential equations:

$$\dot{p}(t) = \delta_p p(t)(a-1) + \delta_p w(t)b$$

$$\dot{q}(t) = \frac{1}{a}\underbrace{\left[(1-a) - \frac{w(t)}{p(t)}b\right]}_{f_m(t)}q(t)$$

$$\dot{w}(t) = \kappa_u\left[1 - \frac{bq(t)}{k}\right]w(t).$$

As we have seen above the dynamics of the model depends on the behaviour of the real wage $\omega(t) = w(t)/p(t)$. We discuss the following simplified version of the model:

$$\dot{\omega} = \delta_\omega\left[\frac{1-a}{b} - \omega(t)\right] + \kappa_u\left[1 - \frac{b}{k}q(t)\right]$$

$$\dot{q} = \frac{(1-a) - \omega(t)b}{a}q(t).$$

The first equation gives the dynamic of the real wage ω. Here, the first term means that the real wage converges to the equilibrium value $(1-a)/b$ whereas the second term reflects the labour market effect. In the case of unemployment $1 - (b/k)q(t) > 0$ there is a pressure on the real wage if $\kappa_u < 0$. The system is non-linear because of the term $\omega(t)q(t)$ in the quantity equation.

Setting $\dot{\omega}$ and $\dot{q}$ equal to zero yields the fix-point:

$$\dot{\omega} = \frac{1-a}{b}, \quad \dot{q} = \frac{k}{b}.$$

Linearizing the system and evaluating at the fix-point gives the Jacobian matrix:

$$\mathbf{J}^* = \begin{bmatrix} -\delta_\omega & -\kappa_u \dfrac{b}{k} \\[2ex] -\dfrac{k}{a} & 0 \end{bmatrix}.$$

The eigenvalues of the system can be calculated as:

$$\lambda_{1,2} = \frac{1}{2}\left(\mathrm{tr}\,\mathbf{J}^* \pm \sqrt{(\mathrm{tr}\,\mathbf{J}^*)^2 - 4\det \mathbf{J}^*}\right),$$

where $\mathrm{tr}\,\mathbf{J}^*$ denotes the trace of the matrix and $\det \mathbf{J}^*$ is the determinant ($\mathrm{tr}\,\mathbf{J}^* = -\delta_\omega \le 0$, $\det \mathbf{J}^* = -\kappa_u(b/a) \ge 0$).

The structure of the eigenvalues can be used to examine the stability of the model. Table 9.A.1 shows the trace, the determinant, and the discriminant Δ of the Jacobian $\mathbf{J}^*$ for different sets of the adjustment parameters δ_ω and κ_u. Let us start with the case in which $\kappa_u > 0$ which would mean that in the case of unemployment the real wage would even rise (or vice versa). If additionally the real wage-to-rent adjustment parameter is less than zero, i.e. $\delta_\omega < 0$ (which would mean that prices diverge from costs) the system is clearly unstable as both eigenvalues become positive. For $\delta_\omega = 0$ or $\delta_\omega < 0$ the model is saddle-point stable (both real eigenvalues have opposite signs).

If $\delta_\omega < 0$, then irrespective of the value of the sign of κ_u the system is unstable as the eigenvalues or the real part of the complex eigenvalues are positive.

For $\delta_\omega = 0$ and $\kappa_u = 0$ both eigenvalues are zero, which means that the system just remains at the starting values and there are no adjustments at all. For $\kappa_u = 0$, i.e. with no effects of unemployment on wages, but $\delta_\omega > 0$ one can see that the first eigenvalue is zero and the second eigenvalue is negative. In economic terms this means that prices adjust to costs but there is no 'mechanism' which assures full employment. The system converges to a steady state but without assuring full employment. In the other case with $\kappa_u < 0$ and $\delta_\omega = 0$ we find complex eigenvalues with real parts equal zero. Thus in this case we can observe stable oscillations. However it is structurally unstable as changes of δ_ω shift the regime either into the unstable or the stable region.

Finally, we discuss the economically meaningful cases with a positive wage-to-rent adjustment and a negative effect of unemployment on the real wage. In this case the trace is negative and the determinant is positive which implies stability of the system. We have to distinguish three cases. First, the discriminant is positive and thus both eigenvalues are negative and different from each other. In the second case we have equal eigenvalues with negative signs. Finally, the third case in which the discriminant is negative and the eigenvalues are complex with negative real parts. In this case we can observe dampened oscillations to the equilibrium path.

Table 9.A.1 Stability analysis

	$\delta_\omega > 0$	$\delta_\omega = 0$	$\delta_\omega < 0$
$\kappa_u > 0$	tr < 0	tr = 0	tr > 0
	det < 0	det < 0	det < 0
	$\Delta > 0$	$\Delta > 0$	$\Delta > 0$
	$\lambda_1 > 0$	$\lambda_1 > 0$	$\lambda_1 > 0$
	$\lambda_2 < 0$	$\lambda_2 < 0$	$\lambda_2 > 0$
$\kappa_u = 0$	tr < 0	tr = 0	tr > 0
	det = 0	det = 0	det = 0
	$\Delta > 0$	$\Delta = 0$	$\Delta > 0$
	$\lambda_1 = 0$	$\lambda_i = 0$	$\lambda_1 > 0$
	$\lambda_2 < 0$		$\lambda_2 = 0$
$\kappa_u < 0$	tr < 0	tr = 0	tr > 0
	det > 0	det > 0	det > 0
	(1) $\Delta > 0$	$\Delta < 0$	(1) $\Delta > 0$
	$\lambda_1 < 0$	Re $\lambda_i = 0$	$\lambda_1 > 0$
	$\lambda_2 < 0$		$\lambda_2 > 0$
	(2) $\Delta = 0$		(2) $\Delta = 0$
	$\lambda_i < 0$		$\lambda_i > 0$
	(3) $\Delta < 0$		(3) $\Delta < 0$
	Re $\lambda_i < 0$		Re $\lambda_i > 0$

NOTES

1. The second formulation is analogous to the solution of a dynamic Leontief model with only circulating capital (see e.g. Pasinetti, 1977).

2. This result also holds if wages are paid *post factum*. In this case the price has to be formulated as $p(t) = (1 + \pi)p(t)a + w(t)b(t)$ and the equilibrium price is $p = wb[1 - (1 + \pi)a]^{-1}$. Demand out of profits and rents which equals investment by assumption then is $f_m = (m/p)q = \pi pa/p = \pi a$. The growth rate then turns out to be $\gamma_q = (1/a)\pi a = \pi$. In the case that $\pi = \pi^{max}$ the economy grows at the maximum growth rate $\gamma_q^{max} = (1/a) - 1 = \gamma^{max}$.

3. A growing labour force is discussed below.

4. A referee pointed out that full employment could also be maintained following a technology shock without adjusting income distribution if either there were inventories which could be decumulated and used for building up the required additional capacities or in case there were no such inventories there could be some temporary savings in circulating capital used which again would facilitate the building-up of additional capacities. In our model which does not distinguish explicitly between fixed and circulating capital (both are captured by the same coefficient a) such a transitory pattern – while possible – would require an additional specification of inputs required as intermediate inputs versus inputs for capacity expansion. We do not want to overload the chapter by such a distinction.

5. A similar condition holds for fixed wage rates and flexible prices:

$$\frac{\dot{p}}{p} = \gamma_b + \frac{a(\dot{\gamma}_b + \dot{\gamma}_\lambda)}{(1-a) - a(\gamma_b + \gamma_k)}$$

If both, wage rate and price, are flexible the condition is:

$$\frac{\dot{w}}{w} - \frac{\dot{p}}{p} = -\gamma_b - \frac{a(\dot{\gamma}_b + \dot{\gamma}_\lambda)}{(1-a) - a(\gamma_b + \gamma_k)}$$

6. This rather mechanic specification represents the Schumpeterian insight that technological innovations happen through transitory changes in the market structures which accompany the introduction and diffusion of new technologies. The specification thus models the macro-dynamics of technical change and does not model the individual firms' pricing behaviour.

7. The model could also allow the inclusion of a changing participation rate, i.e. $\zeta(t)$, but we shall not introduce this in this chapter.

8. In this specification it is assumed that additionally required investment goods (see discussion in Section 9.6.2) are made available from outside the system. Alternatively, there could be an adjustment in the productivity parameter a or in the wage rate, as discussed above, but these alternatives would have implications for the price equations and the distribution of income.

9. For example, out of fear that the high pressure on capacities might lead to a lowering of returns due to a Phillips-curve effect.

10. The role of p_{h^*} and p_{h^-} will only emerge in a more elaborate version of this model when dynamics of financial asset valuation will be explicitly considered.

11. 'Relatively low' can be interpreted here in relation to a scenario without leakage.

REFERENCES

Dutt, A. (1990), *Growth, Distribution and Uneven Development*, Cambridge: Cambridge University Press.

Flaschel, P., R. Franke and W. Semmler (1997), *Dynamic Macroeconomic: Instability, Fluctuation, and Growth in Monetary Economics*, Cambridge, Massachussetts: MIT Press.

Foley, D. (1986), *Money, Accumulation and Crisis*, London: Harwood Academic Publishers.

Goodwin, R. (1986), 'Swinging along the turnpike with von Neumann and Sraffa', *Cambridge Journal of Economics*, **10**(3), 203–10.

Goodwin, R. and L. Punzo (1987), *The Dynamics of a Capitalist Economy*, Cambridge: Polity Press.

Landesmann, M. and R. Stehrer (2000), 'Industrial specialisation, catching-up and labour market dynamics', *Metroeconomica*, **51**(1), 67–101.

Marglin, S. (1984), *Growth, Distribution and Prices*, Cambridge, Massachusetts: Harvard University Press.

Pasinetti, L. (1977), *Lectures on the Theory of Production*, London: Macmillan Press.

Pasinetti, L. (1981), *Structural Change and Economic Growth*, London: Macmillan.

Stehrer, R. (2002), 'Dynamics of trade integration and technological convergence', *Economic Systems Research*, **14**(3), 219–44.

Taylor, L. (1981), *Income Distribution, Inflation and Growth: Lectures on Structuralist Macroeconomic Theory*, Cambridge, Massachusetts: MIT Press.

10. Schumpeterian growth theory and Schumpeter's monetary ideas: a suggested integration[*]

Guido Cozzi

10.1. INTRODUCTION

Endogenous growth theory based on research and development (R&D) purposefully carried out by profit-maximizing firms in competitive situations has derived much inspiration from Joseph A. Schumpeter's ideas about the innovative process. Most notably, Aghion and Howitt (1992) work, by incorporating Schumpeter's (1934 and 1939) 'creative destruction' in a general equilibrium model deserved the definition of 'basic Schumpeterian model' (see e.g. Aghion and Howitt, 1998). However there has been a general theoretical neglect of the role of private money creation in the growth process that Schumpeter considered crucial.

One of the fundamental lessons of Schumpeterian growth theory pioneered by Aghion and Howitt's (1992) contribution is the forward-looking nature of industrial wealth. According to this view the main source of real wealth is productive firms' securities, and these securities in turn derive their value from the expected profit stream arising from the private property of useful ideas as codified in patents, and that are continuously challenged by outsider research firms. In this chapter, I assume that the financial system leverages on this important source of wealth a credit pyramid leading to the creation of private money. I will stylize this by saying that 'banks' can create means of payments up to a fraction/multiple of the capitalized value of the manufacturing firms owned by banks' shareholders. Financial intermediaries – involving several entities that we will label 'banks' with an' obvious definitional abuse – in turn lend newly created bank money to R&D firms challenging the current monopolist. This credit creation process fuels obsolescence that limits bank capital and thereby credit. Hence the ultimate variable that equilibrates private money demand and supply is R&D investment. This is the main channel that this chapter intends to emphasize and through which it tries to cast a bridge between modern Schumpeterian theory and Schumpeter's own monetary ideas.

The theoretical introduction of a role for what we have labeled 'banking' needs a preliminary motivation for money in a picture usually analyzed in an Arrow–Debreu framework. In Schumpeter's book on the essence of money (Schumpeter, 1970) he argued that banks should manage transactions and social accounting even in a stationary economy. Decentralized trade intermediated by the several money media generates frictions of all sorts that justify the existence of payment leads and lags and the necessity of monetary and banking regulation. This is stressed by Schumpeter in several other articles and books too. However, I think that current advances in Schumpeterian growth theory suggest a natural way to go beyond the exogenous imposition of a cash in advance constraint, entailing transaction costs without justification in terms of what would be available under centralized trade.

Aghion and Howitt's (1992) 'arbitrage condition' elegantly stylizes what is required for centralized trade to guarantee the financing of R&D from individual voluntary savings: the knowledge of the parameters affecting directly or indirectly the effective patent life and profits. I think it is useful to compare this with Schumpeter's own vision, which stressed that the innovative process has some peculiarly unpredictable aspects that would make it impossible to manage them in what he called a 'Walrasian equilibrium'. In particular Schumpeter (1934 and 1939) depicts growth and business cycles as the innovative destruction of a 'static' equilibrium and the transition to a new one. I have chosen to microfound the essentiality of monetary exchanges by assuming Knightian uncertainty in an aspect of the innovative activity that makes it impossible to generate it as the outcome of an Arrow–Debreu equilibrium. In particular this chapter assumes that in a given period when researchers are trying to innovate it is not possible to know the probability intensity that after the next innovation a new one will be achievable by each research time unit. The unpredictable aspect of future R&D productivity is this chapter's original part in microfounding the emergence of bank money as a social institution, but I believe it is very much in line with Schumpeter's line of thinking and fairly realistic too.

As a consequence of the assumed element of Knightian uncertainty though all agents are assumed to be rational and selfish, to costlessly and instantaneously know the learnable details of the model and never to make mistakes, and though markets are assumed always to clear instantaneously, a Walrasian equilibrium would entail no innovation at all. The reason is the impossibility of guaranteeing that the value of future obsolescence be low enough to induce conservative – i.e. maximinizers in the face of strong uncertainty – consumers to save, and this feeds back into the marginal value of R&D investment. Though money and banking operate less smoothly than an ideal Arrow–Debreu equilibrium they have the additional virtue of rendering innovation possible. In the spirit of Dubey and Geanakoplos (2001) money offers gains from trade that can outweigh even those of a frictionless centralized trade, and in the spirit of Wallace (1998) and Smith (2001) money is essential in that it allows us to achieve allocations that centralized trade cannot replicate or improve upon, in so far as innovation is desirable.

Despite Knightian uncertainty the model determines a unique equilibrium level of R&D employment, price levels, money growth, right-continuous inflation and sudden deflation processes. Aggregate GDP, employment composition, and income distribution (between unskilled and skilled wages, and profits) are functions of the monetary regulation, of individual intertemporal preferences, production elasticities, and the realization of the a priori unknown R&D productivity parameter. Interestingly, the equilibrium expected growth rate turns out to be well known and constant in all contingencies. Hence bank credit creation is the main engine for stable expected growth, though its interaction with technological stochasticities is at the same time responsible for business cycles and for the reallocation of productive factors and individual incomes.

The chapter will assume perfect information and perfect competition in the banking sector. This clearly reduces realism and forces me to ignore a large and important literature on banking industry imperfections and growth. A seminal paper on finance and growth under imperfect information is King and Levine (1993). For interesting recent work see Galetovic (1994a and 1994b), Huang and Xu (1999), Cetorelli and Gambera (2000), and Cetorelli and Peretto (2000). All these papers assume computable risk, and under this assumption they shed much light on how market and institutional aspects of banking and finance interact with innovation and growth. Unlike them, this chapter instead starts an analysis of finance and growth under Knightian uncertainty. It would be very interesting to join the two approaches. I hope that our admittedly highly artificial economy could suggest some ideas related to transaction money, banks, and growth that might give some useful insights for future work.

This work is organized as follows. Section 10.2 provides a brief reminder of the aspect of Aghion and Howitt (1992) model that will be relevant for the rest of the chapter. Sections 10.3.1, 10.3.2, and 10.3.3 introduce our main assumptions about uncertainty and about the payment system and derives the first consequences on the essentiality of money and of limited liability. Section 10.3.4 computes the equilibrium values of the main macroeconomic variables. Section 10.4 concludes with some comments.

10.2. A REMINDER OF THE BASIC SCHUMPETERIAN MODEL

This chapter effects a variation on the Schumpeterian endogenous growth model developed by Aghion and Howitt (1992). For simplicity and to make the results more transparent we will use its basic version with drastic innovations, one consumption sector, one intermediate good sector, and perfect capital markets. To facilitate the exposition, before introducing the original part of the chapter, I will recall the features of the basic Schumpeterian model that will be useful in the rest of the chapter. This subsection can costlessly be skipped by readers who are familiar with this literature. From Section 10.3 the new features of our model will be introduced and developed.

A final sector is assumed where perfectly competitive firms combine a flow of intermediate goods x of the same quality $t \in N$ and unskilled labour, whose total supply M is normalized to one, to produce a flow of perishable consumption good according to a CRS production function given by $y = A_t f(x, M) = A_t f(x, 1) \equiv A_t F(x)$, with $F(\cdot)$ increasing and strictly concave and satisfying Inada's conditions. We will use throughout the chapter the simple Cobb–Douglas specification:

$$Y = A_t x^\alpha M^{1-\alpha} = A_t x^\alpha.$$

Every new quality of the intermediate good scales total factor productivity A_t up by a factor $\gamma > 1$. Hence $A_{t+1} = \gamma A_t$ for all $t = 0, 1, 2, \ldots$, where t does not represent calendar time, but the currently used generation of the intermediate good. We can normalize by setting $A_0 = 1$.

Time is continuous and unbounded above and the continuum of infinitely lived dynasties of individuals have identical intertemporally additive preferences with a constant subjective rate of time preference $r > 0$; instantaneous utility is linear in consumption; capital markets are costless and perfectly competitive; hence the equilibrium real interest rate is constantly equal to r. Moreover individuals are endowed with flow units of unskilled and skilled labor time which they will supply inelastically to a perfectly competitive labor market. Intermediate goods are produced on a one-to-one basis from skilled labor, and the total supply of skilled labor is equal to $L > 0$. Since preferences satisfy the Gorman conditions, the distribution of labor types and firm property across individuals does not affect the equilibrium behavior of aggregate quantities, on which our analysis is focused.

Every new quality of the intermediate good is discovered by perfectly competitive research firms that employ only skilled labor, each time unit of which produces the next innovation with Poisson arrival rate $\lambda_t > 0$. We generalize Aghion and Howitt's (1992) technology slightly by allowing the flow probability of quality improvement to change depending on the vintage of the intermediate good to innovate. Hence it is possible that some quality improvements are more difficult to develop than others.

The inventor of the new generation of the intermediate good is assumed by Aghion and Howitt (1992) able to instantaneously patent the new invention and to implement its production. We will work under the assumption of 'drastic' innovations, i.e. the quality upgrade γ is so high as to allow the producer of this new quality (its discoverer or someone to whom the blueprint is sold) to completely displace the former intermediate good from the market even by setting a price for it that maximizes monopoly real profits in terms of the consumption good. Though at any instant there is free entry and CRS technology in all markets, the intermediate good sector will be run by a unique monopolist in equilibrium.

In this economy production, skilled labor employment, and consumption decisions by agents are constant during the holding times between two successive innovations: hence we can order all endogenous variables by the quality t of the intermediate good currently in use. The skilled labor market equilibrium condition is $L = x_t + n_t$, where n_t is the total mass of skilled labor employed in the research sector, and x_t is the number of workers producing the intermediate good of quality t, equal to the flow per unit time of output in this sector.

Maximized intermediate good monopolist real profits in period (of stochastic duration) t are:

$$\pi_t \equiv \max \alpha A_t x^{\alpha-1} x - \frac{w_t}{p_t^C} x = A_t \tilde{\pi} \frac{w_t}{p_t^C A_t} = \left(\frac{1}{\alpha} - 1\right) \alpha^2 A_t (L - n_t)^\alpha.$$

where p_t^C is the consumer good nominal price. Aghion and Howitt's (1992) focus on non-monetary economic aspects justified their normalization $p_t^C = 1$. Since we are re-introducing money into the model we will need explicitly nominal prices, which in principle can change over time.

The equilibrium skilled labor real wage is easily obtained as:

$$\frac{w_t}{p_t^C} = \frac{\alpha^2 A_t}{(L - n_t)^{1-\alpha}}$$

and the equilibrium unskilled labour real wage is:

$$\frac{w_t^U}{p_t^C} = (1-\alpha)A_t \left(\frac{L - n_t}{M}\right)^\alpha = (1-\alpha)A_t (L - n_t)^\alpha,$$

where w_t^U denotes the nominal unskilled wage in period t.

The real value V_t of being the current monopolist satisfies the asset equation $V_t r = \pi_t - \lambda n_t V_t$ where π_t, is the monopolist's profit flow and λn_t is the probability intensity of the arrival process of innovation $t + 1$, equal to the integral sum of the arrival rate λ of each unit of mass n_t of independent research time units in the economy. With probability intensity λn_t the new quality arrives and the monopolist is displaced.

Given our assumption on the production function in the consumption sector it is easy to see that $\pi_t = A_t \tilde{\pi}(w_t / A_t)$, where w_t is the wage rate of the skilled labor and $\tilde{\pi}(.)$ gives productivity-adjusted profit π_t / A_t, as a decreasing function of productivity-adjusted real wage $w_t / (p_t^C A_t) \equiv \omega_t$. Moreover it is easily seen that $\pi_t = \tilde{x}(\omega_t)$, with $\tilde{\pi}' < 0$. This implies that the skilled labor market clearing condition for all $t = 0, 1, 2, \ldots$ can be rewritten as:

$$L = \tilde{x}(\omega_t) + n_t$$

Perfect competition in the research sector implies the arbitrage condition $w_t = \omega V_t$ which, in the light of the previous results, becomes:

$$\frac{w_t}{p_t^C} = \lambda_t V_{t+1} \equiv \left(\frac{1}{\alpha} - 1\right) \frac{\lambda_t \alpha^2 A_{t+1}(L - n_{t+1})^\alpha}{r + \lambda_{t+1} n_{t+1}} .$$

The last two equations allow us to completely describe the dynamics of this economy. It will display stochastic growth with expected rate[1] $\lambda_t n_t \ln\gamma$.

10.3. MOVING CLOSER TO SCHUMPETER

10.3.1. Without Banks

According to Schumpeter's theory of economic growth (Schumpeter, 1934) and of business cycles (Schumpeter, 1939), innovation is not typically financed by consumer's voluntary savings, but by new money created by banks that force savings to free up the productive resources (labor in our model) needed to carry out the innovation. As credit/money creation by banks is of crucial importance for Schumpeter it will be central for our monetary model of Schumpeterian growth.

Let us note that in the current Schumpeterian growth theory innovation is assumed to be financed only out of voluntary consumer savings. This is clearly visible in Aghion and Howitt's (1992) arbitrage equation (2.1), where the real value of the firm is the expected present value of its profit flows computed by using the consumer rate of time preference r. More specifically, R&D firms are assumed to issue instantaneous lotteries conditional on the success of their enterprise – i.e. on the successful development of the t + 1st intermediate good – paying out shares of the stock of the firm that will produce it under monopoly, which in turn are evaluated by using the consumer subjective interest r and the exact knowledge of the hazard rate of the future monopolist, $\lambda_{t+1}n_{t+1}$. Notice that risk neutral consumers during period t are assumed to know for sure how many people will be undertaking R&D aimed at overcoming something that has not yet been discovered and their exact probability of success. Notice that for centralized trade to operate well they are required to know not only the flow probability of arrival of the next innovation, but also the probability of innovating again after the realization of the next innovation. Under these conditions, the financing of R&D becomes a routine saving decision.

According to Schumpeter's own ideas of growth and business cycle (Schumpeter 1934 and 1939) the future consequences of the next innovations are not completely foreseeable before the first innovation has been completed. Stated in terms of our model, we can safely say that Schumpeter would be more inclined to think that at least the productivity of R&D in the discovery of the t + 2nd innovation cannot be computed before the success of innovation t + 1. We will therefore introduce the assumption that during period t the individuals know that $\lambda_{t+1} \in \left[\overline{\lambda}, +\infty\right)$, with $\overline{\lambda} \geq 0$, but do not have any further information about the probability distribution of λ_{t+1} – i.e. some degree of Knightian uncertainty characterizes future R&D productivity. When we have to deal with large-scale innovations each such event is unique in the sense that calculable risk methods can be applied at most one (stochastic) period in advance. This implies that it is not any longer obvious how to convince rational consumers to forgo current consumption in exchange for an expected gain nobody is able to calculate.

Given Knightian uncertainty, we have to revise Aghion and Howitt's (1992) assumptions about individual preference to determine behavior. We will adopt the conservative assumption that if the consumer does not know the exact probability distribution of a set of possible outcomes she will choose actions as if the worst outcome was the (almost) sure event. Such preferences (advocated by Hansen and Sargent 2001) imply a *maximin* optimal choice under Knightian uncertainty. Notice that such consumer preferences are extremely risk averse when considering lotteries in which probabilities are strongly unknown whereas they do not imply any risk aversion when pairs of lotteries with computable probabilities are considered. Hence we will assume Aghion and Howitt's (1992) computable risk neutrality coupled with Hansen and Sargent's (2001) conservative attitude towards Knightian uncertainty.

Under our new assumptions the market of R&D funds from consumer savings cannot operate because the worst possible value of the future monopolist is zero: in fact the monopolists' obsolescence is crucial in calculating its stock market value and it has unbounded support by assumption. Consequently R&D firms cannot market options on not yet invented blueprints at any positive price. Hence we can state our first result:

Lemma 1: *No innovation takes place in a Walrasian equilibrium.*

As claimed by Schumpeter (1934 and 1939) in an economy that relies only on consumer saving decisions to fund creative destruction there would be no innovation at all. It is important to note that there exists a unique general equilibrium outcome in this economy with Knightian uncertainty, but this is precisely the Schumpeterian model's 'no-growth' outcome, with $n_t = 0$.

Moreover, for the no-growth equilibrium to be the only one it is not necessary to have the above postulated form of Knightian uncertainty. In fact, even if $\lambda_{t+1}, \lambda_{t+2}, \ldots, \lambda_{t+N}$ were known for an arbitrarily large N, if λ_{t+N+1} is Knightian uncertain the R&D markets close down for all preceding periods. In fact, the forward-looking character of the value of the intermediate monopolist requires that in period t we know the R&D employment of the next period, $t + 1$, to assess the next period's profits. This in turn requires the solution of period $t + 1$'s arbitrage equation that needs knowledge of $t + 2$'s R&D parameters, and so on, up to $t + N$'s parameter knowledge requirement. Hence the reader should not interpret our Knightian uncertainty requirement as stating that when mainframe computers had been invented, R&D productivity in the discovery of lap-top computers was unknown. Instead, it suffices that she accepts the idea that – for example – such R&D productivity was unknown by Gutenberg when he made his first steps into the development of modern printing.

If we want to recover growth in this stylized economy in order to obtain insights about real world innovation we should find other credit channels at least to complement the useless stock market for R&D firms' securities. We note in passing that the stock market where existing firms' equities and bonds are traded is actively operating in this economy, as obsolescence rate of current monopolists is always computable and, as we shall see, strictly positive in the unique equilibrium.

10.3.2. With Banks

Who could finance innovation in the technological framework of our modification of Aghion and Howitt's (1992) economy and in what way? A simple response would be: the government. Letting the public sector replace private innovation would at first sight seem the only solution. However, though publicly funded research centers and universities do a considerable amount of basic and applied R&D it is equally true that private foundations and venture capitalists finance and undertake many R&D enterprises as well. Hence our theory should allow for a private solution to the problem outlined above.

To the question of who, in the absence of consumer's voluntary savings, could ever finance innovation, Schumpeter's (1934 and 1939) answer would be: 'banks will do it'. To the question of how their financing of R&D might be consistent with rationality and optimizing behavior we suggest the introduction of a stylized and admittedly abstract form of banking payment system and credit into the basic Schumpeterian model.

We will assume that bank transaction deposits are used in this economy as the main medium of transaction. Banks can create this type of money costlessly up to a multiple $k > 0$ of the current value of the transferable real assets deposited with them by their shareholders. Bank capital consists of the only real earning assets available in the stylized basic Schumpeterian model with perishable intermediate and consumption goods: the intermediate monopolist's shares. Hence bank deposits are ultimately guaranteed by their equity ownership.

Deposits are created through new loans to firms. Hence an individual can obtain bank deposits only as a consequence of new loans that banks have granted to a firm. For example, firms manufacturing consumption goods using their overdrafts to pay their unskilled workers or for intermediate good input, or R&D firms paying skilled workers.

To sum up, we are assuming that the banking system operates under perfect competition and each bank can produce 'money' at a zero cost. In a minimal interpretation of the model, when a bank is created its shareholders obtain bank's shares in exchange for the intermediate monopolist's equities they possess, necessary to define the limits of its deposits' liabilities. In practice, the bank will administer its monopolist shares on behalf of its own shareholders – as unit trusts – by transferring to them the nominal value of any dividend and capital gain. Moreover the bank will transfer to them any positive margins obtained from lending the money created. As a consequence, depositors will always accept holding only the minimum money balances necessary for consumption purposes, while maintaining all additional wealth in bank equities. In equilibrium no consumer will be holding positive amounts of the monopolist's shares without the intermediation of a bank, but the reserve requirements are justified only by exogenous regulation.

In this model, banks do not provide insurance but they have a seigniorage power for transaction money. Since money creation costs nothing to banks they will pour it into the economic system.

Conceptually distinguishing between the intermediate monopolist's shares and their representatives – money – is what allows our artificially designed 'banking system' to have an important function in the creation of credit and in allowing for the possibility of sustained economic growth. As we shall see this definition of monetary payment system through 'banks' makes credit creation 'essential' (Wallace, 1998; Smith, 2001) without forsaking a rational expectations methodology, perfectly symmetric information, no trade restrictions, and infinitely lived agents.

Given share $g_t \in \,]0,1]$ of the monopolist's stock and given the level of consumer price index $p_t^C(s)$ at time s, the nominal value of banks' assets is:

$$p_t^C(s)g_t\left(\frac{1}{\alpha}-1\right)\frac{\alpha^2 A_t(L-n_t)^\alpha}{r+\lambda_t n_t}. \tag{10.1}$$

Multiple k is set exogenously by institutional regulation – though the reader may think of a more flexible reserve system. Moreover, every intermediate monopolist shareholder is better off underwriting a bank's equity and depositing her stock with the bank. In fact a zero measure depositor cannot affect the monopolist's obsolescence that depends on the economy-wide amount of credit; however, she will reap gains from her bank's lending to outsider R&D firms trying to displace the current monopolist. We note in passing that dispersed ownership of the intermediate monopolistic sector is crucial for our results. More concentrated ownership could lead a coalition of intermediate monopolist shareholders to restrict credit to new R&D firms trying to displace it.[2] Therefore the unique equilibrium value of share $g_t \in \,]0,1]$ of monopolist's equities held by the aggregate banking sector is 1. Hence the aggregate bank money supply is:

$$M^S(s)=p_t^C(s)\left(\frac{1}{\alpha}-1\right)\frac{\alpha^2 A_t(L-n_t)^\alpha}{r+\lambda_t n_t}k, \tag{10.2}$$

and this will be total money supply as we are assuming no other forms of money. We maintain Aghion and Howitt's (1992) assumption that the production period is instantaneous; within that period manufacturing firms borrow money – deposits – from banks at a zero interest rate. We rule out consumption credit creation by banks, as suggested by Schumpeter (1934 and 1939). Therefore in the aggregate, households finance their consumption expenditure from their bank account balances.

After consumers have spent their incomes the final sector firms will repay banks the loans for their own (unskilled labor) wage bill and transfer the rest of their money revenues to the intermediate good firm. This in turn repays banks their (skilled) wage bill loans and finally transfers its nominal profits – equal to the dividends – to the shareholders. When workers and/or shareholders in turn try to spend the nominal value of their wages and dividends some time will elapse until the moment the same bank notes are actually transferred to the final good sector firms. We assume that income circulation absorbs time as an input, as we will shortly see more precisely. As a consequence, if money creation has been taking place steadily the real value of income recipients' money will have depreciated by inflation. Hence firms' factor owners are penalized by the inflationary loss of purchasing power.

When banks lend money to R&D firms their return is risky in time and strongly uncertain in the amount. Being unable to negotiate a precise interest rate, banks negotiate the fraction $\theta_{t+1} \in]0,1]$ of the monopolist's stock they will be repaid in case of success. Hence we are interpreting this aspect of Schumpeter's 'banking' activity as a venture capital activity. Venture capitalists typically finance highly risky R&D projects by asking for a participation in the start-up R&D firms, thereby appropriating a share of their success in exchange for their sinking the capital needed for its R&D start-up. Given Schumpeter's broad interpretation of 'banks' as more general financial institutions, I believe that we would not distort his original thought too much by adopting this more modern interpretation of 'banks' as simplified theoretical objects summarizing the integrated activities of commercial banks, unit trusts, investment or merchant banks, and venture capitalists. For greater clarity, the reader could think of commercial banks buying a well-diversified portfolio of investment banks' shares in exchange for newly created transaction deposits. The investment banks transfer such deposits to the R&D firms which in turn use them to pay their wage bills. If R&D is successful both investment banks and commercial banks earn a profit in terms of shares of the new intermediate good monopolist. If R&D is unsuccessful, the investment banks do not pay out positive dividends for the moment. In the case of unsuccessful R&D the commercial bank is as well off as if it had lent the same amount of deposits to a sequence of solvent manufacturing firms paying no positive interest on them. Simply, on the assets side of the commercial bank's balance sheet we could observe the same value listed as 'investment securities' instead of 'commercial and industrial loans'.

In general, the zero interest margin implied by perfect competition entails that the only source of positive income for the consolidated banking system is the intermediate monopolist's profits. Hence, when a bank lends money to an R&D firm it activates the only form of credit from which the banks as a whole can get positive profits: the only form of credit from which the bank can avoid a complete capital loss in the event an innovation occurs. The reader may wonder what happens if the R&D firm is insolvent due to bad luck in the R&D process. The following will happen: first the bank records a credit loss that subtracts the corresponding amount from its accounting capital. However, the market valuation of the bank's equity remains constant. The reason is that the credit loss does not diminish the intermediate monopolist's dividend stream accruing to the bank: this is the only thing the stock market cares about, and it is never touched by the bank's credit loss. Hence even if the bank's nominal capital is reduced by the loss, it immediately gets revalued due to a higher market's valuation.

Hence while at first sight one would expect banks to restrict their activities after a sequence of unlucky R&D financing, under our definition banks are never hurt by the credit loss. The reader will realize that this result is due to the interpretation of banks as money creators only in *excess* of their intermediate monopolist's stock ownership. These stocks guarantee their unique expected income flow, regardless of their uses of the newly created money. Since profitability is the only thing that matters for bank's capital valuation this has to remain constant regardless of the amount of credit losses in the part of its assets that exceed the monopolist's equity holding. Therefore banks' seigniorage power costs nothing to them – and under perfect competition is valued zero to outsiders – and its credit losses do not diminish bank profitability.

In the lucky case, the R&D firm transfers part of its earnings to the bank, and the latter will experience a positive increment to its capital from this source of gains. However, since conservative maximinizing individuals only value the worst case, such gain is valued at zero in advance.

Notice that since the opportunity cost of lending – indirectly – to R&D firms instead of lending to commercial and industrial firms is zero in terms of expected profit stream (due to perfect competition and continuous time), the banking system is weakly better off financing R&D, because it has at least a probability $\lambda_t n_t > 0$ of getting something positive or zero depending on the next period's amount of R&D employment. However, it is important to note that though before completely determining the monetary equilibrium we are not yet able to exactly determine by how much the positive payoff can exceed zero, indifference between the two uses of bank money does not apply except under the conservative *maximin* preferences when faced with Knightian uncertainty. In fact for all contingencies in which future R&D employment is less than L the R&D firm will repay something positive to the bank in the form of a future dividend stream accruing to the bank's shareholders. Only in the extreme case in which future R&D employment is $n_t = L$ will the value of the intermediate good monopolist be equal to zero. Instead in all contingencies, manufacturing firms' repayments will leave the bank with no additional profits.

Note that with probability $\lambda_t n_t$ per unit time, the innovation occurs and the current monopolist will become valueless: hence the bank will lose all of its current capital stock with this probability intensity. If the bank underwrites R&D firms' shares it will obtain some of the new intermediate monopolist's shares if an innovation occurs. That is, with probability $\lambda_t n_t > 0$ per unit time, the bank's capital stock will be replaced by a new one of a positive or zero value. If instead the innovation does not occur, the bank will earn nothing positive by lending newly created deposits to manufacturing firms nor by underwriting R&D firms' issuances; similarly it loses no profits from either activity. Why so? Because at a zero interest rate the manufacturing firms' repayment allows the bank to lend the same amount to someone else, with no increase in the dividends to its shareholders, because the bank – by institutional regulation – can never use its own deposits to pay its shareholders: seigniorage cannot be used to finance bank owners' consumption. The only use of a repaid loan that might generate new profits for the bank is its transformation into R&D firms' shares. Hence manufacturing loans will be weakly dominated by R&D financing. Therefore we can state:

Lemma 2: *Banks prefer the underwriting of new R&D firms' equities to lending money to manufacturing firms.*

The reader understands that only the *maximin* preference ordering makes banks indifferent: any less conservative preference ordering would entail that banks strictly prefer R&D lending to manufacturing loans. Therefore we will assume that indifference is resolved to a priority given to R&D loans rather than manufacturing loans.

It is important to stress that this activity is not achievable by individual savers but that it is specific to the – perfectly competitive and costless – producers of bank money. In fact the bank can channel its money creation to would-be intermediate monopolists because its creating money does not diminish its shareholders' consumption budget set in any respect. In such a hypothetical economy costless money creation is a privilege conferred to the bank's shareholders in so far as they never use that amount of money for their own consumption process. All other uses are unable to increase their profit flows. We can interpret the kind of banking system described in this chapter as a device for helping the industrial wealthy promote its interests by appropriating further industrial wealth. However, society as a whole may be willing to accept such pro-wealth biased payment arrangements in so far as this allows the no-growth trap to be overcome.

A result of the previous Lemma and of the priority assumed for R&D loans is that circulating capital instantaneously and deterministically repaid by manufacturing firms is lent by consumers at the zero interest rate. Consumers lend bank money to firms by transferring their transaction deposits to them in exchange for an equal amount of demand deposits at an infinite speed. In such a role the consumer is a first rate creditor of the manufacturing firms. We will assume that no friction takes place in such a fully deterministic credit circulation. Friction appears only in technological factor payments (wages – for labor – and dividends – for patent use), but not for monetary service payments.[3]

Given the technological assumptions of the benchmark Schumpeterian model, the demand for R&D credit will be infinitely elastic at all fractions $\theta_{t+1} \in]0,1]$. Since the supply of loanable funds by the banks is inelastic by regulation, it follows that the only equilibrium value of θ_{t+1} will be 1. Therefore banks extract all surplus from the would-be entrepreneurs. As a consequence, after at most one round (one innovation) the banks will own the whole intermediate monopolist's equity. Hence since banks do not make consumption loans in this stylized economy, the value of the consolidated bank sector's capital will equal the stock value of the intermediate monopolist. Since banks are required to create new deposits (as a result of their lending) only up to a given multiple $k > 0$ of their capital, and since such capital has to coincide with the intermediate monopolist's stock market value, this endogenously pins down money supply. Hence equation (10.2) should not be regarded as exogenously imposed, but it is an equilibrium relationship.

Another consequence is that under perfect diversification of each bank's portfolio the stock of intermediate monopolist equities created over time will be owned always by the same people. More precisely, given her share of the current intermediate monopolist value a bank shareholder is expected to gain the same share of the monopolist that will displace the current one. If each bank holds a perfectly diversified portfolio of loans it will earn profits in proportion to its shareholders' wealth.

Newly created money is new credit denominated in the unit of account and lent only to firms for productive purposes. In our simplified setting we are assuming that such credit money is granted to firms only to buy the primary input wage labor and/or to buy intermediate goods from one another. Firms are supposed to honor their debts within the end of the production period, which – as in Aghion and Howitt (1992) – is assumed to implode in one instant. Research firms may go bankrupt if their R&D is unsuccessful, in which case debts will no longer be repaid. Hence – unlike manufacturing firms whose profit and loss account items are fully deterministic – R&D firms need fully exploit limited liability. In fact, if R&D firms' owners were charged the full amount of their firms' debts they would never undertake R&D for in that case R&D investment by entrepreneurs would have the nature of consumer saving, and this is ruled out by Knightian uncertainty. Therefore the lack of knowledge about λ_{t+1} in period t explains not only why money emerges but also why limited liability emerges as a social institution. Hence we can state:

Lemma 3: *Limited liability is essential for innovation.*

All reimbursed money is destroyed: repaid debts destroy deposits (Schumpeter 1970). Therefore the increase in money supply will only derive from the R&D firms' wage bills, which honor their creditors only in shares of new successful monopolies, i.e. in shares of the new patent values. In our banking economy the deposits created through these credits always remain trapped within circulation and add to the pre-existing stock of money balances. Therefore though financing manufacturing firms and R&D firms are viewed as similar activities – both earn zero interest – by the bank sector, it is the second kind of credit that affects the stock of money. Hence R&D investment directly and indirectly involves long-term loans and results in new money creation.

How can money stocks keep circulating in a world where production, input and output market clearing, firms' borrowing, debt repayment, and default take place in just an instant? Though maintaining most of Aghion and Howitt's (1992) timing assumptions, as hinted above we relax Aghion and Howitt's (1992) assumption of an infinite velocity of factor payments by assuming a positive time lag. Let us assume that when firms at time $\tau > 0$ give banks the order to pay workers and shareholders, both categories can spend the just transferred money only from instant s uniformly distributed from time τ to time $\tau + \mu$ on, where $\mu > 0$ denotes an arbitrarily small but positive time lag in consumer income full liquidity. For example this may be due to the fact that the bank of the firm is not the same as that of its employees, that consumers have to walk to shops in discrete time to buy the consumption good, etc. Note that we have not assumed a mechanical lag, but have allowed this lag to vary stochastically in an albeit short interval. This allows heterogeneities and spatial aspects of the real world to be captured. However the main implication of this friction is that money has a finite velocity of circulation $1/\mu > 0$. This is a simplification, but the reader can easily imagine many other ways of modeling some of the sources of payment sluggishness that are present in the real world and that would yield similar qualitative results.

Schumpeter's knowledge of the real working of the financial systems made him repeatedly highlight the leads and lags in the functioning of the payment system. Hence our assumption that some time passes between the moment in which firms are charged factor payments and the moment in which these factors are able to transfer such incomes to final goods firms is not only consistent with his statements, but also stylizing his theory of how inflation works in the reallocation of resources among sectors and in particular to the advantage of innovation.

As a consequence of this assumption the total stock of money in circulation at any instant $s > 0$ is given as follows:

$$M^D(s) = \frac{1}{\mu} \int_0^\mu \left[p_{t(s-r)}^C (s-r) A_{t(s-r)} \left(L - n(s-r) \right)^\alpha + w_{t(s-r)}(s) n_{t(s-r)} \right] dr, \quad (10.3)$$

that is, transaction consumer money demand is the sum of all instantaneous manufacturing and R&D factor payments cumulated during the lag.[4]

In equilibrium money demand and supply are both equal to $M(s)$ and the equilibrium is guaranteed by the instantaneous adjustment of $n_t(s)$, as we shall see shortly.

10.3.3. The Timing of Payments

Summarizing what we have been assuming so far, we can state that our model's broadly defined 'banks' create money by lending circulating capital in the form of the skilled labor wage bill of the intermediate good sector:

$$w_t(s)(L - n_t) = \frac{\alpha^2 A_t}{(L - n_t)^{1-\alpha}} p_t^C(s)(L - n_t)$$

and unskilled labor wage bill employed in the consumption sector:

$$w_t^U(s)U = A_t(1 - \alpha)(L - n_t)^\alpha p_t^C(s);$$

whereas they lend R&D capital in the form of the skilled labor wage bill of the R&D sector:

$$w_t(s)n_t = \frac{\alpha^2 A_t}{(L - n_t)^{1-\alpha}} p_t^C(s)n_t.$$

Manufacturing firms' circulating capital has a safe return and – given Bertrand or perfect competition between banks – earn zero net nominal interest. The R&D capital has a highly uncertain return in terms of the bank's claim to a fraction of the *ex-post* stock value of the successful firm.

The circuit banks–firms–banks/workers operates at infinite speed. As a consequence the previous equations describe credit flows that have zero measure with respect to the existing stocks of bank deposits. Similarly, as soon as consumers buy final goods firms transfer such bank deposits immediately to the intermediate good firm – settling their trade debits at the end of the instantaneous production period – and settling their own bank debts – i.e. the unskilled labor wage bill anticipated by banks at the beginning of the instantaneous production period. The intermediate monopolist refunds banks the skilled wage bill loaned at the beginning of the instantaneous production period and transfers what remains to the bank sections that manage household portfolios in the form of dividends. Hence the circuit consumers–firms–banks operates at infinite speed too.

All this takes place in every instant $s \geq 0$. The amount of skilled and unskilled wages and dividends that firms have paid to the banks at the end of instant s will be transferable by consumers to final good firms only partially: a fraction immediately and other fractions later up to the beginning of instant $s + \mu$, due to the money/consumption transaction lag $\mu > 0$. This kind of lag is the only inefficiency of our stylized bank-administered payment system.

However, at the end of instant s wage and dividend earners can already use their imperfect money flow to operate in the stock market by converting such money into firm equities and bonds, and consumer loans. Consistent with the assumed timing for consumer expenditures, though firms and banks can immediately use such resources, consumers will be able to completely consume any dividends, interests, and consumption loans only at time $s + \mu$. Therefore the price of equities at time s is correctly expressed in terms of time s's money and prices. Hence all relevant consumption/saving decisions take place at the moment in which incomes are paid and not necessarily when they are ready to be spent, if later. As a consequence, all but a zero measure subset of the deposits immediately available for consumption translates into consumer good demand.

Note that in considering consumer choice in the form in which the same amount of money will be received (plain cash or expected cash flows) Knightian uncertainty plays a neutral role, as risk neutral consumers care only about expected monetary flows which are perfectly computable at time s and they adopt a *maximin* strategy (Hansen and Sargent 2001) on the evaluation of future discounted income streams. In fact the intermediate monopolist's shares are evaluated as if they paid no profits after the current monopolist is displaced whereas the bank guarantees that they will be transformed into the new monopolist's shares. However since the value of these shares can be zero with a positive but unknown probability (as we shall see more precisely later) the consumers choose the defensive *maximin* strategy to exchange them as if the worst outcome should happen almost certainly. In fact at that price the infinite elastic savings supply function curves abruptly into a perfectly inelastic one.

10.3.4. Equilibrium

We now have all the elements needed to find the unique rational expectations equilibrium of our monetary Schumpeterian model.

At any date $s \geq 0$, given the bank money balances in the hands of consumers $M(s) > 0$, the final good market equilibrium is:

$$\frac{M(s)}{\mu} = A_t(L - n_t)^\alpha p_t^C(s) \tag{10.4}$$

Notice that the left-hand side of equation (10.4) is the amount of flow money balances circulating in the consumer goods market at any instant, equal to the nominal value of all transactions carried out instantaneously.

Equation (10.4) is our version of the quantity theory of money and allows us to determine current period nominal prices as:

$$p_t^C(s) = \frac{M(s)}{\mu A_t(L - n_t)^\alpha} \tag{10.5}$$

From (10.2) we can state that the amount of circulating money balances does not exceed the limit set by regulation if and only if:

$$M(s) \leq k p_t^C(s) A_t \left(\frac{1}{\alpha} - 1\right) \frac{\alpha^2 A_t(L - n_t)^\alpha}{r + \lambda_t n_t} \tag{10.6}$$

that is if and only if:

$$M(s) \leq k \frac{M(s)}{\mu A_t(L - n_t)^\alpha} A_t \left(\frac{1}{\alpha} - 1\right) \frac{\alpha^2 A_t(L - n_t)^\alpha}{r + \lambda_t n_t} \tag{10.7}$$

Equation (10.7) in equilibrium is satisfied as a strict equality, because perfectly competitive banks leaving no profit opportunity unexploited lend as much credit as they can to harvest potential earnings. This uniquely determines R&D employment as:

$$n_t = \min\left(\max\left[\frac{1}{\lambda_t}\left(\frac{k(1-\alpha)\alpha}{\mu} - r\right), 0\right], L\right) \equiv \bar{n}(\lambda_t) \tag{10.8}$$

where we have taken into account non-negativity and full employment conditions. Equation (10.8) shows that at interior solutions, R&D

employment is an increasing function of monetary policy openness, k, and of profit share in GDP, and a decreasing function of impatience, r, of the payment lag, μ, and of the current R&D productivity λ_t. The reason why R&D success probability somewhat surprisingly affects R&D investment negatively is due to its positive effect on obsolescence and therefore its negative effect on the value of bank reserves. Notice that monetary policy in the form of prudential regulation can have important real effects on GDP composition and growth and on income distribution.

It is important to remark that in this model the force equilibrating money demand and supply at any instant $s \geq 0$ is the flow of new money creation $n_t w_t(s)$ by banks to finance innovation. This clearly cannot affect the stock of money immediately, but the role of the instantaneous flow of new credit is that of modifying obsolescence and consequently to render the real value of banks' assets – i.e. the current intermediate monopolist stock value – of the same size as the existing money required by circulation. In this sense we can say that here money supply adapts to money demand through the effect of R&D credit on real bank assets.

To get interior solutions we would need to assume:

$$\lambda_t \geq \bar{\lambda} > \left(\frac{k(1-\alpha)\alpha}{\mu} - r \right) \frac{1}{L} > 0 \tag{10.9}$$

i.e. that the smallest level of R&D productivity is high enough and that monetary policy is neither too restrictive nor too expansionary. However, it is very unlikely that individuals living in any particular period are able to know for sure that in the future the productivity of R&D will not fall short of a particular positive value. Moreover, a very fine regulation tuning is required to guarantee that inequalities (10.9) hold. Hence our stylized economy might end up in a 'zero growth trap' (Aghion and Howitt 1992) or in a period of no positive consumption. This completely justifies our previous Lemma 2.

Note that holding the reserve requirement fixed, equation (10.8) predicts that in periods characterized by high productivity of R&D we would observe fewer R&D workers whereas in periods of low productivity more R&D workers, but the success probability of aggregate R&D, $\bar{n}(\lambda_t)\lambda_t$, always remains constant.

Therefore a statistician would observe that in periods of high wage inequality and high R&D investment there would be the same growth rate as in periods of low wage inequality and low R&D investment, as observed by Jones' (1995a and 1995b) well-known empirical evidence.[5] Interestingly, despite Knightian uncertainty about λ_t at interior solutions the average growth rate is always determinate at:

$$\lambda_t \bar{n}(\lambda_t) \ln \gamma = \left(\frac{k(1-\alpha)\alpha}{\mu} - r \right) \ln \gamma \qquad (10.10)$$

The negative relation between R&D productivity and R&D employment is the opposite of what is predicted by Aghion and Howitt's (1992) basic Schumpeterian model: the difference is that in their model R&D was financed by voluntary savings, whereas in our model of Schumpeter's (1934 and 1939) theory of economic development, R&D is financed by involuntary savings through banks' privilege of money creation.

Interestingly, Knightian uncertainty over λ_t's full support is crucial for bank credit creation to be essential in this model. In fact let us suppose that consumers were sure that inequalities (10.9) could be satisfied. As a consequence in equilibrium during period t there would exist a minimum value of the next – period $t + l$'s – monopolist and in real terms it is equal to:

$$V_{t+1}^{\min} = A_{t+1} \left(\frac{1}{\alpha} - 1 \right) \frac{\alpha^2 \left[L - n(\bar{\lambda}) \right]^\alpha}{k(1-\alpha)\mu a} > 0 \qquad (10.11)$$

It is important to note that in light of equation (10.11) individual savers would be able to perform a correct valuation of the value of R&D firms: the expectation of future banking behavior allows the stock market to value current R&D labor as $\lambda_t V_{t+1}^{\min}$. If parameters were such that $w_t(s) \le p_t^C(s) \lambda_t V_{t+1}^{\min}$ the R&D firms could get funds from consumers. However with such parameters future banking behavior would no longer be pinned down: disintermediated R&D finances would be inconsistent with Knightian uncertainty again. Therefore the only way to always guarantee the existence of a monetary equilibrium with banks and therefore of positive R&D would be to assume:

$$\frac{\alpha^2 A_t}{\left[L - n(\bar{\lambda}) \right]^{1-\alpha}} > V_{t+1}^{\min} A_{t+1}$$

but this is not possible if λ_t's support has no finite upper limit.

We can now endogenize the inflation rate. We will be working under the assumption that $n_t = \bar{n}(\lambda_t)$.

Since R&D capital borrowed from banks is equal to the R&D sector wage bill:

$$w_t(s) n_t = \frac{\alpha^2 A_t n_t}{(L - n_t)^{1-\alpha}} p_t^C(s) = \frac{\alpha^2 n_t M(s)}{\mu (L - n_t)}$$

we can use (10.5) and conclude that money creation between innovation periods t and $t + 1$ is governed by:

$$M'(s) = w_t(s)n_t = \frac{n_t}{L - n_t} \frac{\alpha^2}{\mu} M(s)$$

Therefore money is right-continuously injected in the economy and off-jumps nominal prices grow exponentially at rate:

$$\pi \equiv \frac{p'(s)}{p(s)} = \frac{M'(s)}{M(s)} = \frac{n_t}{L - n_t} \frac{\alpha^2}{\mu}$$

Note that the higher is R&D employment, the more intense is credit inflation.

From (10.5) we see that prices fall when innovations occur due to two reasons: quality jump $\gamma > 1$ that dilutes money balances on a larger set of producible consumption goods due to higher productivity; possible R&D drop and resulting increase in final consumption flow.

To summarize the main results of this section we can state:

Proposition 1: *In the unique Schumpeterian monetary equilibrium, after any innovation the amount of R&D employment, aggregate GDP, its composition, inflation, and income distribution are uniquely determined right-continuous functions of time. In the interior cases, if research productivity λ_t decreases, R&D employment will rise, nominal prices will initially jump downward and then start rising again continuously at a higher rate than before the innovation whereas the expected growth rate will stay constant. If research productivity λ_t increases, R&D employment will fall, nominal prices will initially jump downward and then start rising again continuously at a lower rate than before the innovation whereas the expected growth rate will stay constant. A lower bank capital requirement leads to more R&D employment, more wage inequality (skill premium), lower monopolist profits, higher expected growth, and higher inflation.*

10.4. FINAL REMARKS

This chapter has tried to highlight an aspect of the growth process analyzed in depth by Schumpeter (1934 and 1939) that still lacks incorporation into current Schumpeterian macroeconomic models: the role of money creation by financial intermediaries. Schumpeter argued theoretically and documented historically the roles that financial intermediaries and banks in particular have played. It is important to note that throughout this chapter 'banks' should be interpreted as a consolidation of the commercial and investment bank sectors. Even more generally, according to Schumpeter's own viewpoint, any financial intermediaries that create liabilities that are accepted by third parties as means of payments can be labeled with his definition of 'banks'. Hence the reader should not interpret banks in the usual juridical and technical meaning, but as a simplification of a much more complex body of financial intermediaries.

Importantly the dependence of a bank's ability to create deposits on its equity ownership is crucial for our model's results. At the time of Schumpeter, gold or real estates were the main real assets, but in the modern globalized world both assets are overwhelmed by the capitalized value of vertically integrated industries. This consideration naturally leads us to update the banking definition of wealth to take into account the fact that the world's real wealth ultimately depends on its productive capacity. As a consequence I have decided to express the minimum capital requirements limiting bank size in terms of the real value of the firms existing in the economy. In our model's stylized economy such wealth is captured by the intermediate monopolist equity, but it is clear how to generalize this assumption to other cases.[6] More precisely, in the basic Schumpeterian model, the only transferable wealth is the currently leading edge patent. Hence we can say that the main 'precious metal' in this economy is codified knowledge.

As we have seen, once we replace government's fiat money or a physical object not subject to obsolescence for the patent value as the main form of wealth the monetary and real implications of the equilibrium change dramatically. In particular, the nominal value of current patents is subject to inflationary revaluations and their real values are affected by the flow of new loans to R&D firms. The reason for this is obsolescence. Hence more credit to R&D implies tighter credit limits for banks: R&D investment is the equilibrating force between money demand and money supply in an economy in which leading-edge knowledge is the most important basis of real wealth.

NOTES

*   I would like to thank Theo Eicher, Augusto Graziani, Marcello De Cecco, and Gianluca Violante for very useful discussions at the early stages of this work. I also thank seminar participants at the University College of London and at the University of Pisa for comments. I am indebted to an anonymous referee for very useful criticism.

1. The original Aghion and Howitt's (1992) framework implies a scale effect in per capita growth rate and in the level of aggregate output, which has been criticized on empirical

grounds by Jones (1995b). However it is easy to amend it along the lines suggested in the literature by assuming that λ_t tends to change inversely proportionally with population. In this case long-run growth rates will only depend on population growth.

2. This suggests an alternative channel for the often observed negative relationship between inequality and growth.

3. However the reader can easily understand that this assumption is not needed for our results to hold. With a lag in circulating capital repayments the real interest rate r would be applied in an obvious way.

4. As an example of a different mechanism leading to the same result one could imagine the following. Factor income expenditure lag could be interpreted entirely deterministically: workers can buy consumer goods only by decumulating their savings and by using the wage received μ time units before. However, if a worker has no immediate liquidity but can document a stream of wage payments that accrue for sure in a short time she can apply for an overdraft with a bank. This allows her to anticipate the formal receipt of her wages. Consistent with Schumpeter's view of the bank function in facilitating payments we could assume that each individual i is allowed to spend in a short time interval ds an amount equal to $M_i(s)/\mu$ of her short-term monetary assets $M_i(s)$. At any time banks can retrospectively evaluate consumer's pending payments and transform her 'imperfect money' (as it only lacks full consumption liquidity) into money flows that are immediately spendable in exchange for consumption goods. Under this second interpretation, by aggregating individual bank accounts, instantaneous consumption expenditure flow at time s is again given by (10.3).

5. Allowing for a growing population we would have to amend the model by adopting one of the solutions to the 'scale effect' problem emerged in the more recent growth literature. The easiest way would be to directly replace λ_t for λ_t/L as R&D productivity parameter. In such a setting the right-hand side of our equation (10.8) yields the fraction of the skilled labor population employed in the R&D.

6. For example, in Grossman and Helpman's (1991) quality ladders economy, the top quality final good property rights are the unique non-labor real wealth. Alternatively, assuming vintage specific physical capital – therefore subject to endogenous obsolescence – would play a similar role.

REFERENCES

Aghion P. and P. Howitt (1992), 'A model of growth through creative destruction', *Econometrica*, 60, 323–51.

Aghion P. and P. Howitt (1998), *Endogenous Growth Theory*, Cambridge, Massachusetts: MIT Press.

Cetorelli N. and M. Gambera (1999), 'Bank market structure financial dependence and growth: international evidence from industry data', Federal Reserve Bank of Chicago, WP 99-8.

Cetorelli N. and P. Peretto (2000), 'Oligopoly banking and capital accumulation', Manuscript, Duke University.

Dubey P. and J. Geanakoplos (2001), 'Inside and outside fiat money, gains to trade, and IS-LM', Cowles Foundation Discussion Paper N. 1257R.

Galetovic A. (1994a), 'Financial intermediation, resource allocation, and long run growth', Discussion Paper, Princeton University.

Galetovic A. (1994b), 'Credit market structure, firm quality, and long run growth', Discussion Paper, Princeton University.

Grossman G. and E. Helpman (1991), *Innovation and Growth in the Global Economy*, Cambridge, Massachusetts: MIT Press.

Hansen, L.P. and T.J. Sargent (2001), 'Acknowledging misspecification in macroeconomic theory', *Review of Economic Dynamics*, **4**, 519–35.

Huang H. and C. Xu (1999), 'Institutions, innovations, and growth', *IMF Working Paper* 99/34.

Jones, C. (1995a), 'Time series test of endogenous growth models', *Quarterly Journal of Economics*, **110**, 495–525.

Jones, C. (1995b), 'R&D-based models of economic growth', *Journal of Political Economy*, **103**, 759–84.

King R. and R. Levine (1993), 'Finance, entrepreneurship, and growth: theory and evidence', *Journal of Monetary Economics*, **32**, 513–42.

Schumpeter J.A. (1934), *The Theory of Economic Development*, Cambridge, Massachusetts: Harvard University Press.

Schumpeter J.A. (1939), *Business Cycles: A Theoretical, Historical and Statistical Analysis of the Capitalist Process*, New York: McGraw-Hill.

Schumpeter J.A. (1970), *Das Wesen des Geldes* [*The Essence of Money*], Gottingen: Vandenhoeck & Ruprecht.

Smith B. (2001), 'Introduction to monetary and financial arrangements', *Journal of Economic Theory*, **99**, 323–51.

Wallace N. (1998), 'Introduction to modeling money and studying monetary policy', *Journal of Economic Theory*, **81**, 323–51.

11. Distribution and policy in the new growth literature

Cecilia García-Peñalosa

11.1. INTRODUCTION

One of the main contributions of the new growth theories is the fact that they have rediscovered a role for government policy. Indeed, the contrast with the Solow–Swan model could not be more stark. In the Solow–Swan model the long-run growth rate of the economy is determined solely by the rate of technological progress, which in turn is viewed as exogenous, unaffected by the actions of consumers or producers, and consequently leaves no role for policy. In the new growth literature, policy intervention is both possible and desirable. It is possible because these theories maintain – in one or other of their versions – that the rate of growth is determined by the decisions of economic agents, such as the accumulation of physical capital, human capital investments, or firms' R&D expenditures, all of which can be affected by taxes and subsidies.

Policy is also desirable. The endogenous growth literature relies either on externalities or on monopoly power on the part of firms, and as a result the competitive equilibrium is not socially optimal. Economic policy can, to some extent, correct the externality or the distortion due to market power and hence increase welfare. Most of the existing models maintain that the competitive growth rate is lower than the socially optimal one.[1] Optimal policy then consists of a system of taxes and subsidies that increases the rate of growth and brings it closer to the first-best.

A number of measures have been argued to promote growth. The simplest approach to endogenous growth is the investment-led model, in which private investment in physical capital generates new knowledge that raises the economy-wide level of productivity. It hence implies that subsidies to capital accumulation can increase the rate of growth. R&D-led models emphasize the role of two types of policies. On the one hand, growth is seen as the result of research expenditures by private firms, and consequently R&D subsidies that increase the amount of research done would also accelerate growth. On the other hand, human capital is argued to be the main input of the research sector and policies that increase educational attainment would also increase the pool of researchers and thus the rate of technical change.

The question I want to address in this chapter is what are the implications of these policies for the distribution of income and consumption across agents. Subsidies to investment, education, or R&D have to be financed through taxes. In the absence of lump-sum taxation, these taxes will be distortionary and will affect different types of agents differently. Moreover, the subsidies will alter relative prices and will, per se, impact on factor rewards and hence on distribution.

The last decade has seen a revival of interest on the relationship between inequality and the rate of growth. The bulk of this literature has examined, both theoretically and empirically, how the given initial distribution of wealth or human capital affects, through a number of mechanisms, investment in human or physical capital and hence growth.[2] The approach I take in this chapter is rather different. I am going to argue that a major contribution of the new growth theories is that they allow us to examine the joint determination of growth and distribution. Because growth is endogenous, it is going to depend on technological and preference parameters, the same parameters that also determine the rewards to the various production factors. If factor ownership varies across agents, we will have a correlation between growth and the personal distribution of income.

The joint determination of growth and the degree of inequality implies that growth-enhancing policies will have distributional implications. In this chapter I consider three possible scenarios. I start in Section 11.2 with a simple investment-led model where growth can be increased through investment subsidies. Agents are assumed to differ in the holdings of physical capital, but all are endowed with the same amount of labour. The subsidies are financed through a consumption tax, as a tax on labour income would imply negative redistribution. We will see that the tax-subsidy system, by altering the price of capital relative to that of the consumption good, is going to affect the value of agents' endowments and hence their relative welfare.

Section 11.3 considers a simple R&D-based model, where the stock of human capital and the rate of technical change are jointly determined. Agents differ in the amount of education they have acquired, and we examine how the distribution of wage income is determined. In this setup, both R&D and education policies can increase the rate of growth, but they will have different effects on the wage of skilled workers relative to the unskilled, as the former increases the demand for and the latter the supply of skills. The next section addresses the question of whether redistribution – in the form of a tax on capital income and a subsidy to labour income – necessarily reduces growth. I argue that, even when capital markets are perfect, this need not be the case once we allow for two sectors and for productivity shocks. Section 11.5 concludes.

11.2.   ENDOGENOUS SAVING PROPENSITIES

Interest in the relationship between distribution and growth started in the 1950s with the work of the post-Keynesian economists. Kaldor (1956, 1957) and Pasinetti (1962) maintained that the saving propensity of capitalists is greater than that of workers, and that consequently aggregate savings depend on the distribution of income. These authors, as all their contemporaries, viewed the rate of output growth as given. With constant saving propensities and the rate of investment determined by the exogenous growth rate, only the distribution of income could adjust to ensure equality between investment and savings. This meant that the rate of growth determines how income is distributed between capitalists and workers. In particular, faster growth requires greater savings, and hence a higher share of income must accrue to capitalists.

The idea that saving propensities depend on the source of income has been reexamined in the context of the new growth literature by Alesina and Rodrik (1994) and Bertola (1993). A feature of the investment-led models of growth is that the interest rate is constant and consequently there are no transitional dynamics. This, in turn, has two implications for the distribution of income. First, the propensity to save out of capital income differs from the propensity to save out of labour income. Second, and as a result of the above, the distribution of (relative) wealth reproduces itself over time. In contrast to the early literature, the endogenous growth formulation obtains saving behaviour from utility maximization, and sees causation as running from the technological parameters determining the interest rate to growth and savings. Growth and distribution are then jointly determined. In this context, unlike in the early literature, policy analysis becomes interesting, as measures aimed at affecting the growth rate will also impact on the distribution of income.

Endogenous Growth
To understand how policy can work in the investment-based growth model, let us follow the framework in Bertola (1993). Consider an economy where output is produced using capital and labour according to:

$$Y_t = A_t K_t^\alpha L^{1-\alpha}, \tag{11.1}$$

A_t being a measure of the level of productivity. Assuming perfect competition in the output and factor markets, the wage and the interest rate are, respectively:

$$w_t = \frac{(1-\alpha)Y_t}{L} \text{ and } r_t = \frac{\alpha Y_t}{K_t}.$$

The economy is populated by L agents indexed by i. All agents have one unit of labour per period. However, they have different initial holdings of wealth, the only asset being physical capital. Initially, agent i owns K_{i0} units of capital, with $\sum_i K_{i0} = K_0$. She maximizes a utility function of the form:[3]

$$U_{i0} = \int_0^\infty \frac{C_{it}^{1-\gamma}-1}{1-\gamma} e^{-\beta t} dt, \ \gamma > 1, \tag{11.2}$$

subject to her capital accumulation constraint:

$$\dot{K}_{it} = r_t K_{it} + w_t - C_{it}, \tag{11.3}$$

where for simplicity we assume there is no depreciation of the capital stock.

The evolution of individual consumption is then given by the familiar Euler equation:

$$\frac{\dot{C}_{it}}{C_{it}} = \frac{r_t - \beta}{\gamma}, \tag{11.4}$$

and her income at time t is simply:

$$Y_{it} = r_t K_{it} + w_t. \tag{11.5}$$

Equation (11.4) implies that aggregate consumption grows at a constant rate only if the interest rate is constant. Assume that technical change is due to an externality stemming from the stock of capital. In particular, let us assume that $A_t = A_0(K_t/L)^{1-\alpha}$, i.e. the higher the stock of capital per worker, the greater A_t is. Then, the economy's rate of balanced growth, g, is simply

$$g = \frac{\dot{Y}_t}{Y_t} = \frac{\dot{K}_t}{K_t} = \frac{\dot{C}_t}{C_t} = \frac{\alpha A_0 - \beta}{\gamma}. \tag{11.6}$$

Equation (11.6) captures the main result of the investment-based endogenous growth models; namely, that with constant returns to aggregate capital, the interest rate is constant. As a result, the rate of growth of consumption is also constant, different from zero, and exhibits no transitional dynamics.

Saving Rates

Under our technological assumptions, the shares of labour and capital in total output are, respectively, $S_L = 1 - \alpha$ and $S_K = \alpha$. We then have that a higher value of α results in a higher growth rate and a lower labour share. Since capital is more unequally distributed than labour, this implies that faster growth is associated with greater income inequality.

Define now the saving rate, s, as the proportion of output saved and added to the capital stock, i.e. $s = \dot{K}_t / (A_0 K_t)$. Using the expression for g above, we have:

$$s = \frac{1}{\gamma}\left(\alpha - \frac{\beta}{A_0}\right). \tag{11.7}$$

There is a negative relationship between the saving rate and the labour share, which is the result of the different saving propensities of individuals with different stocks of capital. To see this, note that the intertemporal budget constraint of individual i is:

$$\int_0^\infty c_{it} e^{-rt} dt \ \leq \int_0^\infty (1-\alpha)\frac{Y_t}{L}e^{-rt}dt + K_{i0},$$

which can be rewritten as:

$$\int_0^\infty c_{i0} e^{-(r-g)t} dt \ \leq \int_0^\infty (1-\alpha)A_0 K_0 L^{-1} e^{-(r-g)t} dt \ + K_{i0}.$$

This expression, together with the Euler equation, implies that the optimal consumption path of agent i grows at rate g starting from:

$$c_{i0} = \left[(r-g)k_i + (1-\alpha)A_0 L^{-1}\right]K_0, \tag{11.8}$$

where $k_i \equiv K_i/K$ is the relative wealth of agent i. The initial savings of individual i are simply $s_{i0} = y_{i0} - c_{i0}$, and grow at rate g. Using equation (11.8), we have:

$$s_{i0} = gK_{i0}. \tag{11.9}$$

We can now examine how factor ownership affects savings. Equations (11.8) and (11.9) tell us that an individual will consume all her labour income plus a fraction of her capital income equal to $(r-g)K_{it}$, and she will save gK_{it} in order to sustain a rate of growth of her capital holdings of g.

It follows that the distribution of (relative) factor ownership remains constant over time. Those with no initial capital, i.e. $k_{i0} = 0$, consume all their wage, $c_{it} = w_t$, and never save. They therefore continue to hold no physical assets. Those who are initially endowed with capital choose a rate of growth of capital g irrespective of their initial wealth. Since the aggregate capital stock also grows at rate g, the relative wealth of each agent, $k_i \equiv K_{it}/K_t$ remains constant and the relative distribution of wealth is unchanged.

The endogenous growth model yields the post-Keynesian result that the saving propensities of capitalists are greater than those of workers. In particular, we have obtained a zero propensity to save out of wage income, a case studied by Kaldor (1956). The difference is that now both the rate of technical progress and the saving rate are determined within the model. This means that causality no longer runs from one to the other. Moreover, both can be simultaneously affected by policy instruments.

Investment Subsidies

It has been widely argued by the new growth literature that investment subsidies raise the growth rate, as they foster the accumulation of the factor that engenders technical change, physical capital. The question is how to finance them when agents are heterogeneous. Financing the subsidy through a tax on wages would imply taxing the factor that is equally distributed, and subsidizing the one unequally distributed, hence resulting in reverse redistribution. An alternative, considered by Bertola (1993), is to finance the investment subsidy through a consumption tax. A priori, we would expect this policy to benefit the owners of capital more than the owners of labour, who see their purchasing power reduced but do not directly benefit from the subsidy since they never save. Yet, as we will see, the endogeneity of the growth rate is going to lead to the opposite outcome.

Let the producer price of consumption good be the numeraire. The price of the consumption good faced by agents is then $p_c = 1 + \tau$, and that of the investment good $p_k = 1 - s$, where τ and v are, respectively, the consumption tax and the investment subsidy. The government budget constraint requires that payments be equal to tax receipts, i.e. $(1 - p_k)\dot{K} = (p_c - 1)C$, which implies a consumption–good price $p_c = (A_0 - p_k g)/(A_0 - g)$. The effect of the tax-subsidy policy on the growth rate is straightforward. The return to one dollar invested is now $r = \alpha A_0 / p_k$, and hence the Euler equation becomes:

$$g = \frac{\alpha A_0 - \beta p_k}{\gamma p_k}. \tag{11.10}$$

which is greater the lower the investment good price is.

The AK technology implies that this policy has no impact on the distribution of income, but, because it changes the relative price of the investment good, it will affect the distribution of consumption and hence of welfare. Consider the budget constraint of individual i, now given by:

$$\int_0^\infty P_c c_{i0} e^{-(r-g)t} dt \leq \int_0^\infty (1-\alpha) A_0 K_0 L^{-1} e^{-(r-g)t} dt + p_k K_{i0}. \quad (11.11)$$

Using equation (11.11), together with the above expressions for the consumption price and g, implies that the initial consumption level of agent i is:

$$c_{i0} = (A_0 - g)\left[k_i + \alpha B(g)\left(\frac{1}{L} - k_i\right)\right] K_0,$$

where $B(g)$ is an increasing function of g. This expression illustrates that a higher rate of growth of consumption requires a lower initial level. A lower p_k thus reduces c_{i0} for all agents, although this negative impact on welfare can be offset by the positive effect of a higher growth rate.

What is interesting is that the tax-subsidy system will affect the distribution of relative consumption. Consider the consumption of agent i relative to the mean – that is, to that of an individual with wealth $k = 1/L$ – which is given by:

$$\frac{c_{i0}}{c_0} = k_i L + \alpha B(g)(1 - k_i L).$$

Since $\partial B/\partial g > 0$, the sign of $\partial(c_{i0}/c_0)/\partial g$ is given by $(1 - k_i L)$. The introduction of the tax-subsidy system will have the effect of *reducing* the relative consumption of individuals with wealth holdings above the average, while those with below-average capital will experience an *increase* in their relative consumption. In other words, the distribution of consumption (and hence of welfare) becomes *less unequal*.

The intuition for this result is apparent in the budget constraint (11.11). On the one hand, the lower relative price of capital reduces the value of physical wealth in terms of the consumption good, and hence reduces the relative total wealth of those with large capital endowments. On the other hand, faster growth and a lower discount rate result in a greater present discounted value of the labour endowment and the consumption flow.

To sum up, in the investment-led growth model the rate of growth and the factor distribution of income are simultaneously determined by technological parameters. We have seen that a higher rate of growth is associated with a lower labour share and, if capital endowments are more unequally distributed than labour endowments, also with greater inequality in the distribution of income. Policy can, however, help ameliorate this tradeoff. A system of investment subsidies financed through indirect taxation can at the same time increase the rate of growth and reduce the extent of consumption inequality.

11.3. BIASED TECHNICAL CHANGE

We have just seen that faster growth is associated with greater inequality, the reason being that the technological characteristics that lead to fast growth – namely, a high α – also lead to a small labour share. In this setup there is no causal relationship between growth and distribution. But is there any reason to suppose that growth can directly affect distribution?

During the last decade, and largely in response to the increase in inequality observed in a number of OECD countries, a number of papers have addressed the question of whether growth itself can impact on the degree of inequality.[4] Now, if the rate of growth is to affect distribution, it must be because technological change is *biased* towards certain factors of production, in the sense that it changes their productivity relative to that of other factors. The concept of biased technical change found its way into economics in the 1940s with the work of Hicks and Harrod, and was incorporated into the neoclassical growth model. If technical change is not neutral, then the rate of growth is to affect distribution through its impact on factor rewards. Yet, until recent years, the distributional implications of biased technical change had received little attention. This was largely due to the widespread use of a Cobb–Douglas production function, which, as we saw in the previous section, results in constant factor shares.

It is straightforward to show that under a more general technology the rate of growth does affect distribution even in the neoclassical model. To see this, consider the previous model with infinitely lived agents, but let the production function take the form $Y = F(K, AL)$, where A measures the level of technology. Technical progress is then said to be *labour-augmenting*, and grows at the constant exogenous rate g. The rate of growth of consumption is given by equation (11.4) above. Along the balanced growth path it must be equal to the rate of technical change, hence:

$$\frac{r_t - \beta}{\gamma} = g \qquad (11.12)$$

We can also obtain that the share of labour in total output is $S_L = 1 - f'(k)k / f(k)$, where $f(k) = F(k,1)$ and $k = K / AL$.

With a Cobb–Douglas production function technical change is necessarily neutral, as the labour share is given by $1-\alpha$. A more interesting case arises when the production function is of the CES form:

$$Y = \left[\alpha K^{-\rho} + (1-\alpha)(AL)^{-\rho} \right]^{-\frac{1}{\rho}},$$

where $\phi = 1/(1+\rho)$ is the elasticity of substitution between capital and labour. Differentiating with respect to the capital stock and substituting for the interest rate in the balanced growth condition (11.12), we obtain the equilibrium capital stock:

$$k^* = \left[\frac{1}{1-\alpha} \left(\frac{\alpha}{\gamma g + \beta} \right)^{\frac{\rho}{1+\rho}} - \frac{\alpha}{1-\alpha} \right]^{-\frac{1}{\rho}}.$$

The share of labour in total output is now given by:

$$S_L = (1-\alpha) \left[\alpha \left(k^* \right)^{-\rho} + (1-\alpha) \right]^{-1},$$

and, through k^*, is a function of the rate of technical change. The sign of $\partial S_L / \partial g$ is given by $-\rho$: faster technical change increases the labour share if $\rho < 0$, and reduces it for $\rho > 0$. The degree of substitutability between factors determines the effect of biased technical change on factor shares, with faster labour-augmenting technical progress increasing the labour share only for high values of the elasticity of substitution.

11.3.1. Human Capital and Biased Technical Change

In this simple formulation all workers are identical, or, if we think of L as measuring efficiency units of labour, they are perfect substitutes. Technical change is therefore neutral as far as different types of labour are concerned. This framework of analysis is unsatisfactory for two reasons. First, inequality in labour incomes is a major component of income inequality and hence we would like to have some understanding of its determinants. Second, it has become apparent that certain types of innovations are particularly suited to be used by workers with particular skills. For example, the new information technologies have been said – and to a large extent shown – to be more complementary with educated than with non-educated workers (see Bartel and Lichtenberg, 1987, and Krueger, 1993).

The argument that the degree of complementarity between new technologies and different types of labour is not the same is not new. In his analysis of the relationship between human capital and inequality, Tinbergen (1975) suggested that inequality is ultimately determined by the opposing effects that technology and education exert, respectively, on the demand for and supply of skilled labour, and hence on the relative wage. He stipulated that the relationship between growth and inequality is determined by the 'race between technological development and education' (1975, p. 97).

Although technological change can exert an upward pressure on the demand for skilled workers and thereby increase their wage premium over unskilled workers, education should eventually lead to an expanded supply of skilled labour and thereby to a fall in the wage differential. In what follows I argue that this is not necessarily the case. The section is based on a joint paper with Theo S. Eicher (see Eicher and García-Peñalosa, 2001) where we formalize Tinbergen's hypothesis to examine how technical change affects relative wages, but because the rate of technical change is itself endogenous some new results emerge. First, we are going to see that a greater stock of skilled labour may be associated with a higher or with a lower relative wage. Second, the effect of growth-enhancing policies on relative wages will depend on whether they target the demand for or the supply of labour.

Production

Suppose that the production function takes the form first introduced by Romer (1987):

$$Y_t = \sum_{i=1}^{D_t} n_{it}^{\alpha} H_t^{1-\alpha}, \tag{11.13}$$

where D represents the number of different intermediate goods used in production, n_i is the quantity of the ith intermediate good employed, and H is the skill-adjusted stock of labour. Technological change takes the form of an expansion of the number of different intermediate goods available, and will be endogenized below. It is possible to show that the quantity of intermediary used is the same for all types, and that it is constant over time, which allows us to rewrite aggregate output as $Y_t = D_t n^{\alpha} H_t^{1-\alpha}$.

The economy consists of skilled workers, denoted S_t, and unskilled workers, U_t, and the population is normalized so that $U_t + S_t = 1$. The two types of labour differ not only in terms of productivities, but also in their technological capabilities. Following Nelson and Phelps' (1966) argument that skilled workers possess a greater capacity to absorb new technologies, we introduce the notion that technological change erodes the aggregate stock of human capital due to its effect on the productivity of uneducated workers.

This assumption is captured by the following expression for the skill-adjusted stock of labour:[5]

$$H_t = \left[\frac{U_t^{-\rho}}{g_t} + \left(S_t^P\right)^{-\rho} \right]^{-\frac{1}{\rho}}, \tag{11.14}$$

where S_t^P denotes skilled labour employed in production, and $g_t = \Delta D_t / D_{t-1}$ is the rate of technological change. As we saw in the previous subsection, the elasticity of substitution is a crucial determinant of the impact of biased technical change on factor rewards. In what follows we assume that $-1 < \rho < 0$. That is, the elasticity of substitution, $\phi = 1/(1+\rho)$, falls in the interval $(1, \infty)$, implying that skilled and unskilled labour in production are imperfect substitutes.

From (11.13) and (11.14) the demand for labour can be derived as a function of the rate of technological change and the relative wage of skilled to unskilled workers, ω_t. That is:

$$\omega_t \equiv \frac{w_t^S}{w_t^U} = \left(\frac{U_t}{S_t^P} \right)^{1+\rho} \frac{\Delta D_t}{D_{t-1}}. \tag{11.15}$$

On the production side, the relative wage depends on two standard factors: relative factor supplies and relative productivity. The later is, however, determined endogenously by the rate of technological change.

Factor Supplies
Agents live for two periods, but work only when young. At the start of their working lives, they decide whether to invest in education or to remain unskilled. The cost of education is of the form cw_t^U/a, where a denotes the agent's ability to learn and c the direct cost of education. We assume that abilities are distributed uniformly in $[0,1]$. More able individuals can learn faster and therefore incur a lower cost.

The income of a skilled worker born at time t can be written as:

$$Y_t^S = w_t^S - \frac{cw_t^U}{a}.$$

Agents choose to invest in skills if Y_t^S exceeds the income obtained by remaining unskilled, $Y_t^U = w_t^U$. Equating these two expressions, and given the distribution of abilities, we obtain an inverse labour supply of the form:

$$\omega_t = 1 + \frac{c}{1 - S_t}. \tag{11.16}$$

Equation (11.16) simply says that the higher the relative wage and the lower the cost of education, the greater the number of educated workers will be.

Technological Change

New technologies are generated through intentional R&D. Let us consider a formulation that has by now become standard in the new growth literature (see Romer, 1990), and assume that $\Delta D_t = S_{t-1}^R D_{t-1}$. The invention of new types of machinery is linear in the number of researchers, S_t^R, and in the existing number of blueprints. I abstract from the micro-foundations of R&D decisions, and simply assume that a fixed fraction of the skilled labour force, β, is employed in R&D.[6] The economy then produces technological blueprints according to:

$$\Delta D_t = \beta S_{t-1} D_{t-1}. \tag{11.17}$$

Substituting for technical change in equation (11.15), and using the labour market constraints $S_t^P + S_t^R = S_t$ and $U_t + S_t = 1$, we obtain the inverse relative labour demand:

$$\omega_t = \frac{\beta S_{t-1}}{(1-\beta)^{1+\rho}} \left(\frac{1 - S_t}{S_t} \right)^{1+\rho}. \tag{11.18}$$

Equation (11.18) implies that the demand for skilled labour is a lagged function of its supply, as the relative wage is decreasing in the current stock of skilled labour but increasing in the last period's stock. The reason for this is that a greater proportion of skilled labour in period $t-1$ results in faster technological change, which means that the productivity of skilled labour is growing more rapidly than that of unskilled labour. This raises the demand for skills at t, and therefore the wage ratio for any given supply.

Stationary States

The equilibrium of the model is obtained by equating the labour supply, given in equation (11.16), to the labour demand, (11.18), which renders a differential equation in S_t and S_{t-1}. Imposing the steady state condition, $S_{t-1} = S_t = S$, we have:

$$1 + \frac{c}{1-S} = \frac{\beta}{(1-\beta)^{1+\rho}} S^{-\rho} (1-S)^{1+\rho}. \tag{11.19}$$

This equation yields S^* as a function of the parameters of the model. Once the equilibrium stock of skilled labour is obtained, it uniquely determines the relative wage and the rate of growth of the economy. Relative wages are given by the supply of labour function. To obtain the rate of output growth, note that in steady state all inputs except the number of intermediate goods available are constant. The steady state growth rate is then $g = \beta S^*$.

We can examine the solution to equation (11.19) graphically in the (ω, S) space. As we see in Figure 11.1, the labour demand is initially upward-sloping since more skilled labour allows for more R&D, which improves the productivity of skilled workers in production. Unskilled labour eventually becomes sufficiently scarce to exert downward pressure on the relative wage and the demand function becomes downward-sloping. It reaches its maximum at $S = -\rho$; a higher elasticity of substitution between skilled and unskilled (that is, a lower ρ), prolongs the upward-sloping section of the relative demand curve, as it slows down the rate at which the scarcity of unskilled labour reduces the relative wage.

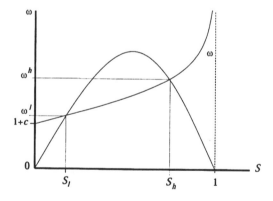

Figure 11.1 Steady state equilibria

The first thing to note is the possibility of multiple equilibria. There is a high-growth equilibrium, S_h, a low-growth (unstable) equilibrium, S_l, and a poverty trap with no human capital and no technical change. Multiplicity emerges as the result of two features of our economy: skilled-biased technical change and the fact that new knowledge is generated by skilled labour. Essentially, a greater supply of skilled workers accelerates technical change, which in turn increases the relative demand for these workers in order to absorb the new technology. Because demand is high, there are enough incentives to invest in education and the greater stock of skilled labour is supported by equilibrium wages. The economy thus finds itself in a virtuous cycle. In the low-growth equilibrium, a low relative wage, caused by the fact that slow technical change implies a small demand for educated labour, generates no incentives to further invest in skills. Through the same mechanism, the economy can even be stuck in a no-growth trap.

The concept of biased technical change that we have just formalized is central to Tinbergen's (1975) hypothesis that the pattern of relative wages over time depends on the strength of the demand for skills exerted by technology and the supply of skills generated by education. What is new is that endogenous technical change creates an interdependence between demand and supply, which, in turn, gives rise to multiplicity.

Multiplicity results in poverty traps, where countries are trapped in a no-R&D equilibrium, even though a high-growth equilibrium would be feasible for the economy's parameter values. Only if the initial stock of labour exceeds the level associated with the unstable, middle equilibrium, does the country converge to the stable R&D equilibrium. If the initial level of skilled labour is not sufficiently high, the country reverts to the development trap in which there is no technical change.

11.3.2. Education Policy versus R&D Policy

Two types of policy have been advocated by the new growth literature as being able to accelerate growth in the R&D-based models: education subsidies and R&D subsidies. In our setup, both have the standard effect on the growth rate, but their distributional implications are not the same.

Suppose first that the government can increase the fraction of the skilled labour force employed in research through subsidies to private R&D firms. This implies a higher value of β, which shifts upwards the labour demand function. The subsidies can be financed through a proportional tax on labour incomes, τ. The arbitrage equation between skilled and unskilled is now $(1-\tau)\left(w_t^S - cw_t^U/a\right) = (1-\tau)w_t^U$.[7] The tax thus reduces the incomes of skilled and unskilled workers by the same proportion, leaving the relative supply function unchanged.

For an economy already in a high-growth steady state, this policy increases the rate of growth and the wage ratio of the economy. Faster technical change is the result of two effects. First, for any S, the fraction of educated workers employed in R&D is higher. Second, in the new high-growth steady state there is a larger stock of skilled labour, as higher inequality induces more individuals to invest in human capital (see Figure 11.2). Faster growth is, thus, achieved at the expense of greater wage inequality. For a low-growth economy, this policy could move it out of its unstable equilibrium and into the high-growth steady state, although it would imply a sharp increase in the relative wage. Note also that the R&D policy would *not* get a country with zero human capital out of its poverty trap.

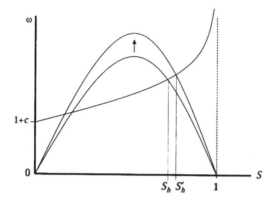

Figure 11.2 R&D subsidies

Suppose now that the government subsidizes the private education cost, reducing it from c to c'. The subsidy can, as before, be financed by a proportional tax on labour incomes. Since the tax is neutral, the only effect of the policy is to shift the inverse labour supply function downwards, as with a lower cost of education more workers are willing to invest in skills for any level of the relative wage. The new high-growth steady state exhibits a larger stock of human capital and hence faster growth. The effect on the relative wage can, however, go either way, as illustrated in Figures 11.3a and 11.3b. If the economy is on the downward-sloping segment of the demand function, then we will witness a reduction in the relative wage, as predicted by Tinbergen. If, on the other hand, the economy is on the upward segment, the higher growth rate will be associated with *increased* wage inequality. The elasticity of substitution between the two types of labour becomes a crucial parameter. A high elasticity of substitution implies that the range over which the demand function is upward-sloping is greater, and hence makes it more likely that a reduction in the cost of education increases the wage premium.

   To sum up, in a model where the source of growth is the level of human capital, technological policies indirectly increase the incentives to become educated by generating a greater skill premium. As a result, faster growth is attained at the expense of greater inequality between the skilled and the unskilled. In the case of education policies, a lower cost of education directly encourages the accumulation of skills. Yet, because the relative demand for labour is increasing in the lagged supply of labour, this does not necessarily imply that the relative wage will fall.

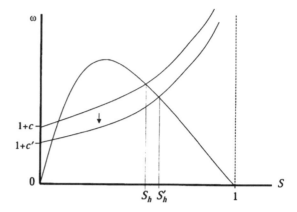

Figure 11.3a   Education subsidies with a low elasticity of substitution

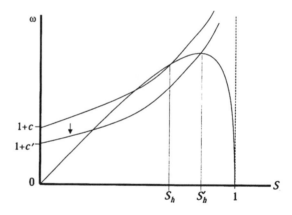

Figure 11.3b   Education subsidies with a high elasticity of substitution

11.4.   REDISTRIBUTION IN VOLATILE ECONOMIES

The textbook approach to redistribution emphasizes the idea, first formalized by James Mirrlees (1971), that there is necessarily a trade-off between productive efficiency and equality due to incentive considerations. The basic incentive argument carries over to the aggregate economy when capital markets are perfect. As we saw in Section 11.2, in a Ramsey–Cass–Koopmans growth model with perfect capital markets, the rate of growth of individual consumption is given by the Euler equation $g = (r - \beta)/\gamma$. If all agents have the same preference parameters, this expression is also the aggregate rate of growth. By making the after-tax rate of interest smaller, greater taxation reduces the return to saving, thus lowering the incentives to accumulate capital and hence the rate of growth.

A number of recent papers have challenged this argument. If capital markets are imperfect, the positive effect of redistribution on agents' investment possibilities may overcome the negative incentive effect and result in faster growth.[8] In this section I want to examine how, even with perfect capital markets, it is possible for redistribution to foster growth.

What follows is based on joint work with Stephen Turnovsky (see García-Peñalosa and Turnovsky, 2001). We consider a Ramsey–Cass–Koopmans model with an externality associated to the capital stock, and we introduce two modifications. First, we consider a two-sector economy, with a modern and a traditional sector, such that only the former uses capital. This means that even with constant returns to aggregate capital, the interest rate is not constant as it depends on how labour is allocated between the two sectors. Second, we assume that the production function in the modern sector is stochastic; that is, in each period there is a shock that increases or reduces the output produced with a given amount of labour and capital.[9] As we are going to see, the endogeneity of employment in the modern sector implies that there is a positive effect of redistribution, as well as the standard negative one.

11.4.1. Volatility and Factor Shares

Consider again the infinitely lived agent economy, but let there be two sectors, a modern sector and a traditional or backyard one. There is a mass 1 of infinitely lived agents in the economy. Assume that all agents are endowed with a unit of time each period that can be allocated either to the modern sector, l, or to operating the traditional technology, $1-l$.

In the modern sector firms are indexed by j. The representative firm produces output according to the stochastic production function:

$$dY_j = AK_j^\alpha (\bar{K}l_j)^{1-\alpha}(dt + du),   (11.20a)$$

where K_j denotes the individual firm's stock of capital, $\bar{K}$ is the aggregate stock of capital, and $\bar{K}l_j$ the efficiency units of labour employed by the firm. The stochastic variable is temporally independent, with mean zero and variance $\sigma^2 dt$ over the instant dt. The realization of the shock is the same for all firms at any particular point in time. All firms are identical, hence they all choose the same level of employment and capital, i.e. $K_j = \bar{K}$ and $l_j = \bar{l}$. A firm's stochastic production function thus exhibits constant returns to scale in private inputs, labour and capital, but aggregate output $\bar{Y}$ is linear in the stock of capital, as:

$$d\bar{Y} = A\bar{l}^{1-\alpha}\bar{K}(dt + du). \tag{11.20b}$$

We assume perfect competition in factor markets, so that wages and rates of return on capital are determined by the usual marginal productivity conditions. In particular, the private rate of return on capital over the time interval $(t, t + dt)$ is specified as $dR = r(dt + du)$, where $r = \alpha A\bar{l}^{1-\alpha}$. The return to labour over the same interval is $dW = w(dt + du)$, with $w = (1-\alpha)A\bar{l}^{-\alpha}\bar{K} \equiv \delta\bar{K}$.

The traditional sector consists of a linear technology that can be operated by a single individual and which uses no capital. Let agent i's output be given by $dQ = Z(1-l)dt$. The backyard technology is thus riskless.[10] We assume that there is an externality from the aggregate level of capital, so that, as before, labour productivity, Z, is proportional to the aggregate capital stock. That is:

$$dQ = q\bar{K}(1-l)dt, \tag{11.21a}$$

and total output in the traditional sector is:

$$d\bar{Q} = q\bar{K}(1-\bar{l})dt. \tag{11.21b}$$

Consumers

A consumer's expected lifetime utility is assumed to take the form:

$$E_0 \int_0^\infty \frac{C_t^{1-\gamma}}{1-\gamma} e^{-\rho t} dt, \ \gamma > 1. \tag{11.22}$$

Her capital accumulation constraint is $dK = KdR + ldW + dQ - Cdt$, which can be expressed as:

$$dK = \left(rK + \delta\bar{K}l + q\bar{K}(1-l) - C \right)dt + \left(rK + \delta\bar{K}l \right)du. \tag{11.23a}$$

Through both the equilibrium wage rate and the rate of return, the dynamic path of the individual's stock of capital depends on the aggregate stock of capital, which in turn evolves according to:

$$d\bar{K} = \left(r\bar{K} + \delta\overline{Kl} + q\bar{K}(1-\bar{l}) - \bar{C} \right)dt + \left(r\bar{K} + \delta\overline{Kl} \right)du. \tag{11.23b}$$

The representative consumer then chooses consumption and the allocation of labour between the two sectors in order to maximize expected lifetime utility, equation (11.22), subject to (11.23). As is well known in this type of models, both r and δ are independent of the capital stock, making the two constraints linear in the capital stock. This linearity is precisely what makes the model tractable.

Macroeconomic Equilibrium

First note that the aggregate resource constraint can be expressed as $dY + dQ = dC + dK$. Using (11.20), (11.21) and (11.23), this equation allows us to write the rate of growth of the capital stock as:

$$\frac{dK}{K} = \left[A\overline{l}^{1-\alpha} + q(1-\overline{l}) - \frac{\overline{C}}{K} \right] dt + A\overline{l}^{1-\alpha} du \equiv gdt + dk.$$

That is, the rate of growth is stochastic, with mean g and variance:

$$\sigma_g^2 = \left(A\overline{l}^{1-\alpha} \right)^2 \sigma^2.$$

The solution to the stochastic growth model can be shown to be given by two equations obtained from the consumers' maximization problem, namely:

$$\delta - \gamma A\overline{l}^{1-\alpha}\delta\sigma^2 = q, \qquad (L)$$

$$g = \frac{r-\beta}{\gamma} + \left[\frac{\gamma-1}{2} + (1-\alpha) \right] \left(A\overline{l}^{1-\alpha} \right)^2 \sigma^2. \qquad (G)$$

Equation (L) is the first order condition with respect to l. It simply states that the risk-adjusted return to labour must be the same in the two sectors. In the absence of uncertainty, it would reduce to $\delta = q$. For risk-averse individuals, uncertainty in the modern sector has the effect of shifting labour to the traditional one. Equation (G) is a modified Euler equation. Inserting the equilibrium value of $\overline{l}$ obtained from (L) yields the average rate of growth.

The presence of uncertainty has both an income and a substitution effect on capital accumulation. For $\gamma > 1$, the income effect dominates and greater volatility tends to increase the rate of growth, as we can see in equation (G). But greater volatility also affects the allocation of labour between sectors, shifting employment away from the modern sector, and thus reducing the interest rate. For reasonable levels of the volatility parameter, this effect is never strong enough to offset the direct impact, implying that greater volatility results in faster growth.

The degree of volatility also affects the labour and capital shares. The share of labour in total output is given by:

$$S_L = \frac{\bar{l}dW + d\bar{Q}}{d\bar{Y} + d\bar{Q}},$$

which is stochastic. Let us consider its deterministic component, that is:

$$E(S_L) = \frac{\bar{l}\delta(\bar{l}) + q(1-\bar{l})}{A\bar{l}^{1-\alpha} + q(1-\bar{l})}.$$

An increase in σ^2 shifts labour away from the modern sector, which increases the marginal product of labour, and hence the overall share of labour in total output. Faster growth is then associated with a larger labour share. Note that this result does not contradict our findings in Section 11.2. In fact, in the stochastic growth model, an increase in α will also result in faster average growth and a lower labour share. Whether high growth rates are accompanied by a high or a low labour share then depends on whether fast growth is due to a high marginal productivity of capital or to high volatility.

11.4.2. Growth and Redistribution

We can now examine whether it is always the case that redistributive policies imply slower growth. Suppose the government redistributes income by taxing capital income at a rate τ, and using the proceeds to subsidize all labour earnings at rate s. The individual capital accumulation constraint then becomes:

$$dK = \left\{r(1-\tau)K + (1+s)[\delta l + q(1-l)]\bar{K} - C\right\}dt + \left[r(1-\tau)K + (1+s)\delta\bar{K}l\right]du \quad (11.24)$$

Because all labour incomes are taxed at the same rate, the allocation of labour between sectors is unaffected, and it is still given by equation (L). Solving the new maximization problem we obtain that the average rate of growth is given by:

$$g = \frac{r(1-\tau)-\beta}{\gamma} + \left[\frac{\gamma-1}{2} + (1-\alpha)(1+s)\right]\left(A\bar{l}^{1-\alpha}\right)^2 \sigma^2. \quad (G')$$

The direct effect of the tax is to reduce the interest rate, while the labour subsidy, by magnifying the effect of the shock on income, tends to foster capital accumulation. This effect can be shown to be weak for reasonable levels of σ^2. The tax-subsidy policy hence reduces the average growth rate.

Suppose now that only wages in the modern sector are subsidized. The allocation of labour is now governed by the following expression:

$$(1+s)\left(\delta - \gamma A \bar{l}^{1-\alpha} \delta \sigma^2\right) = q. \tag{L'}$$

The subsidy now increases the relative return to working in the modern sector, and shifts labour away from the traditional sector. The effect of redistribution on growth is ambiguous. From the (G') schedule, a higher τ reduces the rate of growth. But because it also increases the subsidy and hence the supply of labour in the modern sector, the marginal product of capital increases. There are therefore two effects of the tax-subsidy system on the growth rate; a direct reduction in the net interest rate that tends to depress growth, and an indirect increase in the marginal product of capital due to higher employment, which tends to foster it.

Consider for a moment an economy without risk. The three equilibrium relationships are then:

$$(1+s)\delta = q, \tag{11.25}$$

$$g = \frac{r(1-\tau) - \beta}{\gamma}, \tag{11.26}$$

$$\tau r = s\delta l, \tag{11.27}$$

where the last equation is simply the government budget constraint. These three equations together allow us to express the growth rate as:

$$g = \frac{r - l(q - \delta) - \beta}{\gamma}. \tag{11.28}$$

Differentiating this expression and using equations (11.25) and (11.27), we have:

$$\frac{dg}{d\tau} = \frac{r' - (q - \delta) + l\delta'}{\gamma} \frac{dl}{ds} \frac{ds}{d\tau} = -\frac{r}{\alpha\gamma} < 0.$$

In the absence of risk, redistribution always reduces the growth rate. Can the positive impact of redistribution ever dominate? Calibrating the model, it is possible to show that this is indeed the case. Suppose that the government taxes capital income at 30 per cent and uses the proceeds to subsidize wages in the modern sector at 20 per cent.[11] In a riskless economy, the introduction of the tax subsidy would reduce the growth rate from 3 to 2.7 per cent, implying the usual trade-off between growth and redistribution. As risk increases, the impact of the subsidy on the allocation of labour between sectors becomes stronger, and the effect of the increase in $\bar{l}$ on the interest rate eventually offsets the reduction due to the tax. For high-volatility economies, i.e. $\sigma = 0.4$,[12] the policy raises the share of wages from 76 to 79 per cent and *increases* the growth rate by 0.5 percentage points. That is, redistribution from capital to labour results in faster growth.

The reason is that the presence of risk distorts the allocation of labour, leading to too little employment in the formal sector. This reduces the marginal product of capital and, since capital accumulation is the source of growth, also the average rate of growth. The wage subsidy partially corrects this distortion. When risk is small, this distortion is small, and the effect of the reallocation of labour weak. When risk is large, the allocation of labour is far from the optimum. The subsidy will have a large impact on l and hence on the marginal product of capital, sufficient to offset the negative direct effect of the tax.

11.5. CONCLUSIONS

It has been said that the new growth literature draws on old concepts such as the non-rivalry of knowledge, creative destruction, or learning-by-doing, and that its only contribution has been to formalize existing ideas. In this chapter I have argued that this formalization has important implications. First, it has challenged the notion of causality. We have seen that the new growth theories can reproduce post-Keynesian arguments about different saving propensities of different individuals, as well as Tinbergen's analysis of how the race between education and technical change determines wage inequality. Yet, by drawing attention to the underlying decisions of consumers and producers, this analysis implies that the rate of growth and the distribution of income are jointly determined by preference and technology parameters.

Second, it has allowed us to ask new questions. The formalization of the concept of learning-by-doing has resulted in a growth model that is linear in the capital stock and consequently easy to deal with. As a result, more complex issues can be addressed than in the traditional neoclassical growth model. For example, as we saw in Section 11.3, we have been able to solve a model where production is stochastic, and examine whether there is a correlation between output volatility and factor shares.

Lastly, the new growth theories emphasize the role of policy. Because they examine how the decisions of producers and consumers determine an economy's rate of growth, they imply that government policy, by impacting on these decisions, can affect growth. Since most of this literature concludes that the *laissez-faire* growth rate is lower than the social optimum, policies to accelerate growth are called forth. But because factor rewards and growth are jointly determined, policy will also affect the distribution of income (or consumption, or wages) across agents. We have seen that in investment-led models there may not be a conflict between growth and redistribution. When growth is driven by R&D investments and technical change is biased towards more educated workers, growth-enhancing policies may increase or decrease relative wages depending on whether they take the form of R&D or education subsidies.

One important question remains. In this chapter I have concentrated on how policies affect distribution across contemporaneous agents which have different endowments of capital or skills. However, in an overlapping-generations framework, agents' endowments change over their lifecycle and factor rewards then determine the incomes of different age groups. Growth-enhancing policies then affect the distribution of income between the young and the old and, in a world of changing population structures, it is important to understand how.

NOTES

1. The notable exception is the model of 'creative destruction' of Aghion and Howitt (1992), where a new invention replaces an existing product. There is a negative externality as the producer of the new good does not take into account the destruction of the profits of the incumbent producer, and this may lead to an excessively high rate of technological change.
2. See Galor and Zeira (1993), Perotti (1993), Alesina and Rodrik (1994), Persson and Tabellini (1994), García Peñalosa (1995), and Aghion and Bolton (1997), and also Barro (2000) for empirical evidence. Aghion et al. (1999) review this literature.
3. See Obstfeld (1994) for evidence on the intertemporal elasticity of substitution.
4. See Eicher (1996), Galor and Tsiddon (1997), Greenwood and Yorukoglu (1997), Acemoglu (1998), and Caselli (1999).
5. Galor and Moav (2000) and Gould et al. (2000) also assume that the productivity of uneducated workers depends on the rate of technical change. The main difference is that they consider a production function in which the two types of workers are perfect substitutes, hence the labour demand is monotonic and the equilibrium unique.
6. In Eicher and García Peñalosa (2001) we endogenously determine this fraction.
7. A consumption tax would also leave the labour supply unchanged, as agents are assumed to consume all their income by the end of their lifetime.
8. See Perotti (1993), Banerjee and Newman (1993), and Aghion and Bolton (1997).
9. See Grinols and Turnovsky (1998) and Turnovsky (1999) for a stochastic endogenous growth model.

10. In García Peñalosa and Turnovsky (2001) we consider an economy with shocks to both sectors.

11. The parameter values used are $\alpha = 0.6$, $\gamma = -1.5$, $\beta = 0.04$, $q = 0.3$, and $A = 0.4$.

12. This level of risk implies a standard deviation of the rate of growth of between 9 and 12, depending on the tax, which are close to the highest levels observed in the Summers and Heston data set (see Breen and García Peñalosa, 2000).

REFERENCES

Acemoglu, D. (1998), 'Why do new technologies complement skills? Directed technical change and wage inequality', *Quarterly Journal of Economics*, **113**, 1055–90.

Aghion, P. and P. Bolton (1997), 'A trickle-down theory of growth and development with debt overhang', *Review of Economic Studies*, **64**, 151–62.

Aghion, P. and P. Howitt (1992), 'A model of growth through creative destruction', *Econometrica*, **60**, 323–51.

Aghion, P., E. Caroli and C. García-Peñalosa (1999), 'Inequality and economic growth: the perspective of the new growth theories', *Journal of Economic Literature*, **37**, 1615–60.

Alesina, A. and D. Rodrik (1994), 'Distributive politics and economic growth', *Quarterly Journal of Economics*, **109**, 465–90.

Banerjee, A. and A.F. Newman (1993), 'Occupational choice and the process of development', *Journal of Political Economy*, **101**, 274–98.

Barro, R. (2000), 'Inequality and growth in a panel of countries', *Journal of Economic Growth*, **5**, 5–32.

Bartel, A.P. and F.R. Lichtenberg (1987), 'The comparative advantage of educated workers in implementing new technology', *Review of Economics and Statistics*, **69**, 1–11.

Bertola, G. (1993), 'Factor shares and savings in endogenous growth', *American Economic Review*, **83**, 1184–98.

Breen, R. and C. García-Peñalosa (2000), 'Income inequality and macroeconomic volatility: an empirical investigation', GREQAM, mimeo.

Caselli, F. (1999), 'Technological revolutions', *American Economic Review*, **89**, 78–102.

Eicher, T.S. (1996), 'Interaction between endogenous human capital and technological change', *Review of Economic Studies*, **63**, 127–44.

Eicher, T.S. and C. García-Peñalosa (2001), 'Inequality and growth: the dual role of human capital in development', *Journal of Development Economics*, **66**, 173–97.

Galor, O. and O. Moav (2000), 'Ability based technological transition, wage inequality and economic growth', *Quarterly Journal of Economics*, **115**, 469–97.

Galor, O. and D. Tsiddon (1997), 'Technological progress, mobility, and economic growth', *American Economic Review*, **87**, 363–82.

Galor, O. and J. Zeira (1993), 'Income distribution and macroeconomics', *Review of Economic Studies*, **60**, 35–52.

García-Peñalosa, C. (1995), 'The paradox of education or the good side of inequality', *Oxford Economic Papers*, **47**, 265–85.

García-Peñalosa, C. and S.J. Turnovsky (2001), 'Production risk and the functional distribution of income: tradeoffs and policy responses', *GREQAM Working Paper* 01A30.

Gould, E., O. Moav and B.A. Weinberg (2000), 'Precautionary demand for education, inequality, and technological progress', mimeo.

Greenwood, J. and M. Yorukoglu (1997), '1974', *Carnegie–Rochester Conference Series on Public Policy*, **46**, 49–95.

Grinols, E.L. and S.J. Turnovsky (1998), 'Risk, optimal government finance and monetary policies in a growing economy', *Economica*, **65**, 401–27.

Kaldor, N. (1956), 'Alternative theories of distribution', *Review of Economic Studies*, **23**, 83–100.

Kaldor, N. (1957), 'A model of economic growth', *Economic Journal*, **67**, 591–624.

Krueger, A. (1993), 'How computers have changed the wage structure', *Quarterly Journal of Economics*, **108**, 33–60.

Mirrlees, J.A. (1971), 'An exploration in the theory of optimum income taxation', *Review of Economic Studies*, **38**, 175–208.

Murphy, K.M. and F. Welch (1992), 'The structure of wages', *Quarterly Journal of Economics*, **107**, 285–326.

Nelson, R. and E. Phelps (1966), 'Investments in humans, technological diffusion, and economic growth', *American Economic Review*, **61**, 69–75.

Obstfeld, M. (1994), 'Risk-taking, global diversification, and growth', *American Economic Review*, **84**, 310–29.

Pasinetti, L. (1962), 'Rate of profit and income distribution in relation to the rate of economic growth', *Review of Economic Studies*, **29**, 267–79.

Perotti, R. (1993), 'Political equilibrium, income distribution, and growth', *Review of Economic Studies*, **60**, 755–76.

Persson, T. and G. Tabellini (1994), 'Is inequality harmful for growth? Theory and evidence', *American Economic Review*, **84**, 600–21.

Romer, P.M. (1987), 'Growth based on increasing returns due to specialization', *American Economic Review*, **77**, 56–72.

Romer, P.M. (1990), 'Endogenous technological change', *Journal of Political Economy*, **98**, S71–S102.

Tinbergen, J. (1975), *Income Distribution: Analysis and Policies*, North-Holland: Amsterdam.

Turnovsky, S.J. (1999), 'On the role of government in a stochastically growing open economy', *Journal of Economic Dynamics and Control*, **23**, 873–908.

12. Does investment cause growth? A test of an endogenous demand-driven theory of growth applied to India 1950–96

Ramesh Chandra and Roger J. Sandilands

12.1. INTRODUCTION

From the early development literature of the 1940s and 1950s, notably that of Paul Rosenstein-Rodan (1943, 1961), Ragnar Nurkse (1953) and Arthur Lewis (1954), a mainstream view emerged that capital accumulation was the key to growth. Capital was the 'missing component' which if applied in adequate amounts could help break the vicious circle of poverty. Underdevelopment and low productivity were diagnosed as the result of an acute shortage of material capital, so the key to enhanced productivity lay in measures to boost the savings and investment rates.

For various reasons, there has been growing scepticism that physical capital is the main constraint on development. First, the neoclassical growth accounting exercises have found that increase in capital per worker explains only a small proportion of per capita income growth, a large portion of which is attributed to the unexplained residual or exogenous technical progress. Second, the new endogenous growth theory focuses on the externalities associated with new knowledge and emphasises the importance of human capital and research and development (R&D) in offsetting the tendency to diminishing returns. Thus the above theories all tend to focus on supply constraints: physical or human capital, or the supply of new knowledge. The aim of this chapter is to offer and test a contrasting approach that is based on the demand side. Its essence can be summarised by reference to Adam Smith's famous aphorism that the division of labour is limited by the size of the market, or Allyn Young's extension of this theme – that the division of labour is limited by the division of labour.

The Indian five-year plans did not diverge from the early mainstream view on development issues. India's development strategy since the second plan (1956–61) has come to be known as the Nehru–Mahalanobis strategy. This strategy accorded primacy to the capital goods sector and advocated a socialist framework in which the public sector would play a dominating role. In line with mainstream thinking, India's planners subscribed to the supply-side view of the growth process in which capital accumulation was key (see, for example, Chakravarty, 1987). Given the added assumption of low elasticity of export demand (i.e., elasticity pessimism) and the need to convert high savings into real investment, primacy to capital goods production at home was thought to be the logical outcome.

As a result of policies derived from this thinking, India's planners succeeded in pushing up the rates of saving and investment from around 10 per cent in 1950 to around 22 per cent by 1980; but there was no commensurate increase in the growth rate. Bhagwati (1993) stated that the weak growth performance reflected, not a disappointing saving performance, but rather a disappointing productivity performance.

Thus the theoretical, as also the empirical, question is: Is capital accumulation (or investment) really the main key to growth? The empirical literature seems divided on the issue. The observed strong relationship between fixed capital formation (as a percentage of GDP) and growth rates since World War II led De Long and Summers (1991, 1992) to suggest that the rate of capital formation determines the rate of a country's economic growth. Lipsey and Kravis (1987), on the other hand, find that the observed long-term relationship between the capital formation rate and the growth rate is due more to the effect of growth on capital formation than to the effect of capital formation on growth. In a recent paper Blomström et al. (1996) test the causality between the fixed investment rate and the growth rate by using the Granger (1969) and Sims (1972) framework. They find that, while economic growth precedes capital formation, there is no evidence that capital formation precedes growth.

Given the importance attached to capital formation in India's planning process and the evidence that the observed strong relationship between the fixed capital formation rate and the growth rate since World War II does not prove causality, the objective of this chapter is to explore whether higher investment leads to higher growth in India. Our aim is to investigate which of the two contrasting approaches to development is supported by the Indian data: the capital accumulation approach which gives a causative role to capital accumulation, or the Smith–Young demand-based approach in which capital accumulation is more an effect than a cause of growth. Using data from the National Accounts Statistics, we investigate the issue of causality by using cointegration and error-correction modelling.

The next section of this chapter reviews in greater detail the nature of these contrasts. Methodological issues are discussed in Section 12.3. Section 12.4 then subjects to empirical test, with reference to the important case of post-independence India, the competing hypotheses as to whether it is investment that causes growth, or growth that causes investment. Finally, in Section 12.5 we draw out the policy implications for India's development strategy.

12.2. THE ROLE OF CAPITAL IN DEVELOPMENT: A CRITICAL REVIEW

The post-war period saw the grant of political freedom to many developing countries. The issue of development therefore was pushed to centre stage. The mainstream view emphasised the need to push up the saving and investment rates to achieve growth. For Nurkse (1953), the heart of the problem was that '[t]he so-called underdeveloped areas, as compared with advanced, are underdeveloped with capital in relation to their population and natural resources' (p. 1). Further, his emphasis was on accumulation of physical capital to the neglect of investment in education, health and skills (human capital), and technical progress. A larger share of society's currently available resources had to be diverted to increase the stock of capital to make possible an expansion of consumable output in the future. Nurkse did mention the vicious circle of poverty on the demand side but his solution was a supply-side strategy of balanced growth – 'a more or less synchronised application of capital to a wide range of different industries' – which he took to be an implication of Rosenstein-Rodan's theory. His view was that though 'capital formation is not entirely a matter of capital supply ... this is no doubt the more important part of the problem'. To finance the required investment a high savings ratio (or massive foreign borrowing) would be necessary.

Rosenstein-Rodan (1943, 1961) emphasised indivisibilities and externalities in the production process, and suggested that in underdeveloped countries individual investment decisions would be frustrated by the small size of the market. An incrementalist approach would therefore yield insignificant contributions to growth. Instead, a coordinated 'big push' (the minimum quantum of investment needed 'to jump over the economic obstacles to development') was needed to launch these countries into self-sustaining growth.

Likewise, in Lewis's theory of development the central problem was the process by which a community previously saving and investing only around 4 or 5 per cent of national income was converted into one whose voluntary saving rate was 12 to 15 per cent or more. Here:

[t]he key to the process is the use which is made of the capitalist surplus. In so far as it is reinvested in creating new capital, the capitalist sector expands, taking more people into capitalist employment out of the subsistence sector. The surplus is then larger still, capital formation is still greater, and so the process continues until the labour surplus disappears. (Lewis, 1954, pp. 151–2)

This too was primarily a supply-side view of development; with demand constraints either not considered important or ignored. Lewis discounted Ricardian and Malthusian concerns over a potential fall in the rate of profit, and the consequent emergence of a stationary state, in the following words: 'If we assume technical progress in agriculture, no hoarding, and unlimited labour at a constant wage, the rate of profit on capital cannot fall. On the contrary it must increase, since all the benefit of technical progress in the capitalist sector accrues to the capitalists' (Lewis, 1954, p. 154).

The Harrod–Domar growth model (Harrod, 1939; Domar, 1947) also emphasised saving and investment in growth. Given a constant capital/output ratio, the growth rate is strictly determined by the savings rate. The model indicates the additional savings (or foreign aid) required to achieve a targeted rate of growth.

Along with the desirability of high savings and investment ratios, a major role for state intervention in resource allocation was also thought necessary. The state was expected not only to push up the rates of saving and investment through appropriate policies, but also to intervene directly through public sector investment. Further, the trade-pessimism philosophies of Nurkse (1962), Raúl Prebisch (1950), Hans Singer (1950) and Gunnar Myrdal (1957) implied an import-substitution model of growth, and typically this also involved a greater direct and indirect role for the public sector.

In 1956 Robert Solow produced his seminal paper on neoclassical growth. This invoked an aggregate Cobb–Douglas production function with constant returns to scale but diminishing returns to each input. A related paper (Solow, 1957), following similar work by Moses Abramovitz (1956), attempted to measure the contribution of capital to growth based on the neoclassical assumption that factors are paid their marginal product, but again with diminishing marginal product if one factor should grow faster than cooperant factors. Thus capital deepening (a secular rise in the capital/labour ratio) would involve diminishing returns (unlike the Harrod–Domar assumption of a constant capital/output ratio), and a rise in savings and investment rates would boost growth only temporarily. In the long run, absent (exogenous, unexplained) technical progress, growth could be sustained only at the rate of growth of the labour force. *Per capita* output growth would be zero. However, the temporary effect on growth of a higher rate of capital accumulation would place countries on a higher *level* of income per head even in the long run. The conclusion was that the savings rate should still be encouraged for its levels effect.

Without abandoning the neoclassical framework, modern endogenous growth theory seeks to explain why per capita income growth continues in capital-abundant countries and is often faster than in capital-poor countries. It suggests that capital deepening may avoid diminishing returns thanks to various externalities and productivity gains that are explained endogenously in these models. The aggregate production function then exhibits increasing rather than constant returns to scale. While Allyn Young's (1928) seminal paper on increasing returns is often cited as an early exposition of this general insight (e.g., Romer, 1987, 1989; Murphy et al., 1989a, 1989b; Krugman, 1990, 1993; Shaw, 1992; Aghion and Howitt, 1998), modern theorists claim to explain what he had in mind in greater detail and rigour.

Young's 1928 paper was an amplification of Adam Smith's insight that the division of labour is limited by the size of the market, and of Alfred Marshall's distinction between internal and external economies. He insisted that growth of the market explained the fuller exploitation of the cost-reducing economies to be gained from more specialized, roundabout, capital-intensive methods. Thus demand was at least as important as the supply of inputs in explaining growth. Young's conception of a market, and its growth, was as 'an aggregate of productive activities tied together by *trade*' (Young, 1928, p. 533; italics added). Thus demand involved the exchange of real products for other products, a variant on Say's law that supply creates its own demand:

> [The] capacity to buy depends upon capacity to produce. In an inclusive view, considering the market not as an outlet for the products of a particular industry, and therefore external to that industry, but as the outlet for goods in general, the size of the market is determined and defined by the volume of production. ... Adam Smith's dictum amounts to the theorem that the division of labour depends in large part upon the division of labour ... Thus change becomes progressive and propagates itself in a cumulative way. (Young, 1928, p. 533)

Two of Young's own students have contributed to this cumulative-causation, demand-side approach: Lauchlin Currie (1902–93) who studied under him at Harvard, 1925–27; and Nicholas Kaldor (1908–86) who studied under him at the London School of Economics from 1927 until Young's untimely death in 1929. This chapter is based largely on Currie's interpretations of Young's 1928 paper on the causes of economic progress (Currie, 1966, 1974, 1981, 1997), and offers an alternative to the mainstream views outlined above.[1]

Young attempted to explain growth not in terms of the apparent measured contributions of increased supplies of labour and capital that are subject to diminishing returns absent some exogenous technical progress, but as a process which is self-perpetuating rather than self-exhausting. From Young's insight that 'the division of labour depends in large part upon the division of labour', Currie (1981, 1997) drew the implication that 'growth begets growth': that there is a built-in tendency for the trend rate of growth, whether fast or slow, to be perpetuated unless interrupted by exogenous shocks or significant policy changes that act upon the size of the market and the degree of competition and mobility. In this view, increased factor inputs (and technology too) were largely the consequence of the growth process rather than its cause.

Young thought that while the law of diminishing returns may apply to individual inputs employed by individual firms at a particular time, it did not characterise the dynamic laws of motion of the whole economy. For the individual firm an increase in output may typically appear to be obtainable only at rising marginal cost while also tending to depress the product price. An increase in *aggregate* output, however, may engender productivity-enhancing changes in organisation and methods, via increased specialisation and aggregate exchange (or aggregate real demand)[2] that could offset the microeconomic tendency to diminishing returns that would be expected under the theoretical assumption of static *ceteris paribus* conditions.

In the aggregate, the whole economic environment is in continuous process of transformation (*ceteris non paribus*) through the interactive multiplicity of individual actions. Microeconomic diminishing returns may confront the individual firm as it expands output with given techniques and organisation (so there appears to be a declining but positive marginal product, in physical and value terms). But if the effect of multiple individual actions is to increase aggregate output, then, in Young's theory, microeconomic constraints and rising supply price are converted into macroeconomic opportunities for economic progress with increasing returns and falling unit costs. This was his demand-based view of growth in which specialisation and division of labour (limited by, but also determining, the size and growth of the market) play a crucial role.

Thus Young viewed the overall market size as flexible and extendable. By contrast, while Nurkse (1953) quotes Smith with approval on the link between division of labour and size of market, we have seen that he comes to a mainly supply-based prescription for growth that emphasises capital formation. Currie (1966) took Nurkse and others to task for this excessive preoccupation with capital formation in which investment is 'good' and consumption 'bad'. Nurkse overlooked the possibilities for boosting consumer goods as well as investment goods by providing incentives to the mobilisation and use of chronically underemployed labour and capital resources. In particular, he overlooked the possibility that labour may be unproductive or poorly employed not because of lack of capital but because of lack of effective demand in relation to supply. For example, a girl's labour may be worth almost nothing in agriculture but be quite remunerative as urban domestic labour, while utilising no more capital.

According to Currie, given the gross inequalities in incomes and expenditures in developing countries and also the existence of idle labour, it makes little sense to talk of increasing saving by holding back consumption of the masses. The solution may lie not in restraining consumption but by creating incentives to the provision of more remunerative work, whether in consumption (textiles) or in investment (housing). Increases in saving and investment would follow as derivative rather than initiating factors of growth.

In his 'leading sector' model of growth Currie (1974) distinguishes a 'Keynesian' increase in money demand from an increase in 'Sayian' demand. While the former may be effective in stimulating an economy undergoing depression, it may have little impact on the underlying trend growth of intersectoral demand for products and services. In the classical, Sayian sense of demand, an increase in one sector's output constitutes its real demand for the products of other sectors. When and if this is met by an induced increase in the traded output of other sectors in exchange, then the overall rate of growth is raised by the weighted average of the 'leading' and 'following' sectors' individual growth rates.

By contrast, the Keynesian mechanism may not operate to increase real demand (hence real output) even when there is much slack in the system if this slack arises not because of deficient monetary demand but because of the chronic institutional barriers in underdeveloped countries that impede mobility or the better utilisation of existing equipment. In that case Keynesian demand may be dissipated in general inflation, with no incentives to better and fuller resource allocation. In Currie's words, one may expect that 'measures to ensure better mobility or a better combination of factors will ... lead to an increase in real output even while aggregate money demand may be falling' (Currie, 1974, p. 4).

We have seen that the neoclassical growth-accounting framework emphasises exogenous technical progress as the theoretically and empirically dominant element in growth rather than the traditional inputs of labour and capital because, with diminishing returns, capital deepening leads to a steady state of zero per capita income growth, in the absence of technical change. Modern endogenous growth models retain the neoclassical framework but try to explain the unexplained residual – variously called exogenous technical progress, a 'measure of our ignorance' (Abramovitz, 1956), or 'total factor productivity growth' – by placing even more emphasis on the supply of inputs but with the difference that capital inputs generate positive externalities, especially skilled human capital inputs engaged in the dissemination of 'non-rivalrous' or non-excludable knowledge via investment in research and development activities.

Sandilands (2000) explains that while the modern endogenous growth literature stresses patents, protectionism and subsidies to new knowledge and R&D expenditures, Young showed how the fuller exploitation and adaptation of existing as well as new knowledge is enhanced via greater rather than less competition, and by opening up rather than closing off markets. Thus the modern literature in this respect neglects or misrepresents Young's concept of increasing returns in the process of self-sustaining growth.

Young's vision is of a process in which competition and mobility hasten the overall increase in purchasing power by ensuring that resources flow to where they are used most efficiently – at lowest cost and lowest prices. As the size of the market thus increases so does the incentive to continue the process of innovation with cost and price reductions. These further enhance the size of the market via greater specialisation within and between firms. This calls for new modes of industrial organisation, with or without large investments in physical capital. But in any case the financing of new capital, new processes and new products comes largely from the increased sales revenues in the growing economy. This is an endogenous process in which growth itself breeds further growth, so that growth is self-sustaining rather than self-exhausting.

That is the theory. The need now is to consider the empirical implications of the theory and subject it to test. A major implication is that efficient capital accumulation – the kind that yields increased value to cover its cost, and so to increase GDP – is to a large extent induced by an increase in aggregate demand (as measured by overall real GDP) rather than being the main force determining an increase in GDP. Of course, investment is itself a part of GDP so an increase in investment spending will itself enhance GDP. But investment is only a fraction of GDP and in many countries where growth is strong this fraction is relatively small. After discussing the methodological issues in the next section we shall look at our hypothesis in the light of the Indian experience.[3]

12.3. METHODOLOGY

12.3.1. Definition of Causality

We start by defining Granger's (1969) concept of causality. X is said to Granger-cause Y if Y can be predicted with greater accuracy by past values of X rather than not using such past values, all other relevant information in the model remaining the same. Consider the equation:

$$Y_t = \alpha_0 + \alpha_1 Y_{t-1} + \alpha_2 Y_{t-2} + \beta_1 X_{t-1} + \beta_2 X_{t-2} + u_t.$$

If $\beta_1 = \beta_2 = 0$, X does not Granger-cause Y. If, on the other hand, any of the β coefficients are non-zero, then X does Granger-cause Y. The null hypothesis that $\beta_1 = \beta_2 = 0$ can be tested by using the standard F-test of joint significance. Note that we have taken two-period lags in the above equation. In practice, the choice of the lag length is arbitrary. Varying the lag length may lead to different test results. As a practical guide one can include as many lags as are necessary to ensure non-autocorrelated residuals.

Another well-known test for causality is that of Sims (1972). This makes use of the notion that the future cannot cause the present. Consider another equation:

$$X_t = a_0 + a_1 X_{t-1} + a_2 X_{t-2} + b_1 Y_{t+2} + b_2 Y_{t+1} + b_3 Y_{t-1} + b_4 Y_{t-2} + e_t.$$

Here X rather than Y is the dependent variable and the leading values of Y such as Y_{t+1} and Y_{t+2} are included. Here the F-test is H_0: $b_1 = b_2 = 0$. Rejection of H_0 must imply that X causes Y because non-zero b_1 and b_2 cannot be interpreted as implying that causation runs from leading values of Y to X. Since the Sims test includes leading values, it has the disadvantage of using more degrees of freedom as compared to the Granger test.

Bahmani-Oskooee and Alse (1993) have criticised studies based on the above procedures on the grounds that they do not check the cointegrating properties of the concerned variables. If these variables – investment and GDP in our case – are cointegrated then the standard causality techniques outlined above lead to misleading conclusions because these tests will miss some of the 'forecastability' which becomes available through the error-correction term. Secondly, the traditional tests use growth of the concerned variables and this is akin to first differencing. This filters out long-run information. To remedy the situation they recommend cointegration and error-correction modelling to combine the short-term information with the long run.

12.3.2. Cointegration and Error-correction Modelling

Before cointegration is applied, it is essential to test a time series for stationarity.[4] At an informal level stationarity can be tested by plotting the correlogram[5] of a time series. At a formal level, stationarity can be tested by determining whether the data contain a unit root. This can be done by the Dickey–Fuller (1979), Augmented Dickey–Fuller (ADF) and Phillips–Perron (1988) tests.[6] The ADF test is used here for testing for stationarity as well as for the order of integration of a series.[7]

We shall take the log of concerned variables so that the first differences can be interpreted as growth rates. If two variables *LI* (the log of real investment) and *LY* (the log of real GDP at factor cost) are integrated to the order one, i.e., $I(1)$, then the next step is to find whether they are cointegrated. This can be done by estimating the following cointegrating equations by OLS and testing their residuals for stationarity:

$$LY = a + bLI + u \qquad (12.1)$$

$$LI = \alpha + \beta LY + e. \qquad (12.2)$$

If *LY* and *LI* are both $I(1)$, then for them to be cointegrated *u* and *e* should be stationary or $I(0)$. Once it is established that two variables are cointegrated, the next issue is which variable causes the other. Before the advent of cointegration and error-correction modelling, the standard tests were used widely to determine the direction of causality. However, as noted earlier, the standard Granger and Sims methods are likely to be misleading if the concerned variables are cointegrated. This is because the standard Granger or Sims tests do not contain an error-correction term. The error-correction models are formulated as follows:

$$\Delta LY = f(\text{lagged } \Delta LI, \text{lagged } \Delta LY) + \lambda u t_{-1} \qquad (12.3)$$

$$\Delta LI = f(\text{lagged } \Delta LI, \text{lagged } \Delta LY) + \phi e_{t-1}, \qquad (12.4)$$

where the error-correction terms u_{t-1} and e_{t-1} are stationary residuals from the cointegrating equations. By introducing error-correction terms an additional channel is opened up through which causality is tested. For example, in equation (12.3), growth of real investment (ΔLI) is said to Granger-cause real income growth (ΔLY) either when the coefficients of the lagged ΔLI are positive and jointly significant through the F-test, or if λ is significant, or both. If income growth causes investment growth, either the coefficients of the lagged ΔLY are positive and jointly significant (F-test), or ϕ is significant, or both (equation 12.4). Thus error-correction models allow for the fact that causality can be manifest through the lagged changes of the independent variable, or through the error-correction term, or through both.

In the above analysis, it is important to distinguish between short-term and long-term causality. Following Jones and Joulfaian (1991), Bahmani-Oskooee (1993), Doraisami (1996), and others we interpret the lagged changes in the independent variable to represent the short-run causal impact, while the error-correction term is interpreted as representing the long-run impact.

In the autoregressive models represented by the above equations where there is more than one lag on the right-hand side, one has to devise an appropriate strategy for choosing the optimum number of lags on each variable. One way would be that followed by Hsiao (1987), Bahmani-Oskooee et al. (1991), and Love (1994) by employing Akaike's final prediction error (FPE) criterion to identify the optimum number of lags. Another way would be to include a sufficient number of lags on the right-hand side of the equation to ensure that there is no autoregression in the estimated equation, and then proceed from general to specific search. Yet another way is the 'simple to general' search recommended by Engle and Granger (1987) in which one starts with fewer lags and then proceeds to test for added lags. The idea is that if non-autocorrelated residuals are achieved by a smaller number of lags then that model is preferred to one with a larger number, in the interests of parsimony. Moreover, this method has the added advantage of not overparameterising the model and preserving the degrees of freedom, particularly if the sample size is relatively small. Keeping these considerations in mind, we shall follow the third method of simple to general search.

12.4. RESULTS

We have employed various concepts of investment such as private investment, government investment, total investment and fixed investment to investigate the issue of causality.[8] As noted above, the standard Granger procedure is inapplicable if LY and LI are cointegrated. If the variables are not cointegrated, the standard procedure can be applied. As we shall see below, except for government investment all other proxies for investment cointegrate with real income. So in all cases, except the one involving government investment, cointegration and error-correction modelling will be applied.

Before cointegration can be applied it is essential to test a time series for stationarity as well as its order of integration. Table 12.1 presents the results of the ADF test for unit root. It can be seen that since the ADF test statistic for all level variables is more than the 95 per cent critical value, the null of non-stationarity is accepted. First differences are, however, stationary as the ADF statistic in all cases is less than the 95 per cent critical value. Since first differences are $I(0)$, the original series are all $I(1)$. Given that all level variables are $I(1)$, there is no problem in applying cointegration analysis.

Let us first take up the causality between the growth of government investment (ΔLGI) and income growth (ΔLY). Table 12.2 shows that LY and

Table 12.1 ADF test for unit root

Variable	Test statistic		95% Critical value	
	Levels	First differences	Levels	First differences
LY	−1.216(0)	−7.611(0)	−3.522	−2.936
LGI	−2.285(4)	−4.024(3)	−2.934	−2.936
LPI	0.481(3)	−5.637(2)	−2.934	−2.936
LTI	−0.397(4)	−5.561(3)	−2.934	−2.936
LFI	−0.126(3)	−5.570(2)	−2.934	−2.936

Notes:
1. Computations are performed by using Microfit 4.0 (Pesaran and Pesaran, 1997).
2. Terms in parentheses show the number of augmentations or lags (k) in ADF regressions.
3. k is chosen with the help of a model selection criterion such as Akaike Information Criterion (AIK), Schwarz–Bayesian Criterion (SBC) and Hannan–Quinn Criterion (HQC).
4. Microfit 4.0 uses critical values from Dickey and Fuller (1979).

Table 12.2 Causality between growth of government investment and income growth

ADF test for cointegration

Regression	$\bar{R}^2$	CRDW	ADF	95% CV
$LY = f(LGI)$	0.908	0.302	−1.030(4)	−3.489
$LGI = f(LY)$	0.908	0.324	−1.962	−3.489

Notes:
1. Critical values are from MacKinnon (1991).
2. The critical values for CRDW in the vicinity of 50 observations are 0.78 at 5 per cent and 0.69 at 10 per cent levels of significance, respectively (Engle and Yoo, 1987). CRDW is a useful test for cointegration if the disequilibrium errors of the cointegrating regression are generated by first-order AR process.
3. Causality results based on error-correction models could not be presented as *LY* and *LG* are not cointegrated.

LGI are not cointegrated as the ADF test statistic in both regressions exceeds the 95 per cent critical value. Moreover, the CRDW statistic is also quite low ruling out any cointegration between the concerned variables. So there is no long-term relationship between real government investment and real GDP. Therefore, the methodology of cointegration and error-correction modelling could not be applied. However, the application of simple Granger-causality (minus the error-correction term) suggested that growth of government investment has a negative and significant impact on economic growth; i.e., government investment acts as a negative engine of growth. The sign of the reverse causality was positive and significant; i.e., economic growth had a positive impact on growth of government investment.

Next, we take up the causality between the growth of private investment (ΔLPI) and growth of income (ΔLY). Table 12.3a shows that the CRDW statistic in both regressions is quite large and greater than the 95 per cent critical value of 0.78. The ADF test statistic in both regressions is less than the 95 per cent critical value. The conclusion is that *LY* and *LPI* are

Table 12.3 *Causality between growth of private investment and income growth.*

(*a*) ADF test for cointegration

Regression	$\overline{R}^2$	CRDW	ADF	95% CV
$LY = f(LPI)$	0.958	1.114	−4.600(0)	−3.489
$LPI = f(LY)$	0.958	1.161	−4.897(0)	−3.489

(*b*) Results of error-correction models

Regression	Lags	$E(-1)$	$F(i \rightarrow y)$	$F(y \rightarrow i)$
$\Delta LY = f(\text{lagged } \Delta LPI, \text{lagged } \Delta LY) + \lambda E(-1)$	1	0.081(0.160)	0.740(0.395)	
$\Delta LPI = f(\text{lagged } \Delta LPI, \text{lagged } \Delta LY) + \phi E(-1)$	1	−0.908(0.000)		0.991(0.326)

Notes:
1. $E(-1)$ stands for the error-correction term.
2. *i* stands for rate of growth of investment and *y* for rate of growth of income.
3. In Table 12.3a the terms in the parentheses are the number of lags, while in Table 12.3b they are the probability values.

cointegrated and there is a long-term relationship between these variables. The next step is to estimate error-correction models. The results are shown in Table 12.3b. It can be seen that the error-correction term for the model with ΔLPI as the dependent variable is quite significant and has the correct sign, whereas the error-correction term for the model with ΔLY as the dependent variable is insignificant. This indicates that the direction of causality in the long run runs only in one direction, from ΔLY to ΔLPI. Results of the F-test show that there is no short-term causality in either direction. The conclusion emerging from this analysis is that private investment and GDP exhibit a long-term relationship with each other; and the direction of long-term causality runs from growth of income to growth of private investment.

Now we turn to the causality between growth of total investment (ΔLTI) and growth of income (ΔLY). Table 12.4a shows that LY and LTI enter into a long-term relationship with each other. Again the direction of long-term causality runs from ΔLY to ΔLTI; there is no short-term causality in either direction (Table 12.4b). The same story is repeated if we consider fixed investment, FI (Tables 12.5a and 12.5b).

Some authors (for example Sheehey, 1990) have argued that there is bound to be a problem of built-in correlation between GDP and any category (such as exports or investment) which is a substantial portion of GDP. To

Table 12.4 Causality between growth of total investment and income growth

(*a*) ADF test for cointegration

Regression	$\bar{R}^2$	CRDW	ADF	95% CV
$LY = f(LTI)$	0.968	1.032	−4.217(0)	−3.489
$LTI = f(LY)$	0.968	1.064	−5.218(1)	−3.489

(*b*) Results of error-correction models

Regression	Lags	$E(-1)$	$F(i \to y)$	$F(y \to i)$
$\Delta LY = f(\text{lagged } \Delta LTI, \text{lagged } \Delta LY) + \lambda E(-1)$	1	0.086(0.1158)	0.018(0.893)	
$\Delta LTI = f(\text{lagged } \Delta LTI, \text{lagged } \Delta LY) + \phi E(-1)$	2	−0.760(0.000)		1.404(0.258)

Table 12.5 Causality between growth of fixed investment and income growth

(a) ADF test for cointegration

Regression	$\overline{R}^2$	CRDW	ADF	95% CV
$LY = f(LFI)$	0.983	0.673	−4.607(1)	−3.489
$LFI = f(LY)$	0.983	0.680	−5.065(1)	−3.489

(b) Results of error-correction models

Regression	Lags	$E(-1)$	$F(i \rightarrow y)$	$F(y \rightarrow i)$
$\Delta LY = f(\text{lagged } \Delta LFI, \text{ lagged } \Delta LY) + \lambda E(-1)$	1	0.063(0.432)	0.009(0.923)	
$\Delta LFI = f(\text{lagged } \Delta LFI, \text{ lagged } \Delta LY) + \phi E(-1)$	2	−0.443(0.000)		0.028(0.868)

take account of this objection the above regressions were re-estimated after netting out the relevant investment variable from the GDP. Although the results are not reported here, this adjustment makes no difference to our results. Moreover, when the income variable is defined in terms of per capita income in place of GDP and the investment variable is defined as investment/GDP ratio, the results remain the same. It thus appears that the results are quite robust to the way we define the investment or income variable.

So the basic conclusion which emerges is that in India capital accumulation is the result rather than the cause of growth. This finding is in line with that obtained by other researchers such as Lipsey and Kravis (1987) and Blomström et al. (1996). The findings are also in consonance with the Young and Currie view that saving and investment are derivative rather than initiating factors of growth.

Our finding that the rate of capital accumulation exercises an insignificant influence over the rate of growth of the Indian economy is similar to that obtained by Chandra (2000). In a multivariate model involving the investment ratio and trade policy variables, he finds that the investment ratio has an insignificant impact on per capita income growth. This result contradicts the mainstream view that the investment rate is crucial to explaining growth, and this in turn requires an explanation.

This result, inter alia, may be the outcome of large unutilised capacity in Indian industry. Studies have shown that the protectionist policies of the past have had an adverse impact on capacity utilisation in India. For example,

Paul (1974) and Goldar and Renganathan (1991) found a negative relationship between the effective rate of protection and the rate of capacity utilisation across industries. It appears that protection from foreign competition insulates domestic firms from any competitive pressures to reduce production costs by utilising capacity more fully. Moreover, protectionist policies do not allow imported inputs and intermediates to be readily available, resulting in large unutilised capacity.

Other factors inhibiting fuller utilisation of capacity may include infrastructural bottlenecks (in the form of power shortage or transportation difficulties), shortage of domestic demand, incompatibility of the structure of capacities with the evolving structure of demand, and management deficiencies.

Large unutilised capacity may also result from archaic policies that prevent redeployment of resources from unproductive uses to more productive ones. For example, an industrial unit in India cannot be closed down unless permitted by the government and such permission is rarely forthcoming. Similarly, labour laws are heavily loaded in favour of labour, as a result of which it is almost impossible to retrench labour.[9] Restructuring and redeployment of resources are an essential ingredient of competition; in India laws prohibit this. Competition is not only about easy entry but easy exit as well. In India an exit policy has yet to be evolved. As a result, large parts of her industry remain sick or unviable.

12.5. CONCLUSIONS

Development literature has regarded accumulation of material capital as the key to growth; the emphasis has therefore been placed on increasing the rates of saving and investment in strategies followed by developing countries in the post-war period.

Indian planning has not deviated from this mainstream thinking. Accordingly, policies aimed at pushing up the rates of savings and investment were vigorously pursued. While India succeeded in pushing up these rates from a low of 10 per cent in the 1950s to around 22 per cent by the end of the 1970s, there was no commensurate increase in the growth rate.

Empirical investigation shows that no doubt there is a long-term positive relationship between investment and GDP in India, but the causality is from the latter to the former and not vice versa. The evidence suggests that in India capital accumulation does not cause growth in the long run; rather growth is the cause of capital accumulation, in line with the Young–Currie view.

In the case of government investment and GDP there is no long-run relationship; and the short-run relationship from government investment to growth actually appears to be negative.

The emerging conclusion is that investment may be important; but it is important in a derivative sense and not as a causative factor. Policy makers in India need to pay as much attention to the efficiency (or productivity) of investment as to investment itself. An environment needs to be created whereby those resources that are currently locked up in unproductive uses are allowed to be moved to more productive employments. The markets need to be enlarged and strengthened along with the institutional structures which are required for their efficient functioning. State intervention designed to replace and distort the markets is not likely to yield good results, as the Indian experience suggests.

It is not our intention to suggest that policy makers should de-emphasise investment;[10] rather they should give equal importance to the demand-side view which regards higher saving and investment as a consequence of higher growth and not its primary cause. The policy makers would therefore do well to give up their excessive obsession with a purely capital accumulation (supply-side) approach and adopt a more balanced one which takes account of demand. Because increased demand in the overall sense means increased trade or reciprocal exchange, this requires that countries foster more competitive and internationally open markets.

In this way resources would flow more naturally to where they would yield the greatest social return with lowest prices and cost. The overall size of the market (reciprocal demand) is more rapidly extended if consumers' purchasing power is increased through lower prices and more remunerative employment. These are the fruits of product–market competition, factor–market mobility, low inflation, and flexible prices including realistic exchange rates. As the market grows, so does the opportunity to extend the division of labour in ever more elaborate and productive ways, making innovation and 'factor–productivity growth' endogenous and cumulative. The role of the state would then be to create conditions for the rapid realisation of increasing returns by strengthening and enhancing the market system and its institutions. In this circumstance lies the possibility of economic progress, as Allyn Young would have put it.

NOTES

1. Nicholas Kaldor also developed a critique of equilibrium theory and instead emphasised the role of demand and increasing returns (see, for example, Kaldor, 1972; Toner, 1999). Sandilands (1990, 2000) explains the parallels, but also some important differences, in the

'Youngian' interpretations of Kaldor and Currie. See also the editors' preface in Mehrling and Sandilands (1999), a collection of Young's writings that includes extracts from Kaldor's notes on Young's LSE lectures on growth theory.

2. Increased specialisation necessarily implies increased trade or exchange. Exchange implies a market demand. In the aggregate this is defined by GDP. Thus if capital follows GDP we have that capital follows upon demand in the aggregate, Say–Young conception. (A related issue is how far real Sayian demand is boosted when the government replaces the private marketplace. Note that Say's Law was fully expressed as Say's *Law of Markets*. While Keynes may have shown how Say's Law may be interrupted by cyclical, short-term monetary disturbances, he assuredly did not bury it as a long-term 'law' for a world in which the demand for goods in general is still insatiable, and where government controls do not frustrate the operation of market forces.)

3. Compare Currie (1997) for an empirical investigation of the theory in the context of the United States.

4. A time series is stationary (in the sense of weak stationarity) if its mean, variance and covariances remain constant over time.

5. A correlogram is a graph of autocorrelation of a series at various lag levels. For a stationary time series, the correlogram tapers off quickly; for a non-stationary time series it dies off gradually.

6. Perman (1991) suggests that if the diagnostic statistics (such as normality, autocorrelation etc) from ADF regression are not in order a prima facie case exists for adopting non-parametric adjustments proposed by Phillips and Perron.

7. If a time series has to be differenced once before it becomes stationary, it is integrated to the order one, i.e., $I(1)$. In general, if a time series has to be differenced d times before it becomes stationary, it is integrated to the order d or $I(d)$.

8. Appendices containing data on all the level variables and their rates of growth, together with the graphs, are available from the authors on request.

9. Pro-labour laws are, however, against the long-term interest of labour as they inhibit employers from offering formal employment to labour which cannot be retrenched. Moreover, the labour laws inhibit rapid growth of the industrial sector thereby inhibiting rapid expansion of employment opportunities.

10. Especially of the market-enhancing kind such as on transport and communications. Such public investments were viewed with approval even by Adam Smith.

REFERENCES

Abramovitz, M. (1956), 'Resources and output trends in the United States since 1870', *American Economic Review, Papers and Proceedings*, **46**, May, 5–23.

Aghion, P. and P. Howitt (1998), *Endogenous Growth Theory,* Cambridge, Massachusetts: MIT Press.

Bahmani-Oskooee, M. and J. Alse (1993), 'Export growth and economic growth: an application of cointegration and error-correction modelling', *Journal of Developing Areas,* **27**, July, 535–42.

Bahmani-Oskooee, M., H. Mohtadi and G. Shabsigh (1991), 'Exports, growth and causality in LDCs: a re-examination', *Journal of Development Economics*, **36**, October, 405–15.

Bhagwati, J. (1993), *India in Transition: Freeing the Economy*, Oxford: Clarendon Press.

Blomström, M., R.E. Lipsey and M. Zejan (1996), 'Is fixed investment the key to economic growth?', *Quarterly Journal of Economics*, **111**, February, 269–73.

Chakravarty, S. (1987), *Development Planning: The Indian Experience*, Oxford: Clarendon Press.

Chandra, Ramesh (2000), 'The impact of trade policy on growth in India', Unpublished Ph.D. Thesis, University of Strathclyde, Glasgow.

Currie, L. (1966) *Accelerating Development: The Necessity and the Means*, New York: McGraw-Hill.

Currie, L. (1974), 'The leading sector model of growth in developing countries', *Journal of Economic Studies*, **1**(1), 1–16.

Currie, L. (1981), 'Allyn Young and the development of growth theory', *Journal of Economic Studies*, **8**(1), 52–61.

Currie, L. (1997), 'Implications of an endogenous theory of growth in Allyn Young's macroeconomic concept of increasing returns', *History of Political Economy*, **29**(3), 413–43.

De Long, J.B. and L. Summers (1991), 'Equipment investment and economic growth', *Quarterly Journal of Economics*, CVI, 445–502.

De Long, J.B. and L. Summers (1992), 'Equipment investment and economic growth: how strong is the nexus?', *Brookings Papers on Economic Activity*, **2**, 157–211.

Dickey, D.A. and W.F. Fuller (1979), 'Distribution of the estimators for autoregressive time series with a unit root', *Journal of the American Statistical Association*, **74**, 427–31.

Domar, E.D. (1947) 'Expansion of employment', *American Economic Review*, **31**, March, 34–55.

Doraisami, A. (1996), 'Export growth and economic growth: a re-examination of some time-series evidence of the Malaysian experience', *Journal of Developing Areas*, **30**, January, 223–30.

Engle, R.F. and C.W.J. Granger (1987) 'Cointegration and error correction: representation, estimation and testing', *Econometrica*, **55**, March, 251–76.

Engle, R.F. and B.S. Yoo (1987), 'Forecasting and testing in cointegrated systems', *Journal of Econometrics*, **35**, 143–59.

Goldar, B. and V.S. Renganathan (1991), 'Capacity utilisation in Indian industries', *Indian Economic Journal*, **39**(2), 82–92.

Granger, C.W.J. (1969), 'Investigating causal relations by econometric models and cross-spectral methods', *Econometrica*, **37**, 424–38.

Harrod, R.F. (1939), 'An essay in dynamic theory', *Economic Journal*, **49**, March, 14–33.

Hsiao, M.W. (1987), 'Tests of causality and exogeneity between export growth and economic growth', *Journal of Development Economics*, **18**, 143–59.

Jones, J.D. and D. Joulfaian (1991), 'Federal government expenditures and revenues in the early years of the American Republic: evidence from 1972 and 1860', *Journal of Macroeconomics*, **13**(1), 133–55.

Kaldor, N. (1972), 'The irrelevance of equilibrium economics', *Economic Journal*, **82**, 1237–55.

Krugman, P. (1990) *Rethinking International Trade*, Cambridge, Massachusetts: MIT Press.

Krugman, P. (1993), 'Towards a counter-counterrevolution in development theory', *Annual Conference on Development Economics*, Washington, DC: World Bank, 15–38.

Lewis, W.A. (1954), 'Economic development with unlimited supplies of labour', *Manchester School of Economics and Social Studies*, **XXII**, 139–91.

Lipsey, R. and I. Kravis (1987), *Saving and Economic Growth: Is the United States Really Falling Behind?*, New York: Conference Board.

Love, J. (1994), 'Engines of growth: the exports and government sectors', *World Economy*, **17**, 203–18.

MacKinnon, J.G. (1991), 'Critical values for cointegration tests', in R.F. Engle and C.W.J. Granger (eds), *Long-run Equilibrium Relationships*, Oxford: Oxford University Press.

Mehrling, P.G. and R.J. Sandilands (eds) (1999), *Money and Growth: Selected Papers of Allyn Abbott Young*, London and New York: Routledge.

Murphy, K.M., A. Schleifer and R. Vishny (1989a), 'Income distribution, market size, and industrialization', *Quarterly Journal of Economics*, **104**(August), 537–64.

Murphy, K.M., A. Schleifer and R. Vishny (1989b), 'Industrialization and the big push', *Journal of Political Economy*, **97**(5), 1003–26.

Myrdal, G. (1957), *Economic Theory and Underdeveloped Regions*, London: Gerald Duckworth.

Nurkse, R. (1953), *Problems of Capital Formation in Underdeveloped Countries*, Oxford: Basil Blackwell.

Nurkse, R. (1962), *Patterns of Trade and Development* (Wicksell Lectures, 1959), Oxford: Basil Blackwell.

Paul, S. (1974), 'Industrial performance and government controls', in J.C. Sandesara (ed.), *The Indian Economy: Performance and Prospects*, Bombay: Bombay University Press.

Perman, R. (1991), 'Cointegration: an introduction to the literature', *Journal of Economic Studies*, **18**(3), 3–30.

Pesaran, M.H. and B. Pesaran (1997), *Microfit 4.0*, Oxford: Oxford University Press.

Phillips, P.C. and P. Perron (1988), 'Testing for a unit root in a time series regression', *Biometrica*, **75**(2), 335–46.

Prebisch, R. (1950), *The Economic Development of Latin America and its Principal Problems*, New York: UN Economic Commission for Latin America.

Romer, P. (1987), 'Growth based on increasing returns due to specialization', *American Economic Review*, **77**(2), 56–62.

Romer, P. (1989), 'Capital accumulation in the theory of long-run growth', in R.J. Barro (ed.), *Modern Business Cycle Theory*, Cambridge, Massachusetts: Harvard University Press, pp. 52–127.

Rosenstein-Rodan, P.N. (1943), 'Problems of industrialisation of Eastern and South-Eastern Europe', *Economic Journal*, **53**, 202–11.

Rosenstein-Rodan, P.N. (1961), 'Notes on the theory of the "big push"', in H.S. Ellis and H.C. Wallich (eds), *Economic Development for Latin America*, London: Macmillan, pp. 57–67.

Sandilands, R.J. (1990), *The Life and Political Economy of Lauchlin Currie: New Dealer, Presidential Adviser, and Development Economist*, Durham, North Carolina and London: Duke University Press.

Sandilands, R.J. (2000), 'Perspectives on Allyn Young in theories of endogenous growth', *Journal of the History of Economic Thought*, **22**(3), 309–28.

Shaw, G.K. (1992), 'Policy implications of endogenous growth theory', *Economic Journal*, **102**(May), 611–21.

Sheehey, E.J. (1990), 'Exports and growth: a flawed framework', *Journal of Development Studies*, **27**(1), 111–16.

Sims, C.A. (1972), 'Money, income and causality', *American Economic Review*, **62**(September), 540–52.

Singer, H.W. (1950), 'The distribution of gains between investing and borrowing countries', *American Economic Review*, **40**(May), 473–85.

Solow, R.M. (1957), 'Technical change and the aggregate production function', *Review of Economics and Statistics*, **39**(August), 311–20.

Toner, P. (1999), *Main Currents in Cumulative Causation: The Dynamics of Growth and Development*, London: Macmillan.

Young, A.A. (1928), 'Increasing returns and economic progress', *Economic Journal*, **38**(December), 527–42.

13. When Romer meets Lucas: on human capital, imperfect competition and growth[*]

Alberto Bucci

13.1. INTRODUCTION

Recent theoretical and empirical advancements in economic growth literature suggest that technological progress and human capital accumulation are primary determinants of economic growth. The majority of growth models, however, focus on only one of these engines at a time.[1] Exceptions are represented by Stokey (1988) and Young (1993), Grossman and Helpman (1991, Ch. 5.2), and Eicher (1996), Redding (1996) and Restuccia (1997). Even though all these works take explicitly into account the interaction between endogenous technological change and human capital formation, they still remain limited in many respects. In the first two (Stokey, 1988 and Young, 1993), for example, skill accumulation happens through learning-by-doing and on-the-job training in the production activity, rather than a separate education sector. In Grossman and Helpman (1991, Ch. 5.2), a separate education sector does exist but, strangely enough, it does not require any skilled worker to run. Eicher (1996) develops a rich model in which both human capital and technological innovation are endogenous. However, his paper is solely concerned with steady-state predictions on the relationship between relative supply of skilled labour and relative wage. Restuccia (1997), on the other hand, builds a dynamic general equilibrium model with schooling and technology adoption. But the primary concern of the paper is to study how these two elements may be amplifying the effects of productivity differences on income disparity. Finally, Redding (1996) emphasises the potential interaction between investment in education and investment in research and shows under which conditions such an interaction may give rise to co-ordination problems and underdevelopment traps.

Given all this, it is quite surprising that little attention has been paid until now to the analysis of the economic determinants of the equilibrium shares of human capital devoted to each economic sector employing this factor input within the context of an integrated model of purposive research and development (R&D) activity and human capital accumulation. The aim of this chapter is to fill this gap in the literature.

In order to do this it combines in the simplest possible way the basic Lucas (1988) model of skills accumulation, on the one hand, with the Grossman and Helpman (1991, Ch. 3) and Romer's (1990) models of endogenous technical change, on the other. In more detail, I consider a model economy that is made up of a representative household and firms. For simplicity purposes the representative household consists of only one agent who is involved in four types of activities: consumption goods production, intermediate goods manufacturing, human capital investment and R&D effort. Population is stationary in the economy and consumption goods are produced within a perfectly competitive industry in which prices are taken as given and each input is compensated according to its own marginal product. The intermediate goods sector consists of monopolistic producers of differentiated products entering the production function of the homogeneous final good as an input. The representative household invests portions of its fixed time endowment to acquire formal education. Finally, purposive R&D activity is the source of technological progress in the model. Indeed, technical progress happens through inventing new varieties of horizontally differentiated capital goods within a separate and competitive R&D sector. When a new blueprint is discovered in the R&D sector, an intermediate goods producer acquires the perpetual patent over it. This allows the intermediate firm to manufacture the new variety and practise monopoly pricing forever. In modelling R&D activity we strictly follow Grossman and Helpman (1991, Ch. 3, p. 51), treating technological capital as a private good (we assume that the returns to the creation of new knowledge may be fully appropriated by the inventor). In the original Grossman and Helpman model without knowledge spillovers this specification of the R&D process implies the cessation of growth in the long run. In our model, instead, this does not happen since (unlike Grossman and Helpman, 1991, Ch. 3 and Romer, 1990) in our economy the true engine of growth is represented by human capital accumulation (and not by the R&D externality). In this sense the model we present here shares the same conclusions of many other models with purposive R&D activity and skills accumulation.[2] Another peculiarity of the model is that all the sectors composing this economy employ human capital. This is done because, as already mentioned, it is one of our objectives here to study in detail the economic forces underlying the equilibrium inter-sectoral allocation of such an input.

Our main findings are threefold. First, economic growth depends only on the parameters describing preferences and the skills acquisition technology.

At the same time, and unlike Lucas (1988), the presence of imperfect competition in the intermediate sector has growth effects and influences the allocation of the available human capital stock to the different sectors employing this factor input. Second, as is common in recent endogenous growth theory,[3] our model does not display any *scale effect*, since growth does not depend on the total available human capital stock. Finally, we find that the relationship between the equilibrium growth rate and the share of resources invested in R&D on the one hand, and that between the latter and the mark-up rate on the other, are absolutely non-monotonic.

Our analysis here is related to other works, both in its scope and its methodological approach. Arnold (1998) also develops an endogenous growth model that integrates purposive R&D activity with human capital accumulation. But his work is mainly motivated by the attempt to reject, on theoretical grounds, two main predictions of standard growth models based on R&D (namely that the equilibrium growth rate is very much sensitive to policy changes and to the level of resources used in research). Blackburn et al. (2000) extend Arnold's model (1998) in the direction of a fuller micro-foundation of the R&D process and obtain the same results with no further insights. Then, neither of these two works deal at all with the determinants of the inter-sectoral allocation of skilled workers and with the long-run implications of imperfect competition for economic growth. Indeed, in Blackburn et al. (2000) intermediate firms do not employ human capital directly, since they use forgone consumption to produce. This is the main reason why we consider their framework truly inadequate to answer the questions we would like to tackle in this chapter.

To the best of our knowledge, and within a similar framework, this is the first attempt in this direction. In this respect, we should probably mention a recent work by Jones and Williams (2000) aimed at analysing whether a decentralised economy undertakes too little or too much R&D in the presence of some distortions to the research activity.[4] However, in the above paper there is no human capital accumulation and capital goods and research are produced by employing units of forgone consumption. In addition, in the paper there is no evaluation of the possible long-run links between (im)perfect competition and growth. Finally, another work which comes closer to ours is Bucci (2001). The main difference is that this chapter endogenises the shares of human capital devoted to each economic activity (that are kept exogenous in that approach).

The rest of the chapter is organised as follows. Section 13.2 introduces the basic model and Section 13.3 proposes the equilibrium of it. Section 13.4 examines the steady-state properties of the model and Section 13.5 computes the equilibrium output growth rate. In Section 13.6 we solve for the inter-sectoral allocation of human capital, present some comparative statics results about the main economic determinants of the shares of the reproducible input (skilled work) devoted to each economic activity and briefly discuss the other most important findings of the chapter. Finally, Section 13.7 concludes.

13.2.   THE BASIC MODEL

Consider an economy with three different productive sectors. There exists an undifferentiated consumption good which is produced using skilled labour and capital goods (intermediate inputs). These are available, at time t, in n_t different varieties. In order to produce such inputs intermediate firms employ only human capital. Technical progress takes place as a continuous expansion, through purposive R&D activity, of the set of available horizontally differentiated intermediates. R&D is skill-intensive as well. Unlike the traditional *R&D-based growth models*, I assume that the supply of human capital may grow over time. In this connection, following the pathbreaking papers by Uzawa (1965) and Lucas (1988), I postulate the existence of a representative household that chooses plans for consumption (c), asset holdings (a, to be defined later) and human capital (h). For the sake of simplicity, I also assume that the representative household of this economy has unit measure. In the model there is no physical capital and unskilled labour. Human capital is a homogeneous input and can be employed to produce the final output, intermediates, new human capital and to invent new varieties of capital goods (research).

13.2.1   The Consumption Good Sector

The homogeneous, undifferentiated consumption good is produced within a *competitive industry*. Such an industry is populated by a large number of identical firms and employs the following constant returns to scale aggregate production function:

$$Y_t = AH_{Yt}^{1-\alpha} \int_0^{n_t} x_{jt}^\alpha dj, \quad A > 0, \quad \alpha \in (0,1), \tag{13.1}$$

where A is total factor productivity and α is a technological parameter. Therefore, output at time $t(Y_t)$ is obtained combining skilled work (H_Y) and n different varieties of intermediate inputs, each of which is employed in the quantity x_j. Since the industry is competitive, in equilibrium each variety of intermediates receives its own marginal product (in terms of the *numeraire*, the only final good):

$$p_{jt} = A\alpha H_{Yt}^{1-\alpha} x_{jt}^{\alpha-1}, \quad \forall j \in (0, n_t). \tag{13.2}$$

In equation (13.2) p_{jt} is the inverse demand function faced at time t by the generic j-th intermediate producer. From the same equation the direct demand function for the j-th type of intermediates reads as:

$$x_{jt} = \left(\frac{A\alpha H_{Yt}^{1-\alpha}}{p_{jt}} \right)^{\frac{1}{1-\alpha}}, \quad \forall j \in (0, n_t). \tag{13.3}$$

As is common in the *innovation-based* growth literature, the elasticity of substitution between two generic intermediates coincides with the price-demand elasticity faced by each capital goods producer and is equal to $1/(1-\alpha)$.

13.2.2 The Intermediate Goods Sector

The capital goods industry is *monopolistically competitive* and each intermediate input is produced using the same technology:

$$x_{jt} = Bh_{jt}, \quad \forall j \in (0, n_t), \quad B > 0. \tag{13.4}$$

This production function is characterised by constant returns to scale in the only input employed (human capital) and, accordingly, one unit of skills is able to produce (at each time) the same constant quantity of whatever variety. The parameter B measures the productivity of human capital employed in this sector. Following Romer (1990) and Grossman and Helpman (1991, Ch. 3), I continue to assume that each intermediate good embodies a design created in the R&D sector and that there exists a patent law which prohibits any firm from manufacturing an intermediate good without the consent of the patent holder of the design. The generic j-th firm maximises (with respect to x_{jt}) its own instantaneous profit under the demand constraint (given by equation (13.2)). From the first order conditions, the following can be immediately obtained:

$$w_{jt} = AB\alpha^2 H_{Yt}^{1-\alpha} x_{jt}^{\alpha-1}, \tag{13.5}$$

where w_{jt} is the wage rate paid (at time t) to one unit of human capital employed in this sector.

In a symmetric equilibrium (where $x_{jt} = x_t$, $\forall j \in (0, n_t)$), each local monopolist faces the same wage rate ($w_{jt} = w_t$, $\forall j \in (0, n_t)$). The hypothesis of symmetry is dictated by the way in which each variety of intermediates enters the final output technology and by the fact that all the capital goods producers use the same production function (equation (13.4)). Plugging (13.3) into (13.5) yields:

$$p_{jt} = \frac{1}{\alpha} \frac{w_{jt}}{B} = \frac{1}{\alpha} \frac{w_t}{B} = p_t, \quad \forall j \in (0, n_t). \tag{13.6}$$

Hence, when all the capital goods firms are identical, they produce the same quantity, face the same wage rate accruing to intermediate skilled workers and fix the same price for their own output. The price is equal to a constant *mark-up* $1/\alpha$ over the marginal cost w_t/B.

I define by $H_{jt} \equiv \int_0^{n_t} h_{jt} dj$ the total amount of human capital employed in the intermediate sector at time t obtaining from equation (13.4) and under the hypothesis of symmetry among capital goods producers:

$$x_{jt} = \frac{BH_{jt}}{n_t} = x_t, \quad \forall j \in (0, n_t). \tag{13.7}$$

Finally, the profit function of a generic *j-th* intermediate firm is given by:

$$\pi_{jt} = \left(p_t - \frac{1}{B} w_t \right) x_t = A\alpha (1 - \alpha) H_{Yt}^{1-\alpha} \left(\frac{B \cdot H_{jt}}{n_t} \right)^{\alpha} = \pi_t, \quad \forall j \in (0, n_t) \tag{13.8}$$

Equation (13.8) says that, just like x and p, so too is the instantaneous profit equal for each variety of intermediates in a symmetric equilibrium.

13.2.3 The Research Sector

Producing the generic *j-th* variety of capital goods entails the purchase of a specific blueprint (the *j-th* one) from the competitive research sector, characterised by the following aggregate technology:

$$\dot{n}_t = CH_{nt}, \quad C > 0, \tag{13.9}$$

where n_t denotes the number of capital goods varieties existing at time t, H_n is the total amount of human capital employed in the sector and C is the productivity of the skilled research workers. The production function of new ideas coincides with that employed by Grossman and Helpman (1991) in their Chapter 3 model without knowledge spillovers (pp. 43–57). It implies that in the present framework, knowledge is a completely *private good* (the returns to the discovery of a new blueprint are fully appropriated by the inventor[5]) and *non-cumulative* (in order to invent new varieties of intermediate inputs only skilled labour is employed and not the available stock of disembodied technological capital approximated by the existing number of designs). From a theoretical point of view, in the present context, the use of such an R&D technology specification is harmless and perfectly compatible with a positive and constant growth rate of output in the long-run equilibrium. Indeed, in our model economy not only technological capital but also human capital (the true engine of growth) may be accumulated over time. Consequently, unlike Romer (1990), where the only lever to economic development is represented by R&D activity, we do not need to introduce any kind of pecuniary externality in the research sector in order for growth to be sustainable in the long run. At the same time we think that concentrating our attention in the main text on the simple R&D technology of equation (13.9) helps to avoid potential complications concerning the nature of knowledge spillovers, the way the latter are to be most appropriately modelled and the problem of technology diffusion.[6]

As the research sector is competitive, new firms will enter it until all profit opportunities are completely exhausted. The zero profit condition amounts, in this case, to setting:

$$\frac{1}{C} w_{nt} = V_{nt} \tag{13.10}$$

$$V_{nt} = \int_{t}^{\infty} \exp\left[-\int_{t}^{\tau} r(s)\,ds\right] \pi_{jt}\,d\tau, \qquad \tau > t. \tag{13.11}$$

Symbols used in (13.10) and (13.11) have the following meaning: w_n is the wage rate accruing to one unit of human capital devoted to research; r is the instantaneous real rate of return on the consumers' asset holdings; π_j is the profit accruing to the *j-th* intermediate producer (once the *j-th* infinitely lived patent has been acquired) and V_n is the market value of one unit of research output (the generic *j-th* idea allowing to produce the *j-th* variety of capital goods). Notice that V_n is equal to the discounted present value of the profit flow a local monopolist can potentially earn from t to infinity. Since there is a one-to-one relationship between the number of patents and the number of capital goods producers, it coincides with the market value of the *j-th* intermediate firm.

13.2.4 Consumers

We consider a closed economy in which there exists only one representative infinitely lived household that holds assets in the form of ownership claims on firms and chooses plans for consumption (c), asset holdings (a) and human capital (h). For the sake of simplicity, I assume that the only household populating this economy has unit measure and there is no population growth. This hypothesis implies that, at each t, the household's own stock of human capital h equals the economy aggregate stock of human capital H. Following Lucas (1988), I also assume that the household is endowed with one unit of time and optimally allocates a fraction u of its time endowment to productive activities (research, capital goods and consumption goods production) and the remaining fraction $(1-u)$ to non-productive activities (education). As will be clearer below, given the household's choice of the optimal u (that we denote by u^*), the labour market clearing conditions will determine the decentralised allocation of the productive human capital between manufacturing of intermediate and consumption goods and invention of new ideas (research).

With an instantaneous utility function $u(c_t) = \log(c_t)$, the decisional problem of the household can be written as:

$$\underset{\{c_t,u_t,a_t,h_t\}_{t=0}^{\infty}}{Max} \; U_0 \equiv \int_0^{\infty} e^{-\rho t} \log(c_t)dt, \quad \rho > 0 \qquad (13.12)$$

$$\text{s.t.:} \quad \dot{a}_t = r_t a_t + w_t u_t h_t - c_t \qquad (13.13)$$

$$\dot{h}_t = \delta(1-u_t)h_t, \quad \delta > 0 \quad a_0, \, h_0 \; \text{given.} \qquad (13.14)$$

The control variables of this problem are c_t and u_t, whereas a_t and h_t are the state variables. Equation (13.12) is the intertemporal utility function; equation (13.13) is the budget constraint and equation (13.14) represents the human capital supply function.[7] The symbols used have the following meaning: ρ is the subjective discount rate; c denotes consumption of the homogeneous final good; w is the wage rate accruing to one unit of skilled labour[8] and δ is a parameter reflecting the productivity of the education technology.

With λ_{1t} and λ_{2t} denoting, respectively, the shadow price of the household's asset holdings and human capital stock, the first order conditions are:

$$\frac{e^{-\rho t}}{c_t} = \lambda_{1t}; \qquad (13.15)$$

$$\lambda_{1t} = \lambda_{2t} \frac{\delta}{w_t}; \tag{13.16}$$

$$\lambda_{1t} r_t = -\dot{\lambda}_{1t}; \tag{13.17}$$

$$\lambda_{1t} w_t u_t + \lambda_{2t} \delta (1 - u_t) = -\dot{\lambda}_{2t}. \tag{13.18}$$

Conditions (13.15) through (13.18) must satisfy the constraints (13.13) and (13.14), together with the transversality conditions:

$$\lim_{t \to \infty} \lambda_{1t} a_t = 0; \qquad \lim_{t \to \infty} \lambda_{2t} h_t = 0.$$

13.3. GENERAL EQUILIBRIUM

In order to find out the equilibrium of the model under the symmetry hypothesis $(x_{jt} = B \cdot H_{jt} / n_t = x_t, \ \forall j \in (0, n_t))$ first note that, for given $u*$ (the optimal fraction of skills devoted by consumers to production activities), the optimal allocation of human capital among research, capital and consumption goods production is found by solving simultaneously the following labour market clearing conditions:

$$H_Y + H_j + H_n = u * H, \qquad \forall t \tag{13.19}$$

$$w_j = w_n, \ w_j = w_Y. \tag{13.20}$$

(For notational simplicity I have dropped the index t near the variables depending on time.)

Since human capital is perfectly homogeneous in the model, I impose that: (1) it is paid the same wage rate across all the productive sectors where this input is employed (equation (13.20)); (2) the sum of the human capital stocks allocated to each market is equal to the total stock of productive human capital available at each time (equation (13.19)).

Second, as the total value of the household's assets must equal the total value of firms, the following condition must be checked in a symmetric equilibrium:

$$a = n V_n. \tag{13.21}$$

V_n is defined by (13.11) and satisfies the following asset-pricing equation:

$$\dot{V}_n = rV_n - \pi_j, \tag{13.21a}$$

where:

$$\pi_j = \frac{\alpha H_Y w_Y}{n} \tag{13.21b}$$

and:

$$w_Y = \frac{A(1-\alpha)n}{H_Y^\alpha}\left(\frac{BH_j}{n}\right)^\alpha. \tag{13.21c}$$

Recall that one new idea allows a new intermediate firm to produce one new variety of capital goods. In other words, there exists a one-to-one relationship between the number of ideas, number of capital goods producers and number of intermediate input varieties. This explains why, in equation (13.21), the total value of the household's assets a is equal to the number of profit-making intermediate firms (n) times the market value V_n of each of them (equal to the market value of the corresponding idea). Finally, equation (13.21a) simply suggests that the interest on the value of the j-th generic intermediate firm (rV_n) should be equal, in equilibrium, to the sum of two terms:

- the instantaneous monopoly profit π_j coming from the production of the j-th capital good;
- the capital gain or loss matured on V_n during the time interval $dt\left(\dot{V}_n\right)$.

We can now move to the steady-state equilibrium.

13.4.   STEADY STATE

In this section I characterise the steady-state (or balanced growth-path) equilibrium of the model. A balanced growth-path equilibrium is defined as follows:

Definition: *A balanced growth-path (or steady-state) equilibrium is an equilibrium where each variable depending on time grows at a constant rate over time, human (H) and knowledge (n) capitals are complement, and* H_y, H_j, H_n *grow at the same rate as* H.[9]

With this definition of balanced growth path, when the growth rate of H, g_H, is constant, u is constant as well (see equation (13.14)).[10] This means that, along a balanced growth path, the household will optimally decide to devote a constant fraction of its fixed time endowment to working $u*$ and education $(1-u*)$ activities.

Solving explicitly the consumers' problem, it is possible to show that the following results hold in the long-run equilibrium (see the Appendix for details):

$$r = \delta(2 - \alpha) - \rho(1 - \alpha) \tag{13.22}$$

$$g_{H_Y} = g_{H_j} = g_{H_n} = g_n = g_H = \delta - \rho \tag{13.23}$$

$$g_c = g_a = (2 - \alpha)(\delta - \rho) \tag{13.24}$$

$$\frac{H_j}{n} = \frac{\alpha\delta}{C(1 - \alpha)}, \quad \frac{H_Y}{n} = \frac{\delta}{\alpha C} \tag{13.25}$$

$$u* = \frac{\rho}{\delta}. \tag{13.26}$$

According to result (13.22), the real interest rate r is constant. Equation (13.23) states that along a balanced growth path, the number of new ideas n, the household's total human capital stock H and the human capital stocks devoted respectively to consumption goods production H_Y, to the intermediate sector H_j and to research H_n all grow at the same constant rate, given by the difference between the human capital accumulation technology productivity parameter δ and the subjective discount rate ρ. Equation (13.24) gives the equilibrium growth rate of consumption and household's asset holdings. Equation (13.25) instead gives, respectively, the equilibrium values of the constant H_j/n and H_Y/n ratios, whereas equation (13.27) represents the optimal constant fraction of the household's time endowment that it will decide to allocate to working activities $(u*)$. For the growth rate of the variables in equations (13.23) and (13.24) to be positive and bounded, δ should be strictly greater than ρ and bounded. The condition $\delta > \rho$ also assures that $0 < u* < 1$. The two transversality conditions are trivially checked.

13.5. ENDOGENOUS GROWTH

To compute the output growth rate of this economy in a symmetric, balanced growth equilibrium, I first rewrite equation (13.1) as follows:

$$Y_t = AH_{Y_t}^{1-\alpha} n_t \left(\frac{BH_{jt}}{n_t}\right)^{\alpha} = \Psi H_{Y_t}^{1-\alpha} n_t, \quad \Psi \equiv A\left(\frac{BH_{jt}}{n_t}\right)^{\alpha}.$$

Then, taking logs of both sides of this expression, totally differentiating with respect to time and recalling that in the steady-state equilibrium $g_{H_Y} = g_n = g_H = \delta - \rho$ (see equation (13.23) above), I obtain:

$$\frac{\dot{Y}_t}{Y_t} \equiv g_Y = g_c = g_a = (2-\alpha)(\delta-\rho) = (2-\alpha)g_H.$$

Hence, economic growth depends only on the technological parameter α (the inverse of which can be easily interpreted as a measure of the monopoly power enjoyed by each intermediate local monopolist) and the accumulation rate of human capital (g_H). In this last respect the model supports the main conclusion of that branch of the endogenous growth literature pioneered by Uzawa (1965) and Lucas (1988).[11] As a consequence, our analysis does not display any scale effect, since g_Y depends neither on the absolute dimension of the economy (its total human capital stock), nor on the population growth rate (that, indeed, is equal to zero in our model).[12]

Since I am particularly interested in analysing those factors potentially able to influence the *inter-sectoral competition* for the acquisition of human capital in the present context, we have first to determine an expression for the equilibrium human to technological capital ratio ($R \equiv H/n$). To this end, I use equation (13.19), with $u^* = \rho/\delta$, $H_j/n = \alpha\delta/(1-\alpha)C$ and $H_Y/n = \delta/\alpha C$, and obtain:

$$\frac{H_n}{n} = R\frac{\rho}{\delta} - \frac{\delta}{\alpha C} - \frac{\alpha\delta}{(1-\alpha)C} \implies g_n = C\frac{H_n}{n} = C\frac{\rho}{\delta}R - \frac{\delta}{\alpha} - \frac{\alpha\delta}{(1-\alpha)}.$$

Equating the last expression above to equation (13.23) yields:

$$R \equiv \frac{H_t}{n_t} = \frac{\delta[\delta - \alpha\rho(1-\alpha)]}{\alpha\rho(1-\alpha)C}.$$

In the next section, I compute the equilibrium shares of human capital devoted to research (s_n), capital goods production (s_j), final good manufacturing (s_Y) and human capital accumulation (s_H).

13.6. HUMAN CAPITAL, R&D AND GROWTH

Given R, computed in the last section, the shares of human capital devoted to each sector in the decentralised long-run equilibrium are easily determined:

$$s_j \equiv \frac{H_j}{H} = \frac{H_j}{n} \frac{n}{H} = \frac{H_j}{nR} = \frac{\alpha^2 \rho}{\delta - \alpha\rho(1-\alpha)} \qquad (13.27)$$

$$s_Y \equiv \frac{H_Y}{H} = \frac{H_Y}{n} \frac{n}{H} = \frac{H_Y}{nR} = \frac{\rho(1-\alpha)}{\delta - \alpha\rho(1-\alpha)}$$

$$s_n \equiv \frac{H_n}{H} = \frac{H_n}{n} \frac{n}{H} = \frac{H_n}{nR} = \frac{\alpha\rho(\delta - \rho)(1-\alpha)}{\delta[\delta - \alpha\rho(1-\alpha)]}$$

$$s_H \equiv \frac{H_H}{H} = 1 - u^* = \frac{\delta - \rho}{\delta}.$$

13.6.1. Some Comparative Statics Results

From equation (13.27) the following comparative statics results may be stated (throughout this analysis I'll continue to assume $g_H > 0$, which implies $\delta > \rho > 0$):

$$\frac{\partial s_j}{\partial \alpha} > 0, \quad \frac{\partial s_j}{\partial \delta} < 0, \quad \frac{\partial s_j}{\partial \rho} > 0. \qquad (13.28)$$

Equation (13.28) states that the equilibrium share of human capital devoted to the capital goods sector depends negatively on the human capital accumulation productivity parameter δ and positively on α and the subjective discount rate ρ. I am particularly interested in studying the impact that the monopoly position enjoyed by each local intermediate producer may have on the main variables of the model in the long-run equilibrium. For this purpose, recall that $1/\alpha$ represents the constant mark-up rate charged over the marginal cost by the intermediate producers. Indeed, the higher the level of α, the higher the elasticity of substitution between two generic intermediate inputs (equal to $1/(1 - \alpha)$). This means that they become increasingly similar when α grows and, accordingly, the price elasticity of the derived demand curve faced by a local monopolist (equal, again, to $1/(1 - \alpha)$) tends to be infinitely large when α tends to 1. In a word, the toughness of competition in the intermediate sector is strictly (and positively) dependent on the level of α.

Conversely, the inverse of α can be viewed as a proxy for how uncompetitive the sector is.

Intuitively, what the first part of equation (13.28) tells us is that when α increases, the degree of competition within the capital goods market increases and thus the aggregate intermediate output and the human capital demand coming from this sector increase as well (s_j goes up). Therefore, a re-allocation of the available human capital among all the sectors employing this input indeed occurs.[13]

As for the equilibrium share of human capital devoted to the consumption good sector, we conclude that:

$$\frac{\partial s_Y}{\partial \alpha} < 0, \quad \frac{\partial s_Y}{\partial \delta} < 0, \quad \frac{\partial s_Y}{\partial \rho} > 0.$$

Hence, unlike what happens for s_j, now an increase in the mark-up rate increases the decentralised equilibrium share of human capital devoted to the production of the final good. Again, the economic intuition behind this result is quite simple: an increase in the mark-up rate (hence in the price) of all the intermediate inputs, *ceteris paribus*, makes it more profitable for the final good producers to substitute human capital for capital goods. As a consequence, the demand for this factor input H_Y increases and, for given total human capital stock, s_Y increases as well. The effects of ρ and δ on s_Y are exactly the same as those found on s_j.

Coming now to the comparative statics results for the equilibrium share of human capital devoted to R&D activity s_n, it is possible to show that:

$$\frac{\partial s_n}{\partial \alpha} > 0, \text{ when } 0 < \alpha < 1/2 \quad \text{and} \quad \frac{\partial s_n}{\partial \alpha} < 0, \text{ when } 1/2 < \alpha < 1.$$

This means that the impact that the intermediate sector monopoly power exerts upon s_n is not unambiguous and crucially depends on the absolute size of the monopoly power itself. The relationship between market power and the share of human capital to the R&D sector is illustrated in Figure 13.1.[14]

As is evident from the figure, there exists a critical level of the monopoly power enjoyed by capital goods producers that maximises s_n. Therefore, unlike Jones and Williams (2000),[15] our analysis underlines the fact that in the presence of human capital accumulation and when all the sectors employ skilled workers it is no longer obvious that in the decentralised equilibrium the R&D share is always increasing in the mark-up rate.[16] This striking result can be explained as follows: when the level of competition in the capital goods sector is high, a higher mark-up increases, *ceteris paribus*, the flow of profits accruing to intermediate producers, which in turn increases the market

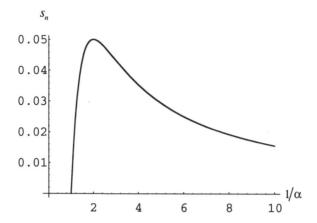

Figure 13.1 *The relationship between the level of competition in the*
intermediate sector $(1/\alpha)$ *and the equilibrium share of human*
capital devoted to research (s_n).

value of one unit of research output, raising R&D investment. On the
contrary, when the level of competition among intermediate firms is low, a
further increase in the mark-up rate leads final output producers to use more
and more human capital. This *substitution effect* of capital goods with skilled
workers in the downstream sector is so strong as to induce a shift of
resources away from the research and intermediate sectors.[17]

Concerning the effect that δ and ρ have on s_n, again it is possible to see
that it is not unambiguous and crucially depends on the absolute value of the
human capital accumulation productivity parameter δ:

$$\frac{\partial s_n}{\partial \delta} > 0 \text{ and } \frac{\partial s_n}{\partial \rho} < 0 \text{ when } \rho < \delta < \rho\left(1 + \sqrt{1 - \alpha(1-\alpha)}\right)$$

$$\frac{\partial s_n}{\partial \delta} < 0 \text{ and } \frac{\partial s_n}{\partial \rho} > 0 \text{ when } \delta > \rho\left(1 + \sqrt{1 - \alpha(1-\alpha)}\right).$$

Finally, the comparative statics results for s_H and R are as follows:

$$\frac{\partial s_H}{\partial \alpha} = 0; \ \frac{\partial s_H}{\partial \delta} > 0; \ \frac{\partial s_H}{\partial \rho} < 0$$

$$\frac{\partial R}{\partial \alpha} > 0 \text{ when } 1/2 < \alpha < 1 \quad \text{and} \quad \frac{\partial R}{\partial \alpha} < 0 \text{ when } 0 < \alpha < 1/2$$

$$\frac{\partial R}{\partial \rho} < 0; \quad \frac{\partial R}{\partial \delta} > 0; \quad \frac{\partial R}{\partial C} < 0.$$

Table 13.1 summarises all the comparative statics results.[18]

Table 13.1   Summary of comparative statics results

	δ	ρ	α	g_Y	g_H	$R \equiv \dfrac{H}{n}$	s_n	s_j	s_Y	s_H
$\rho < \delta < \rho\left(1+\sqrt{1-\alpha(1-\alpha)}\right)$	↑			+	+	+	+	−	−	+
$\delta > \rho\left(1+\sqrt{1-\alpha(1-\alpha)}\right)$	↑			+	+	+	−	−	−	+
$\rho < \delta < \rho\left(1+\sqrt{1-\alpha(1-\alpha)}\right)$		↑		−	−	−	−	+	+	−
$\delta > \rho\left(1+\sqrt{1-\alpha(1-\alpha)}\right)$		↑		−	−	−	+	+	+	−
$0 < \alpha < 1/2$			↑	−	0	−	+	+	−	0
$1/2 < \alpha < 1$			↑	−	0	+	−	+	−	0

13.6.2.   Discussion

First it is worth noting that g_Y, g_H, s_n, s_j, s_Y and s_H do not depend on the productivity with which human capital is employed in the intermediate and research sectors. These variables are also independent of the total factor productivity A. Instead, the ratio of human to technological capital R depends on the parameter C (the higher the research human capital productivity, the higher the amount of resources invested in this sector, the higher the number of available capital goods, and the lower the ratio R).

Looking at Table 13.1 (first row), one can also see that when $\rho < \delta < \rho\left(1+\sqrt{1-\alpha(1-\alpha)}\right)$, then g_Y, g_H, R, s_n and s_H are positively correlated to each other. By contrast, s_n and s_H turn out to be negatively correlated with s_j and s_Y, meaning that within the above mentioned interval when the productivity of human capital in the education sector increases, then the economy allocates more resources to education and research and less resources to intemediates and final output production. This, in turn, has the effect of boosting economic growth (which depends on human capital accumulation) and making human capital relatively abundant with respect to technological capital (R increases).[19] On the other hand, when δ is sufficiently high $\left(\delta > \rho(1+\sqrt{1-\alpha(1-\alpha)})\right)$, s_n, s_j and s_Y are positively correlated with each other and negatively correlated with g_Y, g_H, s_H and R.

Hence, the inference is that when human capital is particularly productive in the education sector, further increases in δ push the investment in education up and reduce the investment (in terms of human capital) in the other three sectors competing for the same input. All this implies a generalised increase in both the steady-state growth rate of the economy and the ratio R. The effect that an increase in ρ has on the main variables of the model is perfectly consistent with what we have just stated.[20]

Overall, the result is that, contrary to Jones and Williams (2000) – where the steady-state share of R&D is monotonically increasing in the steady-state output growth rate – the relationship between s_n and g_Y is non-monotonic in a context where human capital is allowed to grow over time through optimising behaviour of rational agents and human and technological capital are complements. The result stated by Jones and Williams remains true either when the productivity parameter of human capital accumulation is sufficiently low or when the level of competition in the intermediate sector is sufficiently high.

Finally, as for the impact of α (the *proxy* for the monopoly power in the model) on the other variables, we notice in general that an increase in α increases s_j and reduces s_Y without any ambiguity. At the same time, this parameter plays no role either on g_H or s_H. Indeed, as in the recent paper by Blackburn et al. (2000), the market power enjoyed in the monopolistic sector does not play any role in the consumers' decision about how much time to invest in education and training (such a decision being solely driven by the parameters describing preferences and human capital technology and entirely independent of R&D activity). However, variations in α do influence the allocation of human capital between the capital goods, final output and research sectors ($1/\alpha$ is positively correlated with s_Y; negatively correlated with s_j and its relationship with s_n is ambiguous *a priori*, as already explained). More importantly, and unlike the work by Blackburn et al. (2000), the present analysis shows that introducing in the simplest possible way, a model of endogenous technological change within a basic Lucas (1988) model allows us to predict an unambiguously positive relationship between imperfect competition ($1/\alpha$) and growth (g_Y).[21] The intuition behind this result is quite simple. Looking at the production function of the homogeneous final good, one realises that in the steady-state equilibrium (with x constant), an increase in the level of output may be caused either by the growth of H_Y, or the growth of n, or the growth of both. Since the growth of n is itself (for the complementarity hypothesis between human and technological capital) induced by the growth of H (independent of the mark-up rate), the only way for market power to influence output growth is through varying the level of H_Y. In turn, H_Y can be decomposed into two parts:

$$H_Y \equiv s_Y H, \quad s_Y = \frac{H_y}{H}.$$

While the impact of a variation in $1/\alpha$ on human capital accumulation is null, an increase in the market power variable exerts an unambiguously positive effect on s_y. In other words, it is through allocating a higher share of human capital towards the final output sector that monopoly power positively affects growth in the model.

In principle this result may seem counterintuitive since previous papers (notably Aghion et al., 1997a, 1997b, and Aghion and Howitt, 1996, 1998b) clearly maintain that product market competition is unambiguously good for growth. Still, these works consider frameworks where the engine of growth is represented by the continuous improvement in the quality level of already existing goods. In comparison with these approaches what this chapter shows is that results concerning the long-run relationship between competition and growth might well change within a horizontal differentiation model of endogenous growth in which the true engine of growth is human capital accumulation and the choice of utility-maximising agents to invest in formal education complements that of profit-seeking firms to invent new varieties of intermediate goods.

13.7.   CONCLUDING REMARKS

In this chapter I have analysed the steady-state predictions of an endogenous growth model with both purposive R&D activity and human capital accumulation. In the economy, human and technological capital are complements to each other and skilled workers enter as an input in all economic activities. One aim of this chapter was indeed to analyse the economic forces underlying the inter-sectoral allocation of human capital.

The results of the model can be summarised as follows. First of all, the steady-state output growth rate depends solely on the parameters describing preferences and the human capital accumulation technology and is completely independent of R&D activity. As a consequence, the model does not display any scale effect. Many other endogenous growth models nowadays share this property. Second, the share of human capital devoted to research is not monotonically increasing either in the steady-state growth rate or the market power enjoyed by intermediate producers. Indeed, the result found by Jones and Williams (2000) – according to which the share of resources invested in R&D increases without any ambiguity with the aggregate output growth rate – remains true in the present context when both the productivity parameter of human capital accumulation and the level of product market power in the intermediate sector are not sufficiently high. Finally, as for the impact of monopoly power on the other main variables of the model, the presence of imperfect competition among the capital goods producers is found to have positive growth effects and may dramatically influence the allocation of the reproducible factor input (human capital) to the economic sectors employing it. We think this is as important as an alternative result in comparison with other papers that, unlike the approach taken here, consider technological progress as basically stemming from a continuous vertical differentiation process.

For future research, a thorough empirical test on the economic determinants of the long-run allocation of human capital among alternative uses (with particular emphasis on R&D activity) undoubtedly deserves further attention.

APPENDIX

In this Appendix, I derive the set of results (13.22) through (13.26). From now on I will omit the index t near the time-dependent variables.

As already mentioned, from equation (13.14) when g_h is constant, u_t proves constant as well. This means that in equilibrium the household devotes a constant fraction of its own time endowment to working (u) and to education ($1 - u$) activities. Consequently, the optimal u (u^*) will be constant and endogenously determined through the solution to the household decisional problem. From equations (13.16), (13.17), and (13.18) we get:

$$\frac{\dot{\lambda}_2}{\lambda_2} = -\delta, \ \frac{\dot{\lambda}_1}{\lambda_1} = -r.$$

In a symmetric, steady-state equilibrium H_Y, H_j, H_n and n all grow at the same constant rate as H (denoted by g_H). This definition of steady state implies that x (the output produced in the symmetric equilibrium by each local monopolist) is constant over time and (from equations (13.5) and (13.21c)) the wage rate accruing to one unit of skilled labour (w_i) grows at a rate equal to $(1 - \alpha)g_H$. Then, using equation (13.16), we get:

$$\frac{\dot{\lambda}_1}{\lambda_1} = \frac{\dot{\lambda}_2}{\lambda_2} - (1 - \alpha)g_H,$$

that implies:

$$r = \delta + (1 - \alpha)g_H. \tag{13.29}$$

This means that in a steady state equilibrium, the real interest rate r is constant. From equation (13.8) it follows that the profit rate accruing to capital goods producers also grows at the rate $(1 - \alpha)g_H$. In turn, after simple manipulations, this allows us to obtain from equation (13.11):

$$V_n = A\alpha(1-\alpha)\left(\frac{BH_j}{n}\right)^\alpha \frac{H_Y^{1-\alpha}}{\delta}. \tag{13.30}$$

According to the equation above, the market value (the discounted flow of future profits) of a generic *j-th* intermediate firm (equal to the market value of the corresponding *j-th* idea) grows in the long-run equilibrium at the rate $(1 - \alpha)g_H$. Using equations (13.10) and (13.30), it is possible to conclude that:

$$w_n = AC\alpha(1-\alpha)\left(\frac{BH_j}{n}\right)^\alpha \frac{H_Y^{1-\alpha}}{\delta}. \tag{13.31}$$

Employing equations (13.5), (13.20), (13.21c), and (13.31), we get equation (13.25). Combining equations (13.15) and (13.17) we obtain the optimal household's consumption path:

$$\frac{\dot{c}}{c} \equiv g_c = r - \rho = \delta - \rho + (1-\alpha)g_H.$$

From equation (13.13) we get:

$$\frac{c}{a} = r + wu\frac{h}{a} - g_a.$$

Since in the steady-state equilibrium r, u and g_a are constant, the c/a ratio is constant if and only if wh/a is constant, which is certainly the case since h grows at the rate g_H, w grows at the rate $(1 - \alpha)g_H$ and $g_a = (2 - \alpha)g_H$. The last result is obtained recalling that $a = nV_n$ (from equation (13.21)), $g_n = g_H$ (for the complementarity hypothesis between human and knowledge capital) and $g_V = (1 - \alpha)g_H$ (see equation (13.30)). Hence consumption c and asset holdings a grow at the same constant rate along a balanced growth path. This implies that:

$$r - \rho = \delta - \rho + (1-\alpha)g_H = g_c = g_a = (2-\alpha)g_H,$$

from which equations (13.22), (13.23) and (13.24) are obtained. Finally, plugging equation (13.23) into (13.14) equation (13.26) is found.

NOTES

* I 'would like to thank, without implicating, B. Amable, R. Balducci, C. Benassi, R. Boucekkine, G. Candela, D. Checchi, D. de la Croix, J. Ruiz, M. Salvati, A. Scorcu and H. Sneessens for invaluable comments on an earlier draft of this chapter. I also thank the participants at the Economic Theory Seminar of the Catholic University of Louvain (Louvain-la-Neuve, Belgium) and the seminar held at the University of Milan for very useful suggestions. Special thanks are due to the editor (N. Salvadori) and an anonymous referee who have considerably contributed to improve this version of the chapter. Usual disclaimers apply.

1. 'AK-based growth models' (e.g. Lucas, 1988; Jones and Manuelli, 1990 and Rebelo, 1991) imply that sustainable growth is the outcome of reproducible inputs (such as physical and human capital), whereas 'Research and development (R&D)-based models' (e.g. Romer, 1990; Segerstrom et al. (1990); Grossman and Helpman, 1991; Aghion and Howitt, 1992; Jones, 1995a and Young, 1998) all maintain that technological progress, rather than any accumulable input, is the main engine of growth.

2. Notably Arnold (1998) and Blackburn et al. (2000).

3. See Eicher and Turnovsky (1999) for a detailed discussion on *non-scale models of economic growth*.

4. These distortions are represented respectively by the *surplus appropriability problem*, the presence of *knowledge spillovers* and the *creative destruction* and *congestion externalities*.

5. This could happen, for example, thanks to the existence of a perfect patent protection system (based on infinitely lived patents) that allows the successful innovator to accrue the whole gains from his/her R&D efforts and prevents someone from imitating (or even from innovating around the original innovation). See Bucci and Saglam (2000) for a model of endogenous growth where patent lifetime is not infinite.

6. The empirical literature on knowledge spillovers is almost unbounded and particularly controversial. Griliches (1992), for example, supports the idea that they are quite important in the R&D process. On the other hand, the surveys by Keely and Quah (1998) and Keely (2001) cast many doubts on the strength of R&D spillovers in real life (both at the micro and macro level). At the micro level Keely and Quah (1998) conclude that '...*knowledge spillovers do occur. However, the physical clustering of innovation suggests that spillovers do not happen automatically or completely*' (p. 24). At the macro level, instead, they note that '...*spillovers across regions do occur. At the same time, however, these spillovers are generally incomplete*' (p. 25). According to Keely (2001): '...*Although in principle a patent's information spills over to other firms, there is a large empirical literature that suggests such spillovers are in practice neither so immediate nor widespread*' (p. 5). On the basis of such empirical results it is a fair conclusion that our hypothesis on the R&D capital aggregate production function seems to be as extreme as the (opposite) one of immediate and instantaneous spillovers in innovation activity generally adopted by the pathbreaking *R&D-based growth models* (Romer, 1990; Grossman and Helpman, 1991, Ch. 3, pp. 57–65; Aghion and Howitt, 1992).

7. Note that I assume no depreciation for human capital. Also note that, with regard to equation (13.14), I consider the variant of the basic Lucas model (1988) in which spillovers from education are internalised. This is done because I am explicitly assuming that there is only one household (of unit measure) within this economy and population is stationary.

8. In equilibrium there exists only one wage rate accruing to skilled workers since human capital is homogeneous.

9. The hypothesis that human and technological capital are complements (the value of the ratio $R = H/n$ remains invariant along the balanced growth path) may be justified on both

theoretical and empirical grounds. From the theoretical point of view, Redding (1996) clearly shows that the complementarity relationship between skilled workers and technology does represent a crucial element in explaining the existence of poverty traps in many less developed countries, due to the joint presence of low levels of skills and R&D investment in these areas. He also shows that, under particular conditions, the complementarity hypothesis between human capital and R&D is also responsible for the existence of multiple steady states. On the empirical side, instead, many contributions claim the relevance of the skill-technology connections even at the sectoral level (Goldin and Katz, 1998), whereas de la Fuente and da Rocha (1996) also find evidence of strong complementarities between human capital stock and investment in R&D for the OECD countries. Other works where the skill-biased technical progress hypothesis is analysed (both theoretically and empirically) include Bartel and Lichtenberg (1987), Berndt et al. (1992), Bell (1996), Machin et al. (1996), Doms et al. (1997), Bartel and Sicherman (1998) and Machin and Van Reenen (1998).

10. As already stated in Section 13.2.4, given the assumptions on the size of the representative household and the population growth rate, $h \equiv H$ (which implies that I can use g_H instead of g_h).

11. Benhabib and Spiegel (1994), Islam (1995) and Pritchett (1996) all suggest that, unlike Lucas (1988), international differences in per-capita growth rates depend exclusively on differences in the respective human capital stocks each country is endowed with. However, Jones (1995a, 1995b) points out that the *scale effect hypothesis* should be rejected on empirical grounds.

12. The *no-scale-effect prediction* is indeed shared by many other models (e.g. Kortum, 1997; Aghion and Howitt, 1998a, Ch. 12; Dinopoulos and Thompson, 1998; Peretto and Smulders, 1998; Segerstrom, 1998; Young, 1998; Howitt, 1999; Blackburn et al., 2000; Bucci, 2001, among others). See Jones (1999) and Eicher and Turnovsky (1999) for recent surveys.

13. In other words, when the monopoly power enjoyed by intermediate local monopolists rises, then a decentralised market equilibrium will allocate less and less resources to capital goods production (which, indeed, is not the true engine of growth within this economy).

14. In the graph I have set $\delta = 0.10$ and $\rho = 0.08$. As long as one assumes $\delta > \rho$, the behaviour of $s_n(1/\alpha)$ does not change at all in qualitative terms.

15. Where there is no human capital accumulation and the inter-sectoral competition for the same resource (forgone consumption) is restricted to the intermediate and research sectors.

16. As in the present model, in Jones and Williams (2000) the mark-up is determined by the elasticity of substitution between intermediate capital goods, too.

17. Notice, indeed, that in this case $0 < \alpha < 1/2$, $\partial s_j / \partial \alpha > 0$, $\partial s_n / \partial \alpha > 0$ and $\partial s_Y / \partial \alpha < 0$. In a moment, I will also show that $\partial s_H / \partial \alpha = 0$ for each value of α.

18. The first and second rows of Table 13.1 show what happens to g_Y, g_H, R, s_n, , s_j, s_Y and s_H when δ increases and falls, respectively, in the following two intervals:

$$\rho < \delta < \rho\left(1 + \sqrt{1 - \alpha(1 - \alpha)}\right) \text{ and } \delta > \rho\left(1 + \sqrt{1 - \alpha(1 - \alpha)}\right).$$

In rows number 3 and 4 I do the same with ρ. Finally, in the last two rows I analyse what happens in the long run to the main variables of the model when α increases and again I keep the two intervals distinct: $0 < \alpha < 1/2$ and $1/2 < \alpha < 1$.

19. Evidently R can also be written as: $R = \alpha\delta / \left(s_j(1 - \alpha)C\right)$. An increase in δ determines an increase in the numerator, a reduction in the denominator (through the effect on s_j) and an unambiguous increase in R.

20. Indeed, in the interval:

$$\rho < \delta < \rho\left(1 + \sqrt{1 - \alpha(1 - \alpha)}\right),$$

variables g_r, g_H, R, s_n and s_H are positively correlated with each other and negatively correlated with s_j and s_r.. Instead, in the interval:

$$\delta > \rho\left(1 + \sqrt{1 - \alpha(1 - \alpha)}\right),$$

variables g_r, g_H, R and s_H are positively correlated with each other and negatively correlated with s_n, s_j and s_r.

21. In another paper (Bucci, 2003) it is shown that the same relationship is highly ambiguous when one considers a generalisation of R&D-based growth models with horizontal differentiation, deterministic research activity and no human capital accumulation.

REFERENCES

Aghion, P. and P. Howitt (1992), 'A model of growth through creative destruction', *Econometrica*, **60**(2), 323–51.

Aghion, P. and P. Howitt (1996), 'Research and development in the growth process', *Journal of Economic Growth*, **1**, 49–73.

Aghion, P. and P. Howitt (1998a), *Endogenous Growth Theory*, Cambridge, Massachusetts: MIT Press.

Aghion, P. and P. Howitt (1998b), 'Market structure and the growth process', *Review of Economic Dynamics*, **1**, 276–305.

Aghion, P., M. Dewatripont and P. Rey (1997a), 'Corporate governance, competition policy and industrial policy', *European Economic Review*, **41**, 797–805.

Aghion, P., C. Harris and J. Vickers (1997b), 'Competition and growth with step-by-step innovation: an example', *European Economic Review*, **41**, 771–82.

Arnold, L.G. (1998), 'Growth, welfare, and trade in an integrated model of human capital accumulation and R&D', *Journal of Macroeconomics*, **20**(1), 81–105.

Bartel, A.P. and F.R. Lichtenberg (1987), 'The comparative advantage of educated workers in implementing new technology', *Review of Economics and Statistics*, **69**, 1–11.

Bartel, A.P. and N. Sicherman (1998), 'Technological change and the skill acquisition of young workers', *Journal of Labour Economics*, **16**(4), 718–55.

Bell, B.D. (1996), 'Skill-biased technical change and wages: evidence from a longitudinal data set', *Oxford Labour Market Consequences of Technical and Structural Change Discussion Paper* no. 8.

Benhabib, J. and M.M. Spiegel (1994), 'The role of human capital in economic development: evidence from aggregate cross-country data', *Journal of Monetary Economics*, **34**(2), 143–73.

Berndt, E.R., C.J. Morrison and L.S. Rosenblum (1992), 'High-tech capital formation and labor composition in U.S. manufacturing industries: an exploratory analysis', *NBER Working Paper* no. 4010.

Blackburn, K., V.T.Y. Hung and A.F. Pozzolo (2000), 'Research, development and human capital accumulation', *Journal of Macroeconomics*, **22**(2), 189–206.

Bucci, A. (2001), 'On scale effects, market power and growth when human and technological capital are complements', *International Review of Economics and Business*, **48**(1), 21–47.

Bucci, A. (2003), 'Horizontal innovation, market power and growth', *International Economic Journal*, forthcoming.

Bucci, A. and C.H. Saglam (2000), 'Growth-maximizing patent life-time', Université Catholique de Louvain, Departement des Sciences Economiques, Discussion Paper no. 2000-19.

de la Fuente, A. and J.M. da Rocha (1996), 'Capital humano y crecimiento: un panorama de la evidencia empirica y algunos resultados para la OCDE', *Moneda-y-Credito*, **203**, 43–84.

Dinopoulos, E. and P. Thompson (1998), 'Schumpeterian growth without scale effects', *Journal of Economic Growth*, **3**(4), 313–35.

Doms, M., T. Dunne and K. Troske (1997), 'Workers, wages and technology', *Quarterly Journal of Economics*, **112**(1), 253–90.

Eicher, T.S. (1996), 'Interaction between endogenous human capital and technological change', *Review of Economic Studies*, **63**(1), 127–44.

Eicher, T.S. and S. Turnovsky (1999), 'Non-scale models of economic growth', *Economic Journal*, **109**, 394–415.

Goldin, C. and L.F. Katz (1998), 'The origins of technology-skill complementarity', *Quarterly Journal of Economics*, **113**(3), 693–732.

Griliches, Z. (1992), 'The search for R&D spillovers', *Scandinavian Journal of Economics*, **94**(0), S29–S47.

Grossman, G.M. and E. Helpman (1991), *Innovation and Growth in the Global Economy*, Cambridge, Massachusetts: MIT Press.

Howitt, P. (1999), 'Steady endogenous growth with population and R&D inputs growing', *Journal of Political Economy*, **107**(4), 715–30.

Islam, N. (1995), 'Growth empirics: a panel data approach', *Quarterly Journal of Economics*, **110**, 1127–70.

Jones, C.I. (1995a), 'R&D-based models of economic growth', *Journal of Political Economy*, **103**(4), 759–84.

Jones, C.I. (1995b), 'Time series tests of endogenous growth models', *Quarterly Journal of Economics*, **110**(2), 495–525.

Jones, C.I. (1999), 'Growth: with or without scale effects?', *American Economic Review, Papers and Proceedings*, **89**, 139–44.

Jones, C.I. and J.C. Williams (2000), 'Too much of a good thing? The economics of investment in R&D', *Journal of Economic Growth*, **5**(1), 65–85.

Jones, L. and R. Manuelli (1990), 'A convex model of equilibrium growth: theory and policy implications', *Journal of Political Economy*, **98**, 1008–38.

Keely, L.C. (2001), 'Using patents in growth models', *Economics of Innovation and New Technology*, **10**(6), 449–92.

Keely, L.C. and D. Quah (1998), 'Technology in growth', *Centre for Economic Performance, Discussion Paper* no. 391.

Kortum, S.S. (1997), 'Research, patenting, and technological change', *Econometrica*, **65**(6), 1389–1419.

Lucas, R.E. (1988), 'On the mechanics of economic development', *Journal of Monetary Economics*, **22**(1), 3–42.

Machin, S., and J. Van Reenen (1998), 'Technology and changes in skill structure: evidence from seven OECD countries', *Quarterly Journal of Economics*, **113**(4), 1214–44.

Machin, S., A. Ryan and J. Van Reenen (1996), 'Technology and changes in skill structure: evidence from an international panel of industries', *Centre for Economic Policy Research Discussion Paper* no. 1434.

Peretto, P. and S. Smulders (1998), 'Specialization, knowledge dilution, and scale effects in an IO-based growth model', *Center for Economic Research Discussion Paper* no. 9802.

Pritchett, L. (1996), 'Where has all the education gone?', World Bank, *Policy Research Working Paper* no. 1581.

Rebelo, S. (1991), 'Long run policy analysis and long run growth', *Journal of Political Economy*, **99**, 500–21.

Redding, S. (1996), 'The low-skill, low-quality trap: strategic complementarities between human capital and R&D', *Economic Journal*, **106**, 458–70.

Restuccia, D. (1997), 'Technology adoption and schooling: amplifier income effects of policies across countries', Working Paper, University of Minnesota, mimeo.

Romer, P.M. (1990), 'Endogenous technological change', *Journal of Political Economy*, **98**(5), Part 2, S71–S102.

Segerstrom, P. (1998), 'Endogenous growth without scale effects', *American Economic Review*, **88**(5), 1290–1310.

Segerstrom, P.S., T.C.A. Anant and E. Dinopoulos (1990), 'A Schumpeterian model of the product life cycle', *American Economic Review*, **80**(5), 1077–91.

Stokey, N. (1988), 'Learning by doing and the introduction of new goods', *Journal of Political Economy*, **96**(4), 701–17.

Uzawa, H. (1965), 'Optimum technical change in an aggregative model of economic growth', *International Economic Review*, **6**, 18–31.

Young, A. (1993), 'Invention and bounded learning by doing', *Journal of Political Economy*, **101**(3), 443–72.

Young, A. (1998), 'Growth without scale effects', *Journal of Political Economy*, **106**(1), 41–63.

14. The enigma of medieval craft guilds: a model of social inertia and technological change[*]

Maria Rosaria Carillo and Alberto Zazzaro

14.1. INTRODUCTION

It is widely recognised by economists that the main force underlying economic growth processes is technological change. However, it is equally acknowledged that technological change generally represents a serious threat to the economic, political and social interests of many individuals and many institutions (consumers, workers, firms, artisans, professionals) which are therefore organised to seek, in various ways, at times even using violence, to impede it.

Schumpeter (1934), for example, considered social resistance to change one of the greatest obstacles encountered by entrepreneurs in introducing new combinations of means of production. Such resistance, noted Schumpeter, essentially consists in the existence of legal or political impediments and is expressed by groups threatened by the innovation. Simon Kuznets (1972a, p. 446) was even more explicit: 'there may be, and there have been cases where the resistance [to the competitive and destructive effects of technological innovations] was so great, and the price of overcoming it so high, that economic growth did not proceed at an adequate pace'.[1] However, the author who perhaps most decisively underlined the checking effect that interest groups may have on the process of technological innovation and growth was Mancur Olson (1982, p. 63), according to whom, 'distributional coalitions slow down a society's capacity to adopt new technologies and to reallocate resources in response to changing conditions, and thereby reduce the rate of economic growth'.

Despite these early advances, only recently has economic growth theory introduced social resistance to innovation on the part of interest groups into its models and analytical schemes. In this new strand of literature the type of barrier which is usually examined is that involving opposition to new technologies already designed and employed elsewhere.[2] Economic intuition is straightforward and in line with the less formal arguments proposed in the past: market regulation and the monopoly rights enjoyed by employees and firms operating in existing industries make it very costly for other firms to enter the industry and discourage adoption of more productive technologies. The reasons for such regulation and protective strength lie in the political power enjoyed by those who operate with the old technology (Acemoglu and Robinson, 2000) and in their electoral influence (Adamopoulus, 2001; Aghion and Howitt, 1998; Bellettini and Ottaviano, 1999; Krusell and Rios-Rull, 1996). However, they may also be the consequence of cumulative economic delay which has limited the number of existing firms and favoured the development of vested interests of those offering their services to the firms in question (Parente and Prescott, 1999; Parente, 2000). Whatever the reason, the conclusion seems to be invariably the same: every form of social and political inertia which is created in the economic system when new technologies are being adopted reduces social welfare and makes the countries affected relatively less affluent compared with those which are free from technology adoption barriers, reducing the level of steady state per capita income and possibly the growth rate.

Is such a drastic conclusion acceptable? To what extent have formal organisations of special interests been able in history to block the introduction of innovation? Though their ability to slow down technological change is acknowledged, can we say for sure that the institutions and social forces opposed to innovation have always been a negative factor for social welfare and a barrier to economic growth?

Of course, in order to attempt to question the conclusions of a model, we need to question the assumptions underpinning it. The recent economics literature on social barriers to technological change is based on two crucial assumptions: (*a*) introducing innovations does not generate negative externalities in the economic system; (*b*) adopting new technologies does not require firm-specific investments. We are obviously dealing with two considerable simplifications of reality which however, if taken on their own, would be no greater than those that all economic theories are forced to introduce in their analytical schemes. The point is that the existence of negative externalities and the presence of firm-specific investments are precisely those elements which may justify, in terms of economic efficiency, the presence of institutions to safeguard special interests and the existence of social barriers to innovation. Thus, in the presence of negative externalities and firm-specific investments, the action of institutions to protect vested interests may favour the growth process or at least bring it close to its socially optimal level.

In the next section we will briefly review the experience of medieval craft guilds. From the twelfth century onwards, for the subsequent six or seven centuries, the craft guilds were, throughout Europe, formal organisations to protect widespread vested interests, invested with great social and political power. As will be seen, the conclusions reached by economic historians concerning their influence on the economic life of the period and on technological development are highly ambivalent and underline the various factors that may have turned guilds into welfare- and growth-enhancing organisations.

In the following two sections, we will present a model of endogenous growth with successive non-overlapping generations, in which we introduce the existence of social inertia to the development and adoption of new technologies similar to those represented by medieval craft guilds. As in the Romer model (1990), we assume that the only final good of the economy is produced with the use of a certain number of intermediate goods. Each of these goods, in turn, is produced by a monopolist with the use of labour alone (Aghion and Howitt, 1992). Besides the monopolistic rents, the producer of the intermediate good enjoys a certain social prestige and political power. The former is intentionally accumulated by an institution operating on behalf of monopolists and is, in part, also transferred to those working in the intermediate goods sector. For a given amount of social lobbying effort, however, social prestige tends to diminish as the number of firms operating in the intermediate goods sector increases.

Political power is instead used by incumbent firms to block the entry of new firms and new intermediate goods. To start up new firms, new intermediate goods need to be introduced, which requires firm-specific investments. Once the new goods are designed, the barriers set by the incumbents still have to be overcome. Therefore, incumbents and entrants play a rent-seeking game at the end of which the number of intermediate goods produced in the subsequent period is determined.

The economic intuition of our model is therefore typical of neo-Schumpeterian literature. The monopoly power enjoyed by firms that manage to design and introduce new goods is the stimulus to innovation without which the economy does not grow. The difference lies in the fact that in our model, monopolists benefit not only from monopoly rents but also from a certain social prestige which nevertheless tends to diminish with the increase in the number of firms supplying that type of good. Hence the ambivalent effect of social inertia: what drives monopolists to block entry, namely the lessening of social prestige, is also what encourages potential entrants to employ resources in designing new goods and what makes the economy grow.[3]

14.2.   THE CRAFT GUILDS IN MEDIEVAL EUROPE

The best known and most widely studied example of institutions established to protect vested interests is undoubtedly that of occupational (merchant and craft) guilds of medieval Europe.[4] The system of guilds developed in Italy in the twelth and thirteenth centuries, and rapidly spread throughout Europe. The guilds were formal associations, established on a voluntary basis, with the aim of regulating how a trade might be performed, both by fixing quality standards and sale prices for goods and services, and to explicitly regulate how production should be organised and the terms of entry to a trade. Their powers of control were often established by law; in exchange, the guilds were called upon to pay taxes or royalties (Pirenne, 1933).

However, besides regulating the economic life of the period, the guilds were also firmly established social and political institutions. Each member enjoyed economic protection as regards income level, continuity and the independence of his own work. Belonging to a guild meant acquiring a distinct moral identity and important social prestige (Black, 1984, p. 14). The profound solidarity that bound the members of a guild was due both to religious and social incentives and to ties of kinship (fostered, for example, by the many marriages that united guild members) perhaps to a greater extent than to mere economic incentives (Thrupp, 1963, pp. 238–9; Black, 1984, pp. 12–13).

In time the guilds began to acquire considerable political weight as well, generating 'a distinct group of administrators who cultivated political skill' (Thrupp, 1963, p. 238). Although always considered private associations, the guilds took an extremely active part in the work of city administration and their officers were often considered 'as quasi-public officials' (Thrupp, 1963, p. 232). It was not rare for their more distinguished members to assume public office (Simonde de Sismondi, 1827). Indeed, the guilds actively and rationally cultivated their political power and social prestige, undertaking social relation activities (Thrupp, 1963, p. 249).

Associations of this type were common even before the emergence of craft guilds. A prime example consists in the *collegia* of the Roman period, even if their aims were chiefly non-economic, concerning the handing-down of the craft rather than its protection (Pirenne, 1933; Finley, 1973; Hickson and Thompson, 1991). Above all, associations comparable with guilds are commonly found today in the form of professional orders, thus making the study of the experience of medieval craft guilds also relevant to contemporary economies.[5]

A major part of historical reconstruction, and probably the most authoritative, seems unanimous that medieval craft guilds on the whole had a negative effect on the economic prosperity of the regions into which they spread. The traditional economic interpretation supplied by historians considers craft guilds as monopoly institutions which limited competition with their statutes on apprenticeship and with their constraints on the organisation of workshops and labour (such as the maximum number of apprentices per master, the ban on employing workers registered with other guilds, the prohibition on adopting certain production methods or introducing certain types of production), thereby seriously reducing citizen welfare, but being especially detrimental to the entrepreneurial spirit of local populations. According to Carlo Cipolla (1952, 1970), for example, one of the elements found in all episodes of stagnation and economic decline between the sixteenth and eighteenth centuries affecting first Spain and then Italy and lastly the Netherlands is the strong mental and social resistance to change on the part of such populations, resistance that was created and stimulated by the system of guilds. In Italy, noted Cipolla (1952, p. 183), 'the excessive powers of the obsolete guilds and of the old corporative legislation compelled ... industry to adhere to antiquated and out-of-date methods in business and production'.[6] Cipolla (1952, 1959) reports various enlightening examples of obstacles placed in labour organisation on the part of guilds, such as that of a Genoese silk spinner, Paolo de Simone, who in 1570 was prevented by the dyers' guild, with the support of the city administration, from employing a dyer in his own workshop lest this might open the way to the proletarianisation of dyers. Then there is the case of the Collegio Lanificio in Venice who, faced with the ban by local guilds of manufacturing woollen clothes according to the new English or Dutch style, which had rapidly supplanted local manufactures on retail markets, was forced to formally request that the masters be left free to produce the types of clothes that they felt most appropriate with production methods which they deemed best.

By contrast, according to other authors, the elimination of the privileges of the artisan guilds, the removal of their political power and more permissive laws favouring individual initiative are the factors that contributed to the rapid development of the Netherlands in the seventeenth century and the Industrial Revolution in England in the following century.[7] According to David Landes (1969), for example, the fact that in England the control of the guilds over production and apprenticeship had already been largely dissolved by the end of the seventeenth century is one of the most convincing reasons as to why the Industrial Revolution started up precisely in England. Unlike in other European countries, notes Mokyr again (1990, p. 241), 'the British government was by and large unsupportive of reactionary forces that tried to slow down the Industrial Revolution'.[8]

Despite the authoritativeness of the hostile opinions expressed vis-à-vis medieval craft guilds, the historical evidence is far less clear and unambiguous than one might be led to believe. There are various examples, such as Portugal and Spain in the fifteenth and sixteenth centuries, Denmark and Sweden in the seventeenth and eighteenth centuries, of rapid increases in growth following the strengthening of the power of guilds in their favour (Kellenbenz, 1977; Hickson and Thompson, 1991). Besides, as noted by Hickson and Thompson (1988) and Epstein (1998), if craft guilds were definitely opposed to economic prosperity and growth, why would it have had so many imitators and spread so rapidly throughout Europe?

In actual fact, there are various reasons for believing that craft guilds did not only constitute a check on economic growth. First, the guilds had never had the power to completely block the process of innovation, which had always developed in country areas outside the walls of cities, where their statutes did not apply (Simonde de Sismondi, 1827; Thrupp, 1963). Clearly, the innovators could be refused the status of guild member. This prevented them from enjoying prestige and considerable social and political benefits which were tied to membership of a guild (Black, 1984; Thrupp, 1963), but did not prevent them from undertaking that particular occupation (Pirenne, 1933). However, often, as in the city of London, there was the opportunity for new entrants to appeal to the city council: by demonstrating their skill in the profession, their application to join a guild might be successful (Hickson and Thompson, 1991). Thus, the ability of guilds to block the entry of new masters or journeymen could not be carried out across the board but had to be negotiated on each occasion with the political authorities.

Second, the existence of guilds was a device, in some ways rationally designed but in others only hit upon by chance, to reduce transaction costs and internalise both positive and negative externalities. The guilds, for example, undertook the important task of preventing undue expropriation on the part of bureaucrats with little respect for the laws in force (Hickson and Thompson, 1988; Greif et al., 1994), transferring the reputation of the whole trade to products and masters who were not well-known outside domestic markets (Gustafsson, 1987; Persson, 1988) and facilitating access to credit (Pfister, 1998). However, the guilds and the rights to restrict access to the craft were also a means of efficiently internalising the positive externalities related to defensive expenditure to protect cities and the accumulated physical capital (Thrupp, 1963; Thompson, 1974, 1979; Hickson and Thompson, 1991) and negative externalities regarding the destruction of human skills caused by technological advances (Epstein, 1998). Moreover, by lengthening the times required by apprentices to reach a stable position, the constraints imposed by guilds had the effect of limiting births and thereby making the spectre of Malthusian traps more remote (Simonde de Sismondi, 1827).

Third, concerning innovation policies, the attitude of guilds was not always suffocating. Although the guilds system may well not have acted as a stimulus to the entrepreneurial spirit, undoubtedly, as Sylvia Thrupp also recalls (1963, p. 279), the external conditions of the age generally made caution necessary and also 'entrepreneurs who stood outside [guilds] ranks made no better showing'. 'It would be an error' – writes Thrupp (1963, p. 231) – 'to identify medieval guilds solely with so desperate a conservatism. Their policies could move also in opposite directions, open to innovation and favouring the masters who had capital'.

For example, the guilds system, by driving artisans' workshops to crowd within fairly restricted areas, favoured the creation and diffusion of technological externalities (Poni, 1990; Epstein, 1998). Furthermore, by closely defining the activities that each occupation could undertake, the system favoured specialisation in production, the division of labour and technological progress (Epstein, 1998). Finally, the same struggles to slow down innovation and protect the masters of the trade which the guilds so often waged managed to act as a stimulus for those who intended to develop a new product or a new production method. In other words, in medieval times the guilds and their regulations, as regards innovation, played a very similar role to that played by patents today.[9]

It is precisely this ambiguity of the effects that social inertia had with regard to technological innovation that will be the focus of the next sections.

14.3. THE MODEL

14.3.1. An Informal Account

A class of growth models that can be used to represent the ambiguous effects of social inertia on technological change comprises the monopolistically competitive models. The main building block of the model we present in this section is the variety-based model due to Romer (1990).

Unlike the Romer's model, in our model there is no capital accumulation and there is, instead, a succession of non-overlapping generations. Each generation, j, lives for two periods. At the beginning of the first period there is a constant number N of workers, each endowed with one indivisible unit of skilled labour, and a variable amount of entrepreneurs–firms, each endowed with the technology and ability to organise production.

In the economy there are three productive sectors. A final-good sector, whose inputs consist of a variety of a unique specialised craft good; an intermediate craft-good sector, whose inputs consist of skilled workers only; and a sector which designs and develops new varieties of the craft good, which also requires only the use of skilled workers.

All the entrepreneurs and workers who produce the intermediate input belong to a craft guild, the former with the qualification of master, the latter with that of apprentice.

In the first period of each generation *j* all productive sectors operate. The number of intermediate goods or workshops or masters (for the sake of simplicity, we assume that these quantities are exactly the same) coincides with the number existing at the end of the previous generation. Thus the idea is that each master at the end of his own life has a descendant to whom he is able, due also to the protection of the guild, to transfer his tacit knowledge and the technical secrets to carry out the trade.

Each craft workshop enjoys an absolute monopolistic power. This, we may imagine, is partly guaranteed by the tacit knowledge required to produce that particular variety of craft good and partly by the statute of the guild that prohibits its own members from imitating, even where it was technically possible, goods produced by other members. Apart from monopoly profits, masters also enjoy a certain social prestige which, in line with what was stated in the previous section, we imagine is intentionally boosted by the guild and which is extended, albeit to a lesser extent, to those who work there as apprentices.

Still in the first period, outside the guild, hence without enjoying the protection and social prestige that membership ensures, a certain number of individuals employed as journeymen work to design new products. However, the creation of a new product is not enough to ensure its actual production in the subsequent period. Moreover, it is also necessary to enter and become part of the guild. However, since the increase in the number of masters operating in the guild diminishes its social prestige, the guild will attempt to block the opening of new workshops.[10] The entrants, for their part, will appeal to the local political authorities to force the guild to accept their entry, and between the two parties a rent-seeking game will take place where each will use their own lobbying power to influence the authorities' decision.

In each generation, in the second period, only production of the consumption good and intermediate goods is undertaken, while there is no further research carried out. All those who worked as journeymen in the sector outside the guild offer their labour to workshops that produce intermediate goods, which thus in the second period, in equilibrium, absorb all the labour force.

The number of workshops existing in the second period depends on the outcome of the rent-seeking game. If the competition is won by the guild, the number of the workshops remains unchanged and the innovations will be lost. Otherwise, the number of workshops will increase according to the number of new goods invented, as will the production of the final consumption good.

14.3.2. The Economy

The economy consists of a continuum of individuals of measure N, which lives for two periods and is endowed with one indivisible unit of skilled labour, the disutility of whose supply is nil. Any individual is characterised by the same linear intertemporal utility function which relates the flow of utility to the quantity of consumption and to the social prestige accruing from the job performed. The intertemporal preference rate, $r > 0$, is constant and, in equilibrium, coincides with the rate of interest at which firms collect savings.

The consumption good, which acts as numeraire, is produced in a perfectly competitive market according to the following production function:

$$Y_t^j = \int_0^{A_t^j} \left(x_{it}^j \right)^\alpha di \quad 0 < \alpha \le 1, \tag{14.1}$$

where j indicates the generation, t the period of life and i the variety of craft goods employed in the production of the final good. A_t^j is the number of goods actually produced in the period t. In the first period the latter coincides with the number of intermediate goods produced by masters of generation $j-1$ in the second period of their life, and handed down to masters of generation j. In the second period if innovators are able to enter the guild, the number of intermediate goods will increase; otherwise it will remain constant. In symbols:

$$A_1^j = A_2^{j-1}$$

$$A_2^j = \begin{cases} A_1^j & \text{if the guild impedes the entrance of new masters} \\ A_1^j + \Delta A^j & \text{otherwise.} \end{cases}$$

Each variety of the craft good is produced by the same linear production function:

$$x_{it}^j = n_{x_{it}}^j, \tag{14.2}$$

where $n_{x_{it}}^j$ denotes the number of apprentices involved in the production of the i-th craft good in period t and generation j. Having assumed that each craft good has the same productivity in the production of the consumption good and their marginal productivity being independent of each other, in equilibrium all the workshops will always produce the same amount of output and will enjoy the same profits. This implies that hereafter we can omit the index i without ambiguity.

In the first period, a certain number of individuals are employed in an activity researching and developing new varieties of the craft good whose production function is the following:

$$\Delta A^j = \lambda A_1^j n_{r_1}^j, \tag{14.3}$$

where $n_{r_1}^j$ is the number of workers employed as journeymen in the research, and λ is a productivity parameter.

As in Romer (1990), the productivity of research increases with the number of the intermediate goods already produced, giving rise to a positive externality which sustains the growth process. As equation (14.3) shows, the employment of a journeyman definitely gives rise to the production of λA_1^j new intermediate goods. Therefore, the introduction of new intermediate goods can be seen, following Romer, as a research activity that produces new goods. Otherwise, it may be fairly interpreted as a process of adoption of a new technology that is incorporated in new goods and whose application requires firm-specific investments.[11]

14.4. THE CRAFT GUILD

All the masters and apprentices who at a certain moment work in the intermediate craft-good sector belong to a guild. The latter performs various functions on behalf of its members. In particular, apart from protecting the monopoly power of each workshop, the corporation regulates access of new masters to the guild and safeguards the image and social prestige of the craft. Clearly, these two activities are intimately bound and both require intense political and social lobbying. For the sake of analytical simplicity, however, we will deal with them separately, under the assumption that the political power and social power of the guild can be cultivated separately without the one affecting the other. Let us begin with social power.

14.4.1. Social Lobbying

In the economic literature there are various contributions focusing on the demand for social status on the part of socially minded individuals and the effects that this has on the performance of the economy in the presence of the social ranking of professions (Fershtman and Weiss, 1993; Weiss and Fershtman, 1998). Nevertheless, in the literature in question, social ranking of occupations is generally considered an exogenous element on the basis of which individuals make their own choices. In reality, however, the social prestige of occupations is at least partly an endogenous variable, intentionally demanded by the formal organisations representing them, like the guilds of yesteryear and the professional orders of today (Larson Sarfatti, 1977).

Thus, let us imagine that the guild may play a role of social relations, with a view to enhancing the social prestige of the craft and its more distinguished members, the masters. The costs of this activity (measured in units of effort) are proportional to the organisational effort ℓ devoted to it. However, the benefits, besides depending increasingly on the guild's organisational effort, diminish with the increase in the number of masters belonging to it. As usual, the organisational effort of the guild in social lobbying will be such as to maximise the difference between benefits and costs:

$$\max_{\ell_t}\left(\frac{S_m}{A_t}\ell_t^\beta - c\ell_t\right),$$

where $0 < \beta < 1$ indicates the productivity of the organisational effort, S_m/A_t its effectiveness at the margin and c its marginal cost (as each generation is identical to the other, to simplify the notation hereafter we omit the index j). The optimal lobbying effort is therefore:

$$\ell_t^* = \left(\frac{\beta S_m}{cA_t}\right)^{\frac{1}{1-\beta}}. \tag{14.4}$$

The social lobbying performed by the guild thus increases as its effectiveness increases (i.e. with the increase in S_m) and as its costs diminish. Nevertheless, as the guild expands (i.e. A_t increases) the organisational effort to social relations is reduced, in that its effectiveness is reduced. Finally, an increase in social lobbying productivity has a positive effect, but only until the number of guild members becomes excessive.[12]

In equilibrium, the social prestige accruing to masters is $SP_m = (S_m/A_t)\ell_t^*$. However, the social prestige of the craft, which the guild maximises in consideration of the masters' prestige, is also partly transferred to apprentices:

$$SP_a = \frac{S_a}{A_t}\ell_t^*,$$

where SP_a is the social prestige of the apprentices and $S_a/A_t < S_m/A_t$ the effectiveness for them of social lobbying undertaken by the guild. Therefore, the level of social stratification within the craft, SP_m/SP_a, does not depend on the optimal social lobbying effort of the guild but only on the ratio between its effectiveness for masters and apprentices S_m/S_a.

14.4.2. Political Lobbying

Besides being engaged in social lobbying, the guild is also committed to political lobbying with a view to regulating the entry of new masters within the craft. As in our model the entry of new masters has no positive effect on the incumbents; in each generation the aim of the guild will be to block new entrants. This will be opposed by those who have devised new varieties of the craft good. As already stated, in order to supply the product they have created the latter must first become members of the guild. In light of the certain refusal they will encounter, the entrant masters cannot but appeal to the political authorities so as to force the guild to accept them as members.

This situation can be formalised as a rent-seeking game, where innovators and the guild compete to gain the favour of politicians and administrators by devoting resources to lobbying.[13] For analytical simplicity, let us assume that also the potential masters act as a single agent or, which amounts to the same thing, that the acceptance or exclusion of a new master on the part of the guild is extended to all those who designed new products in that generation. The guild and entrants thus act so as to maximise respectively the benefits of all incumbent masters and all potential masters. The cost of political lobbying is proportional to the effort made and the number of incumbents or entrants.

Let e_r and e_x stand for the resources, in terms of effort, devoted to political lobbying by the entrant masters and the guild. The probabilities of success of the two groups assume the traditional logit form introduced by Tullock (1980), but are not perfectly symmetric. More precisely, let us assume that political lobbying is a constant return activity in the effort of lobbying groups, but that the marginal productivity of the effort is not the same.[14] Hence the probability that new masters enter the guild and the probability that the guild succeeds in impeding this entrance are respectively:

$$q = \frac{e_r}{e_r + \sigma e_x}, \quad (1-q) = \frac{\sigma e_x}{e_r + \sigma e_x}, \qquad (14.5)$$

where σ denotes the relative ability of the guild to undertake political lobbying.

The pay-off functions are:

$$u_x = \frac{\sigma e_x}{\sigma e_x + e_r} A_1 V_{x_2}^{A_1} + \frac{e_r}{\sigma e_x + e_r} A_1 V_{x_2}^{A_1 + \Delta A} - A_1 e_x$$

and:

$$u_r = \frac{e_r}{\sigma e_x + e_r} \Delta A V_{x_2}^{A_1 + \Delta A} - \Delta A e_r,$$

where A_1 and ΔA are respectively the number of incumbent and of entrant masters, $V_{x_2}^{A_1}$ and $V_{x_2}^{A_1+\Delta A}$ the per-master value of conducting a craft workshop in the case in which entry is refused and in the case in which it is accepted.

Since the guild has already established political relations in the past its contractual bargaining and lobbying capacity is greater than that of the entrant masters. Formally we express this situation by hypothesising that the marginal productivity of lobbying is greater for the guild (i.e. $\sigma > 1$) and by assuming that the rent-seeking game is sequential, that is that the guild has the first-mover advantage and constrains the innovators to respond to its action.[15]

Given the pay-off functions, the reaction function of the entrant masters group is:

$$e_r^* = \sqrt{\sigma e_x V_{x_2}^{A_1+\Delta A}} - e_x, \tag{14.6}$$

while the level of effort which maximises the guild's pay-off function is:

$$e_x^* = \frac{\sigma\left(V_{x_2}^{A_1} - V_{x_2}^{A_1+\Delta A}\right)^2}{4V_{x_2}^{A_1+\Delta A}}. \tag{14.7}$$

Proposition 1: *The rent-seeking game has a unique equilibrium in pure strategies if and only if*

$$V_{x_2}^{A_1+\Delta A} > \frac{\sigma V_{x_2}^{A_1}}{2+\sigma}. \tag{14.8}$$

In this case the lobbying effort exerted by the guild increases, and the probability that the new masters enter the intermediate craft-good market decreases, as the difference between the values of being masters before and after the entrance of new masters and the lobbying capacity of the guild increase.

Proof: On substituting (14.7) in (14.6) it is evident that if inequality (14.8) holds, then $e_r^* = 0$. In this case, it would also be optimal for the craft guild not to devote effort to lobbying, thus making $e_r^* = 0$ a non-optimal response (and so on). Moreover, substituting (14.7) and (14.6) in (14.5) we have the result that the probability of the new masters managing to enter the guild and offering new products is:

$$q^* = 1 - \frac{\sigma\left(V_{x_2}^{A_1} - V_{x_2}^{A_1+\Delta A}\right)}{2V_{x_2}^{A_1+\Delta A}}. \tag{14.9}$$

Therefore, the larger the difference between the values of being masters, and the stronger the political power of the guild, the fewer the resources that the innovators will invest in lobbying, and the lower the probability that they obtain entry into the intermediate craft-good market. In such cases there would be considerable social barriers to innovation and the benefits of innovation would thus be very low, trapping the economy in an equilibrium of very low growth (if any).

14.5. THE EQUILIBRIUM

In symmetrical equilibrium, the demand functions of the different varieties of craft goods are identical and may be calculated starting from the profit maximisation of firms producing the final commodity. In particular, recalling from (14.1) that the final good acts as numeraire, the inverse demand function for any craft good is:

$$p_{x_t} = \alpha x_t^{\alpha - 1}. \tag{14.10}$$

In turn, the masters who operate in the craft-good sector choose the number of apprentices to employ, maximising their profits, $\pi_{x_t} = p_{x_t} x_t - w_{x_t} n_{x_t}$. Substituting equations (14.2) and (14.10) in the latter expression, in equilibrium the wages paid to apprentices are equal to:

$$w_{x_t} = \alpha^2 x_t^{\alpha - 1}$$

and the masters' profits are:

$$\pi_{x_t}^* = \alpha(1 - \alpha) x_t^{\alpha}.$$

As stated above, however, the social benefits arising from belonging to the guild must be added to the economic benefits. In particular, let us assume that social prestige is a multiplicative variable of salaries and profits. In equilibrium, therefore, taking due account of the optimal social lobbying effort conducted by the guild (see equation (14.4)), the total benefits apprentices and masters receive in each period of their lives are respectively:

$$U_{x_t} = \left(\frac{\beta}{c}\right)^{\frac{\beta}{1-\beta}} \left(\frac{S_a}{A_t}\right)^{\frac{1}{1-\beta}} \alpha^2 x_t^{\alpha - 1}$$

$$V_{x_t} = \left(\frac{\beta}{c}\right)^{\frac{\beta}{1-\beta}} \left(\frac{S_m}{A_t}\right)^{\frac{1}{1-\beta}} \alpha(1 - \alpha) x_t^{\alpha}. \tag{14.11}$$

The expected benefits of research are the total benefits that the researchers can secure by producing in the second period the new goods invented multiplied by the probability of gaining access to the guild. Therefore, assuming free entry to the research sector, and taking into account equation (14.3), in equilibrium the wage paid to the journeymen employed in this sector is:

$$w_r = q^* A_1 \lambda \frac{V_{x_2}^{A+\Delta A}}{1+r}. \qquad (14.12)$$

The labour market is in equilibrium when all individuals find employment. In the first period, the research sector is also active and the number of intermediate craft goods is that inherited from the past generation, the labour market equilibrium is given by the following expression: $N = n_r + A_1 \bar{x}_1$. In the second period, the research sector is no longer active and all the workers find employment in the intermediate sector. Therefore, if innovators win the rent-seeking game and enter the guild the equilibrium condition is $N = (A_1 + \Delta A) \bar{x}_2$. On the contrary, if the guild manages to block the entry of new masters, the equilibrium is $N = A_1 \bar{x}_2$.

Finally, as in the second period all the workers are employed in the craft sector, in the first period, in equilibrium, the utility deriving from employment as apprentice or journeyman in the two sectors must be the same. That is:

$$w_r = \frac{S_a}{A_1} \left(\frac{\beta S_m}{c A_1} \right)^{\frac{\beta}{1-\beta}} \alpha^2 x_t^{\alpha-1}. \qquad (14.13)$$

14.6. THE PACE OF TECHNOLOGICAL CHANGE AND LONG-RUN GROWTH

In our economy, the growth in the production of the final good from one generation to another is related to the number of new intermediate goods which are introduced on the market. As stated above, this depends on the resources employed in research, conditional upon the fact that innovators manage to win the rent-seeking competition and gain access to the guild.

The equilibrium equation of the research sector together with the equilibrium conditions of the labour market allow us to determine the number of workers who in each generation in equilibrium will be employed in the research sector.

Therefore, substituting equation (14.11) in equation (14.9) and then the latter and equation (14.13) in equation (14.12), we obtain the optimal number of workers who, in equilibrium in each generation, are employed as journeymen in research:

$$S_a \alpha \left(N - n_r^* \right)^{\alpha-1} = \frac{\lambda S_m (1-\alpha) N^\alpha}{2} \left[\frac{(2+\sigma)}{\left(1+\lambda n_r^*\right)^{\frac{1}{1-\beta}+\alpha}} - \sigma \right]. \quad (14.14)$$

As may be easily verified, the marginal costs of research (the expression on the left-hand side of equation (14.14)), increases with n_r, while the marginal benefits (the right-hand side) decrease with it. Thus, if in $n_r = 0$ $LHS_{(14)} < RHS_{(14)}$ holds, the number of workers employed in research is that determined by condition (14.14). Otherwise, $n_r^* = 0$ and the economy remains trapped in an equilibrium without growth.

As regards the effects of social inertia on the pace of technological change, straightforward exercises in comparative statics allow us to reach the following proposition:

Proposition 2: *An increase in social stratification within the craft (i.e. an increase in S_m and a decrease in S_a) weakly increases the resources employed in research and favours technological change. An increase in the productivity of social lobbying of the guild and an increase in its political lobbying capacity (i.e. an increase in β and in σ) reduce the probability of entering the guild and, consequently, reduce the resources employed in research and slow the pace of technological change.*

Proof: It follows trivially from (14.14).

As mentioned previously, the effects of social inertia on the rate of an economy's technological progress are ambiguous. The presence of social barriers acts as a check to innovation insofar as it reduces, for those involved, the probability of succeeding in gaining its benefits and increase its costs. Indeed, the social prestige accruing to those who find employment within the guild as apprentices drives up the wages of journeymen in the research sector. On the other hand, for those who manage to overcome obstacles placed by those who have an interest in maintaining the status quo, social barriers increase the performance of innovation precisely because they ensure high social prestige and reduce the probability that in the future other individuals may introduce further innovation.

Naturally, more intense research increases the ex-post rate of growth of the economy. However, an ex-ante increase in n_r^* reduces the probability of innovations being actually introduced; in other words it reduces the probability of innovators winning the rent-seeking competition and makes the effect on expected growth rate ambiguous.

Formally, the growth rate expected between one generation and the next is given by:

$$E(g_Y) = q^* \frac{Y_2^j - Y_2^{j-1}}{Y_2^{j-1}}. \tag{14.15}$$

In symmetrical equilibrium, in each period, and in each generation, production of the final commodity is $Y_t^j = A_t^j \left(\overline{x}_t^j \right)^\alpha$. Substituting this expression and equations (14.9) and (14.12) in (14.15), then:

$$E(g_Y) = \frac{1}{2}\left[2 + \sigma - \sigma\left(1+\lambda n_r^*\right)^{\frac{1}{1-\beta}+\alpha} \right]\left[\left(1+\lambda n_r^*\right)^{1-\alpha} - 1 \right]. \tag{14.16}$$

Proposition 3: *Sufficient condition for an increase in resources employed to bring about an increase in the expected growth rate of the economy is:*

$$\left(1+\lambda n_r^*\right)^{1-\alpha} > \frac{2-\beta}{1+\alpha(1-\beta)}.$$

Proof: The proposition can be straightforwardly verified by differentiating equation (14.16) with respect to n_r^*, and conducting some tedious algebraic manipulations.

In other words, in economies in which the productivity of innovation is so low or in which the social barriers to innovation are so high as to make n_r^* very small, the relative benefits that the craft guild would obtain from blocking the entry of new masters may be particularly high. In such cases, the beneficial effect on growth of any stimulus to innovation whatsoever would be ex-ante more than compensated by a reduction in the probability of actually managing to introduce innovations into the economy. In all other cases, however, the stimuli for innovation increase, both ex-ante and ex-post, the growth rate of the economy.

14.7. CONCLUSIONS

Processes of technological innovation, whether involving the adoption of existing technology or the creation of new products or production methods, call into question many vested interests. The introduction of such innovation thus has to overcome social inertia and institutional barriers set by those who have such interests at stake. These factors, in some ways, will reduce the resources that a society devotes to innovation. However, the same inertia and social barriers end up ensuring protection for those who undertake the innovative process today, who will be able to reap the benefits of such protection tomorrow.

According to recent historical reconstructions, mechanisms of this type were also created in medieval times, when industry and the economy were strictly controlled by craft guilds. In this chapter, starting from a description of the experience of medieval craft guilds, we presented a simple variety-based model of endogenous growth in which we assume that an institution (the craft guild) which represents the interests of the existing industrial élite (the masters) undertakes social and political lobbying to enhance its prestige and prevent the entry of new masters. The main result that we obtain is the ambiguity of the effects of social barriers on technological change. The greater the guild's capacity of social and political lobbying the fewer the resources committed to research. By contrast, the more effective is social lobbying and the greater the social stratification created by it, the greater are the expected rewards from research and the resources devoted to it.

NOTES

*   We are grateful to Yadira Gonzales de Lara, Moshe Hazan, Alberto Niccoli, Erasmo Papagni, Earl Thompson and two anonymous referees for their very helpful comments and suggestions. All views expressed herein and all errors are our own.

1.   See also Kuznets (1968; 1972a).
2.   This strand of literature, started by the works of Parente and Prescott (1994) and Krusell and Rios-Rull (1996), was then developed in various directions by Acemoglu and Robinson (2000, 2002), Adamopoulus (2001), Hansen and Prescott (1998), Ngai (2000), Parente (2000), Parente and Prescott (1999, 2000), and Prescott (1998). Another chiefly empirical line of research, however, focuses on the effects that interest groups and policy distortions may have, modifying the relative price of investments, on the process of capital accumulation (Mankiw et al. 1992; Easterly, 1993; Jones, 1994; Chari et al. 1996; McGrattan and Schmitz, 1998; Restuccia and Urrutia, 2000; Restuccia, 2001).
3.   Without undertaking any welfare analysis, our model actually removes only the second assumption which is typical of technology adoption models with social barriers, namely the absence of firm-specific investments. For a model that analyses the role of institutions in the

presence of negative externalities tied to the introduction of innovations, see Carillo and Zazzaro (2000).

4. For a detailed review, see Thrupp (1963) and Black (1984).

5. In a companion paper we have analysed the process of professionalisation and the role of professional orders in economic growth (Carillo and Zazzaro, 2002).

6. Other strongly held opinions on the negative effect that the guilds had on economic growth in medieval Europe are expressed, amongst others, in Hobsbawm (1971), Pirenne (1933), Postan (1972) and Cipolla (1970).

7. This positive link between the constraints on the powers of guilds and economic prosperity has been underlined, amongst others, by Landes (1969), Mokyr (1990, 1993, 1994), Rosenberg and Birdzell (1986) and Van der Wee (1977).

8. '... the rights of individuals to use their personal efforts and property in trade and manufacturing without having to answer to their competitors' – Rosenberg and Birdzell (1986, p. 31) write – 'became embedded in English law. By the late eighteenth century, when the introduction of the factory system seriously disrupted some types of earlier handicraft production, there was rarely any way to prevent innovation except by force'.

9. 'The most significant premodern incentive for invention' – Epstein (1998, p. 704) writes – 'was thus the capacity to capture the rents provided by a technical secret; and the most effective source of these rents was the craft guilds'.

10. Of course, the link between the crowding of the guild and social prestige may hardly be considered univocal. Initially, the prestige of the guild will be enhanced as the number of masters belonging to it increases. In this phase the guild would not operate as a factor of inertia to technological change, as it has no interest in blocking the opening of new workshops. Hence, the model may be understood as an analysis of the role of guilds once the initial development phase is past.

11. It is worth noting that Parente (2001) criticises the interpretative capacity of neo-Schumpeterian growth models in that such models assume that each country is forced to produce innovations on its own behalf in order to introduce new products. In reality, what such models assume is only that the introduction of new products, whether it be the result of original innovation or only the adoption of technology already existing in other countries, requires firm-specific investments.

12. Formally:

$$\frac{\partial \ell_t^*}{\partial \beta} \geq 0 \quad \Leftrightarrow \quad \log\left(\frac{\beta S_m}{cA_t}\right) \geq -\frac{(1-\beta)^2}{\beta}.$$

13. Since Tullock's (1980) study, a large body of literature has developed on rent-seeking games. For a recent survey see Nitzan (1994).

14. This particular form of the success function has been used by Baik (1994).

15. For treatment of the rent-seeking game in a model *à la* Stackelberg, see Dixit (1987) and Pérez-Castrillo and Verdier (1992).

REFERENCES

Acemoglu, D. and J.A. Robinson (2000), 'Political losers as a barrier to economic development', *American Economic Review*, **90**, 126–30.

Acemoglu, D., S. Johnson and J.A. Robinson (2001), 'Reversal fortune: geography and institutions in the making of the modern world income distribution', *NBER Working Paper Series*, no. 8460, NBER.

Acemoglu, D. and J.A. Robinson (2002), 'Economic backwardness in political perspective', mimeo, MIT.

Adamapoulos, A.T. (2001), 'Barriers to development and special interests', manuscript, University of Toronto.

Aghion, P. and P. Howitt (1992), 'A model of growth through creative destruction', *Econometrica*, **60**, 323–51.

Aghion, P. and P. Howitt (1998), *Endogenous Growth Theory*, Cambridge, Massachusetts: MIT Press.

Baik, K.H. (1994), 'Effort levels in contests with two asymmetric players', *Southern Economic Journal*, **61**(2), 367–78.

Bellettini, G. and G.I.P. Ottaviano (1999), 'Special interests and technological change', *Working Paper*, no. 340/81, Università di Bologna.

Black, A. (1984), *Guilds and Civil Society in European Political Thought from the Twelfth Century to the Present*, London: Methuen & Co.

Carillo, M.R. and A. Zazzaro (2000), 'Innovation, human capital destruction and firms' investment in training', *Manchester School*, **68**(3), 331–48.

Carillo, M.R. and A. Zazzaro (2002), 'Professionalism and growth', in R. Balducci and S. Staffolani (eds), *Income Distribution, Growth and Unemployment*, Naples: ESI, pp. 209–21.

Chari, V.V., P.J. Kehoe and E.R. McGrattan (1996), 'The poverty of nations: a quantitative investigation', *Staff Report*, no. 204, Federal Reserve Bank of Minneapolis.

Cipolla, C.M. (1952), 'The decline of Italy: the case of a fully matured economy', *Economic History Review*, **5**(2), 178–87.

Cipolla, C.M. (1959), 'Il declino economico dell'Italia', in C.M. Cipolla, *Storia dell'economia italiana. Saggi di storia economica*, vol. I, Turin: Einaudi. Reprinted in C.M. Cipolla, *Le tre rivoluzioni e altri saggi di storia economica e sociale*, Bologna: Il Mulino, 1989, pp. 85–104.

Cipolla, C.M. (ed) (1970), *The Economic Decline of Empires*, London: Methuen & Co.

Dixit, A. (1987), 'Strategic behavior in contests', *American Economic Review*, **77**(5), 891–8.

Easterly, W. (1993), 'How much do distortions affect growth?', *Journal of Monetary Economics*, **32**(2), 187–212.

Epstein, S.R. (1998), 'Craft guilds, apprenticeship, and technological change in preindustrial Europe', *Journal of Economic History*, **58**(3), 684–713.

Fershtman, C. and J. Weiss (1993), 'Social status, culture and economic performance', *The Economic Journal*, **103**, 946–59.

Finley, M.I. (1973), *The Ancient Economy*, Los Angeles: University of California Press.

Greif, A., P. Milgrom and B.R. Weingast (1994), 'Coordination, commitment, and enforcement: the case of the merchant guild', *Journal of Political Economy*, **102**(4), 745–76.

Gustafsson, B. (1987), 'The rise and economic behaviour of medieval craft guilds: an economic-theoretical interpretation', *The Scandinavian Economic History Review*, **35**(1), 1–40.

Hall, R.E. and C.I. Jones (1999), 'Why do some countries produce so much more per worker than others', *Quarterly Journal of Economics*, **114**(1), 83–116.

Hansen, G.D. and E.C. Prescott (1998), 'Malthus to Solow', *NBER Working Paper Series*, no. 6858, NBER.

Hickson, C.R. and E.A. Thompson (1988), 'A new interpretation of guilds, tariffs, and laissez-faire', *Working Paper*, no. 461, UCLA.

Hickson, C.R. and E.A. Thompson (1991), 'A new theory of guilds and European economic development', *Explorations in Economic History*, **28**(1), 127–68.

Hobsbawm, E.F. (1971), *Primitive Rebels: Studies in Archaic Forms of Social Movement in the Nineteenth and Twentieth Centuries*, third edition, London: Norton.

Jones, C.I. (1994), 'Economic growth and the relative price of capital', *Journal of Monetary Economics*, **34**(3), 359–82.

Kellenbenz, H. (1977), 'The organizations of industrial production', in E.E. Rich and C.H. Wilson (eds), *The Cambridge Economic History of Europe*, vol. V, Cambridge: Cambridge University Press, pp. 462–548.

Krusell, P. and J. Rios-Rull (1996), 'Vested interests in a positive theory of stagnation and growth', *Review of Economic Studies*, **63**(3), 301–29.

Kuznets, S. (1968), *Towards a Theory of Economic Growth, with Reflections on Economic Growth of Modern Nations*, New York: W.W. Norton & Co.

Kuznets, S. (1972a), 'Innovations and adjustments in economic growth', *Swedish Journal of Economics*, **74**, 431–51.

Kuznets, S. (1972b), 'Modern economic growth: finding and reflexions', *American Economic Review*, **63**, 247–58.

Landes, D. (1969), *The Unbound Prometheus: Technological Change and Industrial Development in Western Europe from 1750 to the Present*, Cambridge: Cambridge University Press.

Larson Sarfatti, M. (1977), *The Rise of Professionalism: A Sociological Analysis*, Berkeley: University of California Press.

Mankiw, N.G., D. Romer and D.N. Weil (1992), 'A contribution to the empirics of economic growth', *Quarterly Journal of Economics*, **107**(2), 407–37.

McGrattan, E.R. and J.R. Schmitz Jr. (1998), 'Explaining cross-country income differences', *Research Department Staff Report*, no. 250, Federal Reserve Bank of Minneapolis.

Mokyr, J. (1990), *The Lever of Riches: Technological Creativity and Economic Progress*, New York: Oxford Economic Press.

Mokyr, J. (1993), 'Editor's introduction: the new economic history and the industrial revolution', in J. Mokyr (ed.), *The British Industrial Revolution: An Economic Perspective*, Boulder, Colorado: Westview Press, pp. 1–131.

Mokyr, J. (1994), 'Progress and inertia in technological change', in J.A James and M. Thomas (eds), *Capitalism in Context: Essays on Economic Development and Cultural Change in Honor of R.M. Hartwell*, Chicago: Chicago University Press, pp. 230–54.

Ngai, L.R. (2000), 'Barriers and the transition to modern growth', manuscript, University of Pennsylvania.

Nitzan, S. (1994), 'Modelling rent-seeking contests', *European Journal of Political Economy*, **10**(1), 41–60.

Olson, M. (1982), *The Rise and Decline of Nations*, New Haven, Connecticut and London: Yale University Press.

Parente, S.L. (2000), 'Landowners, vested interests, and the endogenous formation of industry insider groups', manuscript, University of Illinois, Urbana-Champaign.

Parente, S.L. (2001), 'The failure of endogenous growth', manuscript, University of Illinois, Urbana-Champaign.

Parente, S.L. and E.C. Prescott (1994), 'Barriers to technology adoption and development', *Journal of Political Economy*, **102**(2), 298–321.

Parente, S.L. and E.C. Prescott (1999), 'Monopoly rights: a barrier to riches', *American Economic Review*, **89**(5), 1216–33.

Parente, S.L. and E.C. Prescott (2000), *Barrier to Riches*, Cambridge, Massachusetts: MIT Press.

Pérez-Castrillo, J.D. and T. Verdier (1992), 'A general analysis of rent-seeking games', *Public Choice*, **73**(3), 335–50.

Persson, K.G. (1988), *Pre-industrial Economic Growth: Social Organization and Technological Progress in Europe*, Oxford: Blackwell.

Pfister, U. (1998), 'Craft guilds and proto-industrialization in Europe, 16th to 18th centuries', in S.R. Epstein, H.G. Haupt, C. Poni, H. Soly and C.E. Núñez (eds), *Guilds, Economy and Society*, Proceedings of the Twelfth International Economic History Congress, Madrid, session B1, Sevilla: Universidad de Sevilla, pp. 11–23.

Pirenne, H. (1933), *Economic and Social History of Medieval Europe*, New York: Harcourt Brace.

Poni, C. (1990), 'Per la storia del distretto industriale serico di Bologna (secoli XVI–XIX), *Quaderni Storici*, **25**(1), 93–167.

Postan, M.M. (1972), *The Medieval Economy and Society*, Los Angeles: University of California Press.

Prescott, E.C. (1988), 'Needed a theory of total factor productivity', *International Economic Review*, **39**(3), 525–51.

Restuccia, D. (2001), 'Barriers to capital accumulation in a model of technology adoption and schooling', manuscript, University of Toronto.

Restuccia, D. and C. Urrutia (2000), 'Relative prices and investment rates', *Journal of Monetary Economics*, **47**(1), 93–121.

Romer, P.M. (1990), 'Endogenous technological change', *Journal of Political Economy*, **98**(5), Part 2, S71–102.

Rosenberg, N. and L.E. Birdzell (1986), *How the West Grew Rich: The Economic Transformation of the Industrial World*, New York: Basic Books.

Schumpeter, J.A. (1934), *Theorie der Wirtschaftlichen Entwicklung*, fourth edition, Berlin: Duncker & Humblot.

Simonde de Sismondi, J.-C.-L. (1827), *Noveaux principes d'économie politique ou de la richesse dans ses rapports avec la population*, second edition, Paris: Treuttel and Würs.

Thompson, E.A. (1974), 'Taxation and national defense', *Journal of Political Economy*, **82**(4), 755–82.

Thompson, E.A. (1979), 'An economic basis for the "national defense argument" for aiding certain industries', *Journal of Political Economy*, **87**(1), 1–36.

Thrupp, S. (1963), 'The gilds', in M.M. Postan, E.E. Rich and E. Miller (eds), *The Cambridge Economic History of Europe, Volume III: Economic Organization and Policies in the Middle Ages*, Cambridge: Cambridge University Press, pp. 230–80.

Tullock, G. (1980), 'Efficient rent seeking', in J.M. Buchanan, R.D. Tollison and G. Tullock (eds), *Towards a Theory of the Rent-seeking Society*, College Station: Texas A.M. University Press, pp. 97–112.

Van der Wee, H. (1977), 'Money, credit, and banking systems', in E.E. Rich and C.H. Wilson (eds), *The Cambridge Economic History of Europe*, vol. V, Cambridge: Cambridge University Press, pp. 290–393.

Weiss, J. and C. Fershtman (1998), 'Social status and economic performance: a survey', *European Economic Review*, **42**, 801–20.

15. Effective demand and growth in a one-sector Keynesian model[*]

Nelson H. Barbosa-Filho

15.1. INTRODUCTION

Income growth is fundamentally a supply phenomenon in mainstream economic theory. Little or no attention is paid to demand on the assumption that income always converges to its potential level, which is tautologically defined by the long-run trend of income itself through some *ad hoc* assumptions about the equilibrium levels of employment, capacity utilization, and multifactor productivity.[1] In fact, given the growth of the labour force and the optimal propensity to save, technological change explains long-run growth variations in mainstream models and, since the seminal work of Romer (1986), the 'new growth theory' developed into a series of models that make productivity growth endogenous. Fair but not enough.

The history of capitalist economies indicates that demand has an important role in explaining growth. The so-called 'short-run' growth variations caused by demand may actually involve several years and have permanent effects in the long run. More importantly, mapping input and productivity indexes to income *ex post* does not explain fully what causes income *ex ante*. One of the central ideas of Keynes's *General Theory* is that, in capitalist economies, one does not necessarily produce what one can in capitalist economies, but actually what one expects to sell at a profit. Mainstream growth theory offers us a good analysis of how inputs can be combined to attend demand but, to understand the latter, we have to look elsewhere.

Keynesian economists tend to put demand at the centre of their growth theories. The labels and models vary across authors but the unifying principle is the same: aggregate demand determines aggregate income in capitalist economies, both in nominal and real terms. Based on this principle and building upon the structuralist models of Taylor (1991), this chapter presents a one-sector model where autonomous expenditures drive growth and determine the level of economic activity and income distribution.[2] The aim is to investigate under which conditions growth can be demand-led and stable.

The other sections of this chapter are organized as follows. Section 15.2 presents the basic assumptions and definitions of the model. Section 15.3 analyses the alternative closures of the investment function. Section 15.4 presents a 2 × 2 dynamical model of demand-led growth. Section 15.5 concludes the analysis with a summary of the main points of this chapter.

15.2. BASIC ASSUMPTIONS AND DEFINITIONS

Consider a one-sector economy where real income can be expressed as:

$$Q = C + I + A, \tag{15.1}$$

where Q is income, C the part of consumption induced by income, I investment, and A the non-capital autonomous expenditures, that is, net exports plus autonomous consumption. Government expenditures are implicit in the three demand categories and imports of goods different than the domestic one do not enter in the identity because they are not produced locally.[3]

Assuming that $C = (1-s)Q$ is a function of Q, (15.1) can be rewritten as:

$$Q = \frac{I + A}{s}, \tag{15.2}$$

where, for simplicity, s is a constant positive parameter between zero and one.[4] In growth terms we have:

$$q = \theta i + (1-\theta)a, \tag{15.3}$$

where by definition $\theta = [I/(I + A)]$ and q, i, and a are the exponential growth rates of Q, I, and A, respectively.

It is straightforward that the θ ratio is itself a function of i and a since:

$$\frac{d\theta}{dt} = \theta(1-\theta)(i-a) \tag{15.4}$$

and, therefore:

$$\theta = \frac{1}{1 + \chi \exp[(a-i)t]}, \tag{15.5}$$

where t is time, and χ is a constant given by the initial value of θ.[5]

Combining (15.3) with (15.5) we have three cases:

(a)   when $i = a$, the growth rate of income is stable;
(b)   when $i > a$, the growth rate of income converges to the growth rate of investment; and
(c)   when $i < a$, the growth rate of income converges to the growth rate of non-capital autonomous expenditures and remains permanently above the growth rate of investment.

Thus, in cases (a) and (b), the growth rates of income and capital tend to the same value at the steady state and, therefore, the economy tends to a stable income/capital ratio. In contrast, income grows faster than capital at the steady state of case (c) and, therefore, the economy tends to an infinite income/capital ratio. Given that capitalist economies display stable income/capital ratios, the latter is just a mathematical possibility with no economic sense. The sensible economic case is for i and a to fluctuate around the same value.

Now, since A was defined to include non-capital expenditures not induced by income, assume that its growth rate is an exogenous variable. The intuition is that A depends on factors such as discretionary macroeconomic policy, wars, speculative booms and busts and so on, so that it can be considered exogenous in the context under analysis.

The natural question at this point becomes whether and how the growth rate of investment converges to the growth rate of non-capital expenditures? To answer it, let u be the income/capital ratio and k the exponential growth rate of the capital stock.[6] Assuming for simplicity that there is no capital depreciation:

$$k = su - h, \tag{15.6}$$

where h is the ratio of autonomous expenditures to the capital stock, that is, the share of the capital stock 'wasted' (not accumulated) to attend net exports and autonomous consumption.[7]

Given that s is constant, $u = (k + h)/s$ and, therefore, the dynamics of h and k determine the evolution of u. If we assume that investment is a function of u,[8] the dynamics of h and k also determine the evolution of i and, consequently, the stability of demand-led growth depends on the joint dynamics of these variables. More formally, note that by definition: .

$$\frac{dh}{dt} = h(a - k) \quad \text{and} \tag{15.7}$$

$$\frac{dk}{dt} = k(i - k). \tag{15.8}$$

Not surprisingly, a non-trivial stationary solution occurs when $a = k = i$ and, given that a is exogenous, the stability of h and k depends crucially on the derivative of i in relation to u. In other words, the stability of demand-led growth depends on how investment responds to changes in the income/capital ratio.

15.3. THE INVESTMENT FUNCTION

In the previous section we assumed that investment is a function of the income/capital ratio. The reason is that investment tends to be a function of the rate of profit, which in its turn tends to be affected by the level of economic activity. Using the income/capital ratio as a proxy of the latter,[9] we can then express investment as a function of the income/capital ratio or, in terms of the growth model of the previous section, the growth rate of investment as a function of the income/capital ratio.

Formally, let r be the rate of profit, in the simple one-sector context under analysis:

$$r = \left(1 - \frac{W}{B}\right)u, \tag{15.9}$$

where W is the real wage and B the income/labour ratio, that is, the average labour productivity.

Notwithstanding the Capital Critique, it is common to assume that investment is a positive function of the rate of profit in Keynesian models and we shall follow this assumption here.[10] However, since the rate of profit is itself a function of the income/capital ratio, this does not tell us whether investment is a positive or negative function of the income/capital ratio. In short, the sign of the derivative of investment in relation to u depends on the sign of the derivative of r in relation to u. The intuition is that the real wage and labour productivity may also be affected by the level of economic activity, so that the rate of profit may be either a positive or negative function of the income/capital ratio.

In terms of the model of section one, assume that $i = i(r)$ is a function of r with $di/dr > 0$. Since $r = r(W, B, u)$ is a function of W, B, and u and assuming that $W = W(u)$ and $B = B(U)$ are also functions of u:

$$\frac{di}{du} = \frac{di}{dr}\frac{dr}{du} = \frac{di}{dr}\left[\left(1 - \frac{W}{B}\right) - \frac{W}{B}(\eta_W^u - \eta_B^u)\right]. \tag{15.10}$$

where naturally $\eta_W^u = (W/u)(dW/du)$ and $\eta_B^u = (B/u)(dB/du)$ are the 'u-elasticity' of the real wage and labour productivity, respectively.

Given the assumption that i is a positive function of r and the fact that the labour share of income (W/A) is a variable between zero and one, the sign of (15.10) depends on how the real wage and labour productivity respond to variations in the income/capital ratio. In Keynesian models we find two alternative closures for each issue.

First, regarding the u-elasticity of the real wage, we have either $\eta_W^u < 0$ according to Kaldor's (1955–56) demand theory of income distribution or $\eta_W^u > 0$ according to Keynesian variants of the Marxian reserve army assumption. In general terms and assuming that prices and wages are both pro-cyclical variables, the Kaldorian closure implies that prices are more responsive to business fluctuations than wages, whereas the Marxian closure implies the opposite. Given that both closures tend to be based on a theory of class conflict, the fundamental difference lies on the impact of business fluctuations on the power structure of capitalist economies. Since this is an empirical question, we cannot rule out any closure a priori.

Second, regarding the u-elasticity of labour productivity, we have either $\eta_B^u < 0$ according to the neoclassical foundations of some Keynesian models or $\eta_B^u > 0$ according to some Keynesian variants of Smith's assumption of increasing returns. The neoclassical closure is based on the assumption that labour productivity is a positive function of the capital/labour ratio, which in turn is a negative function of the level of economic activity. In contrast, the 'Smithian' closure is based on the assumption that an increase in the level of economic activity leads to scale and learning economies and, in this way, results in an increase in labour productivity. The difference lies in the specification of the production function and, similar to what happens with the u-elasticity of the real wage, we cannot rule out any alternative a priori.

Note that, even if we could determine the sign of η_W^u and η_B^u a priori, we still might not be able to determine the sign of (15.10) because this also depends on the magnitude of the elasticity parameters. In fact, only in the event of a 'Kaldorian' real wage and 'Smithian' labour productivity can we say for sure that (15.10) is positive.

15.4.   THE DYNAMICS OF DEMAND-LED GROWTH

In Section 15.2 we defined the dynamics of the ratio of non-capital expenditures to capital h and the growth rate of capital k in terms of the growth rates of investment i and non-capital expenditures a. Assuming that the latter is an exogenously variable, in Section 15.3 we analysed how the growth rate of investment i may be affected by the income/capital ratio u. The remaining task is to put the two together and analyse the dynamics of demand-led growth.

First, as usual when dealing with nonlinear models, assume that there exists at least one non-trivial equilibrium point (h^*, k^*), with both variables positive. The reason is that the income/capital ratio, the marginal propensity to save, and the growth rate of capital stock tend to be stationary variables in capitalist economies.

Second, let $h_d = h - h^*$ and $k_d = k - k^*$ measure the deviation from such an equilibrium point. The linearized version of (15.7) and (15.8) is thus:

$$
\begin{bmatrix} \dfrac{dh_d}{dt} \\[2mm] \dfrac{dk_d}{dt} \end{bmatrix} = \begin{bmatrix} 0 & -h^* \\[2mm] k^*\left(\dfrac{\partial i}{\partial h}\right) & k^*\left(\dfrac{\partial i}{\partial k} - 1\right) \end{bmatrix} \begin{bmatrix} h_d \\[2mm] k_d \end{bmatrix}
\tag{15.11}
$$

and the stability conditions are:

$$
k^*\left(\frac{\partial i}{\partial k} - 1\right) < 0 \quad \text{and} \tag{15.12}
$$

$$
kh^* \frac{\partial i}{\partial h} > 0. \tag{15.13}
$$

To analyse the economic meaning of the above, note that since $u = (h + k)/s$ and $i = i(u)$ is a function of u,

$$
\frac{\partial i}{\partial h} = \frac{di}{du}\frac{du}{dh} = \frac{di}{du}\frac{1}{s}. \tag{15.14}
$$

By analogy, $\partial i/\partial k = (di/du)(1/s)$ and, not surprisingly, the stability of the system boils down to how the growth rate of investment reacts to changes in the level of economic activity.

Using the stability conditions as a guide, we have three possible cases, namely:

(a) $di/du < 0$: the equilibrium point is a saddle point, as shown in Figure 15.1;

(b) $0 < di/du < s$: the equilibrium point is a stable node or focus, as shown in Figure 15.2; and

(c) $di/du > s$: the equilibrium points is an unstable node or focus, as shown in Figure 15.3.

In other words, zero and the marginal propensity to save are the critical values for the derivative of the investment function in relation to the income/capital ratio.[11]

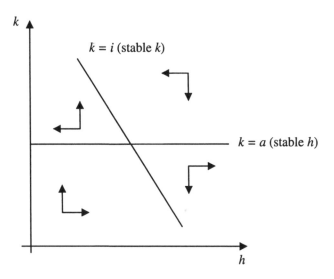

Figure 15.1 – Phase diagram of h *and* k *about a saddle point*

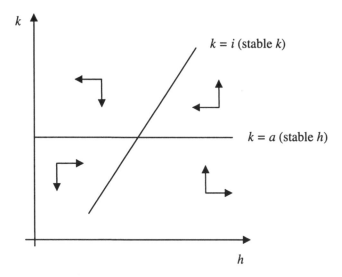

Figure 15.2   Phase diagram of h *and* k *about a stable node or focus*

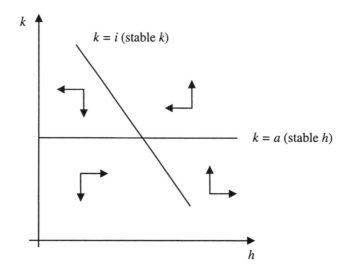

Figure 15.3   Phase diagram of h *and* k *about an unstable node or focus*

Considering the economic meaning of each case separately, case (*a*) occurs when an increase in the level of economic activity leads to a substantial increase in the labour share and, in this way, reduces the rate of profit. The result is a potentially unstable system since, only for shocks along the equilibrium path, will the state variables be stationary.

By analogy, case (*c*) occurs when an increase in the level of economic activity leads to a substantial increase in the rate of profit and, through this, increases the growth rate of investment. The result is an unstable system where investment feeds back into itself along the lines analysed by Harrod (1939).

Finally, case (*b*) occurs when there exists an accelerator mechanism of income on investment ($di/du > 0$), but such a mechanism is not strong enough ($di/du < s$) to produce the 'knife-edge' dynamics of case (*c*). In this context, growth is demand-led and stable, that is, exogenous changes in the growth rate of investment and non-capital autonomous expenditures lead to stable growth fluctuations.

To illustrate the above point, consider an increase in the exogenous component of the growth rate of investment, as shown in Figure 15.4.[12] The 'stable-*k*' line moves up and the short-run result is growth fluctuations while the economy converges to its new steady state. The long-run result is a reduction in *h* with no change in the growth rate of income.

By analogy, an increase in the growth rate of autonomous expenditures moves the 'stable-*h*' line up, as shown in Figure 15.5. The short-run result is also growth fluctuations but, in contrast to the previous example, the long-run result is an increase in both *h* and *k*. In other words, autonomous expenditures drive income growth in the case (*b*).[13]

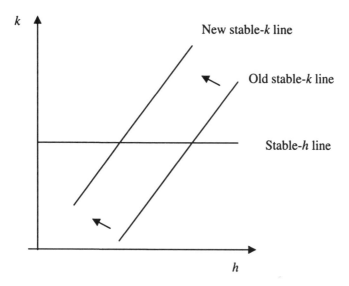

Figure 15.4   Impact of an increase in the exogenous components of the growth rate of investment

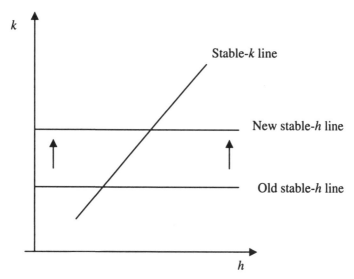

Figure 15.5   Impact of an increase in the growth rate of autonomous expenditures

Since $u = (h + k)/s$, in both cases the income/capital ratio adjusts to the new steady state. In Figure 15.4 u falls because h falls and, in Figure 15.5, u increases because both h and k increase.

The remaining question relates to the feasibility of the equilibrium point since supply constraints necessarily impose an upper bound on the income/capital ratio. Using (15.6) to represent this, let u_{MAX} be the maximum income/capital ratio allowed by the current technology. Figure 15.6 shows the feasible region for the state variables.

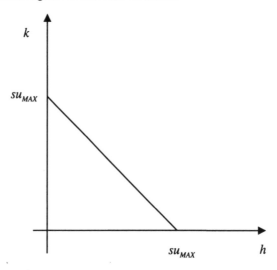

Figure 15. 6   The 'hk' frontier

As long as the economy remains below its 'hk' frontier, growth may be demand-led and stable. Once the economy reaches that frontier, growth is supply constrained and, therefore, determined by the usual factors analysed by mainstream theory. Whether the maximum income/capital ratio is itself a function of the level of economic activity depends on the assumptions implicit in the production function.[14]

15.5.   CONCLUSION

The supply emphasis of mainstream growth theory does not preclude an analysis of demand-led growth. In fact, mainstream growth theory tells us how income is generated to attend aggregate demand with little or no attention to the determinants of aggregate demand itself. One of the aims of Keynesian growth models is precisely to analyse the latter and, as we saw in the previous sections, demand-led growth is consistent with a stable income/capital ratio, provided that investment is a positive function of the level economic activity and does not show unstable dynamics *à la* Harrod (1939). In this context, waves of demand expansion and capital accumulation are represented by exogenous changes in the growth rate of investment and non-capital autonomous expenditures, with the level of economic activity and income distribution following residually. Depending on the growth rate of effective demand, the model of this chapter shows how a one-sector economy may be either at 'slow-growth' or 'fast-growth' equilibrium.

NOTES

*   The author would like to thank Amitava Dutt, Duncan Foley, Eugene Canjels, Lance Taylor, Tony Thirlwall, Gennaro Zezza, and two anonymous referees for their comments and suggestions. The usual disclaimer applies.

1. For an example of the assumptions implicit in estimates of potential income, see Clark (1979) and Congressional Budget Office (1995).

2. The choice of one sector aims to capture the most intuitive aspects of Keynesian growth models. For a multi-sector analysis, see, for instance, Kurz (1985).

3. The implicit simplifying assumption is either that imports are just for consumption or that there is just one good in the world economy. In the first case capital accumulation is not directly affected by imports, whereas in the second case trade surpluses or deficits are included in A.

4. For the case where s is a function of income distribution, see Barbosa-Filho (2001).

5. Let $\theta(0)$ be the value of θ when $t = 0$, from (5) $\chi = (1-\theta(0))/\theta(0)$.

6. Formally, $u = Q/K$, and $k = (dK/dt)(1/K)$, where K is the capital stock.

7. Formally, $h = A/K$. Note that (15.6) is nothing more than an extension of Harrod's (1939) growth identity to include autonomous expenditures since, to obtain it, one just has to normalize $(dK/dt) = Q - C - A$ by K and use the assumption that $C = (1 - s)Q$.

8. This assumption will be analysed in Section 15.3.

9. The implicit assumption is that capital tends to be the relatively scarce factor in capitalist economies, so that the income/capital ratio is a better proxy of the level of economic activity than the rate of employment.

10. As we will see in Section 15.4, the Capital Critique can be incorporated in the possible dynamical configurations without loss of generality.

11. If we acknowledge the Capital Critique and include the possibility of $di/dr < 0$, we still have the same three dynamical configurations.

12. More formally, let $i = \gamma + \zeta u$ be a linear function of u. Figure 15.4 illustrates the impact of an increase in γ.

13. Note that, obviously, this comes from the assumption that a is constant. When a is a function of u we have the most general system, that is, a system where investment and autonomous expenditures drive income growth. The choice of a to be the driving force aims to emphasize the often ignored case where growth can be stable and yet completely driven by exogenous demand.

14. Post-Keynesian models are usually based on a Leontief production function, according to which the maximum income/capital ratio is an exogenous parameter. In contrast, in a Cobb–Douglas function the maximum income/capital ratio tends to be a negative function of the effective income/capital ratio, as shown in Barbosa-Filho (2001).

REFERENCES

Barbosa-Filho, N.H. (2001), 'Effective demand and growth: an analysis of the alternative closures of Keynesian models', *CEPA Working Paper* 2001–05, New School University.

Clark, P.K. (1979), 'Potential GNP in the United States: 1948–80', *Review of Wealth and Income*, **25**(2), 141–65.

Congressional Budget Office (1995), *CBO's Method for Estimating Potential Output*, Washington, DC: Congressional Budget Office.

Harrod, R. (1939), 'An essay on dynamic theory', *Economic Journal*, **49**, 14–33.

Kaldor, N. (1955–56), 'Alternative theories of distribution', *Review of Economic Studies*, **23**, 83–100.

Kurz, H.D. (1985), 'Effective demand in a "classical" model of value and distribution: the multiplier in a Sraffian framework', *Manchester School of Economic and Social Studies*, **53**(2), 121–37.

Romer, P. (1986), 'Increasing returns and long-run growth', *Journal of Political Economy*, October, 1002–37.

Taylor, L. (1991), *Income Distribution, Inflation, and Growth: Lectures on Structuralist Macroeconomic Theory*, Cambridge, Massachusetts: MIT Press.

16. Neo-Kaleckian growth dynamics and the state of long-run expectations: wage- versus profit-led growth reconsidered*

Mark Setterfield

16.1. INTRODUCTION

The neo-Kaleckian model is an established framework for studying the determinants of long-run macroeconomic outcomes in an environment in which effective demand matters. In neo-Kaleckian theory, growth is demand-led because the rates of accumulation, utilisation and profit are all influenced by an independent (of saving behaviour) investment function, even in the long run.

There exist numerous investigations of the structure of the neo-Kaleckian model, its properties and the results associated with it.[1] Little attention has been paid to the importance of historical time and uncertainty in neo-Kaleckian growth dynamics, however, despite explicit acknowledgement that both are part of the fabric of the economy that neo-Kaleckians are modelling (see, for example, Lavoie, 1992, pp. 282–4). As a result, discussions of changes in the state of long-run expectations (SOLE) and the influence that these may have on the rates of accumulation, utilisation and profits, are largely absent from the neo-Kaleckian growth literature.

The purpose of this chapter, then, is twofold. First, variations in the SOLE are introduced into the adjustment dynamics of neo-Kaleckian growth theory. This transforms the canonical neo-Kaleckian model from a traditional equilibrium model (in which equilibrium outcomes are defined and reached independently of the path taken towards them) into one in which outcomes are path-dependent and the rate of growth is conceived as being determined by sequential processes unfolding in historical time. It is shown that this model is capable of generating growth cycles rather than a steady-state growth rate (as in the canonical model).

Second, one of the main results of neo-Kaleckian growth theory – the paradox of costs, according to which increases in wages raise the rates of accumulation, utilisation and profits – is re-examined. The sensitivity of this result to the precise form of the investment function is well known (Bhaduri and Marglin, 1990; Marglin and Bhaduri, 1990; Lavoie, 1992; Blecker, 2002). The purpose here is to rethink the question as to whether growth is wage-led or profit-led in light of the assumed variability in firms' SOLE. In particular, it is shown that in the wage-led growth environment of the canonical neo-Kaleckian model, the potential for changes in the state of long-run expectations makes it harder to generate faster growth by redistributing income towards wages, but reinforces the negative growth consequences of redistributions towards profits. This suggests that the variability of firms' SOLE makes it harder to increase and easier to decrease the growth rate through the redistribution of income.

The remainder of the chapter is organised as follows. Section 16.2 describes the canonical neo-Kaleckian model and its results. Section 16.3 introduces variability in the SOLE to the adjustment dynamics of this model, with the result that growth cycles can emerge. In Section 16.4, the impact of changes in the SOLE on the wage-led growth result of the canonical model is investigated. Finally, Section 16.5 offers some conclusions.

16.2. THE CANONICAL NEO-KALECKIAN MODEL

Modern neo-Kaleckian growth models share important characteristics with the Cambridge growth theory of the 1950s and 1960s (see especially Robinson 1956, 1962). However, a crucial difference between these strands of post-Keynesian growth theory is their treatment of the rate of capacity utilisation. In neo-Kaleckian theory, the rate of capacity utilisation is treated as being variable even in the long run, and as exerting an influence on investment activity that operates independently of its influence on investment via the rate of profit.[2] The earliest formulations of models exhibiting these characteristics are usually attributed to Del Monte (1975), Rowthorn (1981) and Dutt (1984), from which the contemporary neo-Kaleckian growth literature has subsequently developed.[3] Discussion and debate within this literature revolves around what can be described (following Lavoie, 1992, Ch. 6) as a canonical neo-Kaleckian growth model, of the form:

$$g^s = s_\Pi r \tag{16.1}$$

$$g^i = \gamma + g_u u^e + g_r r^e \tag{16.2}$$

$$r = \frac{\pi u}{v} \tag{16.3}$$

$$g^s = g^i \tag{16.4}$$

$$r_t^e = r_{t-1} \tag{16.5}$$

$$u_t^e = u_{t-1}, \tag{16.6}$$

where g^s is the rate of growth of savings and g^i the rate of accumulation, s_Π is the propensity to save out of profits, $\gamma > 0$ is the rate of accumulation that occurs regardless of expected utilisation and profitability, r and r^e are the actual and expected rates of profit respectively, u and u^e are the actual and expected rates of capacity utilisation, π is the profit share of income and v is the full capacity capital/output ratio. Both v and the corresponding labour/output ratio are treated as fixed. That is, production is implicitly modelled in terms of a Leontieff production function. Equation (16.1) is the Cambridge equation describing the rate of growth of savings as a function of the rate of profit and the propensity to save out of profits, while equation (16.2) describes the rate of accumulation as an increasing function of the expected rates of capacity utilisation and profits. Equation (16.3) is true by definition (on which, see endnote 2), while equation (16.4) insists that the rate of growth of savings is always equal to the rate of growth of investment.[4] Finally, equations (16.5) and (16.6) describe the adjustment of expectations between periods.[5]

The model above yields the following steady-state solutions for the rates of growth and capacity utilisation respectively:

$$g^* = \frac{s_\Pi \pi \gamma}{\pi(s_\Pi - g_r) - g_u v} \tag{16.7}$$

$$u^* = \frac{v\gamma}{\pi(s_\Pi - g_r) - g_u v}. \tag{16.8}$$

These solutions are positive and stable as long as their common denominator is positive, or in other words, as long as $s_\Pi > g_u(v/\pi) + g_r$. This stability condition has the straightforward and familiar interpretation that the growth of saving is more responsive to changes in the rate of capacity utilisation than the growth of investment. Moreover, differentiating equations (16.7) and (16.8) with respect to π reveals two of the central results of the canonical neo-Kaleckian growth model:

$$\frac{\partial g^*}{\partial \pi} = \frac{-s_\Pi \gamma g_u v}{(\pi(s_\Pi - g_r) - g_u v)^2} < 0 \qquad (16.9)$$

$$\frac{\partial u^*}{\partial \pi} = \frac{-v\gamma(s_\Pi - g_r)}{(\pi(s_\Pi - g_r) - g_u v)^2} < 0. \qquad (16.10)$$

Equation (16.10) states that the canonical model is stagnationist: increases in the profit share (i.e., reductions in real wages) depress the utilisation rate.[6] Meanwhile, equation (16.9) demonstrates that the model displays wage-led growth: increases in the profit share (i.e., reductions in real wages) depress the rate of growth.

16.3. NEO-KALECKIAN GROWTH DYNAMICS AND THE STATE OF LONG-RUN EXPECTATIONS

A central feature of the canonical neo-Kaleckian growth model is the investment function in equation (16.2). The precise form of this investment function has been the subject of considerable debate, not least since the claim of Bhaduri and Marglin (1990) and Marglin and Bhaduri (1990) that it overstates the influence of the rate of capacity utilisation on the rate of accumulation.[7] Against this, neo-Kaleckians have responded that Bhaduri and Marglin's preferred investment function overstates the influence of the profit share (as opposed to the profit rate) on accumulation and yields results that are sensitive to the choice of functional form, while the canonical neo-Kaleckian investment function better fits the stylised facts of firm behaviour and macroeconomic outcomes (Lavoie, 1992, pp. 332–44; Mott and Slattery, 1994; Blecker, 2002, pp. 5–12).

The purpose of this and the following section is to draw attention to a different feature of equation (16.2) and its implications for neo-Kaleckian growth dynamics. As discussed by Robinson (1962), Asimakopulos (1991, Ch. 8) and Lavoie (1992, p. 286), the structure of this investment function is properly conceived as being determined by a given state of long-run expectations (SOLE), in an environment in which decisions are made sequentially in historical time and expectations are formed under conditions of fundamental uncertainty. However, the canonical neo-Kaleckian growth model is usually presented as a traditional equilibrium model, describing the existence and stability of equilibrium rates of accumulation, utilisation and profit determined by exogenously given data. It is not obvious that this methodology is consistent with the view that the structure of the investment function in equation (16.2) is influenced by firms' SOLE, and that macrodynamic processes occur in historical time (Asimakopulos, 1991, Ch. 8). Why, for example, should the given SOLE that is assumed to inform the structure of equation (16.2) remain unchanging in response to disequilibrium adjustments, or even the repeated realisation of equilibrium outcomes? Moreover, no account is taken of the potential variability of the SOLE and its impact on the structure of the investment function when comparative dynamic exercises are performed using the canonical neo-Kaleckian model.

It is important to note that these objections have been addressed (in part) by Lavoie (1992, pp. 282–5). Following Kregel (1976), Lavoie argues that post-Keynesians need reject neither the notion of equilibrium nor the techniques of equilibrium analysis when modelling economic outcomes, as long as the distinct (from both the classical and neoclassical approaches) methodological features of post-Keynesian economics, which advise both the use and interpretation of these concepts and techniques, are properly understood. This is precisely the position of the current author on this matter (Setterfield, 1997).[8] However, just as post-Keynesians need not *dispense* with equilibrium and equilibrium analysis, nor need they *confine* themselves to this set of modelling techniques. Indeed, given the post-Keynesian emphasis on the importance of historical time and uncertainty, it is hard to see why they should want to do so. Moreover, Lavoie's response does not address the neglect of variations in the SOLE and its impact on the structure of the investment function in neo-Kaleckian comparative dynamics. In sum, there is reason to believe that post-Keynesians should seek to transcend the equilibrist methodology that advises the canonical neo-Kaleckian model, and take account of the potential variability of the SOLE in comparative dynamic exercises whenever an equilibrium framework is utilised.

To see how the first of these objectives might be realised, consider again the canonical neo-Kaleckian model in equations (16.1)–(16.6). Suppose now that we rewrite equation (16.2) as:

$$g^i = \gamma(\alpha_i) + g_u u^e + g_r r^e. \tag{16.2a}$$

In equation (16.2a), the first term in equation (16.2) has been re-written as $\gamma = \gamma(\alpha_i)$, where α_i denotes the SOLE. In other words, γ is now to be interpreted, not as a constant, but as a shift parameter which varies with the SOLE. Introducing the SOLE in this fashion is consistent with the distinction that is made in theories of decision making under uncertainty between agents' forecasts of the future (as captured by the variables u^e and r^e in equation (16.2a)) and their propensity to act on the basis of these forecasts (see, for example, Gerrard, 1995). It is also consistent with traditional neo-Kaleckian interpretations of the coefficients of equation (16.2) as being determined by firms' animal spirits (see, for example, Lavoie, 1992, p. 286).[9]

Combining equations (16.1), (16.2a), (16.3), (16.5) and (16.6) yields the following reduced-form neo-Kaleckian model:[10]

$$g_t^s = \frac{s_\Pi \pi}{v} u_t \tag{16.11}$$

$$g_t^i = \gamma(\alpha_t) + g_u u_{t-1} + g_r \frac{\pi}{v} u_{t-1}. \tag{16.12}$$

By substituting equation (16.11) into (16.12) and using (16.4), the model can be summarised as the first order difference equation:

$$g_t^i = \gamma(\alpha_t) + \frac{1}{s_\Pi} \left(\frac{g_u v}{\pi} + g_r \right) g_{t-1}^i. \tag{16.13}$$

It is now obvious that the model is underdetermined – nothing can be said about the behaviour of g_t^i in equation (16.13) without we first describe the behaviour of α_t. Suppose, then, that the behaviour of α_t is described as follows:

$$\alpha_t = \alpha_t(u_{t-1}, u_{t-1}^e). \tag{16.14}$$

Equation (16.14) is rendered explicit in Table 16.1 below, wherein the conditions under which α will be revised from one period to the next are described.[11]

Table 16.1 Revisions in the SOLE in response to disappointed expectations

Nature of disappointment	Value of α_t
$u_{t-1} - u_{t-1}^e \geq c$	
$u_{t-1} - u_{t-1}^e > -c$ and $u_{t-2} - u_{t-2}^e \leq -c$	$\alpha_t = \alpha_{t-1} + \varepsilon_t$
$u_{t-1} - u_{t-1}^e \leq -c$	
$u_{t-1} - u_{t-1}^e < c$ and $u_{t-2} - u_{t-2}^e \geq c$	$\alpha_t = \alpha_{t-1} - \varepsilon_t$

In Table 16.1, c is a conventional value that is assumed constant for purposes of analytical convenience, while $\varepsilon_t \sim (\mu_{\varepsilon_t}, \sigma_{\varepsilon_t}^2)$, In other words, any change in the SOLE between periods is based on a draw from a distribution with time-dependent moments – a representation that is intended to capture conventional decision making in the presence of effective choice.[12] Hence the mean of this distribution, μ_{ε_t}, represents the conventional reaction of decision makers to disappointed expectations. Because conventions do not completely determine behaviour, however, it is assumed that the precise value of ε can differ from μ_{ε_t} at any given point in time, so that $\sigma_{\varepsilon_t}^2 \neq 0$. Meanwhile, although conventions are relatively enduring, they do not persist indefinitely. Nor, in an environment of effective choice, need the precise pattern of deviance from the convention μ_{ε_t} (as captured by $\sigma_{\varepsilon_t}^2$) remain constant. As such, the moments of the distribution of γ are time-dependent. Moreover, by hypothesis, changes in these moments cannot be described a priori. This follows from the assumption of effective choice, according to which the objects of choice (such as conventional behaviours) can change in novel ways. The system summarised in equations (16.13) and (16.14) remains, therefore, formally open.

Table 16.1 suggests that the revision of the SOLE between periods is a function of the discrepancy between the actual and expected rate of capacity utilisation in the previous period (which, if non-zero, will also result in a discrepancy between the actual and expected rate of profit – see equation (16.3)). Specifically, the SOLE improves if the difference between the actual and expected utilisation rates equals or exceeds the conventional value c, or if this difference exceeds $-c$ having failed to exceed this value in the period before last. Similarly, the SOLE deteriorates if the difference between the actual and expected rates of capacity utilisation is equal to or less than $-c$, or if this difference falls below c having equalled or exceeded this value in the period before last.

Because they describe an open system, it is not possible to portray the growth outcomes arising from equations (16.13) and (16.14) in terms of a traditional, determinate equilibrium, which can be defined and reached independently of the path taken towards it. The recursive interaction of these equations can be used to describe path-dependent growth outcomes, however. To see this, suppose that $u_1^e = u_0$ initially, and that the resulting rate of accumulation in equation (16.12), $g_1^i = \gamma(\alpha_1) + g_u u_0 + g_r(\pi/v)u_0$, gives rise to an actual rate of capacity utilisation u_1 in equation (16.11) such that $u_1 - u_0 = k_1 > c$. This is illustrated in Figure 16.1.

In response to these initial conditions, two things will happen to the rate of accumulation. First, as the expected rate of capacity utilisation is revised upwards on the basis of equation (16.6), the rate of accumulation will increase as a result of 'movement along' the g^i schedule in equation (16.12).

This is captured in Figure 16.1 by the increase in g from g_1 to g'. *Ceteris paribus*, repeated adjustments of this nature would result in convergence towards the sort of steady-state outcome described in equation (16.7). But other things are not equal: a second change in the rate of accumulation will result from a shift in the g^i schedule in equation (16.12) in response to a revision in the SOLE ($\alpha_2 = \alpha_1 + \varepsilon_2$), as described in equation (16.14) and Table 16.1. This second adjustment is captured by the increase in g from g' to g_2 in Figure 16.1.

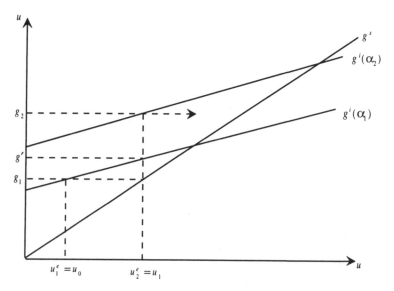

Note: $u_1 - u_0 = k_1 > c$

Figure 16.1 Adjustment dynamics in a neo-Kaleckian model in which the state of long-run expectations is variable

In order to further describe the behaviour of the rate of accumulation at this point, we need to know whether or not:

$$u_2 - u_1 \geq c = (u_1 - u_0) - k_1 + c$$

or:

$$\Delta u_2 - \Delta u_1 \geq -(k_1 - c). \tag{16.15}$$

We know that $\Delta u_1 = k_1$ by hypothesis. Meanwhile, substituting equation (16.11) into equation (16.12) on the basis of equation (16.4) and evaluating the result, we arrive at:

$$u_2 = \frac{v\gamma(\alpha_2)}{s_\Pi \pi} + \frac{v}{s_\Pi \pi}\left(g_u - g_r\frac{\pi}{v}\right)u_1,$$

from which it follows that:

$$\Delta u_2 = \frac{v}{s_\Pi \pi}\gamma'\varepsilon_2 + \frac{v}{s_\Pi \pi}\left(g_u - g_r\frac{\pi}{v}\right)k_1,$$

where $\gamma' = d\gamma/d\alpha$ and $\varepsilon_2 = \alpha_2 - \alpha_1$ by hypothesis. Therefore:

$$\Delta u_2 - \Delta u_1 = \frac{v}{s_\Pi \pi}\gamma'\varepsilon_2 + \left[\frac{v}{s_\Pi \pi}\left(g_u - g_r\frac{\pi}{v}\right) - 1\right]k_1.$$

Referring back to equation (16.15), it now follows that, in order for the condition $u_2 - u_1 \geq c$ to be satisfied, we must observe $\varepsilon_2 \geq \varepsilon_{2\min}$, where:

$$\frac{v}{s_\Pi \pi}\gamma'\varepsilon_{2\min} + \left[\frac{v}{s_\Pi \pi}\left(g_u - \frac{g_r\pi}{v}\right) - 1\right]k_1 = -(k_1 - c).$$

Evaluating this expression for $\varepsilon_{2\min}$, we find that:

$$\varepsilon_{2\min} = \frac{s_\Pi \pi c - (vg_u + \pi g_r)k_1}{v\gamma'}.$$

Finally, rewriting for any period t, we arrive at:

$$\varepsilon_{t\min} = \frac{s_\Pi \pi c - (vg_u + \pi g_r)k_{t-1}}{v\gamma'}. \qquad (16.16)$$

Starting from the initial conditions stated earlier, then, and if $\varepsilon_t \geq \varepsilon_{t\min}$ for all $t > 1$, a cumulative expansion in the rate of accumulation will occur as a result of a series of adjustments of the type depicted in Figure 16.1, in which, over time, the rate of accumulation simultaneously moves towards and redefines the conditions and hence position of its steady-state equilibrium value.

These increases in the rate of accumulation need not continue indefinitely, however.[13] Hence suppose that in some period n, we have $\varepsilon_n < \varepsilon_{n\min}$. This means, of course, that we will observe $u_n - u_{n-1} = k_n < c$. Since $u_{n-1} - u_{n-2} = k_{n-1} \geq c$ by virtue of the cumulative expansion that has taken place in prior periods, equation (16.14) and Table 16.1 suggest that we will now have $\alpha_{n+1} = \alpha_n - \varepsilon_{n+1}$. The possibility arises that we will subsequently observe:

$$u_{n+1} - u_n \leq -c = (u_n - u_{n-1}) - k_n - c$$

or:

$$\Delta u_{n+1} - \Delta u_n \leq -(k_n + c), \tag{16.17}$$

which, by equation (16.14) and Table 16.1, will result in further deterioration in the SOLE and set up the possibility of a series of cumulative contractions in the rate of accumulation – a possibility that will actually materialise if $\varepsilon_t \geq \varepsilon_{t\,min}$ for all $t > n+1$. This situation is illustrated in Figure 16.2.

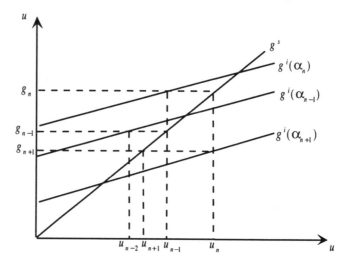

Note: $u_{n-1} - u_{n-2} \geq c;\ u_n - u_{n-1} < c;\ u_{n+1} - u_n \leq -c$

Figure 16.2   An upper turning point in the growth cycle

Under what circumstances will the conditions in equation (16.17) occur? Given that:

$$\Delta u_{n+1} - \Delta u_n = \frac{v}{s_\Pi \pi} \gamma' \varepsilon_{n+1} + \left[\frac{v}{s_\Pi \pi} \left(g_u - g_r \frac{\pi}{v} \right) - 1 \right] k_n,$$

we wish to find the value of ε^*_{n+1} such that:

$$\frac{v}{s_\Pi \pi} \gamma' \varepsilon^*_{n+1} + \left[\frac{v}{s_\Pi \pi} \left(g_u - g_r \frac{\pi}{v} \right) - 1 \right] k_n = -(k_n + c).$$

Solving for ε^*_{n+1}, we arrive at:

$$\varepsilon^*_{n+1} = \frac{s_\Pi \pi c + (v g_u + \pi g_r) k_n}{v \gamma'}.$$
(16.18)

Hence if $\varepsilon_{n+1} \geq \varepsilon^*_{n+1}$ and $\varepsilon_t \geq \varepsilon_{t\,\min}$ for all $t > n + 1$, we will observe an upper turning point in the cumulative expansion of the rate of accumulation followed by a series of cumulative contractions in the growth rate. Since the reaction function in equation (16.14) is symmetrical, it is clear that an equation similar to equation (16.18) could be deduced which would provide the conditions necessary for a lower turning point followed by the onset of a cumulative expansion in the rate of accumulation. In other words, what has been demonstrated is that the model summarised in equations (16.13) and (16.14) is capable of generating growth cycles. Moreover, this cyclical growth is path-dependent: neither the amplitude nor the period of the cycle, nor even the trend rate of growth, can be deduced a priori. Instead, they can only be observed ex post, as a product of the historical sequence of adjustments that results from the recursive interaction of equations (16.13) and (16.14).

16.4. WAGE- VERSUS PROFIT-LED GROWTH RECONSIDERED

An important issue in neo-Kaleckian growth theory is the impact of income redistribution on growth. As noted earlier, the canonical neo-Kaleckian model suggests that growth is wage-led. But this canonical model takes no account of the potential variability of the SOLE with respect to changes in income shares. The question therefore arises as to what the impact of redistribution on growth is when the potential variability of the SOLE *is* taken into account.

According to Keynes (1936, p. 264), a general reduction in nominal wages (and hence, *ceteris paribus*, a decrease in the real wage and increase in the profit share) may in and of itself produce a more optimistic tone in the minds of entrepreneurs (i.e., an improvement in the SOLE). The corollary of this is the intuitive result that an increase in nominal wages (decrease in the profit share) is presumably likely to create a more pessimistic tone.

However, there is more to be said about the case of a general reduction in nominal wages. Keynes warns that because a general decrease in nominal wages cannot be effected simultaneously (in the absence of a central planner), individual groups of wage earners are likely to resist nominal wage cuts, perceiving them to be a reduction in their *relative* nominal wages. Hence anticipations of conflict over reductions in nominal wages, involving losses to production and so forth, may mean that a *decline* in nominal wages will actually induce pessimism regarding expected future returns, rather than the 'optimistic tone' noted earlier. Moreover, suppose that nominal wage cuts today result in firms anticipating the possibility of price cuts in the future, as a result of falling nominal demand. Because production takes time – so that nominal costs and revenues are not realised simultaneously – the prospect of committing resources to production at today's prices while having to sell at tomorrow's (possibly lower) prices may become less appealing. Once again, a cut in nominal wages may induce pessimism rather than the 'optimistic tone' originally identified by Keynes.[14]

In sum, it is plausible to conceive that *either* an increase *or* a decrease in nominal wages (i.e., *any* redistribution of income) may result in a deterioration in the SOLE. This is presumably one of the reasons that ultimately lead Keynes to argue that:

> to suppose that a flexible wage policy is a right and proper adjunct of a system which on the whole is one of *laissez-faire*, is the opposite of the truth ... I am now of the opinion that the maintenance of a stable general level of money wages (and hence, *ceteris paribus*, prices and income shares) is, on a balance of considerations, the most advisable policy. (Keynes, 1936, pp. 269–70)

One way of interpreting all this is to think of wages and prices, and hence income shares, as constituting *distributional regimes* that, together with other institutions such as the structure of the employment relationship, the industrial relations system, the norms governing the conduct of macroeconomic policy and so forth, form the *macrofoundations* of a capitalist economy (Colander, 1996). These macrofoundations create a structural context within which decisions are made and executed. Furthermore, the structural stability of an economy's macrofoundations – including the distributional regime – is conducive to its macroeconomic performance. Hence:

> many of the social conventions that current markets have, such as relatively fixed nominal wages and prices, play a role in ... extra market systemic coordination ... Wage flexibility can undermine the coordinating functions of existing markets. (Colander, 1999, pp. 217–18)

Following Keynes and Colander, then, we may postulate that a distributional regime forms part of the macrofoundations or 'operating system' of a capitalist economy (Colander, 1999, pp. 213–14), in the context of which production, employment, investment and other decisions are made. Moreover, perturbations to this operating system – such as increases or decreases in the profit share – are generally inimical to the SOLE. Let us refer to this latter point as the Keynes–Colander effect, according to which $d\alpha < 0$ whenever $d\pi \neq 0$, or in other words:

$$\frac{d\alpha}{d\pi} < 0 \text{ if } d\pi > 0$$

and:

$$\frac{d\alpha}{d\pi} > 0 \text{ if } d\pi < 0.$$

We can now re-examine the impact of income redistribution on growth in neo-Kaleckian theory in light of this Keynes–Colander effect.

To begin with, assume that the economy is initially growing at an equilibrium rate, given by:

$$g_1^* = \frac{s_\Pi \pi \gamma(\alpha_1)}{\pi(s_\Pi - g_r) - g_u v}, \tag{16.19}$$

where α_1 denotes a particular SOLE and g_1^* is the equilibrium rate of growth corresponding to this SOLE. Using equation (16.19), we can now recalculate the impact of redistribution on growth taking into account the Keynes–Colander effect. Hence differentiating equation (16.18) with respect to π yields:

$$\frac{\partial g^*}{\partial \pi} = \frac{-s_\Pi \gamma g_u v}{(\pi(s_\Pi - g_r) - g_u v)^2} + \frac{s_\Pi \pi \gamma'(d\alpha / d\pi)}{\pi(s_\Pi - g_r) - g_u v}. \tag{16.20}$$

The first term on the right-hand side (RHS) of equation (16.20) is identical to the solution to equation (16.9) and is, of course, negative. However, the sign of equation (16.20) also depends on the second term on the RHS, which captures the impact of the Keynes–Colander effect on growth. Hence if $d\pi > 0$ so that $(d\alpha/d\pi) < 0$, then equation (16.20) is unambiguously negative: a reduction in real wages lowers the rate of growth. In this case, the Keynes–Colander effect reinforces the impact of declining real wages on growth as captured by the canonical neo-Kaleckian model, and a result consistent with the notion of wage-led growth emerges. This is illustrated in Figure 16.3.[15]

Suppose, however, that $d\pi < 0$ so that $(d\alpha/d\pi) > 0$. In this case, the second term on the RHS of equation (16.20) is positive, and the sign of equation (16.20) becomes ambiguous. It is possible that the first term on the RHS of equation (16.20) will dominate, in which case equation (16.20) will be negative. In this case, a rise in real wages boosts growth. Again, this is the traditional wage-led growth result associated with the canonical neo-Kaleckian model. But a second possibility is that the impact of the Keynes–Colander effect on growth – the second term on the RHS of equation (16.20) – will dominate. In this case, equation (16.20) is positive and a rise in real wages will actually lower the rate of growth. This situation is illustrated in Figure 16.4.[16]

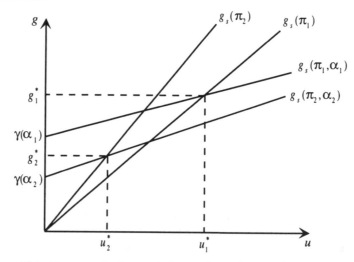

Figure 16.3 The canonical wage-led growth result is reinforced when $d\pi > 0$

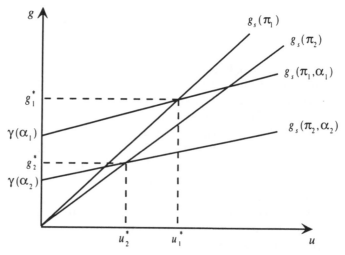

Figure 16.4 The canonical wage-led growth result can disappear when $d\pi < 0$

In sum, when the canonical neo-Kaleckian growth model is augmented by a Keynes–Colander effect, according to which any change in income shares is inimical to the SOLE, we find that a redistribution of income away from wages always lowers the rate of growth (as in the canonical model), but a re-distribution of income towards wages only raises growth under certain circumstances. The significance of these findings is twofold. First, following Blecker (2002), they suggest that some of the results (in this case, the potential disappearance of unambiguously wage-led growth) associated with Marglin–Bhaduri-type growth models, in which the investment function exhibits a 'strong profit share effect', can be derived *without* departing from the treatment of the relationship between g, r and u in the canonical neo-Kaleckian investment function. This is interesting because, as noted earlier, neo-Kaleckians have traditionally objected to the Marglin–Bhaduri results on the basis that the canonical neo-Kaleckian model embodies a superior investment function. Since the canonical neo-Kaleckian investment function is retained in the modelling exercise above, the traditional Kaleckian objection does not apply to the results derived from this exercise – although there may, of course, be other grounds for objecting to the Keynes–Colander effect on which the results *are* based.

Second, the findings above suggest that the variability of firms' SOLE may make it harder to increase and easier to decrease the growth rate through the redistribution of income. Just as Keynes (1936) warned against the inefficacy of flexible wages and prices as a means of achieving and maintaining full employment, so, it seems, neo-Kaleckians might have reason to warn against the potential inefficacy of redistributing income as a means of boosting growth – even as they continue to warn against the ease with which income redistribution can result in lower growth. If the SOLE really is variable in an environment of historical time and uncertainty, and if the Keynes–Colander effect captures the impact of redistribution on the SOLE, then there may be more reliable methods of raising the rate of growth than redistributing income.[17]

16.5. CONCLUSION

Neo-Kaleckian theory seeks to model growth in an environment of historical time and uncertainty. Despite this, little or no account has been taken of the implications of variability in the state of long-run expectations (SOLE) for either the adjustment dynamics of neo-Kaleckian growth models, or the results of comparative dynamic exercises undertaken with these models. The chief purpose of this chapter has been to remedy this shortcoming. It has been demonstrated that when changes in the SOLE are modelled as a reaction to discrepancies between the actual and expected rates of capacity utilisation, the canonical neo-Kaleckian model (which is essentially a traditional equilibrium model) can be transformed into an open system with path-dependent growth outcomes, which may exhibit growth cycles of indeterminate amplitude and period about an indeterminate trend. Moreover, when account is taken of the potential sensitivity of the SOLE with respect to changes in income shares, the wage-led growth results of the canonical neo-Kaleckian model are modified. Specifically, if income shares form 'distributional regimes' that are part of the institutional macrofoundations of a capitalist economy, and if any perturbation of these macrofoundations is inimical to the SOLE, a decrease in real wages will reduce the rate of growth by even more than the canonical neo-Kaleckian model predicts. But an increase in real wages will only boost growth under certain circumstances. This means that it may be easier to reduce and harder to increase the rate of growth by means of redistributing income than the canonical neo-Kaleckian model suggests, and that efforts to raise the rate of growth might have more reliable results if they were directed towards policies other than income redistribution.

NOTES

*   I would like to thank, without implicating, the participants in the Conference (and in particular, Sergio Nisticò and Amitava Dutt) and two anonymous referees for their helpful comments on an earlier draft.

1.   See Section 16.2 below for further details.
2.   If the rate of profit influences investment behaviour – as it does in both Cambridge and neo-Kaleckian growth theory – then it necessarily follows that investment is sensitive to the rate of capacity utilisation, since by definition:

$$r = \frac{\Pi}{K} = \frac{\Pi}{Y} \cdot \frac{Y}{Y_c} \cdot \frac{Y_c}{K} = \frac{\pi u}{v}$$

   where Π denotes profits, K is the capital stock, Y and Y_c are the actual and full capacity levels of output respectively, π is the profit share of income, u is the capacity utilisation rate, and v is the (full capacity) capital/output ratio.
3.   See Lavoie (1992, Ch. 6) and Blecker (2002) for surveys of this literature and its antecedents.
4.   As Lavoie (1992, p. 287) notes, this is a strong assumption which rules out the possibility of a Harrodian discrepancy between the actual and warranted rates of growth. As will become clear below, the canonical neo-Kaleckian model is also un-Harrodian in the sense that it characterises growth as a stable process. See, however, Lavoie (1992, pp. 288–90) on how unstable versions of the model developed above may contribute to the explanation of actual growth experience.

5. Any description of expectations formation that is consistent with the sequential decision making that we would expect to observe in an environment of historical time and uncertainty could be postulated here. For the sake of analytical convenience, the simplest form of the adaptive expectations mechanism has been utilised in equations (16.5) and (16.6).

6. Note that equation (16.10) is strictly negative since the stability condition stated earlier ensures that $s_\Pi > g_r$.

7. Eliminating what Marglin and Bhaduri (1990) term the 'strong accelerator condition' of the canonical neo-Kaleckian model does not eliminate its stagnationist and wage-led growth results. It does, however, reduce the coincidence of these results to one case amongst many.

8. See also Chick and Caserta (1997) for a similar view.

9. It is, of course, entirely possible that the coefficients g_u and g_r will be as, if not more, susceptible to revision in light of changes in the SOLE. This possibility is overlooked here for the sake of analytical convenience.

10. It is more conventional to write reduced forms of the neo-Kaleckian model in terms of growth and profit rates, or profit and capacity utilisation rates. Indeed, the reduced-form model above could be rewritten in terms of growth and profit rates without effecting any fundamental alteration of the results derived below. Equations (16.11) and (16.12) are written in terms of growth and capacity utilisation rates simply to focus attention on the behaviour of the two variables that are the subjects of the stagnationist and wage-led growth results derived earlier.

11. In cases other than those described in Table 16.1 – for example, if $u_{t-1} - u^e_{t-1} < c$ and $u_{t-2} - u^e_{t-2} < c$ – then $\alpha_t = \alpha_{t-1}$. In these cases, the shifts in the g^i schedule in equation (16.12) that are described below will cease and the model will converge to a path-dependent equilibrium, the precise position of which will depend on the prior historical sequence of changes in α. Cases of this nature are not discussed further in what follows, but see Setterfield (1999, pp. 496–8) for a related analysis.

12. Effective choice exists when choices can be novel, and a decision maker could, in any given set of circumstances that are subject to choice, always have chosen to act differently. The existence of effective choice renders social systems intrinsically open (i.e., causes need not always have the same effects) and subject to fundamental uncertainty. It is thus part of the ontological basis for postulating the existence of fundamental uncertainty in post-Keynesian economics. See also Setterfield (2000) for a further discussion of the ontological precepts of post-Keynesianism and their relationship to the SOLE reaction function described above.

13. Indeed they cannot, since changes in the rate of accumulation are accompanied by changes in the rate of capacity utilisation and the latter is bounded above and below.

14. See also Palley (1996, p. 83).

15. Figures 16.3 and 16.4 illustrate the impact of income redistribution on the position of the equilibrium rate of growth. Any such changes in the position of equilibrium will, of course, create initial conditions of disequilibrium, as a result of which the ensuing tendency for g to increase or decrease may be compounded by adjustment dynamics of the sort described in the previous section, where the SOLE – and hence the conditions and position of the equilibrium growth rate, and the behaviour of the actual growth rate – is sensitive to discrepancies between u^e and u along disequilibrium adjustment paths. This possibility is not pursued here for reasons of analytical convenience.

16. In Figure 16.4, the dominance of the Keynes–Colander effect on the RHS of equation (16.20) is associated with a decline in equilibrium u as well as g. It should be noted that this is a possible but not necessary result of the conditions postulated here. In other words, it is possible for an increase in real wages to raise the rate of capacity utilisation even as it lowers the growth rate. This raises the possibility of a 'conflictive stagnationist' result, in

which workers who prefer employment opportunities now rather than later find themselves at odds with firms who wish to maintain the rate of accumulation and hence profit.

17. At least from an analytical standpoint – whether or not the impact of the Keynes–Colander effect on growth will dominate in the event of an *actual* raise in real wages is, of course, a matter for empirical investigation.

REFERENCES

Asimakopulos, A. (1991), *Keynes's General Theory and Accumulation*, Cambridge: Cambridge University Press.

Bhaduri, A. and S.A. Marglin (1990), 'Unemployment and the real wage: the economic basis for contesting political ideologies', *Cambridge Journal of Economics*, 14, 375–93.

Blecker, R. (2002), 'Distribution, demand, and growth in neo-Kaleckian macro models', in M. Setterfield (ed.), *The Economics of Demand-led Growth: Challenging the Supply-side Vision of the Long Run*, Cheltenham: Edward Elgar.

Chick, V. and M. Caserta (1997), 'Provisional equilibrium and macroeconomic theory', in P. Arestis, G. Palma and M. Sawyer (eds), *Markets, Unemployment and Economic Policy: Essays in Honour of Geoff Harcourt*, Vol. II, London: Routledge, pp. 223–37.

Colander, D. (1996), 'The macrofoundations of micro', in D. Colander (ed.), *Beyond Microfoundations: Post Walrasian Economics*, Cambridge: Cambridge University Press, pp. 57–68.

Colander, D. (1999), 'A post-Walrasian explanation of wage and price inflexibility and a Keynesian unemployment equilibrium system', in M. Setterfield (ed.), *Growth, Employment and Inflation: Essays in Honour of John Cornwall*, London: Macmillan, pp. 211–25.

Del Monte, A. (1975), 'Grado di monopolio e sviluppo economico', *Rivista internazionale di scienze sociali*, 83, 231–63.

Dutt, A.K. (1984), 'Stagnation, income distribution, and monopoly power', *Cambridge Journal of Economics*, 8, 25–40.

Gerrard, B. (1995), 'Probability, uncertainty and behaviour: a Keynesian perspective', in S. Dow and J. Hillard (eds), *Keynes, Knowledge and Uncertainty*, Aldershot, Brookfield: Edward Elgar, pp. 177–96.

Keynes, J.M. (1936), *The General Theory of Employment, Interest and Money*, London: Macmillan.

Kregel, J. (1976), 'Economic methodology in the face of uncertainty: the modelling methods of Keynes and the Post Keynesians', *Economic Journal*, 86, 209–25.

Lavoie, M. (1992), *Foundations of Post-Keynesian Economic Analysis*, Aldershot, Brookfield: Edward Elgar.

Marglin, S.A. and A. Bhaduri (1990), 'Profit squeeze and Keynesian theory', in S.A. Marglin and J.B. Schor (eds), *The Golden Age of Capitalism*, Oxford: Oxford University Press, pp. 153–86.

Mott, T. and E. Slattery (1994), 'The influence of changes in income distribution on aggregate demand in a Kaleckian model: stagnation vs. exhilaration reconsidered', in P. Davidson and J. Kregel (eds), *Employment, Growth, and Finance*, Cheltenham: Edward Elgar, pp. 60–82.

Palley, T.I. (1996), *Post Keynesian Economics: Debt, Distribution and the Macro Economy*, London: Macmillan.

Robinson, J. (1956), *The Accumulation of Capital*, London: Macmillan.

Robinson, J. (1962), *Essays in the Theory of Economics Growth*, London: Macmillan.

Rowthorn, R.E. (1981), 'Demand, real wages and economic growth', *Thames Papers in Political Economy*, London: Thames Polytechnic.

Setterfield, M. (1997), 'Should economists dispense with the notion of equilibrium?', *Journal of Post Keynesian Economics*, **20**, 47–76.

Setterfield, M. (1999), 'Expectations, path dependence and effective demand: a macroeconomic model along Keynesian lines', *Journal of Post Keynesian Economics*, **21**, 479–501.

Setterfield, M. (2000), 'Expectations, endogenous money and the business cycle: an exercise in open systems modelling', *Journal of Post Keynesian Economics*, **23**, 77–105.

Index